UNRELIABLE HISTORY

By the same Author

THE BLACK PRINCE
GASTON DE FOIX
MAHASENA
PROSERPINE
DESIDERIO
COLLECTED POEMS
WITH THE RUSSIANS IN MANCHURIA
A YEAR IN RUSSIA
THE RUSSIAN PEOPLE
LANDMARKS IN RUSSIAN LITERATURE
AN OUTLINE OF RUSSIAN LITERATURE
RUSSIAN ESSAYS AND STUDIES
THE GLASS MENDER
FORGET-ME-NOT AND LILY OF THE VALLEY
ORPHEUS IN MAYFAIR
DEAD LETTERS
DIMINUTIVE DRAMAS
LOST DIARIES
ROUND THE WORLD IN ANY NUMBER OF DAYS
SELECTED POEMS
THE GREY STOCKING, AND OTHER PLAYS
R.F.C. H.Q.
OVERLOOKED
PASSING BY
THE PUPPET SHOW OF MEMORY
H.M. EMBASSY, AND OTHER PLAYS
A TRIANGLE
COMFORTLESS MEMORY
C
HILDESHEIM
PUNCH AND JUDY, AND OTHER ESSAYS
HALF A MINUTE'S SILENCE
TRANSLATIONS ANCIENT AND MODERN, WITH ORIGINALS
CAT'S CRADLE
DAPHNE ADEANE
TINKER'S LEAVE
LAST DAYS AT TSARSKOE SELO
ALGÆ
WHAT I SAW IN RUSSIA
CECIL SPENCER
IN MY END IS MY BEGINNING
THE COAT WITHOUT SEAM
ROBERT PECKHAM
FRIDAY'S BUSINESS
LOST LECTURES
SARAH BERNHARDT
THE LONELY LADY OF DULWICH

UNRELIABLE HISTORY

BY

MAURICE BARING

WILLIAM HEINEMANN LTD
LONDON——————TORONTO

FIRST PUBLISHED 1934

PRINTED IN GREAT BRITAIN
AT THE WINDMILL PRESS, KINGSWOOD, SURREY

CONTENTS

DIMINUTIVE DRAMAS

DEAD LETTERS

LOST DIARIES

DIMINUTIVE DRAMAS

DEDICATED TO

A. I.

WHOSE UNWRITTEN CHRONICLES ARE BETTER
THAN BOOKS AND WHOSE UNPREMEDITATED
SUGGESTION HITS A TARGET BEYOND
THE REACH OF ARTISTS AND THE
KEN OF CRITICS

I

CATHERINE PARR

OR

ALEXANDER'S HORSE

SCENE.—*London. Breakfast chamber in the Palace.* KING HENRY VIII *and* CATHERINE PARR *are discovered sitting opposite to each other at the breakfast table. The* KING *has just cracked a boiled egg.*

KING HENRY. My egg's raw. It really is too bad.

CATHERINE. Yesterday you complained of their being hard.

KING HENRY. And so they were. I don't want a hard egg, and I don't want a raw egg. I want them to be cooked just right.

CATHERINE. You are very difficult to please. The egg was in boiling water for three minutes and a half. I boiled it myself. But give it me. I like them like that. I will boil you another.

KING HENRY. No, it's too late now. But it is a fact that you have no idea how to boil an egg. I wish you'd let them do them in the kitchen.

CATHERINE. If they're done in the kitchen you

complain because they're not here when you come down, and if they are here, you say they're cold.

KING HENRY. I never say anything of the kind. The cook boils eggs beautifully.

CATHERINE. She shall boil them to-morrow.

KING HENRY. One would have thought that a woman of your experience might at least know how to boil an egg. I hate a watery egg. (*Pensively*) Poor dear Katie used to boil eggs beautifully.

CATHERINE. Do you mean Catherine Howard or Katharine of Aragon?

KING HENRY. I was alluding to poor, dear, misguided Katie Howard. Katharine of Aragon never was my wife. The marriage was not valid.

CATHERINE. Well, Catherine Howard ought to have known how to boil eggs, considering her mother was a kitchenmaid.

KING HENRY. That is utterly untrue. Her mother was a Rochford.

CATHERINE. You're thinking of Anne Bullen.

KING HENRY. Yes, yes, to be sure, Katie's mother was a Somerset.

CATHERINE. You're thinking of Jane Seymour.

KING HENRY. Not at all. Jane Seymour was a sister of Somerset's.

CATHERINE. All I know is that Catherine Howard's mother was a kitchenmaid. And I think it's very unkind of you to mention her to me. I suppose you mean that you wish she were alive, and that you loved her better than you love me.

KING HENRY. I never said anything of the kind. All I said was that she knew how to boil eggs.

CATHERINE. You clearly meant to say that she had all the qualities which I lack.

King Henry. You are most unfair. I never meant to hint at any such thing. All I said was that I hate a watery egg, and my egg this morning was raw.

Catherine (*rising and going to the door in a temper*). Well, the best thing you can do is to get rid of me, and to marry some one who knows how to boil an egg.

King Henry. Catherine, come back! I really didn't mean to offend you. You know how to boil eggs very well.

Catherine (*sitting down*). One takes an endless amount of trouble, and that's all the thanks one gets. Don't think that I shall ever boil your eggs for you again, because I shan't.

King Henry. I was thinking we might have a little music this morning. I have composed a new ballad which I should like to try over with you. It's for viol and lute and voice. We might try it.

Catherine. I'm not sure if I have time. What is it called?

King Henry. It's called "The Triumph of Love," and it begins:

> Come list to Alexander's deed,
> Great Jove's immortal son,
> Who, riding on a snow-white steed,
> To Babylon did come.

Catherine. "Son" doesn't rhyme with "come."

King Henry. It's not meant to. It's assonance.

Catherine. Do you mean Alexander the Great?

King Henry. Yes, of course.

Catherine. The only thing is, his horse was black.

KING HENRY. No, my dear, you're mistaken; his horse was white.

CATHERINE. Black—black as jet.

KING HENRY. But I know for a fact it was white.

CATHERINE. Alexander's horse was black. Everybody knows it was black.

KING HENRY. It was white. You can ask any one you like.

CATHERINE. It was black. He was famous for his black horse. There are hundreds of pictures of him on his *black* horse—my father has got one.

KING HENRY. Then the painter made a mistake. Plutarch, Xenophon, Aristotle all mention his *white* horse.

CATHERINE. Black.

KING HENRY. But, my dear, how obstinate you are! I *know* it is white——

CATHERINE. Black, *coal*-black.

KING HENRY. Have you read Xenophon?

CATHERINE. You are thinking of something else. Even when we were children my father always showed us the picture of Alexander's *black* horse.

KING HENRY. Well, I can easily prove it to you. There's a Plutarch here in the bookcase. (*He goes to the bookcase and takes out a book.*)

CATHERINE I remember it particularly well because my brother had a black horse and we called it "Bucephalus," after Alexander's *black* horse.

KING HENRY (*turning over the leaves of the book*). If it had been black it would never have been called Bucephalus—it would be absurd to call a black horse Bucephalus.

CATHERINE. Not so absurd as calling a white horse Bucephalus.

KING HENRY. He would never have chosen a black horse. He was superstitious——

CATHERINE. Just because you're superstitious and believe in Saints, and worship images, you think every one else is. As a matter of fact, he chose a black horse on purpose to show he didn't care a pin about superstitions——

KING HENRY. Here it is—" *χαλεπὸς εἶναι καὶ κομιδῇ δύσχρηστος*"—" The horse was wild and extremely difficult to manage." In fact, he had all the characteristics of the white Thessalian horses of that day.

CATHERINE. But it doesn't say it was white. And Thessalian horses are famous for being black.

KING HENRY. You really are too obstinate for words. I will find you the proofs in Xenophon. It is distinctly stated that the horse is *white*. It is an historical fact. Nobody has ever disputed it.

CATHERINE. But Plutarch, you see, practically says it was black.

KING HENRY. Plutarch says nothing of the kind. Besides, I now remember talking about this with Wolsey, who was an excellent scholar. I distinctly remember his saying one day: " As white as Bucephalus." It's quite a common phrase among scholars.

CATHERINE. He must have said " As black as Bucephalus."

KING HENRY. Of course, if you mean to say I tell lies——

CATHERINE. I don't mean that you tell lies, but you are mistaken—that's all.

KING HENRY. But I tell you that there is no mistake possible. I know it as well as I know my own name.

CATHERINE. Your memory plays you tricks. Just now you couldn't remember Catherine Howard's mother's name.

KING HENRY. That's nothing to do with it. Besides, I did remember it. I made a slip, that's all. But this is an historical fact which I've known all my life.

CATHERINE. I quite understand your memory failing you. You have so many names to remember. I expect you were confusing Alexander's black horse with King Alfred's white horse—the white horse of Wantage.

KING HENRY. Good gracious! If you had a smattering of education you wouldn't say such things! It comes of having no religion and no education, and of not knowing Latin. A Lutheran education is worse than none. Even Anne of Cleves knew Latin.

CATHERINE. Thank Heavens, I don't know Latin! Stupid, superstitious language, fit only for bigots and monks!

KING HENRY. I suppose you mean I am a bigot.

CATHERINE. You can turn what one says into meaning anything you like. As a matter of fact, all I said was that the horse was black.

KING HENRY. I'd rather be a bigot than a Lutheran heretic.

CATHERINE. You know you're wrong and you try to escape the point. That's just like a Tudor. No Tudor could ever listen to reason.

KING HENRY. I must ask you not to insult my family.

CATHERINE. You've insulted mine, which is a

far older one. My family has no blood on its escutcheon.

KING HENRY. I won't stand this any longer. (*He gets up, opens the door, and calls*) Denny, Butts, Page, who is there?

Enter a PAGE

PAGE. Your Majesty.

KING HENRY. Go and tell the Lord Chamberlain to make the necessary arrangements for transporting the Ex-Queen to the Tower.

PAGE (*puzzled*). Yes, your Majesty. Does your Majesty mean the late Queen's remains?"

KING HENRY. I said the *Ex*-Queen, you stupid boy—Queen Catherine Parr.

PAGE. Yes, your Majesty.

KING HENRY. And tell him to give orders to the Governor of the Tower to have everything ready for the Ex-Queen's execution.

PAGE. Is the same ceremonial to be observed as in the case of Queen Catherine Howard, your Majesty?

KING HENRY. Yes; only there need only be one roll of drums instead of two—at the end. (*The* PAGE *goes to the door.*) And on the way ask Dr. Butts whether Alexander the Great's horse was black or white.

CATHERINE. It was black. (*The* PAGE *bows and goes out.*) Well, since I'm to be executed, I daresay you will allow me to go and pack up my things. By the way, you left your lute in my sitting-room yesterday. I will bring it down.

KING HENRY. Wait a minute, there's no hurry.

CATHERINE. I beg your pardon, I have very little time, and a great many letters to write.

KING HENRY (*hesitating*). And I wanted to have some music.

CATHERINE. You don't expect me to accompany you now, I suppose? You had better find some one else. I have got other things to think about during my last moments on earth.

KING HENRY (*laughing uneasily*). I was only joking, of course, my dear. You don't mean to say you took it seriously.

CATHERINE. I am afraid I don't appreciate that kind of joke.

KING HENRY. Come, come; let bygones be bygones, and let us have some music. I want to play you my ballad.

Enter the PAGE

PAGE. If you please, your Majesty, I can't find the Lord Chamberlain, and Dr. Butts says your Majesty was quite correct as to the colour of Alexander the Great's horse.

KING HENRY (*beaming*). Very good; you can go. You need not deliver the message to the Lord Chamberlain. (*The* PAGE *bows and retires.*) And now, my dear, we'll go and play. You see, I knew I was right.

[*The* KING *opens the door with a bow.*

CATHERINE. It was black, all the same.

KING HENRY (*indulgently, as if speaking to a child*). Yes, yes, my dear, of course it was black, but let's go and have some music.

[*They go out*

CURTAIN.

II

THE DRAWBACK

SCENE.—*A Corner in Kensington Gardens. A summer evening. Discovered, sitting on a seat, a girl, aged 21, pretty and neat, and a good-looking young man, aged 27, dressed in a top hat and a black morning coat.*

HE. But are you quite sure you will not change your mind?

SHE. I never change my mind once it is made up. I often take a very long time to make up my mind, but once I've made it up I never change. Now my sister Alice is quite different. She never knows her mind from one minute to the other.

HE. But your father——

SHE. Papa always does what I want. Besides, directly he knows you it will be all right. And when he knows that you're at the Bar he will be delighted. He always wanted me to marry a lawyer. You see Papa was at the Bar in his young days—I daresay your father was too.

HE (*embarrassed*). No, yes—I mean no. That's to say he is in a way indirectly connected with the Bar; but my father's principal hobby is playing on the harp. He gives himself up almost entirely to that now.

SHE. I see.

HE. Have you told your father yet?

SHE. You told me I wasn't to until I'd seen you again.

HE. Yes, of course. I thought you might have changed your mind.

SHE. As if that were likely.

HE. And then, if you remember, I told you when I, when you, when we settled everything that there was a—er—drawback.

SHE. As if any drawback could possibly make any difference.

HE. I thought it might.

SHE. You mean to say that it is something which might make me wish to change my mind?

HE. Exactly.

SHE. That shows you know me very little—but what is it?

HE. You see it's a kind of confession.

SHE. I know what it is; you want to tell me you once loved some one else.

HE. No, not that, I swear I never did. I may have thought once or twice that I was in love, but until I met you I never knew what love, what real love, was.

SHE. And those other times when you thought you were in love—were there many of them?

HE. It only happened twice; that's to say three times, only the third time didn't count.

SHE. And the first time, who was she?

HE. I was quite young, only a boy. She was a girl in an A.B.C. shop.

SHE. Was she pretty?

HE. Not exactly.

SHE. Did you propose to her?

HE. Yes, but she refused.

SHE. And that's all that happened?

HE. That's all.

SHE. And the second time?

HE. It was the parson's daughter down in the country.

SHE. Did you make love to her?

HE. No, not really, of course, but we were friends.

SHE. Did you kiss her?

HE. Only once, and that was by accident. But it was all years ago.

SHE. How many years ago?

HE. Let me see; two, no, no, it must have been four years ago. I'm not sure it wasn't five. She married the curate.

SHE. And the third time?

HE. Oh! that was nothing.

SHE. Who was she?

HE. She was an artist—a singer.

SHE. A concert singer?

HE. Almost; that's to say she wanted to be one. She sang in a music-hall.

SHE. Oh!

HE. Only a *serious* turn. She wasn't dressed up or anything. She sang "The Lost Chord" and songs like that. She was called "The New Zealand Nightingale."

SHE. And you knew her?

HE. Very slightly. I had tea with her once or twice. And then she went away.

SHE. Back to New Zealand?

HE. Yes, back to New Zealand.

SHE. Now I've made you confess everything.

Aren't you glad you've got it off your mind? I don't mind a bit, and I like you for being so honest.

HE. But it's not that at all. It's nothing to do with me.

SHE. Then who has it got to do with?

HE. My father.

SHE. You mean he wont approve of me?

HE. Of course I don't mean that. He'd simply love you.

SHE. He's going to marry again.

HE. No, it's not that.

SHE. He doesn't want you to marry.

HE. No, it's nothing to do with me.

SHE. Then I don't understand.

HE. It's something to do with him.

SHE. He's consumptive.

HE. No; his health is excellent.

SHE. He's lost his money.

HE. No; he's very well off. You see it's something to do with his social position. A matter of—I don't quite know how to put it.

SHE. But, Georgie, you don't think I'm such a snob as to care twopence for social position and conventions of that kind? Your father is your father—that's all that matters, isn't it?

HE. I know, I know, but there are prejudices.

SHE. Is it something your father's done? Has he been in the Bankruptcy Court? I wouldn't care a pin.

HE. No, it's nothing he's done. It's something he *is*.

SHE. He's a Socialist!

HE. No.

SHE. Is he a Roman Catholic?

HE. Oh, no! He's Church of England.

SHE. I know; he's a Liberal.

HE. No; he says the Liberals are just as bad as the Conservatives.

SHE. Then he's a little Englander.

HE. On the contrary; he's outside politics. He belongs to no party.

SHE. He's a foreigner—by birth, I mean.

HE. Not at all.

SHE. He's not a Mormon?

HE. No. It's nothing to do with politics or religion or that kind of thing. It's his profession.

SHE. His profession! But I thought—as if I cared about his profession!

HE. But you might—there are some professions——

SHE. You see, I know he's honest.

HE. Oh! you needn't have any fear. He's perfectly honest, respectable, and respected.

SHE. Then what is it?

HE. I'd rather you guessed it.

SHE. How absurd you are! I know what it is; he's somebody's agent.

HE. No.

SHE. Then he's a schoolmaster.

HE. No.

SHE (*tentatively*). Of course, I know he was never in trade?

He. No, never. He has had nothing to do with it

SHE. Is he on the stage?

HE. No; he disapproves of actors.

SHE. He's a Quaker.

HE. I told you it's nothing to do with religion.

SHE. Then, he's a photographer. Some photographers almost count as artists.

HE. No.

SHE. Then it is something to do with art.

HE. His profession certainly needs art and skill.

SHE. He's not a conjurer?

HE. Conjurers are scarcely respectable.

SHE. I know, of course. He's a jockey.

HE. No.

SHE. A bookmaker.

HE. No.

SHE. A veterinary surgeon.

HE. No.

SHE. Does he ever give lessons?

HE. Only to his assistants, whom he's training.

SHE. He's a prize-fighter.

HE. Oh, no!

SHE. He's an Art-dressmaker.

HE. No. You see it's something some people might mind.

SHE. What can it be. A dentist.

HE. No.

SHE. How stupid of me. He's a literary man.

HE. He's never written a line.

SHE. But you told me. I remember now. He plays the harp. He's something musical; but nobody could mind that. He's a dancing-master.

HE. No.

SHE. A commercial traveller.

HE. No.

SHE. Of course not; it's something to do with art. But what could one mind?

HE. Not exactly art. It's more skill.

SHE. Is he a chiropodist?

HE. No.

SHE. Or a Swedish masseur?

HE. Nothing like it.

SHE. Is it anything to do with officials?

HE. Yes, in a way.

SHE. Then I've guessed it. He's a detective.

HE. No.

SHE. He's in the Secret Service.

HE. No.

SHE. It's something to do with the police.

HE. Not exactly.

SHE. With prisons.

HE. In a way.

SHE. He's a prison inspector.

HE. No.

SHE. A prison chaplain.

HE. No; he's not in Orders.

SHE. The prison doctor who has to feed the Suffragettes.

HE. No.

SHE. I've guessed. He's a keeper in a lunatic asylum.

HE. You're getting cold again.

SHE. Then it's something to do with prisons?

HE. Yes.

SHE. He's a warder.

HE. No.

SHE. I don't know who else is in a prison, except the prisoners.

HE. He doesn't live in the prison.

SHE. But he goes there sometimes?

HE. Yes.

SHE. I give it up.

HE. His duty is a disagreeable one, but some one has to do it.

SHE. He's the man who has to taste the prisoners' food.

HE. I didn't know there was such a person.

SHE. You must tell me. I'll never guess.

HE (*blurting it out*). Well, you see, he's the hangman.

[*A Pause.*

SHE. You mean he——

HE. Yes, he——

SHE. Oh, I see.

HE. Some people might mind this. He's going to retire very soon—on a pension.

SHE. Yes?

HE. And, of course, he very seldom——

SHE. Yes, I suppose——

HE. It's all quite private, of course.

SHE. Yes, of course [*A Pause.*
(*Looking at her watch*) Good gracious! I shall be late for dinner. It's nearly seven o'clock. I must fly. I was late yesterday.

HE. Shall I—shall we meet to-morrow?

SHE. No, not to-morrow. I'm busy all to-morrow.

HE. Perhaps the day after.

SHE. Perhaps I had better tell you at once what I was going to write to you.

HE. You think the drawback——

SHE (*indignantly*). I wasn't thinking of that. But I do think you ought to have told me directly about those others.

HE. What others?

SHE. Those women—the A.B.C. shop, the clergyman's daughter, and that music hall singer.

HE. But you said you didn't mind.

SHE. I minded too much to speak about it. A

music-hall singer! The New Zealand Nightingale! Oh! to think that you, that I——Oh! the shame of it.

HE. But——

SHE. There's no but. You've grossly deceived me. You played with my feelings. You led me on. You trifled with me. You've treated me scandalously. You've broken my heart. You've ruined my life.

HE. But let me say one word.

SHE. Not one word. A girl in an A.B.C. shop! A clergyman's daughter! and a music-hall singer!

HE. You really mean——

SHE. I've heard quite enough. Thank you, Mr. Belleville. Please to understand that our acquaintance is at an end. Good evening. (*She bows and walks away.*)

CURTAIN.

III

PIOUS ÆNEAS

SCENE.—*A room in* DIDO'S *Palace at Carthage. Discovered :* ÆNEAS, *wearing a cloak of Tyrian purple ;* SERESTUS *and* SERGESTUS.

ÆNEAS (*in a sharp military tone*). Is everything ready?

SERESTUS. Aye, aye, sir.

ÆNEAS. No leave for either watch to-night. We shall probably go to sea to-morrow morning at four. I'll let you know later.

SERESTUS. Aye, aye, sir.

ÆNEAS. That's all. Don't any of you get talking, and you, Sergestus, report seven minutes to noon to me.

SERGESTUS. Aye, aye, sir.

[SERGESTUS *and* SERESTUS *salute and go out L.*

[ÆNEAS *unrolls a chart.*

DIDO *enters through a curtain C.* ÆNEAS *hastily conceals the chart.*

DIDO (*cheerfully*). Well?

ÆNEAS. Good morning.

DIDO. Are you busy? If so I won't disturb you.

ÆNEAS. No, no, I'm not at all busy.

DIDO. I thought you were reading something when I came in.

ÆNEAS. I was only looking through some accounts.

DIDO. Aren't you cold in this room? Wouldn't you like a fire?

ÆNEAS. No, thank you. I don't feel the cold.

DIDO. It's blowing so hard to-day. I've been for a walk.

ÆNEAS. Oh, is it? I haven't been out this morning.

DIDO. I went for quite a long walk, past the quays.

ÆNEAS. Do you think that was wise? You ought to be careful in this cold weather.

DIDO. I like the cold. It reminds me of the day you came. Do you remember how cold you all were?

ÆNEAS. Yes.

DIDO. I'm sure you're busy. I'm sure I'm disturbing you.

ÆNEAS. Not in the least, I promise you.

DIDO. Æneas.

ÆNEAS. Well?

DIDO. I've guessed!

ÆNEAS (*uneasy and alarmed*). What? I don't understand.

DIDO (*smiling*). Your little surprise.

ÆNEAS. What surprise?

DIDO. I meant not to say, but I can't help it. I found it out this morning by accident. I think it's too dear of you to take all this trouble for me, and to send a *whole* fleet to Tyre to bring me back that purple dye which you promised me—the same colour as your cloak, which *I* gave you. I meant to pretend I didn't know, but I am so touched I can't help it.

ÆNEAS. Oh! the expedition to Tyre. Yes, I was thinking——

DIDO. And when do they start?

ÆNEAS. It isn't quite settled. It depends.

DIDO. Couldn't we go a part of the way with them?

ÆNEAS. No, I'm afraid that's quite out of the question. The time of year, you see, is so bad. I don't think you would enjoy it at all. It's very cold and the sea will be rough.

DIDO. I love a rough sea. Couldn't we go as far as Sicily with them? They're going to stop there.

ÆNEAS. I don't think you could leave Carthage just at this moment, could you?

DIDO. No, that's true. We couldn't very well leave Carthage just now, could we? Because King Iarbas has sent another threatening message.

ÆNEAS. Again?

DIDO. Yes; he threatens to attack Carthage at once. He cannot get over the fact that we really are married, and that I have a brave, dear, faithful, darling husband to love and protect me for ever and ever.

ÆNEAS. It certainly is most awkward.

DIDO. What? What does it matter to us what he says and does?

ÆNEAS. Well, the fact is that I shall probably have to go with the fleet.

DIDO. Then I'll come with you.

ÆNEAS. My dear Elissa, that's impossible.

DIDO. You don't mean to say that you're going to leave me—your wife—alone and unprotected, to face the invasion of a powerful, savage, and angry king when there is absolutely no necessity for your going at all?

ÆNEAS. I can't possibly leave the fleet to Palinurus—our only pilot. Quite between ourselves he doesn't know how to navigate—he once mistook the Charybdis beacon for a star . . . it was after supper. . . .

DIDO. Dearest, I quite understand. You must put off the expedition. I promise you not to mind. I don't really want the purple dye. We'll wait till the season is more propitious. It was most dear of you to think of it.

ÆNEAS. But I'm afraid it can't be put off.

DIDO. Why?

ÆNEAS. Well, you see I have absolutely promised—I have definitely pledged myself—I have given my word of honour to visit my brother Eryx in Sicily.

DIDO. You can put that off until the spring.

ÆNEAS. I'm afraid it would be too late then. You see the whole matter is most complicated. Eryx expects me. I promised him to go, and if I don't go now——

DIDO. What will happen?

ÆNEAS (*vaguely*). He won't be there.

DIDO. Why? Is he going away?

ÆNEAS. And then there's another matter which is still more important. I simply must visit my father's tomb in Sicily.

DIDO. You might have thought of that before.

ÆNEAS. I have constantly—but I put it off.

DIDO. As you have put it off so long already, you may just as well put it off a little longer.

ÆNEAS. Yes, but there's Jove.

DIDO. What has Jove got to do with it?

ÆNEAS. He wishes me to go. He is anxious that I should go to Sicily and (*pauses*) to Italy.

DIDO. Why to Italy?

ÆNEAS. It's entirely for my boy's sake, Ascanius . . . to establish a home for him.

DIDO. And how long will you stay there?

ÆNEAS. It depends how things turn out.

DIDO. A month?

ÆNEAS. I'm afraid it will be a little longer than that.

DIDO. Six weeks?

ÆNEAS. You see it all depends on Jove.

DIDO. I ask you as a favour to put off the whole thing until the spring.

ÆNEAS. You know I would do anything you ask me, but I'm afraid I can't do that. I would if I could, but I can't.

DIDO. You mean you are determined to go to Italy.

ÆNEAS. It's the last thing I wish to do personally, but Jove——

DIDO. Please leave Jove out of the discussion.

ÆNEAS. After all I must go there some time or other.

DIDO. You are tired of me.

ÆNEAS. How can you say such a thing?

DIDO. I knew it at once. You are going to Italy, and you're never coming back.

ÆNEAS. Of course I shall come back some time.

DIDO (*violently*). Then it's true! I knew you were tired of me! I've known it for a long time; but I never thought you could be so despicably mean as to try to go away without saying a word.

ÆNEAS. But I never dreamt——

DIDO. You build a fleet on the sly, in the middle of winter, to go to a strange country where you have no ties.

ÆNEAS. I beg your pardon, there's my brother——

DIDO. When wind and weather are at their worst, simply and solely to get away from me——

ÆNEAS. But I swear——

DIDO. Oh! you don't expect me to believe for a moment all that nonsense about Jove. If you wanted to stay you wouldn't think twice about Jove. You don't care a pin what may happen to me. You have set everybody against me; even my relations, my brother, all the Numidians, and the whole of Libya. You've ruined my reputation and given me over to my enemies, and then you put it all upon Jove.

ÆNEAS. I beg you to listen, Elissa. I had never for a moment meant to conceal my journey.

DIDO. Then why tell all those silly lies about Tyre and the purple dye?

ÆNEAS. I never said a word about Tyre and the purple dye. It was you.

DIDO. How can you tell such lies? When I asked you if the fleet was going to Tyre you distinctly said Yes.

ÆNEAS. What I did say was that I was obliged to go to Sicily to visit my father's tomb. That is the simple truth. You can't expect me to wish the whole world to think me unfilial! As it is, I haven't had a night's rest for months. My father's ghost appears to me every night.

DIDO. You expect me——

ÆNEAS. Please let me finish. And only yesterday I received a direct command from Jove, saying I was to go to Italy at once and found a kingdom there. Of course, if this only concerned myself I shouldn't care, but there's my son Ascanius to be thought of. I have no right to defraud him of his kingdom. If it were a question of inclination of course I should stay here, and Italy's the last place I want to go to. If I went anywhere I should go to Troy; but Jove has made my duty plain, and after all a man must do his duty.

DIDO. Your duty! And I suppose it was a part of your duty to deceive me, to ruin me, to stir up enemies against me, and then to leave me defenceless! Me, your wife!

ÆNEAS (*angrily*). I must point out that I warned you at the time that our marriage was in no sense legal or valid—it could never be recognised as an alliance.

DIDO (*calmly*). You are quite right. It is entirely my fault. I thought you were a man of honour. I believed your word. I thought you were a man. I was mistaken. You are only a Trojan. I found you shipwrecked, an outcast, starving, helpless, at death's door. I saved your fleet. I rescued your comrades from death. I saved you from destruction. And this is my reward. The Greeks were right when they burned Troy to the ground, killed your men and made your women into slaves. They were right to spare you, because you are not a man. Your place is with the menials. Please don't think I shall prevent you going to Italy. Don't imagine for a moment I am going to argue with you. By all means go and found a kingdom. I trust you will enjoy it and that it will turn out better than Troy. I am sure you know best, and I am sure you know what is best, and I am sure you are right. Don't imagine that I mind, or that I shall miss you, for I shan't. I am not in the least annoyed at your going, I am only surprised and vexed to find that a man who I thought was honourable, and truthful, and brave should turn out to be dishonourable, a liar, a coward —and a mean coward. I am angry with myself for having made such a mistake about a man, and that you, by your foolish, silly, transparent lies and shuffling should have shown me what a poor opinion you have of me. I wish you a very pleasant journey, and I hope you will do your duty in Italy as well as you have done it in Carthage.

[*She goes out C.*

ÆNEAS (*wiping his forehead with a handkerchief*). That's over!

Enter SERGESTUS *R.*

SERGESTUS. Seven minutes to noon, sir.

ÆNEAS. It's all right. We go to sea to-morrow.

SERGESTUS. Aye, aye, sir.

[ÆNEAS *goes out, whistling the tune "Good-bye, Carthage, I must leave you."*

CURTAIN.

IV

THE DEATH OF ALEXANDER

SCENE FROM A TRAGEDY.—"*The Life and Death of Alexander.*" Anon. [Old Plays. Printed for *Peter Buck*, at the sign of the *Temple*, near the *Inner-Temple-gate* in *Fleet-street*, 1701.]

ACT V. SCENE IV.—*Babylon. A bed-chamber in* ALEXANDER'S *Palace.* ALEXANDER *sleeping in bed;* ROXANA *attending.*

ROXANA. Full thrice hath Phœbus bath'd in Neptune's flood,
Thrice hath the pale-fac'd moon increas'd and wan'd,
But Alexander is uncomforted.
Not watchful care, nor drugs, nor natural simples
Can hold at bay the sickness which pursues him.
Methinks that treason whets his murderous knife,
And meditates a foul and bloody deed.
I dare not sleep. Have pity on my woes,
Immortal gods! I know not friends from foes!

Enter a SLAVE

SLAVE. Madam.

ROXANA. I know thou bringest some ill news.

SLAVE. Good madam, there is treason in the palace.
The Queen Statira, envious of thy issue,

Is plotting murder. She hath a strange syrup,
Brew'd by a wizard in Arabia,
More direful than the hebenon which Medea
Did cull in Colchos by the yawning graves.
She purposes, when sleep shall seize thee wholly,
To give my Lord o' the juice.

ROXANA. I thank you, slave,
I thank you, here is gold.

SLAVE. I thank you, madam.

[*Exit* SLAVE. ROXANA *feigns sleep.*

Enter QUEEN STATIRA

STATIRA. My Lord, I come to say a last farewell.
Perchance the lying mist which seal'd thine eyes
Shall dissipate and we may be aton'd;
And, deaf to false Roxana, thou'lt prefer
Thy Royal spouse, and cancel and defy
Her bastard's claim.

ROXANA. Hence! hence, foul murd'ress hence!
Thou cursed thief who in the midnight season
Dost come to filch Great Alexander's soul
With mixture dire of hellish property,
Begone! Thy treason is made palpable,
Thy baleful juice is harmless as pure water,
And thy dread weapon, turning on thyself,
Shall compass thine own ignomy.

STATIRA. Vain fool!
Thy scolding frights me not. I am Statira.
Nor canst thou with false accusation
Raze from this brow the seal of royalty,
Nor take away the sov'ranty of birth.
Albeit supplanted by a saucy caitiff,

Albeit slighted, I was once a Queen;
And I am still the daughter of Darius,
The King, whom kneeling Emperors called the Great.
Farewell, my Lord, with no more dreadful purpose
Have I come hither, than to say farewell.
I was thy spouse, and I will not importune
A faithless husband with a faithfulness
Unprofitable. So my Lord, farewell.
[*Exit* STATIRA. ALEXANDER *wakes.*

ALEXANDER. Roxana, take thy lute. My soul is heavy.
Sing me asleep with music, let me rest.

SONG

'Twas in the merry month of May,
When the sweet birds do sing,
That Proserpine—ah! lack-a-day!—
Did go a-gathering.
She stoop'd and cull'd the violet,
The pansy and the oxlip wet.

But gloomy Dis the maid espied,
And yoked his horses six,
And in his wagon drove a bride
Across the doleful Styx.
'Twas in the merry month of May
She gathered flowers. Ah! lack-a-day!

ALEXANDER. I thank you, 'tis a lulling melody
I am a-weary. Sleep, impiteous sleep,
Unmitigable, uncorruptible gaoler,
Come, cloak my senses with thy leaden robe,
Lead me to durance in thy drowsy cell.

Enter DOCTOR

DOCTOR. How doth my Lord?
ROXANA. Ill, ill beyond the power
Of simples, drugs, and physician's art.
In slumb'ry perturbation he'll converse
With images of his distemper'd fancy;
Or he will bid me touch the instrument
And soothe his fever'd spirit with a strain.
DOCTOR. Are you not weary? It is now three nights
That you have watch'd.
ROXANA. The canker of sharp grief,
The sleepless sorrow gnawing at my heart
Doth countervail outwearied nature's claim.
I shall not sleep till Alexander wakes
To health, or till he sleeps to wake no more.
But, softly. See, he stirs.
DOCTOR. Good night, sweet lady.
ROXANA. Good night to you.
[*Exit* DOCTOR. ROXANA *sleeps.*
ALEXANDER. The galleys ride at anchor!
To-morrow we'll set sail for Italy,
Nor rest until we've pitch'd our tent in Rome
And snatch'd the insolent jewel of the West.
But yesterday the Afric oracle
Bespake to me an unconfined sway,
An orb and empery unparallel'd.
And thence, when the barbarians of the West
Are mild as leashed hounds beneath our yoke,
And when each sev'ral province hath subscrib'd,
To India we'll retrace our eager steps
And reach the undiscover'd sea beyond.
By the lush banks of Ganges, Alexander

Shall build a temple to his royal sire,
Great Jupiter. Thence we'll to Babylon,
And plant there our abiding seat of rule—
In the fix'd centre of the universe.
North, south, and east and west shall our dominion,
Like the spread rays of gold Hyperion,
Pierce to the distant corners of the globe.
Oh look, Seleucus, look, Hephæstion,
Look, the swarth King in jewell'd burgonet,
All clinquant, mounted on an elephant,
Advances with his congregated host.
On, veterans! On, on, Bucephalus!
The ford! The ford! The villains fly! Come, Ho!
Clitus, awake, Roxana, O.

ROXANA. My Lord?

ALEXANDER. Didst thou cry out?

ROXANA. My Lord, I was asleep,
And knew not that I cried.

ALEXANDER. Give me to drink.
Methought I was once more in India,
Crying my veterans to victory
Across the enchafed surges of Hydaspes.
My spirit fails. Come near to me, Roxana,
That I may breathe my last in fond adieu.

ROXANA. Drink, my Lord, of this potion. It is mix'd
Of herb-grace by a sure apothecary.

ALEXANDER. Farewell, Roxana. Hie thee to my mother,
Olympias, and tell her that I die
Her name upon my lips, a dutiful son.
Salute her with deep duty, say I needed
Her tenderness; say that I am the shadow,

The mockery and ruins of her boy
Who manag'd and bestrid Bucephalus.
Remain with her, and let our only child
Be nurs'd and school'd in martial exercise,
And taught, as I was taught, philosophy.
Farewell, adieu! The last of all the Greeks
Hath gone to meet Achilles.

ROXANA. O my Lord!

Enter MESSENGER

MESSENGER. Most gracious liege, the veterans are here,
They press without.

ALEXANDER. They shall be welcome. Ho!
Come quickly, veterans, or I am dead.

ROXANA. My Lord! My husband!

Enter VETERANS

ALEXANDER. Friends, farewell to you,
Friends all and brothers all and countrymen,
Born of one soil in Macedonia,
Tell Macedon of how we fought together
Beyond Hydaspes. Grieve not overmuch,
That with the world half-conquer'd I must die,
Not fighting, but in bed, and like a woman.
I, to whom earth's huge globe was all too small,
Must occupy a niggard urn of dust.
I am for India. Come, Bucephalus,
One charge and we are masters of the world!

[*Dies.*

ROXANA. Great Alexander's dead. That soaring spirit
Which fretted in the confines of the world.

Hath broken from its circumscribing clay.
Hyperion himself was not so bright,
Nor Mars so bold. Our Orient sun hath set.
Ashy eclipse shall darken the stale world :
Asia and Egypt to the furthest Ind,
And Greece, and Macedon, where he was born,
Shall mingle tears of everlasting woe.
Come bear his body hence, and build a pyre
More lofty than the walls of Babylon ;
And when the funeral's done, we'll bear his urn,
Obsequiously in sad procession,
Across the Libyan desert, to the grove
Where stands the Temple of his father Jove.

CURTAIN.

V

THE GREEK VASE

SCENE.—*A garret on the top floor of a squalid house in the Trastevere, Rome. Discovered:* GIOVANNI, *a young sculptor, lying in bed, pale and emaciated; he coughs incessantly. The room is quite bare. There are only two chairs and one cupboard. It is very cold. There is no fire. By the bedside sits a prosperous dealer. He wears a frock-coat and a gold pince-nez.*

GIOVANNI (*wearily*). But I tell you it's not for sale.

THE DEALER. You might let me look at it.

GIOVANNI. What is the use? I tell you I won't sell it.

THE DEALER. There can be no harm in your showing it to me.

GIOVANNI (*coughing*). Not to-day. Can't you see that I'm very ill and that talking tires me?

THE DEALER. Very well. I will call again to-morrow.

GIOVANNI. You won't find me at home.

THE DEALER. Are you going away?

GIOVANNI. Yes, on a long journey.

THE DEALER. Abroad?

GIOVANNI. Abroad.

THE DEALER. To what country?

GIOVANNI. They have prescribed me change of air. They say it is the only thing which can cure me.

THE DEALER. You are going to the seaside?

GIOVANNI. On the contrary. I am going to be near a river.

THE DEALER. The Arno? Pisa, I suppose?

GIOVANNI. No.

THE DEALER. Not Paris; that would be bad for you.

GIOVANNI. Why do you think Paris would be bad for me?

THE DEALER. In the first place it's very cold there now, and then I don't think a large town is what you need.

GIOVANNI. You are anxious that I should not go to Paris.

THE DEALER. I? Not at all. Why? I merely meant that I thought you needed country air.

GIOVANNI. Yes, a villa on the Riviera for the winter, and another for the summer at Amalfi with a garden of roses; or a chalet in the Tyrol; or perhaps an island in the Tropics with palm trees and a yacht to sail about in—all that would do me good, wouldn't it? One doesn't have to pay for little luxuries like that, does one? They drop from heaven into the pockets of starving artists.

THE DEALER. Now, if you would only be reasonable and show me that vase. I am sure we could make enough money for you to take a trip to Albano. The air there is beautiful.

GIOVANNI. Very well, you may see it. It's in the cupboard.

[*The* DEALER *goes to the cupboard and takes out a large black circular Greek vase with figures painted on it. He observes it carefully.*

THE DEALER. This is not, of course, up to your best form. I won't say that it is valueless. There is, however, very little market now for this kind of thing, and if I bought it I should probably have it on my hands for years.

GIOVANNI. You needn't trouble about that. The vase is not for sale.

THE DEALER. But in the peculiar circumstances, and since we have done business together for so many years, I am willing to make an exception in this case. How much do you want for it?

GIOVANNI (*savagely*). I tell you it's not for sale.

THE DEALER. Now, be reasonable. I will give forty lire for it.

GIOVANNI. You amuse me immensely.

THE DEALER. The vase is of no particular use to me, and the fashion changes so quickly. Collectors now are mad about Egypt and Japan. Greece is finished. It's old, finished. Why, collectors now prefer even Roman things to Greek. Giordani says——

GIOVANNI. You are wasting your breath.

THE DEALER. I will give you forty-five lire. Mind you, that's an enormous price, because, I repeat, the vase is not up to your usual standard.

GIOVANNI. Please put the vase down on this chair, there, next me. (*The* DEALER *puts the vase down on the chair next to* GIOVANNI.) Thank you. Now I wish you would go away. I am tired. You tire me. (*He coughs.*)

THE DEALER. Now, instead of a vase, if it had only

been a Japanese idol or a Renaissance figure, it would be a very different matter.

GIOVANNI. When you bought my Simonetta you said there was no demand for Renaissance work.

THE DEALER. That was three years ago. It was perfectly true then. The fashion changes so quickly.

GIOVANNI. I won't sell the vase.

THE DEALER. Then, how do you propose to live?

GIOVANNI. Perhaps I have found a patron.

THE DEALER. Ah! Who is he?

GIOVANNI. You would like to know, wouldn't you?

THE DEALER. I wouldn't believe it of you. I know you are far too honest to violate all the canons of business etiquette and to play off one patron against another. You have always dealt with me, and I have always treated you handsomely—most handsomely—you must admit that.

GIOVANNI. How much did you give me for my large terra-cotta bust of Pallas?

THE DEALER. I was mad when I bought that bust. I sold it for a quarter of what I gave you. I had the greatest difficulty in getting rid of it.

GIOVANNI. How much exactly did you give me for it?

THE DEALER. Of course, I could never give you so much as that again.

GIOVANNI (*impatiently*). How much was it?

THE DEALER. I believe it was eighty-five lire. I must have been mad. But times were better then. There is no market for that kind of thing now, none whatever.

GIOVANNI. So much the better for you, then, as you won't lose money over my vase.

THE DEALER. For old acquaintance' sake, I offer you fifty lire; there, you see?

GIOVANNI. You make very good jokes.

THE DEALER. Do you mean to say you think that's too little?

GIOVANNI. I said you make very good jokes. You're a witty fellow.

THE DEALER. You artists are so improvident. You never know how many soldi there are in a lira.

GIOVANNI. You see we don't have very much experience in counting lire. (*He coughs.*)

THE DEALER. Ah! if you only counted the soldi the lire would take care of themselves.

GIOVANNI. We don't always have the chance of counting soldi.

THE DEALER. To think of the position you might be in now if you had only observed the elementary rules of thrift.

GIOVANNI. And to think of the position you are in by my not having done so!

THE DEALER. Yes; here am I obliged, positively forced, to offer you for a trumpery vase at least three times its value, and I give you my word of honour that in offering you fifty-five lire for the vase—for I am going to go as far as that—I shall be out of pocket—out of pocket. Do you understand?

GIOVANNI. I quite understand, only if I were you I shouldn't bring in the word "honour."

THE DEALER. I don't understand.

GIOVANNI. You wouldn't.

THE DEALER. Well, fifty-five lire; it's a bargain!

GIOVANNI. Suppose we talk about something else.

THE DEALER. You are all the same, you

artists. . . . You never will listen to reason. You never will understand that business is business and not——

GIOVANNI. Charity.

THE DEALER. In this case it is charity, pure charity. I would not dream of buying the vase from any one else.

GIOVANNI. I don't expect you would.

THE DEALER. Why, Leonardi sold me only yesterday a little ivory Perseus for thirty lire.

GIOVANNI. I made that Perseus, and you know it; otherwise you wouldn't have bought it.

THE DEALER. Well, I'm a busy man, and I can't waste my time arguing with you. I'll give you sixty lire. That's my last word.

GIOVANNI. It's a great pity you didn't go on the stage.

THE DEALER. You think I'm trying to cheat you. Surely——

GIOVANNI. No, I don't *think* anything of the kind.

THE DEALER. Now, come, let me take the vase. You've got no use for it here. Think what a nice little trip to Albano will do for you.

GIOVANNI (*coughing*). You can't imagine how greatly you tire me.

THE DEALER. I never knew such an obstinate fellow as you are. I'll make it seventy, but this is positively my last word. You can take it or leave it.

GIOVANNI. Oh! Leave it for Heaven's sake. Leave the vase, and leave me. (*He coughs.*)

THE DEALER. You're surely not going to sell it to some one else: you wouldn't be so mean!

GIOVANNI. Who knows?

THE DEALER. That kind of bluff, my friend, won't do with me. I am too old a bird to be caught by a trick. Come now, I offer you seventy lire—seventy whole lire. Do you understand?

GIOVANNI. It's impossible. The vase is disposed of.

THE DEALER. Sold! Impossible! You couldn't do such a thing. You couldn't play me such a shabby trick. Who has bought it?

GIOVANNI. Nobody has bought it.

THE DEALER. You are trifling. It isn't fair. You are wasting my time. You know I'm a busy man.

GIOVANNI. And you are wasting my time, and I am a dying man. They say I can't live twenty-four hours.

THE DEALER. What nonsense! There, you see how foolish you are! Now I tell you what I'll do. I'll give you two hundred lire for the vase. It's unheard of, but in view——

GIOVANNI. I am a dying man, and this is our last bargain. It has consequently no effect on future dealings. The time at your disposal is short; dying men don't bluff, you must have the vase; all this makes your price jump up. Listen to me a moment (*He takes a cutting from a newspaper out of his pocket.*) This is a cutting from an English illustrated newspaper. A friend sent it me. It is the reproduction of a photograph, and under it is written: "The terra-cotta bust of Pallas, a work of the central period of Greek perfection, the age of Pericles, after having been rejected by the British Museum, has been purchased for the Louvre for the sum of £6,000. While congratulating the French nation on their acquisition, we cannot help asking ourselves what the British Museum authorities," etc. I skip. But wait—Here is a further comment which may interest you. "Some of our criticasters have thrown doubts on the authenticity of the vase." Now look at the photograph. Perhaps you recognise the bust.

THE DEALER. You don't mean to say you think——

GIOVANNI (*in a low voice*). Be quiet. You see this vase. (*He takes the vase.*) It's not for sale. It never will be. Do you know why? Because it's my masterpiece, and because it's mine. This is what I'm going to do with it. (*He takes the vase and throws it to the ground, shattering it to fragments.*) and now I can die in peace. Go!

THE DEALER. But——

GIOVANNI. Go! (GIOVANNI *turns his head to the wall.*) [*Exit* DEALER, *mumbling.*

CURTAIN.

VI

THE FATAL RUBBER

SCENE.—*A Room in the Palace of the Louvre. Discovered, seated at a card-table:* CHARLES VI. *King of France,* ISABEAU DE BAVIERE, *the Queen, the* DAUPHIN, *and* CATHERINE, *his sister.*

THE KING. I think we might have some clean cards.

THE QUEEN. I won't play with those thick English cards, it takes hours to shuffle them. Besides, I think it's unpatriotic.

THE KING. Rubbish! Games are outside politics.

THE QUEEN. I think it is unpatriotic just now, when the war's gcing on, and I always shall think so.

THE DAUPHIN (*yawning*). What game are we going to play to-night?

THE KING. Pont d'Avignon.

THE QUEEN. Pont d'Avignon.

THE DAUPHIN. Biribi.

CATHERINE. Nain Jaune.

THE QUEEN. We shall, of course, play Pont d'Avignon. Your father wishes it.

THE KING. Cut for partners. (*They cut.*)

THE DAUPHIN. You and I play together, Papa.

[*They change seats so as to be opposite one another.*

THE KING. Cut for deal. (*They cut.*)

THE DAUPHIN. It's Papa's deal. (*The* KING *deals.*)

THE KING. I leave it.

THE DAUPHIN. I make no trumps.

CATHERINE. I double.

THE DAUPHIN. I redouble.

THE QUEEN. We're content.

THE KING. You've no business to say "we're content."

THE QUEEN. We play Hearts, of course, in doubled no trumps.

THE KING. Never; we always play the highest of the shortest. Besides which it's Catherine who doubled.

THE QUEEN. I play Hearts. The Queen of Hearts is called after me, so of course you must play Hearts, Catherine.

THE KING. You ought to have said that before. Besides in this case the rule doesn't apply.

CATHERINE (*playing the two of Hearts to the Dauphin*). Put your cards down, Charles.

[*The* DAUPHIN *puts his hand down. He has got no Hearts; the ace, King, Knave, ten, and five of Clubs; ace, Queen, ten, and six of Diamonds; Queen, Knave, ten, nine of Spades.*

THE KING. That's not a no-trumper. You might have made no trumps if it had been your make. As for redoubling, it's too absurd.

[*The* QUEEN *takes the trick with the Queen of Hearts; neither the* KING *nor the* DAUPHIN *has got any.*

THE QUEEN. No Hearts. How odd! Then all the rest are ours. I've got nine Hearts now.

THE KING. I beg your pardon. It's not at all so certain.

THE QUEEN. Very well, we'll play it.

CATHERINE. I can see your cards, Papa.

[*They play; the* QUEEN *rakes in her tricks; in the last round but one the* KING *throws away the ace of Diamonds instead of the ace of Clubs, thereby enabling* CATHERINE *to make the King of Diamonds.*

THE QUEEN (*triumphantly*). The Grand Slam!

THE DAUPHIN. You wouldn't have made it if Papa had played properly, and not thrown away his ace of Diamonds.

THE KING. I couldn't have done anything else, and it wouldn't have made the slightest difference.

THE DAUPHIN. We should have saved the slam, that's all.

THE KING. In the first place you ought never to have redoubled.

THE DAUPHIN. I held excellent cards.

THE KING. You had nothing at all—absolutely nothing.

THE DAUPHIN. Two aces; ace, King, Knave, ten of Clubs——

THE KING. I had the ten of Clubs.

CATHERINE. No, papa, I had the ten.

THE DAUPHIN. I'm quite positive I had the ten.

THE QUEEN. As a matter of fact I had the ten of Clubs.

THE KING. I know I had the ten. It's not the slightest use discussing the matter.

CATHERINE. Oh, Papa, how can you say that? Of course you hadn't.

THE KING. I played this game before you were born, and I suppose I know if a hand is a no-trumper or not.

THE DAUPHIN. I had a much better hand than Catherine's. She had no right to double.

CATHERINE. I had everything——

THE DAUPHIN. Besides which it wasn't fair.

CATHERINE. What wasn't fair?

THE DAUPHIN. To play Hearts.

THE KING. You're quite right, Charles, it wasn't fair.

THE DAUPHIN. You would never have played Hearts, if Mamma hadn't told you to.

THE QUEEN. I never told the child anything. I only played according to the rules.

THE KING. In the first place the rule didn't apply, and in the second place it's not the rule. It's a stupid convention invented by the Italians.

THE QUEEN. I always have played Hearts in doubled no trumps, and I always shall.

THE KING. You might just as well give your partner a kick under the table.

CATHERINE. I should have played Hearts in any case.

THE DAUPHIN. What a lie!

CATHERINE. It's you who tell lies. You said you'd the ten of Clubs.

THE DAUPHIN. We've always played from the shortest suit before.

THE KING. Besides which, you never said a word about it until you saw your cards.

THE QUEEN. Of course not, because I always play Hearts. It's so much the best game.

THE KING. If you did that with other people they'd consider it cheating.

THE DAUPHIN. It was cheating.

CATHERINE. You needn't talk about cheating,

Charles. You cheated this morning at tennis—twice.

THE DAUPHIN. I didn't. You don't understand the score. No woman does.

THE KING. Women have got no morals about cards whatsoever.

THE QUEEN. As a matter of fact we should have won anyhow, if Catherine had played Hearts or not.

CATHERINE. Of course we should.

THE DAUPHIN. Oh! Really!

THE KING. You couldn't possibly have made the odd trick.

THE QUEEN. We should have made at least four tricks; we couldn't help it.

THE KING. And you talk the whole time—no wonder one loses.

THE DAUPHIN. It's quite impossible to play when they interrupt.

THE KING. And touch the cards.

THE Dauphin. And tell each other what to play.

THE KING. And argue about every trick.

THE DAUPHIN. And then never tell the truth.

THE QUEEN. If I were you, Charles, I would learn the rudimentary elements of the game.

THE KING. And not double when you've got nothing.

CATHERINE. And not revoke.

THE DAUPHIN. When did I revoke?

CATHERINE. Last night.

THE DAUPHIN. I didn't.

CATHERINE. I suppose it wasn't a real revoke, just like I suppose you had the ten of Clubs just now.

THE DAUPHIN. So I had.

CATHERINE. You wouldn't dare play like that if we were playing for money.

THE DAUPHIN. Very well. If you think I cheat I shan't play at all.

[*He goes out of the room and slams the door.*

THE KING. We'll play without him.

CATHERINE. I'd much rather play without him. Charles is quite impossible at cards—in fact at all games.

THE QUEEN. Whose deal is it?

THE KING. We must begin a fresh rubber. When one plays three, a game counts for a rubber.

THE QUEEN. Charles!

THE DAUPHIN (*opening the door*). What is it?

THE QUEEN. Come back at once. Don't be so silly. Your father wants to play.

THE DAUPHIN. It's no good my playing if you all say I cheat.

CATHERINE. I never said you cheated.

THE QUEEN. Come back directly. (*The* DAUPHIN *comes back and sits down at the table sulkily.*)

THE KING. Whose deal is it?

CATHERINE. Mine.

THE DAUPHIN. Mine.

CATHERINE. Papa dealt last time.

THE DAUPHIN. No; you dealt and I doubled.

CATHERINE. Papa dealt and left it.

THE DAUPHIN. You dealt, because I remember you nearly made a misdeal.

CATHERINE. I never make misdeals.

THE DAUPHIN. Always.

CATHERINE. Very well. You'd better play without me.

[*She goes out and slams the door.*

THE KING. Oh, dear! Oh, dear! They'll drive me mad!

THE QUEEN (*going to the door*). Catherine, come back this moment. Because Charles chooses to make a fool of himself that's no reason why you should.

CATHERINE. I don't want to play. It's no fun playing with Charles.

THE KING. Oh! do let's go on with the game. Do try not to quarrel so, children. (CATHERINE *comes back and sits down.*)

CATHERINE. I'll come back this time, but if he says I cheat again, I shall never play again as long as I live.

THE QUEEN. Hush! It's Catherine's deal.

CATHERINE. There, you see!

THE QUEEN. Hush!

[CATHERINE *deals.*

THE QUEEN (*looking at her cards*). I shouldn't at all mind if it was left to me this time.

THE KING. You've no business whatever to say a word.

THE QUEEN. As if it made any difference!

THE KING. It makes an enormous difference.

THE QUEEN. Not in this case.

THE KING. That's nothing to do with it. It's the principle that's wrong.

CATHERINE. I leave it.

THE KING. There you see!

CATHERINE. Papa, I couldn't do anything else.

THE QUEEN. I make no trumps.

[*The* DAUPHIN *leads a card; the* QUEEN *puts down her cards, revealing an excellent lead;* CATHERINE *hesitates a moment what to play from dummy's hand, the* QUEEN *touches one of dummy's cards to show.*

THE KING. Isabeau, the dummy has no business to touch the cards. That *is* cheating if you like.

THE QUEEN (*rising up in great dignity*). I've played cards for twenty-five years and have never yet been called a cheat in my own house.

[*She walks to the door.*

CATHERINE. Mamma, Mamma, do come back.

THE DAUPHIN (*walking after her*). Oh! Do come back!

THE KING (*getting up*). Don't be so absurd. You're all of you one worse than the other!

THE QUEEN. No, no, he called me a cheat.

THE KING. I never did anything of the sort.

THE QUEEN. No wonder the children never speak the truth when they've got such a father!

THE KING. Now sit down and let's go on.

[*They sit down. The* KING *plays.* CATHERINE *plays from her hand, and then the* DAUPHIN. CATHERINE *again hestitates about dummy's card, and the* QUEEN *again touches a card showing her what to play.*

THE DAUPHIN. Papa, Mamma's cheated again.

THE QUEEN (*getting up*). I won't have you say that.

CATHERINE (*shouting*). Oh! Charles!

THE DAUPHIN (*screaming*). But she showed you——

[*The* KING *gets up and throws the cards to the other end of the room, kicks over the card-table, and rushes to the door screaming.*

THE QUEEN (*terror-stricken*). Heaven have mercy upon us, your father's gone mad!

CURTAIN.

VII

THE REHEARSAL

SCENE.—*The Globe Theatre,* 1595. *On the stage the* AUTHOR, *the* PRODUCER, *and the* STAGE MANAGER *are standing. A rehearsal of "Macbeth" is about to begin. Waiting in the wings are the actors who are playing the* WITCHES, BANQUO, MACDUFF, *etc. They are all men.*

THE STAGE MANAGER. We'd better begin with the last act.

THE PRODUCER. I think we'll begin with the first act. We've never done it all through yet.

THE STAGE MANAGER. Mr. Colman isn't here. It's no good doing the first act without Duncan.

THE PRODUCER. Where is Mr. Colman? Did you let him know about rehearsal?

THE STAGE MANAGER. I sent a messenger to his house in Gray's Inn.

THE FIRST WITCH. Mr. Colman is playing Psyche in a masque at Kenilworth. He won't be back until the day after to-morrow.

THE PRODUCER. That settles it. We'll begin with the fifth act.

THE FIRST WITCH. Then I suppose I can go.

THE SECOND WITCH. } And I suppose we
THE THIRD WITCH } needn't wait.

THE STAGE MANAGER. Certainly not. We're going on to the fourth act as soon as we've done the fifth.

BANQUO. But I suppose you don't want me.

THE STAGE MANAGER. And what about your ghost entrance in Act IV? We must get the business right this time; besides, we'll do the second act if we've time. Now, Act V, Mr. Thomas and Mr. Bowles, please.

THE FIRST WITCH. Mr. Bowles can't come to-day. He told me to tell you. He's having a tooth pulled out.

THE STAGE MANAGER. Then will you read the waiting gentlewoman's part, Mr. Lyle. You can take this scrip.

[*The* FIRST WITCH *takes the scrip.*

Where is Mr. Thomas?

THE FIRST WITCH. He said he was coming.

THE STAGE MANAGER. We can't wait. I'll read his part. We'll leave out the beginning and just give Mr. Hughes his cue.

THE FIRST WITCH (*reading*). "Having no witness to confirm my speech."

THE STAGE MANAGER. Mr. HUGHES.

THE FIRST WITCH. He was here a moment ago.

THE STAGE MANAGER (*louder*). Mr. Hughes.

Enter LADY MACBETH (MR. HUGHES, *a young man about* 24)

LADY MACBETH. Sorry. (*He comes on down some steps L.C.*)

THE PRODUCER. That will never do, Mr. Hughes; there's no necessity to sway as if you were intoxicated, and you mustn't look at your feet.

LADY MACBETH. It's the steps. They're so rickety.

THE PRODUCER. We'll begin again from " speech."

[LADY MACBETH *comes on again. He looks straight in front of him and falls heavily on to the ground.*

I said those steps were to be mended yesterday.

[*The* FIRST WITCH *is convulsed with laughter.*

LADY MACBETH. There's nothing to laugh at.

THE PRODUCER. Are you hurt, Mr. Hughes?

LADY MACBETH. Not much. (*The steps are replaced by two supers.*)

THE PRODUCER. Now from " speech."

[MR. HUGHES *comes on again.*

THE PRODUCER. You must not hold the taper upside down.

LADY MACBETH. How can I rub my hands and hold a taper too? What's the use of the taper?

THE PRODUCER. You can rub the back of your hand. You needn't wash your hands in the air. That's better.

[*The dialogue between the* DOCTOR *and the* GENTLEWOMAN *proceeds until* LADY MACBETH'S *cue: " hour."*

Enter the DOCTOR (MR. THOMAS). *He waits R.*

LADY MACBETH. " Here's a damned spot."

THE STAGE MANAGER. No, no, Mr. Hughes, " Yet here's a spot."

THE PRODUCER. Begin again from " hands."

GENTLEWOMAN. " It is an accustomed action with her, to seem thus washing her hands. I've known her to continue in this three-quarters of an hour."

LADY MACBETH. " Yet here's a damned spot."

THE STAGE MANAGER. It's not " damned " at all. That comes later.

LADY MACBETH. It's catchy. Couldn't I say " mark " instead of " spot " in the first line?

THE DOCTOR (*coming forward*). That would entirely spoil the effect of my " Hark ! " You see " mark " rhymes with " Hark." It's impossible.

THE PRODUCER. Oh ! It's you, Mr. Thomas. Will you go straight on. We'll do the whole scene over presently. Now from " hour."

LADY MACBETH. " Yes, here's a spot."

THE STAGE MANAGER. It's not " Yes," but " Yet," Mr. Hughes.

LADY MACBETH. " Yet here's a spot."

THE DOCTOR (*at the top of his voice*) " Hark ! "

THE PRODUCER. Not so loud, Mr. Thomas, that would wake her up.

THE DOCTOR (*in a high falsetto*). " Har-r-rk ! She spe-e-e-aks. I will . . . set . . . down."

THE PRODUCER. You needn't bleat that " speaks," Mr. Thomas, and the second part of that line is cut.

THE DOCTOR. It's not cut in my part. " Hark, she speaks."

LADY MACBETH. " Yet here's a spot."

THE STAGE MANAGER. No, Mr. Hughes; " out damned spot."

LADY MACBETH. Sorry.

THE PRODUCER. We must get that right. Now from " hour."

LADY MACBETH. " Yet here's a spot."

THE DOCTOR. "Hark! she speaks."

LADY MACBETH. "Get out, damned spot! Get out, I say! One, two, three, four: why there's plenty of time to do't. Oh! Hell! Fie, fie, my Lord! a soldier and a beard! What have we got to fear when none can call our murky power to swift account withal? You'd never have thought the old man had so much blood in him!"

THE AUTHOR. I don't think you've got those lines quite right yet, Mr. Hughes.

LADY MACBETH. What's wrong?

THE STAGE MANAGER. There's no "get." It's "one; two": and not "one, two, three, four." Then it's "Hell is murky." And there's no "plenty." And it's "a soldier and *afeared,*" and not "a soldier and a *beard.*"

THE AUTHOR. And after that you made two lines into rhymed verse.

MR. HUGHES. Yes, I know I did. I thought it wanted it.

THE PRODUCER. Please try to speak your lines as they are written, Mr. Hughes.

Enter MR. BURBAGE, *who plays Macbeth.*

MR. BURBAGE. That scene doesn't go. Now don't you think Macbeth had better walk in his sleep instead of Lady Macbeth?

THE STAGE MANAGER. That's an idea.

THE PRODUCER. I think the whole scene might be cut. It's quite unnecessary.

LADY MACBETH. Then I shan't come on in the whole of the fifth act. If that scene's cut I shan't play at all.

THE STAGE MANAGER. We're thinking of transferring the scene to Macbeth. (*To the* AUTHOR.) It wouldn't need much altering. Would you mind rewriting that scene, Mr. Shakespeare? It wouldn't want much alteration. You'd have to change that line about Arabia. Instead of this "little hand," you might say: "All the perfumes of Arabia will not sweeten this horny hand." I'm not sure it isn't more effective.

THE AUTHOR. I'm afraid it might get a laugh.

MR. BURBAGE. Not if I play it.

THE AUTHOR. I think it's more likely that Lady Macbeth would walk in her sleep, but——

MR. BURBAGE. That doesn't signify. I can make a great hit in that scene.

LADY MACBETH. If you take that scene from me, I shan't play Juliet to-night.

THE STAGE MANAGER (*aside to* PRODUCER). We can't possibly get another Juliet.

THE PRODUCER. On the whole, I think we must leave the scene as it is.

MR. BURBAGE. I've got nothing to do in the last act. What's the use of my coming to rehearsal when there's nothing for me to rehearse?

THE PRODUCER. Very well, Mr. Burbage. We'll go on to the Third Scene at once. We'll go through your scene again later, Mr. Hughes.

MR. BURBAGE. Before we do this scene there's a point I wish to settle. In Scene V, when Seyton tells me the Queen's dead, I say: "She should have died hereafter; there would have been a time for such a word"; and then the messenger enters. I should like a soliloquy here, about twenty or thirty lines, if possible in rhyme, in any case ending with a tag. I should like it to be about Lady Macbeth.

Macbeth might have something touching to say about their happy domestic life, and the early days of their marriage. He might refer to their courtship. I must have something to make Macbeth sympathetic, otherwise the public won't stand it. He might say his better-half had left him, and then he might refer to her beauty. The speech might begin:

O dearest chuck, it is unkind indeed
To leave me in the midst of my sore need.

Or something of the kind. In any case it ought to rhyme. Could I have that written at once, and then we could rehearse it?

THE PRODUCER. Certainly, certainly, Mr. Burbage. Will you write it yourself, Mr. Shakespeare, or shall we get some one else to do it?

THE AUTHOR. I'll do it myself if some one will read my part.

THE PRODUCER. Let me see; I forget what is your part.

THE STAGE MANAGER. Mr. Shakespeare is playing Seyton. (*Aside.*) We cast him for Duncan, but he wasn't up to it.

THE PRODUCER. Mr. Kydd, will you read Mr. Shakespeare's part?

BANQUO. Certainly.

THE PRODUCER. Please let us have that speech, Mr. Shakespeare, as quickly as possible. (*Aside.*) Don't make it too long. Ten lines at the most.

THE AUTHOR (*aside*). Is it absolutely necessary that it should rhyme?

THE PRODUCER (*aside*). No, of course not; that's Burbage's fad.

[*Exit the* AUTHOR *into the wings.*

MR. BURBAGE. I should like to go through the fight first.

THE PRODUCER. Very well, Mr. Burbage.

THE STAGE MANAGER. Macduff—Mr. Foote——

MACDUFF. I'm here.

MR. BURBAGE. I'll give you the cue:

" Why should I play the fool and like a Roman
Die on my sword, while there is life, there's hope;
The gashes are for them."

MACDUFF. " Turn, hell-hound, turn."

MR. BURBAGE. I don't think Macduff ought to call Macbeth a hell-hound.

THE PRODUCER. What do you suggest?

MR. BURBAGE. I should suggest: " False Monarch, turn." It's more dignified.

MACDUFF. I would rather say " hell-hound."

THE PRODUCER. Supposing we make it " King of Hell."

MR. BURBAGE. I don't think that would do

THE PRODUCER. Then we must leave it for the present.

MACDUFF. " Turn, hell-hound, turn."

[*They begin to fight with wooden swords.*

THE STAGE MANAGER. You don't begin to fight till Macduff says " Give thee out."

MR. BURBAGE. I think we might run those two speeches into one, and I might say:

" Of all men I would have avoided thee,
But come on now, although my soul is charged
With blood of thine, I'll have no further words.
My voice is in my sword."

Then Macduff could say:

" O bloodier villain than terms can well express."

THE PRODUCER. We must consult the author about that.

MR. BURBAGE. We'll do the fencing without words first.

[*They begin to fight again.* MACDUFF *gives* MR. BURBAGE *a tremendous blow on the shoulder.*

MR. BURBAGE. Oh! oh! That's my rheumatic shoulder. Please be a little more careful, Mr. Foote. You know I've got no padding. I can't go on rehearsing now. I am very seriously hurt indeed.

MACDUFF. I'm sure I'm very sorry. It was entirely an accident.

MR. BURBAGE. I'm afraid I must go home. I don't feel up to it.

THE STAGE MANAGER. I'll send for some ointment. Please be more careful, Mr. Foote. Couldn't you possibly see your way to take Scene III, Mr. Burbage?

MR. BURBAGE. I know Scene III backwards. However, I'll just run through my speech.

THE STAGE MANAGER. What? "This push will cheer me ever"?

MR. BURBAGE (*peevishly*). No, not that one. You know that's all right. That tricky speech about medicine. Give me the cue.

THE STAGE MANAGER. "That keep her from her rest."

MR. BURBAGE. "Cure her of that:
Canst thou not minister to a sickly mind,
Pull from the memory a booted sorrow,
Rub out the troubles of the busy brain,
And with a sweet and soothing antidote
Clean the stiff bosom of that dangerous poison
Which weighs upon the heart?"
There, you see, word-perfect. What did I say?

THE STAGE MANAGER. Yes, yes, Mr. Burbage. Here's Mr. Shakespeare.

THE AUTHOR. I've written that speech. Shall I read it?

THE PRODUCER. Please.

MR. SHAKESPEARE (*reads*). "To-morrow, and to-morrow, and to-morrow,
Creeps in this petty pace from day to day,
To the last syllable of recorded time;
And all our yesterdays have lighted fools
The way to dusty death. Out, out, brief candle!
Life's but a walking shadow, a poor player
That struts and frets his hour upon the stage,
And then is heard no more; it is a tale
Told by an idiot, full of sound and fury,
Signifying nothing."

MR. BURBAGE. Well, you don't expect me to say that, I suppose. It's a third too short. There's not a single rhyme in it. It's got nothing to do with the situation, and it's an insult to the stage. "Struts and frets" indeed! I see there's nothing left for me but to throw up the part. You can get any one you please to play Macbeth. One thing is quite certain, I won't. [*Exit* MR. BURBAGE *in a passion.*

THE STAGE MANAGER (*to the* AUTHOR). Now you've done it.

THE AUTHOR (*to the* PRODUCER). You said it needn't rhyme.

THE PRODUCER. It's Macduff. It was all your fault, Mr. Foote.

LADY MACBETH. Am I to wear a fair wig or a dark wig?

THE PRODUCER. Oh! I don't know.

THE AUTHOR. Dark, if you please. People are

always saying I'm making portraits. So, if you're dark, nobody can say I meant the character for the Queen or for Mistress Mary Fytton.

THE STAGE MANAGER. It's no good going on now. It's all up—it's all up.

CURTAIN.

VIII

THE BLUE HARLEQUIN

(WITH APOLOGIES TO MR. MAETERLINCK)

SCENE.—*A London street; the houses are scarcely visible in the diaphanous mist. On the right, darkling, is a sausage shop; on the left a green-grocer's. The shop windows glimmer like opals.*

Enter a POLICEMAN. *He is dressed in a cerulean tunic, and his truncheon is transparent and glows like a beryl.*

THE POLICEMAN. It was not on my beat. It was not on my beat.

Enter the PANTALOON. *He is very old.*

THE PANTALOON. I am very old. I am so old that I cannot remember things. I cannot remember names.

THE POLICEMAN. Move on.

THE PANTALOON. I am always moving on. I feel like a sea-gull.

THE POLICEMAN. Move on. I have already told you to move on.

THE PANTALOON. He told me to move on. He said I would be obliged to move on. I am so old that I forget what they say to me.

THE POLICEMAN. Your beard is like grass. It is like the grass that grows over men's graves. I do not like your beard.

THE PANTALOON. You have no beard. Your face is smooth. It has a hole on one side of it like a cheese. The moon has a hole on one side of it. It is foggy in the street.

[*Pointing to the door of the sausage shop.*

Behind that door there is no fog.

THE POLICEMAN. Nobody has ever opened that door. The key of that door is lost. The lock is broken. It is a useless door.

THE PANTALOON. Years ago that door had a key. There was a little red stain on the key. It wanted cleaning.

THE POLICEMAN. It was a rusty key.

THE PANTALOON. It was a latch-key.

THE POLICEMAN. It was lost on a Thursday.

THE PANTALOON. On the Friday they came to clean the key, but it was too dark to clean it.

THE POLICEMAN. On Saturday morning there was no time. On Saturday afternoon the shops were shut.

THE PANTALOON. The shops were shut all Sunday.

THE POLICEMAN. Monday was Bank Holiday. They went away on Monday.

THE PANTALOON. It rained all day on Monday. It poured with rain. The rain was damp. It had come from a damp place. It was wet rain.

THE POLICEMAN. They told me he was wanted.

THE PANTALOON. They asked me what time it was. I said: "I am so old I have forgotten what time it is. I cannot remember things."

THE POLICEMAN. They came back on Monday night. When they came back they had forgotten all about the key.

THE PANTALOON. I said if you want to know what time it is you must ask the policeman. The policeman knows.

THE POLICEMAN. He knows.

THE PANTALOON. What time is it?

THE POLICEMAN. It is seven minutes to five. It will soon be five minutes to five.

THE PANTALOON. She goes out at five, every day, for a walk.

THE POLICEMAN. She will walk through the fog at five. She is sure to come. I am certain she will come.

THE PANTALOON. She will tell him he is wanted.

THE POLICEMAN. If he comes on to my beat I will take up him.

THE PANTALOON. He will never come on to your beat.

Enter the CLOWN *with a red-hot poker, which shines like a carbuncle*

THE CLOWN. It is strange that we should meet here again. We always meet at the same place and at the same hour.

THE PANTALOON. I am so old I had forgotten I should meet you. When you walked down the street I thought you were some one else. I thought I had never seen you before.

THE CLOWN. It is so foggy in the street and my poker is getting cold.

THE PANTALOON. If you put it in the fire it will get warm again.

THE CLOWN. There is no fire in the street. The policeman says we may not light a fire in the street. It is dangerous. It frightens the people.

THE PANTALOON. Last time they lit a fire in the street it was the 5th of November.

THE CLOWN. The policeman was not there on the 5th of November.

THE PANTALOON. It was not on his beat.

THE CLOWN. His beat is far away—on the sand.

THE PANTALOON. There is a cave near his beat.

THE CLOWN. There is a public-house near his beat. There is a public-house quite close to his beat. It has two doors.

THE PANTALOON. One is marked "Public." He never opens that door.

THE CLOWN. The other is marked "Private." He opens it and it swings backwards and forwards.

THE PANTALOON. The people inside complain of the draught. They are always complaining.

THE CLOWN. She waits for him on the other side of the railings.

THE PANTALOON. The railings are very strong. They are black railings. They are in front of the area. She hands things to him through the railings. She gives him things to eat and things to drink.

THE CLOWN. It is on his beat.

THE PANTALOON. No, it is not on his beat, but it is quite close to his beat. Your poker has got cold.

THE CLOWN. I will warm it. I will warm it on the back of the policeman. He has a broad back.

[*He rubs the* POLICEMAN *with the poker.*

THE POLICEMAN. That poker is warm. It is

much warmer than you think it is. (*The* CLOWN *rubs him again.*) When you do that I feel strange. I feel as if a ruby were burning near me.

THE CLOWN. I am warming you with my poker. It is good to be warm. It is so cold in this street. It never used to be so cold. It is foggy. The fog makes me hungry and thirsty. I am so hungry that I would like to eat a sausage.

THE PANTALOON. I am so hungry that I would like to eat many sausages, first one and then another. I could eat six sausages.

THE CLOWN. Let us go and take some sausages. There are some sausages hanging in that shop. I cannot see them through the fog, but I know there are some sausages there.

THE PANTALOON. I can see the sausages. They are all huddled together like pigeons.

THE CLOWN. They are close together like little wood-pigeons. I like sausages. But before we go I will warm the policeman. He is so cold.

THE PANTALOON. It is not on his beat.

[*The* CLOWN *rubs the* POLICEMAN *with his poker.*

THE POLICEMAN. When you do that I feel as if this had happened before. I feel as if I were in a strange room full of doors and lighted candles. I do not like the feeling.

[*The* PANTALOON *and the* CLOWN *go into the sausage shop.*

Enter COLUMBINE

COLUMBINE. I had nine sisters. They were all blind, and they were all born on a Friday. Friday is an unlucky day.

THE POLICEMAN. I have been waiting for you. I thought you had gone to him. He is wanted. I thought you had gone to tell him he is wanted.

COLUMBINE. You will never find him.

THE POLICEMAN. I have been looking for him since Wednesday. I am tired of looking. It was not on my beat.

COLUMBINE. You will never find him. He knows you are looking for him. When he sees you coming round the corner of the street he runs away round the other corner. He runs quicker than you. Nobody runs so quickly as he does.

THE POLICEMAN. I saw the end of his wand yesterday. It was quite white. It was as white as the milk in the pails.

COLUMBINE. The milk in the pails is not always white. Sometimes it is yellow. But his wand is white. He hits people with it and he runs away. He runs so fast nobody can catch him.

THE POLICEMAN. I saw the spangles of his clothes the day before yesterday. They were all gold. I looked again and I thought they were silver spangles. I thought his clothes were red at first. Afterwards they seemed to be green as leaves in the orchard they cut down.

COLUMBINE. Why did they cut it down?

THE POLICEMAN. Because it was green. There are too many green orchards.

COLUMBINE. He changes his clothes so quickly nobody knows what he has got on.

THE POLICEMAN. His clothes are like the scales of fishes. They are like the scales of grey fishes in the old pond. The old pond is full of fishes. It ought to be dredged.

COLUMBINE. Nobody will ever dredge the old pond. The children fish in it.

THE POLICEMAN. His clothes are like the wings of birds. Like the wings of owls, that fly about in the tower, hooting. The tower is full of owls. It ought to be pulled down.

COLUMBINE. Nobody will ever pull down the tower. The owls kill the mice.

THE POLICEMAN. His clothes are like red sparks. Like the sparks that fly from the horses' hoofs in the crooked lane. The crooked lane is full of horses. It ought to be made into a field.

COLUMBINE. It will never be made into a field. Too many people use the crooked lane. It leads to the mill. It is the shortest way to the mill.

THE POLICEMAN. His clothes are like the blue pebbles the old women drop into the stream. The stream is full of pebbles. It ought to be dried up.

COLUMBINE. It will never be dried up, because the old women wash their clothes in it. It is not pebbles they throw into it. It is blue from the blue-bag. They throw it in to whiten the linen.

THE POLICEMAN. I do not know. It is not on my beat. Some people say it is pebbles. Their linen is all in holes. It is frayed linen.

COLUMBINE. His linen is never frayed.

THE POLICEMAN. His clothes hide his linen. You cannot tell what colour his clothes are. Sometimes they are blue and sometimes they are red.

COLUMBINE. Some people say they are grey clothes—grey like the sand.

THE POLICEMAN. They told me they were blue I am sure his clothes are blue.

Enter the CLOWN *through the window*

THE CLOWN. I would have brought you some sausages. I would have brought you a hundred sausages. They are made of pork. The pig was killed on a Friday.

COLUMBINE. Everything always happens on a Friday. I was born on a Friday.

THE CLOWN. I would have brought you more sausages than I can eat myself. I would have brought you more sausages than you can eat.

THE POLICEMAN. Nobody can eat more than a certain amount of sausages. That is why they are so sad in this street. I can eat a great many sausages.

COLUMBINE. It is a bad thing to eat too many sausages.

THE CLOWN. It is not right to go into a shop, to take away the sausages, and to eat them. The shopkeeper called him a thief because he took away the sausages.

THE POLICEMAN. It is not on my beat.

COLUMBINE. He was very hungry.

THE CLOWN. He had no right to take away all the sausages. There were none left for us. If he had not taken away all the sausages I could have brought them to you. He jumped down the chimney. It was cleaned yesterday. He took away all the sausages. He took away the sausages I would have brought you. I had meant to bring them all.

THE POLICEMAN. What colour were his clothes?

THE CLOWN. I was so frightened when he took away the sausages that I did not notice the colour of his clothes. I think they were red clothes.

THE POLICEMAN. Were they not blue clothes?

THE CLOWN. They may have been blue clothes.

He jumped down the chimney and drew out his knife. It was a steel knife, and there were spots on the blade. He cut the string of the sausages from the ceiling. They were all huddled together in the ceiling like birds . . . like birds in the winter.

Enter the PANTALOON

THE PANTALOON. He has taken away all the sausages. I was going to bring you sausages to eat. They were hanging from the roof like little fat mice. But I am so old—I forget things. Then he came with his knife and cut them down. You must take him up. He has stolen the sausages. They were not his sausages.

THE POLICEMAN. It is not on my beat. What colour were his clothes?

THE PANTALOON. I am so old I forget things. I think they were green clothes.

THE POLICEMAN. Were they not blue clothes?

THE CLOWN (*to the* POLICEMAN). You are so cold. I will warm you with my poker. It is a red-hot poker.

THE POLICEMAN. Whenever you do that I feel strange. [*The* CLOWN *rubs him with the poker.*

THE POLICEMAN. I will take away your poker. I do not like to be made to feel strange so often.

[*The* CLOWN *runs away and jumps through the shop window. The* POLICEMAN *runs after him. At that moment the* HARLEQUIN—*he is all blue —darts round the street corner and runs off with* COLUMBINE.

THE POLICEMAN. He has run away with her. They said he would come when I was not looking.

I shall never catch him. His clothes were blue. (*To the* PANTALOON) I will take you up instead. I will say you took the sausages. I will not speak the truth. You will speak the truth. You will say he took the sausages. But they will not believe you. They will believe me. Now you shall come with me, along.

THE PANTALOON. I am so old. I feel as if all this had happened before.

THE POLICEMAN. I will say it was on my beat.

[*As he leads off the* PANTALOON, *the* CLOWN *jumps out of the window and hits him with the red-hot poker.*

THE POLICEMAN. Whenever he does that I feel strange.

[*The* PANTALOON *escapes and fades into the fog.*

CURTAIN.

IX

THE MEMBER FOR LITERATURE

It having been settled that a Member for "Literature" should be elected to the House of Commons, a plebiscite was taken among the members of all the literary clubs and societies in London.

The result was that Mr. M—x B—b—m, Mr. H—ll C—e, Mr. R—d—d K—p—g, *and* Mr. J—e K. J—e *all received exactly the same number of votes. In order to settle which of them should be chosen, it was decided that these four authors should each in turn address the same public meeting, after which the election should be by ballot, and the author chosen by the audience at the meeting should be the Member for Literature.*

Scene.—*A hall at Battersea. On the platform are a* Chairman, *a small Committee, and the four* Authors *in question.*

Mr. M—x B—b—m (*rises to address the meeting*). No politician I.

A Voice from the Back of the Hall. Then why the —— —— do you come here to talk politics?

Mr. M—x B—b—m. That, gentle public, is what I wish carefully to avoid doing. You can lead me to the hustings, but you cannot make me think

—politically. Therefore bear with me a little. Examine yourselves and you will see that, were you in my position, you would do exactly what I am going to do now. Candidature has been thrust upon me. I am forced to speak to you, I am indeed anxious to speak to you so that you may be able to choose one of the three distinguished literary men, whom you see before you on this platform, to be your Literary Member, and I wish to prevent your choice falling upon me.

I will put before you in chosen sentences, which I have carefully arranged beforehand, the reasons why I think you should not elect me. I do not want to be elected. To elect me would indeed be an unfriendly act. Such a choice would not only cause me inconvenience, but it would bring to yourselves neither profit nor pleasure. Be sure I should never think of your interests, be surer still I should never attend the tedious sittings at St. Stephen's. I have listened to eloquence at the Oxford Union and to the gentle rhetoric of Cambridge. Not for me are the efforts of the half-witted and the wholly inarticulate at Westminster, who stammer where old Gladstone used to sing. If you have views I am not privy to them, and from your sympathies I am aloof. I know well enough that you—no more than I—care a red farthing whether the label of your Member be Liberal or Conservative. What you do care for, and what leaves me frigid, is the figure whom you can encourage by chaff or vex by sarcasm.

You want to hear that Lloyd George ought to be thrown into a den of Suffragettes—(*Hear, Hear*)—or that Winston Churchill is good and old. (*Hear, Hear.*) You want to hear it not adumbrated, but said emphatically and without the introduction of a *nuance*, either that Mr. Balfour is infallible or that he is invincibly ignorant. (*Cheers and groans.*)

Now, I care not whether Mr. Balfour be right or wrong. I murmur to myself the jest of Pilate, and I do not wait for the answer. And as to the province of affairs which concerns you here, the province of the Budget, the Fiscal Question, Home Rule, the House of Lords, the Disestablishment of the Welsh Church, and other fallalas, it is for me a vague land into which Leonardo da Vinci never looked forward, and about which I have not experienced the least curiosity; nor do I care whether Mr. Balfour be inspired by an angel or an ape. (*Liberal cheers.*)

As to Mr. Asquith's claims, I am just as undecided and just as indifferent. (*Conservative cheers.*) I know nothing about the Education Bill or the Children's Bill; I have heard that one of these measures will make "Hunt the Slipper" compulsory for children under five years old, and that there is somewhere a clause being moulded which will prevent boys over sixteen years of age from playing marbles in the public thoroughfares. But since before long children will have votes for themselves and be represented in Parliament—(*cries of "Votes for Children"*)—we can surely for the present leave these perplexing questions gently suspended until they shall be dealt with by those whom they more nearly concern. (*A little boy is carried out struggling and waving a megaphone.*)

But you will say—our Imperial Policy? Well, I will be frank, I am in favour of the restoration of the Heptarchy. Had I my way even Rutland should have, not only Home Rule—(*Liberal cheers*)

—but a King, by Divine Right absolute. Of course, I wish our present King to remain a super-King of all the little Englands, of the 52 (or is it 365?) counties of England. (*Loud cheers.*) As for the Colonies, blood may be thicker than water, but water, happily for us, is broader than blood—(*loud cheers*)—and I have always been thankful that we are separated from America, and from our other high-spirited offsprings, by so broad an ocean as the Atlantic. Our Colonies are our children. Their place is in the nursery or at school. There let us leave them to their ninepins, their whipping-tops, their rocking-horses, and their marbles. Their exploits can only weary us who are their grown-up parents, we who are obliged to read their tri-monthly reports, and to pay wages which we can ill afford for their nurses and their ushers.

I hear a lady murmuring the words "Budget" and "Fiscal Question"—magical words, it is true. But we need hardly discuss them, because whatever we say or do there will always be a Budget; there will always be a Fiscal Question, and a vague alternative to it preached by an indignant and sanguine Opposition.

Whatever our taxes may be, and however we have to pay them, they will always have to be paid, and I for one shall never pay them with ecstasy. (*Cheers.*) Formerly the poor had the exclusive right of paying taxes; now it is rumoured that the rich have usurped that privilege, and so grossly abused it that, the rich having become poorer than the poor, the poor must needs pay a super-tax. (*Groans and cries of "Shame."*) Well, I only desire that there may always be people so much richer than myself that they will pay me cheerfully and generously for taking pains to write what few will trouble to read. When the day comes that there will be no more rich—(Oh, dreadful day !)—Max's occupation will be gone, because even were I then to draw flaming seascapes in coloured chalk on the paving-stones of Piccadilly, there will be no one richer than myself to drop a bad halfpenny into the saucer which shall hang under the card, so needlessly telling the passer-by what the pictures themselves proclaim : that the artist is blind.

I think I have now lightly shaken by the hand the questions which, as the phrase goes, are at issue, and although I have not given you my reasons in clauses, headings, and sections, I hope I have made it perspicuous to you that I do not wish to be a member of Parliament, and that were I to be chosen, I should not lift my eye-glass to justify your choice; I would not sacrifice the whiff of a cigarette for all the perfumes of St. Stephen's. But as a postscript, I am in favour of full-dress debates; and by that I mean debates in the House of Lords where the Peers are dressed in robe and coronet; and these debates, were I King of England, should be compulsory and frequent. And as one postscript leads to another, I will tell you that were a more competent Guy Fawkes to blow up the House of Commons, and were it never to arise from its ashes, I should say " Ouf ! "

[*He sits down. Discreet cheers.*

MR. H—LL C—E (*rises*). Mr. Chairman, ladies and gentlemen, loath as I have always been to obtrude upon the public gaze——

A VOICE. Why, it's Shakespeare !

ANOTHER VOICE. No, it tain't. It's the Wax Bust.

MR. H—LL C—E. Loath as I have always been——

A VOICE. As a Manxman, are you, or are you not, in favour of Votes for Women?

MR. H—LL C—E. Loath as I am——

THE SAME VOICE. He's not in favour of Votes for Women and he's a Manxman! (*A terrific blast is blown on toy trumpets and megaphones.*)

ANOTHER VOICE. Tails for Manx Cats.

MR. H—LL C—E. Loath as I am——

VOICES. Votes for Women. (*Loud uproar—some women are ejected.*)

[*After a hurried confabulation it is settled that* MR. R—D—D K—P—G *shall address the audience, and that* MR. H—LL C—E *shall speak later.*

MR. R—D—D K—P—G (*rises*). There was once an Aunt-Hill. It was a small Aunt-Hill, and from the summit to the base of it the distance was about as long as the slip of an E.P. Tent.

The Aunts were busy. They worked all day and sometimes all night. Now when Aunts work all night it's worth going to see. The hill grew bigger and bigger, and tunnels were burrowed, and after some months the Aunts had annexed a whole forest. They were pleased with themselves.

" The sun doesn't set on our Aunt-Hill," said one Aunt.

" Our Aunt-Hill is the key of the Eastern forest," said another. The Kingdom of the Aunts grew so large that they sent some of their younger workers to make Aunt-Hills beyond the forest. This they did, and their Aunt-Hills grew big, too. Then the

Aunts were pleased and said: "We are the greatest Aunts in the World." But one of the Aunts—he wrote things for the other Aunts to read—said: "Take care, you were small once; and if you don't go on working you'll be small again." But the Aunts said he was a fool. Then the Aunts began to get slack and look on at their little Aunts playing at rolling the acorn.

Now in a neighbouring forest a rival Aunt set up a hill and began training an army.

Then the Aunt who wrote things said: "Take care, these new Aunts will grow strong and take away your Aunt-Hill." But the Aunts didn't listen, they went on looking at the Aunts playing at rolling the acorn. And one of the leading Aunts said: "He's a scaremonger, don't listen. He's a 'Jing-aunt.' Its Unauntish to say such things." So nobody cared, and the new Aunts came and took the old Aunts' Aunt-Hill and made them all into slaves.

[Mr. R—d—d K—p—g *sits down.* (*Cheers.*)

Mr. J—e K. J—e (*rises*). Mr. Chairman, ladies and gentlemen——

A Voice. Does your mother know you're out?

Mr. J—e K. J—e. Yes, but my mother-in-law doesn't. (*Terrific cheers.*) Gentlemen, I don't think I need say any more. I'm the only man so far who has said to you a single word you've understood. (*Cheers.*) So I think I'll let well alone. My politics are Home Rule at Home, and down with Mothers-in-Law. (*Renewed cheering.*)

[Mr. J—e K. J—e *sits down.*

[*After brief consultation on the platform,* Mr. H—ll C—e *rises again.*

MR. H—LL C—E. Loath as I am——

MANY WOMEN. What about Votes for Women?

[*There is an uproar; a scuffle and a fight. It is impossible to continue the business, so the question as to who shall be elected is put to the Meeting. The people proceed to vote by ballot. The votes are then counted by the Committee in a room adjoining the platform. After an interval the* CHAIRMAN *comes on to the platform.*

THE CHAIRMAN. Ladies and gentlemen, I will now have the pleasure of reading out the result of the Election. The figures are as follows:—

MR. J—E K. J—E (elected)	333
MR. R—D—D K—P—G	12
MR. M—X B—B—M	3
MR. H—LL C—E	2

[*The Meeting breaks up amidst terrific cheers.*

CURTAIN.

X

CALIGULA'S PICNIC

SCENE.—*A large banqueting table in the centre of a bridge, which stretches for three miles between Puteoli and Baiæ. The* EMPEROR CALIGULA *is reclining in the place of honour. There are hundreds of guests.*

RUFUS (*an intensely eager, bearded man to his neighbour* PROTEUS, *a dandy*). As I was saying, the whole point of the question is this: all diseases come from the secretion in the blood of certain poisons. Now since we imbibe these poisons from certain foodstuffs, what I say is—Cut off the poison at the supply.

PROTEUS (*helping himself to roast boar with stuffing*). Yes, yes, perfectly.

RUFUS. Cut off the poison at the supply. Prevent; don't try to cure when it's too late. You follow me?

PROTEUS (*absently*). Exactly. (*He gives himself an additional helping of roast boar.*)

RUFUS. But there you are, helping yourself to poison again. (RUFUS *gives up* PROTEUS *and turns to his other neighbour.*)

HYGERIUS (*on* PROTEUS'S *right, an aged Senator*). May I trouble you for the peacock?

PROTEUS. I beg your pardon. (*He passes the peacock.*)

HYGERIUS. I suppose these peacocks are imported.

PROTEUS (*not interested*). I suppose so.

HYGERIUS. Now what I say is, the land's the question.

PROTEUS (*foreseeing a discourse on political economy*). The General is trying to catch your eye.

HYGERIUS. Where? Where? I don't see him.

PROTEUS. Right at the other end of the table. (*To his vis-à-vis*, DEMOPHILUS, *an officer*) Were you lucky yesterday?

DEMOPHILUS. No, I lost. They told me Chilon was a certainty.

PROTEUS. Ah! Chilon.

DEMOPHILUS. He didn't do himself justice.

PROTEUS. Over-trained?

HYGERIUS (*to his vis-à-vis*, PETRONIUS, *a fashionable philosopher*). Now you no doubt agree with me that nowadays the whole problem of agriculture——

PETRONIUS (*upsetting a large bowl of wine on the table on purpose*). A thousand pardons! It was too awkward of me.

[*Slaves come and mop up the mess.*

SEVERUS (*a literary man, sitting on* HYGERIUS'S *left, to* PETRONIUS). "Spilt wine shall buy the favour of the Gods," as Particus says.

PETRONIUS. Have you seen Cossatius's play?

SEVERUS. Yes, it's clever, but——

HYGERIUS. That kind of play ought not to be tolerated. It undermines the principles of morality.

SEVERUS. Morals have nothing to do with art.

HYGERIUS. I repeat that these kinds of plays are the ruin of the Empire.

PETRONIUS. I see you are on the side of the "Extensionists."

HYGERIUS. I don't know what you mean by an "Extensionist," but if you mean a Roman and a patriot——

PETRONIUS. No, I mean a Greek and a swindler.

PROTEUS. Excellent eels—try them.

RUFUS. Let me beg you not to touch them; they are full of poison.

DEMOPHILUS (*alarmed*). Poison! Who's poisoned them?

PETRONIUS. Rufus means they give you gout.

PROTEUS. I once knew a man who ate twenty-seven eels for a bet.

DEMOPHILUS (*really interested*). Oh! Did he win?

PROTEUS. Yes; but he died afterwards. Hush! the speeches are beginning.

PETRONIUS. Oh dear! Oh dear!

[*The* PREFECT OF PUTEOLI *rises farther up the table.*

THE PREFECT. Friends and citizens, and more especially, citizens of Puteoli and Baiæ: It is with feelings of peculiar emotion that I rise to propose that toast, which of all toasts is the nearest to the heart and leaps most readily to the lips of a Roman—I mean, of course, the toast of our beloved Emperor. I may say that in all the vast extent of this Empire, of which we are so justly proud, the Emperor has no more loyal subjects than those of Baiæ and—(*cheers*)—of Puteoli. (*Cheers.*) Although in the past we of Puteoli may not always have been able to see eye to eye with our neighbours of Baiæ, in matters of local administration, to-day, happily, all such rivalry has ended. And to whom is this due? To whom but the Emperor, who, with his knowledge of the Roman heart, has had the happy, the graceful, nay, more, the truly Imperial and the truly Roman idea of joining the two cities by this elegant and monumental bridge. (*Loud cheers.*) We of Puteoli are not quick to forget the benefits we have received in the past from the Imperial Family. And some of us who are here present remember that auspicious and never-to-be-forgotten day when the Emperor's illustrious father, the ever-memorable Germanicus—(*loud and prolonged cheers*)—I say many of us here present will recall that thrice-memorable occasion when the illustrious Germanicus—(*loud cheers*)—paid us a visit. Romans, I have no wish to rake up things which are better forgotten; I have no desire to abuse the ashes of him who, whatever his faults and his failings may have been, is now for ever beyond the reach of our recrimination. We Romans have a proverb which says: "Of the dead nothing but good"—(*cheers*)—and you, citizens of Puteoli and Baiæ, have ever strictly observed, both by precept and by practice, the wisdom that has been handed down to us in the popular phrases of the Roman people. (*Cheers.*) Therefore, it is with no fear of being misunderstood, and in no carping or unjust spirit, that I say that the example which our beloved Emperor Caligula is daily setting us, both in peace and in war, and in all the arts and graces of life—this example is, I say, as it were, heightened when we—and we of Puteoli and Baiæ are especially sensible of the fact—when we think of the shortcomings and the mistakes of the late and unfortunate Tiberius—(*hisses and groans*)—shortcomings and mistakes to which our present Emperor put so swift an end, and out of whose ashes he bade our Empire and our Government, our internal affairs and our foreign policy, rise rejuvenated and splendid like the Phœnix. (*Cheers.*) Citizens, I will detain you no longer. All I will say is this: so long as we have at the head of us one who is the pattern of what a Roman gentleman should be, one who is at the same time the elder brother and the father of his people, so long as this shall be, so long will the Roman Empire, throughout all its length and breadth, act together in that same spirit of fraternal love and unity, bound by ties as strong as that with which our Emperor has to-day united and linked the people of Baiæ to the people of Puteoli. Citizens, I propose the health of the divine Emperor. (*Loud cheers. The toast is drunk with enthusiasm.*)

HYGERIUS. A first-rate speech.

THE PREFECT OF BAIÆ *rises.* Citizens, it is with the keenest sense of my unfitness to so exalted a task that I rise to propose the toast which is second on our list, that toast which of all others, with the exception of that which we have just drunk, is most grateful to Roman ears, namely, the Army. (*Cheers.*) Although not a soldier myself, my heart is with the Army; but I will go farther, I will say that all of us, whatever our avocations may be, whether we be lawyers, merchants, engineers, painters, poets, philosophers, are in a sense soldiers of the Emperor. (*Cheers.*) And Peace, citizens, has its battles as well as War. (*Loud Cheers.*) To-day we are gathered together to celebrate one of those battles—a battle which has ended in a triumph. (*Cheers.*) [DEMOPHILUS (*aside*). What battle?] I allude to the completion of this handsome bridge—(*cheers*)—

which is a notable—I may even say an unparalleled example—of the triumph of man's will over the elements. As the immortal poet Camerinus—(*cheers*) —has said :

O'er vanquished Nature Man shall spread his sway,
And force the fretful ocean to obey

(*Cheers.*)

And while the utmost credit is due to the skill and patience with which the engineers, Demonax and Hegias, of Corinth, have executed their stupendous task, still greater praise is due to the Emperor, in whose fertile brain the great idea had its origin, and without whose unceasing aid and constant interest it could never have been completed. (*Cheers.*) We of Baiæ know how keen was that interest, how valuable that aid, and we will never forget it. I have said, citizens, we are all of us in a sense soldiers, and it is a sight like this, an occasion such as to-day's, that brings home to every Roman the self-sacrifice, the patience, the stubborn will, and the dogged persistence—qualities all of them essentially military —of the Roman race. I therefore propose the health of the Army, coupled with the name of its glorious Commander-in-Chief, the Emperor. (*Loud cheers. The toast is drunk.*)

SEVERUS. He misquoted Camerinus.

[*A* PRÆTORIAN OFFICER *rises.*

THE PRÆTORIAN OFFICER. Citizens, my trade is to speak and not to act—I mean to act and not to speak. (*Loud cheers.*) I am a humble particle of what has so rightly been called the great dumb one. (*Cheers.*) I thank you all very much for drinking

D

the last toast, and I in my turn have great pleasure in proposing the toast which comes next on the list, namely, the toast of Literature. (*Cheers.*) I am not much of a literary man myself, but I greatly enjoy reading the description of battles in the works of that poet who, though not a Roman by birth, is practically a Roman—I mean Homer—(*cheers*)—and also in the great epic of our Roman Homer, I mean Camerinus. (*Loud cheers.*) I propose the toast of Literature, coupled with that of the divine Emperor, who, as we all know, is a first-rate author himself. (*Cheers.*)

[EROTIANUS, *an elderly poet, rises to reply.*

EROTIANUS. Citizens, great and immortal names have been mentioned to-day. Homer, Camerinus, have lent by the very mention of their names a diviner light to this already illustrious occasion. Nor has our gallant friend in his masterly oration failed to remind us of the talents, the brilliant and exceptional literary gifts, of our noble master. (*Cheers.*) I am the last person who should address you on this theme. (*Cries of No, No.*) We had hoped that Seneca—(*cheers*)—whose verses are for ever on our lips, would be present. Unfortunately a bad cold has detained him in Rome. Æsculapius has conquered the Muses —(*cries of Shame*)—and instead of a brilliant literary light you have the flicker of a new artisan in the field of letters. (*Cries of No, No.*) I am, if I may say so, no more than a humble shepherd on the slopes of Parnassus. But, citizens, those slopes are so high, and so wide that there is room on them for the greatest, such as Homer and Ovid—(*cheers*)—and for the more humble but none the less painstaking, such as Virgil and myself. (*Cheers.*) I will now proceed to read to you a short epic in six cantos which I have prepared for this occasion. (*Cheers. He clears his throat.*) It is called "The Bridge." (*Cheers.*)

[*The* EMPEROR *makes a signal, upon which a regiment of Prætorians, concealed in a neighbouring tent, rush among the guests armed with swords and sharp tridents, and proceed to toss them into the sea. The meal breaks up in confusion. Some of the guests escape, but a large number are drowned, including* EROTIANUS.

CURTAIN.

XI

THE AULIS DIFFICULTY

SCENE.—AGAMEMNON'S *tent at Aulis. Discovered:* AGAMEMNON *seated at a camp table writing.*

Enter IPHIGENIA

IPHIGENIA. Do you want to speak to me, papa?

AGAMEMNON (*nervously*). Yes, yes, a moment. (*A pause.*)

IPHIGENIA. Well?

AGAMEMNON. Sit down—on that chair—it's more comfortable there. . . . I . . . er . . . (*A pause.*)

IPHIGENIA. If you've got nothing particular to say, papa, I'll go, if you don't mind; because mamma wants me to help her with the dinner. The cook is quite helpless——

AGAMEMNON. Wait a minute. I do want to speak to you very particularly. . . . (*A pause.*) . . . It's a lovely day again to-day.

IPHIGENIA. Really, papa——

AGAMEMNON. It's not so irrelevant as you think. You see, there's not a breath of wind.

IPHIGENIA. I know. They say it's quite impossible for you to start.

AGAMEMNON. We shall have been here two months next Tuesday.

IPHIGENIA. You mean next Saturday.

AGAMEMNON. Tuesday or Saturday, it's all the same.

IPHIGENIA. It's a mercy we did stop here. Mamma says that your linen was in a dreadful state, and that if she hadn't come out she doesn't know how you would have managed.

AGAMEMNON. Yes, I don't say that the stay hasn't been of some use; but now it is absolutely essential that we should get to Troy.

IPHIGENIA. Why don't you start to-day?

AGAMEMNON. Whenever we put to sea there's either no wind at all, or a gale which drives us straight back home.

IPHIGENIA. It is very tiresome, but it can't be helped, can it?

AGAMEMNON. Well, that's just it. I'm afraid it can be helped.

IPHIGENIA. What do you mean, papa?

AGAMEMNON. To cut a long story short, Calchas consulted the Oracle this morning, and it appears, he says, I mean the Oracle said, or rather the goddess——

IPHIGENIA. Which goddess?

AGAMEMNON. Artemis.

IPHIGENIA. Oh, she's impossible.

AGAMEMNON. Well, as I told you, Calchas says that it is Artemis who is causing the delay by sending us adverse winds, and——

IPHIGENIA. Can't something be done?

AGAMEMNON. That is precisely the point. The goddess has, through the Oracle, suggested a way out of the difficulty, and it concerns you.

IPHIGENIA. Me? What can I have to do with it?

AGAMEMNON. Now, my dearest Iphigenia, I want you to be reasonable. You always were a sensible girl, and I want to you bring all your good sense to bear on this . . . in this . . . er . . . trying occasion.

IPHIGENIA. I don't understand.

AGAMEMNON. I will go straight to the point. Artemis says that we shall never leave Aulis unless you consent to go through the form of being sacrificed to her.

IPHIGENIA. What do you mean by " going through the form " ?

AGAMEMNON. I mean chat in all probability . . . in fact, quite certainly, the sacrifice would be purely a formal one, and that there is every chance . . . in fact, I may say it is almost certain that one of the other gods or goddesses would intervene at the last moment and prevent the sacrifice from being fatal.

IPHIGENIA. You mean to say that there is not the slightest chance of my being killed—that it's only a farce?

AGAMEMNON. I won't go so far as that . . . but I will say that as far as we know every precedent in the past——

IPHIGENIA. Oh, bother the precedents. What I want to know is this: Is there the slightest chance of my being *really* sacrificed?

AGAMEMNON. It is highly improbable, of course; only you *must* consent; you must behave exactly as if you were going to be sacrificed; you must express your entire willingness to lay down your life for your country; and knowing what a patriotic, obedient, filial child you are, I am certain this will be a positive pleasure to you.

IPHIGENIA. I won't.

AGAMEMNON. You mean you won't even pretend to——

IPHIGENIA. I won't have anything to do with it at all—I think it's monstrous, and I'm sure mamma will agree with me.

AGAMEMNON. My dearest child, let me beg of you not to say a word about this to your mother just yet.

IPHIGENIA. Of course, I shall tell her. (*Enter* CLYTÆMNESTRA.) Here is mamma. Mamma——

CLYTÆMNESTRA. What is all this?

IPHIGENIA. Papa says I must be sacrificed to Artemis, in order that they may have a smooth passage to Troy, and to prevent Ajax being sea-sick. I say I won't. (*She begins to cry.*)

CLYTÆMNESTRA (*taking her in her arms*). Of course you shan't, my love—my darling. (*To* AGAMEMNON) What is this ridiculous nonsense?

AGAMEMNON. I assure you it is not my doing. I merely repeated what Calchas had said. He consulted the Oracle, and it appears that Artemis is vexed: she is, in fact, very much displeased. She says we shall never leave Aulis unless Iphigenia consents to go through the form of being sacrificed—of course it's only a matter of form—but she must consent.

CLYTÆMNESTRA. I see. As long as I'm here my child shall not degrade herself by being a party to any ridiculous farce of this nature. I don't care a bit if we do stay here. You ought never to have come here for one thing. I always said it was absurd from the first—just because of Helen's silly escapade. If you can't get a fair wind you'll have to go home; but you shan't touch Iphigenia.

Enter a MAID

THE MAID (*to* CLYTÆMNESTRA). The cook wants to know whether the fish are to be boiled or fried.

CLYTÆMNESTRA (*angrily*). I told her fried. (*To* AGAMEMNON) I must go and look after her. I'll be back in a moment.

[*Exit* CLYTÆMNESTRA.

AGAMEMNON. There, you see what you've done. You've set your mother against the whole plan.

IPHIGENIA (*crying*). I hope I have. Of course, if you want to kill me, please do . . . just (*sobbing*) as if I were a sheep.

AGAMEMNON. My dear child, do be calm. Who ever talked of killing——

Enter CALCHAS

AGAMEMNON. She won't hear of it.

CALCHAS. My dear child, please be sensible and think of the interests at stake. Remember you are grown up, and we grown-up people have to face these things.

IPHIGENIA. I don't care what you say, I won't be sacrificed—I won't be killed like a sheep.

CALCHAS. Even if the worst came to the worst, I promise you you would feel no pain. I assure you we have reached a pitch of perfection in the working of these things which makes all accidents impossible. Besides, think of the honour and the glory.

AGAMEMNON. And it's not as if she would be killed *really*.

CALCHAS. It's extremely improbable; but even

if she were to lose consciousness and not recover, I am sure most girls would envy her. Just think, your statue would be put up in every city in Greece.

AGAMEMNON. All the poets would celebrate her.

CALCHAS. You see it's not as if she were married.

AGAMEMNON. She has always refused every one.

CALCHAS. And now it's too late.

AGAMEMNON. Girls are so independent nowadays.

CALCHAS. They think nothing of tradition, country, or of the respect they owe their parents. They are ungrateful.

AGAMEMNON. They never think of what they owe the goddesses. In my time . . .

Enter ODYSSEUS

IPHIGENIA. I don't care what you say. I won't be sacrificed. (*She bursts into tears.*)

[ODYSSEUS *whispers to* AGAMEMNON *and* CALCHAS *to withdraw. They go out.*

ODYSSEUS. And how is our little Iphigenia to-day?

IPHIGENIA (*drying her eyes*). Quite well, thank you; only papa wants to kill me.

ODYSSEUS. Kill you, my dear child! I assure you you are mistaken. Nobody, and least of all your father, could dream of such a thing. You are the life and soul of the expedition. It was only this morning I wrote to Penelope to tell her how well you were looking and what a difference it made to all of us your being here.

IPHIGENIA. Papa wants me to be sacrificed.

ODYSSEUS. You can't have understood your father. Let me explain it to you. You know what Artemis is: she's a charming goddess—quite charming—only she's touchy. Well, she happens to be very much put out at this moment by the attention that has been paid to the other goddesses; and by a very regrettable oversight her sacrifice has been neglected once or twice lately. Of course she is put out; but, believe me, the situation only requires tact—just a little tact . . . and we all want you to help us. . . . You see, if you don't help us we are lost, and the whole expedition may be ruined, all just for the want of a little tact at the right moment. Now, nobody can help us as well as you can. You see Artemis has taken a peculiar fancy to you. She admires you enormously. I happen to know this on the very best authority. She thinks you are far more beautiful than your Aunt Helen. At the same time she is just a shade hurt that you never take any notice of her. Now, what we want you to do is to consent to our stratagem: a delicate piece of flattery which will soothe Artemis and make everything all right. All you will have to do is to wear the most beautiful dress—white and silver—and a band of wrought gold studded with rubies round your head, and to walk with your wonderful hair reaching almost to your feet, in a procession of weeping maidens to the Temple; and there, after the usual prayers and chants, you will sing a hymn to Artemis, especially composed for the occasion, to a flute accompaniment; then, in the gaze of all the crowd, you will kneel down before the altar, and Artemis, flattered and pleased, will carry you off in a cloud, and substitute a sheep or something else for you. Every one will praise you; you will have had all the amusement of the festival, all the glory and honour of the sacrifice, and none of the inconvenience.

IPHIGENIA (*pensively*). It would be rather fun. Are you sure I shouldn't risk being killed really? Calchas said I probably would.

ODYSSEUS. Calchas knows nothing about it at all. I promise you that it's just as safe as if you were going to sing at the festival of Bacchus.

IPHIGENIA. But what will happen to me afterwards?

ODYSSEUS. That must be a secret between you and me. Artemis has arranged that a charming young man shall carry you away. I need not mention his name, as you know it too well. It begins with an A. But the marriage must remain a secret until after the siege.

IPHIGENIA. All right, I will do it. I mean I will pretend to consent, but there must be no question of its really coming off. That you must swear.

ODYSSEUS. I swear we shall sacrifice a sheep instead of you, or if the worst comes to the worst Achilles' slave, who is so like you.

IPHIGENIA. And then I shall really marry Achilles.

Enter CLYTÆMNESTRA

ODYSSEUS (*to* CLYTÆMNESTRA). It's all settled; only don't discuss it with Agamemnon. He doesn't quite know how to deal with goddesses. He is—you forgive me saying so—a little bit heavy.

CLYTÆMNESTRA (*to* IPHIGENIA). You don't mean to say you've consented. I forbid it. . . . I am your mother, and I positively forbid you to do any such thing.

IPHIGENIA. I'm of age. I'm old enough to judge what I can do and what I can't do. It's my duty, and it's a question of principle; and if I choose to be sacrificed, nobody has the right to prevent me. And I *do* choose. The one thing I've always longed for all my life has been to die for my country.

[*Exit* IPHIGENIA *in a passion.*

[ODYSSEUS *looks at* CLYTÆMNESTRA *and smiles.*

CLYTÆMNESTRA. Serpent!

CURTAIN.

XII

DON JUAN'S FAILURE

SCENE.—*The hall in an English Country House. Van Dyck Period.*

LUCASTA. My mother will be down directly, if you don't mind waiting.

DON JUAN. On the contrary, I could wait a hundred years in the company of one whom I know not whether she be a goddess or a mortal.

LUCASTA (*blushing*). It's very kind of you to say so, sir, but I am very busy this morning. I am wanted at the farm to see about the cows.

DON JUAN. Fortunate cows! But cannot they wait a moment? Surely there is no desperate hurry?

LUCASTA. I am late already, sir, and I am loath to keep people waiting.

DON JUAN. How nice, how considerate and charming of you. I adore those who are loath to keep others waiting. It is the revelation of a delightful nature. I am sure we shall be friends. I feel as if we had always known one another.

LUCASTA. Oh, sir, but I do not even know your name! I only know you are the Spanish nobleman who was expected.

DON JUAN (*proudly*). My name is one you may perhaps have heard of. I am Don Juan of Seville.

LUCASTA. One of our ponies is called Don Juan—the old one. It takes the children out in a cart: but he's lame now.

DON JUAN (*vexed*). You must let me give you a horse, a fiery steed fit to carry you, for I'm sure you ride like Diana, and you shall call that Don Juan.

LUCASTA. Thank you, sir, but my mother says one must never accept gifts from strangers.

DON JUAN. But I am not a stranger. You must not look upon me as a stranger. You must look upon me as a friend.

LUCASTA. Mistress Markham says that one has no right to call people friends until one has known them for seven years.

DON JUAN. Who is Mistress Markham?

LUCASTA. She is our governess.

DON JUAN. She knows nothing about it. Believe me, all governesses are fools.

LUCASTA. Not Mistress Markham. She knows everything—even the Greek irregular verbs.

DON JUAN. Well, let us admit, then, that there is only one thing she doesn't know.

LUCASTA. What, sir?

DON JUAN. The birth, the growth, and the nature of our friendship. May not I claim to be a friend? You surely do not wish to regard me as an enemy?

LUCASTA (*after reflecting*). Well, I suppose there's no harm; because I do not suppose it is wrong to make friends with old people.

DON JUAN (*laughing uneasily*). I am old enough to claim friendship with you; but I am not so old as all that. Do I look so very old?

LUCASTA (*blushing*). Oh no, sir. I never meant that, I'm sure. All I meant was that you were old compared with my friends.

DON JUAN. Have you many friends?

LUCASTA. Oh yes! There's Harry, who has just left school; and Philip, he is a student at Oxford; and Valentine, he is about to join the Yeomanry; and my cousin Dick, he is my greatest friend.

DON JUAN. How old is he?

LUCASTA. He left school six months ago. He's going to be a great soldier, like Sir Philip Sidney.

DON JUAN. Oh! and are you very fond of him?

LUCASTA. Very. He plays tennis better than any one. Do you play tennis, sir?

DON JUAN. I'm afraid I don't.

LUCASTA. Bowls?

DON JUAN. I'm afraid not either.

LUCASTA. Rounders?

DON JUAN. I'm afraid I don't play any games except draughts and lansquenet.

LUCASTA. Lansquenet and draughts are indoor games. We don't count them. Cousin Dick says they are all very well for women.

DON JUAN. You see, I never have time for that kind of thing.

LUCASTA. Are you an officer, sir?

DON JUAN. Oh no!

LUCASTA. A sailor?

DON JUAN. No; I hate the sea.

LUCASTA. I suppose you are a discoverer. Spaniards are such great travellers.

DON JUAN. No; I have only travelled in Europe and for pleasure.

LUCASTA. How stupid of me, sir. You are, of course, a diplomatist.

DON JUAN. No: I am merely a gentleman at large.

LUCASTA. Do you mean you follow no profession?

DON JUAN. No profession exactly, but many occupations.

LUCASTA. But how do you contrive to pass the time?

DON JUAN. Well, you see, we Spaniards are different from you English. We are less practical, and more—what shall I say?—more fiery, more impatient, more romantic. We consider it quite enough for a man who is a Spaniard and a nobleman as I am, nay, more, we consider that such a man can have no nobler occupation than to devote his life, his heart, his brain to the constant and daily service and worship of a beautiful woman.

LUCASTA. Oh, I see; you are engaged to be married.

DON JUAN. No, alas!

LUCASTA. Haven't you got enough money to marry on?

DON JUAN. It's not that: my purse is equal to my station.

LUCASTA. Her parents, I suppose, have refused their consent.

DON JUAN. I have not yet asked them.

LUCASTA. I wish you all success, sir.

DON JUAN. But you don't understand, most charming and gracious of Englishwomen. It is true that I love. I am consumed with a love which will never diminish nor die, a love that burns within me like a raging fever; but I have not yet dared to speak it. The divine and adorable creature whom I worship does not suspect the cruel plight I am in. She ignores my flame.

LUCASTA. Why do you not tell her, sir?

DON JUAN. Ah! That is so easily said! But what if she were to take offence? What if I were by a too sudden and abrupt declaration of the passion that consumes me to nip in the bud all chance of my love finding a response in her breast? What if I by a too hasty word were to shatter my hopes for ever?

LUCASTA. Is she so very young? Pardon me, sir, if I am wrong in asking.

DON JUAN. You could never do wrong. No fault could ever mar those faultless lips. (LUCASTA *blushes.*) I will tell you she is very young, and I have only seen her once.

LUCASTA. Then it was a case of love at first sight?

DON JUAN. Yes, but love is a weak word to express the great wave which has carried me away.

LUCASTA. They say that love at first sight is often mutual.

DON JUAN. I pray Heaven that it may be so in this case; but I doubt if she has guessed my sweet and bitter secret. She is so young, so innocent.

LUCASTA. Is she fair or dark, sir?

DON JUAN. Her hair is the colour of your hair, and, like yours, it has the glitter of sunshine, with miraculous shades and adorable crisping curls like those that wreathe your brow. Her skin is like yours; that is to say, a rose lately sprinkled with dew. Her eyes are the colour of your eyes; that is to say, they have the radiance of the azure sky and depth of the summer sea. Her nose is the pictured semblance of your nose, delicate as a flower, tip-tilted, transparent, enchanting. Her lips are like your lips; they put to shame ripe cherries, red roses, and rubies; and her teeth are like your teeth, more perfect than Orient pearls. She has your carriage, your grace and rhythm of movement, the stately poise of your head, and the divine contour of your form. She has the radiance of your smile and the laughing music of your speech.

LUCASTA. It is very kind of you, sir, to compare me to so well-favoured a person.

DON JUAN. I am not comparing you to her. I am comparing her to you. Until this morning I did not know that such beauty could live and breathe.

LUCASTA. Did you see her this morning for the first time?

DON JUAN. Yes, it was this morning; to-day is the fatal day that has changed the earth for me to a giddy ladder suspended between heaven and hell.

LUCASTA. Then I know who it is. It is Electra Harrington our neighbour. You saw her on your way here.

DON JUAN. Believe me, it was no Electra Harrington. Electra Harrington would be a wrinkled hag in comparison with the goddess whom I worship. But tell me, do you think I might dare to plead my cause? Do you think there is the frailest hope of her listening to my suit?

LUCASTA. Why not? I am sure, sir, any girl would feel very much flattered at the attentions of a nobleman such as yourself.

DON JUAN. But you said I was old.

LUCASTA. Oh, sir, I told you I never meant that.

All I meant was that you were grown-up and a man, and not a schoolboy like Philip.

DON JUAN. Then you think that a maiden could look at me without disgust?

LUCASTA. Oh, sir!

DON JUAN. Even if at first I found her heart hard as adamant, if she will only let me plead my cause I feel certain I can soften it. That is all I ask—a hearing.

LUCASTA. I should tell her at once, sir, in your place. Girls are often bashful. (*She blushes.*)

DON JUAN. Then there is another grisly fear that haunts me. She may already have given her heart away. She may already have a betrothed.

LUCASTA. That is not likely if it's any of the girls in our county. They are all so young; and the others are married—except Dianeme, and then she's a fright, so it could hardly be her.

DON JUAN. Then you think I ought to be bold?

LUCASTA (*clapping her hands*). Oh yes, do be bold!

[DON JUAN *seizes* LUCASTA *and endeavours to kiss her. She gives him a very smart box on the ears.*

LUCASTA. Sir, what does this unpardonable liberty mean? I thought you were a gentleman and a nobleman.

DON JUAN (*kneeling*). Forgive me. I thought you had understood. I thought you must have guessed —don't interrupt me, only hear me—I thought you must have known when I described to you my heart's desire; when I told you that you had her every feature; but I was mad. It was unpardonable of me; but hear me all the same, Lucasta; adorable, lovely, perfect Lucasta, I love you; I love you passionately. I offer you my hand, my life, my fortune.

LUCASTA. Please get up, sir. I hate men who kneel—they look so silly; and if you are going to talk nonsense any more I shall go upstairs.

DON JUAN (*rising*). Then you mean that I may not even hope?

LUCASTA (*bursting into peals of laughter*). Forgive me, but I can't help it.

DON JUAN. It is really no laughing matter. (*He draws his sword.*) I am ready to stab myself.

LUCASTA (*still shaking with laughter*). Please do not be so foolish. Why, you're much older than my father. Here is my mother.

Enter the COUNTESS OF WESSEX, *a handsome lady. She curtsies deeply.*

LUCASTA (*aside to her mother*). Oh! he's so funny.

[*She runs away, vainly suppressing a peal of laughter.*

CURTAIN.

XIII

CALPURNIA'S DINNER-PARTY

SCENE.—*A room in* JULIUS CÆSAR'S *house. Discovered:* JULIUS CÆSAR *and* CALPURNIA.

CALPURNIA. Catullus has accepted, so that will make us thirteen.

CÆSAR. I won't sit down thirteen to dinner; it isn't fair to one's guests.

CALPURNIA. What nonsense! They none of them mind.

CÆSAR. I beg your pardon. I happen to know that Cicero is intensely superstitious. Of course I don't mind personally, but one must think of others.

CALPURNIA. Then what shall we do?

CÆSAR. Ask some one else.

CALPURNIA. Then you must get another man. You are sure to see some one at the Forum.

CÆSAR. I will ask Calvus.

CALPURNIA. How like a man. In the first place he is in mourning.

CÆSAR. Who for?

CALPURNIA. Quintilla, of course.

CÆSAR. We need not go into that.

CALPURNIA. He won't go anywhere—at present—but even if it wasn't for that, don't you see that it would quite spoil the dinner to ask Calvus with Catullus?

CÆSAR. Why?

CALPURNIA. Because they both write poetry.

CÆSAR. What does that matter?

CALPURNIA. Of course, if you want to spoil the dinner——

CÆSAR. Must it be a man?

CALPURNIA. Yes; we have got quite enough women.

CÆSAR. Why not ask Atticus?

CALPURNIA. Then we should have to ask Pilia.

CÆSAR. She hates going out.

CALPURNIA. It is impossible to ask him without her—and I won't ask her; she would ruin the dinner. Besides, I told you we can't have another woman.

CÆSAR. What about Cinna?

CALPURNIA. Cornelia's got him. She always gives a dinner the same night as I do, so as to take away the people I want from me.

CÆSAR. I can't think of anybody.

CALPURNIA. You will see some one at the Forum; but mind you are careful, and don't ask some one nobody else knows, or some one whom they all hate.

CÆSAR. There's nobody in Rome just now.

Enter a SLAVE, *with a letter for* CALPURNIA

THE SLAVE. They are waiting for a verbal answer.

[CALPURNIA *takes the letter and reads it.*

CALPURNIA. It is from Lucullus; he wants us to dine with him to night—quite a tiny dinner, he says—he wants us to taste some oysters from Britain.

CÆSAR. I suppose we can't put off our guests?

CALPURNIA. Certainly not. It *is* unlucky. (*She sits down at a table and writes an answer.*) It is the sort of thing that's sure to happen. I wish you hadn't asked all these people.

CÆSAR. I didn't ask a soul.

CALPURNIA (*to the* SLAVE). There's the answer.

The SLAVE *bows and retires. He returns again immediately with another letter, which he gives to* CALPURNIA.

CALPURNIA. Is there an answer?

THE SLAVE. The slave is waiting.

CALPURNIA (*reading out*). "MOST ILLUSTRIOUS AND CELESTIALLY FAVOURED CALPURNIA"—it is from the Persian Ambassador—"Pity me. The gods are most cruel and unpropitious. Owing to the extraordinary carelessness of my private secretary I find that I have been engaged for several weeks to dine with Lucullus to-night. As I only know him slightly, I am sure you will understand that in this case I must sacrifice pleasure to duty, and miss a brilliant and charming evening. Alas, alas, pity me!—Your slave, ZOROASTER SORHAB JEMSHID." (*To the* SLAVE) Say I quite understand. (*Exit* SLAVE.) Jemshid always, always throws one over.

Enter the SLAVE *with two letters. He gives one to* CÆSAR *and one to* CALPURNIA

THE SLAVE. Both waiting for an answer.

CALPURNIA. Who is yours from?

CÆSAR. Mark Antony. (*He reads*) "DEAR OLD BOY—I am frightfully sorry, but I can't dine with you to-night. I have had a tooth pulled out this morning, and the doctor says I mustn't go out, worse luck. My respects to Calpurnia. I will look in to-morrow if I am well enough. Don't bother to come and see me, as I can't talk.—M.A."

CALPURNIA. He's dining with Lucullus, of course. If you had only let me engage that cook from Gaul, nobody would ever throw us over.

CÆSAR. Who is yours from?

CALPURNIA. Lucilius. (*She reads*) "MOST ILLUSTRIOUS AND EXQUISITE CALPURNIA—I have got into the most frightful muddle. Last Monday, Lucullus asked me to dinner to-night, and I accepted. Then the next day I wrote to him and said I could not dine with him after all, as I had to go into Court the day after, and I should have to work all night. The day after I wrote this letter my case was put off, and then you kindly asked me to dinner, and of course I accepted; and now Lucullus has found out that I am dining with you, and thinks I threw him over for you. He says he's a man short, and that as I was engaged to him first, I simply must come to his dinner. So I am writing to know whether you could possibly let me off? And, as I have already been obliged to throw Lucullus over twice lately, I am sure you will understand that I cannot very well come to you to-night. I am too sorry for words.—LUCILIUS."

CÆSAR. I suppose the answer is "Very well" in both cases.

CALPURNIA. Yes. (*Exit* SLAVE.) Of course they will all throw us over now.

CÆSAR. Well, in that case, the matter would be solved, and we could dine with Lucullus.

CALPURNIA. But they won't *all* throw us over. Portia's certain to come.

Enter the SLAVE *with two letters. He gives them to* CALPURNIA

THE SLAVE. No answer.

CALPURNIA (*eagerly*). This is from Clodia. I wonder what lie she will tell. (*Reads*) "DARLING CALPURNIA—I am *too, too* miserable. Everything has gone stupidly wrong. When you asked me to dinner and said Friday, I thought Friday was the 10th, and now I see it is the 11th, and I have been engaged for ages to that tiresome old Lucullus. Of course I would throw him over *at once*, but Metellus won't hear of it, and he says it will serve me right if you never ask us again. So like a husband! It is *too* unlucky, darling, isn't it? You will feel for me, I am sure.—Your loving CLODIA." Well, Catullus won't come now.

CÆSAR. Is the other letter from him?

CALPURNIA. No. Of course they wouldn't send them together. It is from Cicero; if he can't come, our dinner's ruined. (*She reads*) "MOST HONOURED AND EXCELLENT CALPURNIA—Owing to a quite unusual press of business I much regret to say that I shall be compelled to forgo the pleasure of enjoying your kind hospitality to-night. The misfortune is all the more heavy since I shall not only miss the pleasure of enjoying your charming society, but also the opportunity of discussing several matters of importance with Cæsar, which I was particularly anxious to do. Believe me, I am consumed with regret, but I will not waste your time in vain excuses and apologies, which seem only to increase my vexation without diminishing the inconvenience I fear I may be causing you. Hail and farewell.—M. T. CICERO."

Enter the SLAVE *with a letter for* CÆSAR

THE SLAVE. No answer. (*He goes out.*)

CÆSAR (*opening the letter*). It is from Catullus. (*Reading*) "A terrible catastrophe has happened. Going home last night from the Esquiline I got my feet wet, and this has affected my style; my hexameters are beginning to limp and my elegiacs are gouty. The doctor says the only thing which can cure me is a quiet night's rest and some oysters from Britain. But it is unlikely that I shall find any in Rome. In view of these distressing circumstances I fear I must put off coming to-night to your dinner-party. Quite seriously, I am unwell. With a thousand compliments to Calpurnia.—Wretched CATULLUS." "*P.S.*—I was half engaged to Lucullus to-night, so if you see him later, tell him I *was* going to dine with you."

CALPURNIA. How silly he is! I shall never ask him again.

CÆSAR. Who is there left?

CALPURNIA. Now, there are only Brutus and Portia, Cassius and Cynthia.

Enter the SLAVE *with a letter for* CALPURNIA. *She takes it.*

THE SLAVE. No answer. (*He goes out.*)

CALPURNIA. It is from Cynthia. I thought she would throw us over too. (*Reads*) "DEAREST CALPURNIA—Lucullus says you and Cæsar and Catullus and Clodia are all dining with him. Is that right? Am I dining with him or with you? Please arrange it with him. I will do exactly what you like.—Your loving CYNTHIA." Now we have only got the bores left, Cassius, Brutus and Portia. I don't suppose we can very well put them off.

CÆSAR. I think we might in this case. You see,

it is perfectly true that our guests have all thrown us over, and it is much too late now to get any one else.

CALPURNIA. Very well. You must write to Cassius and I will write to Portia.

CÆSAR. And then we can dine with Lucullus.

CALPURNIA. Just as you think best; but if Brutus and Portia find it out they will never forgive us.

CÆSAR. What nonsense! Besides, perhaps Lucullus will ask them.

CALPURNIA. Never. (*Reading out as she writes*) DEAREST PORTIA—It is too unlucky, we are obliged to put off our dinner-party after all, because everybody has thrown us over; we are dreadfully disappointed, as we had so looked forward to seeing you. We shall have our little dinner on the 19th instead—Friday week. We do so hope you and Brutus are free.—Yours, Calpurnia.

CÆSAR. That's all right. I will write to Lucullus and say we will come, if he has still got room for us.

CALPURNIA. Just as you like; but remember that Brutus is touchy and that Portia never forgives.

CURTAIN.

XIV

LUCULLUS'S DINNER-PARTY

SCENE.—*A room in* LUCULLUS'S *house. Discovered:* LUCULLUS (*an old man*) *and his* COOK.

LUCULLUS. Of course, I don't say that it wasn't a good dish; but it was not Neapolitan peacock.

THE COOK. They were straight from Naples; the same as we've always had, sir.

LUCULLUS (*irritated*). I'm not talking about the bird, but about the dish. You know as well as I do that Neapolitan peacock without anemone seed is not Neapolitan peacock. And then the nightingales' tongues were over-roasted. They ought to be roasted for twenty-three minutes and not one second longer.

THE COOK. They were only twenty-four minutes on the roast.

LUCULLUS. There, you see, it was that extra minute that spoilt them. You might just as well not roast them at all as roast them for twenty-four minutes. And then there were too many butterflies' wings round the sturgeon.

THE COOK. The chief slave——

LUCULLUS. I've told you over and over again, till I'm tired of saying it, that the chief slave has nothing to do with the arrangement of the dishes.

That is your affair. The chief slave can arrange the table, but he must not touch the dishes. The look of a dish is just as important as the taste of it. And then there was a pinch too much salt in the wild boar sauce.

THE COOK. The first sauceman has just lost his wife.

LUCULLUS. That's not my affair. Please make it clear that this must not happen again. The fact is, Æmilius, you're falling off—last night's dinner wasn't fit to eat; it was filthy; the kind of food one gets at Cæsar's—sent for from round the corner.

THE COOK. If I may be so bold as to say so, we were saying in the kitchen that these rehearsals of dinners the night before the real dinner make us nervous——

LUCULLUS. All I can say is, if you can't cook a good dinner twice running you'd better get another place. The dinner wasn't fit to eat, and if it's anything like that to-night I advise you to give up trying to cook and to take to wrestling. That's all; you can go.

[*The* COOK *blushes scarlet and goes out.*

Enter a SLAVE

THE SLAVE. Can you see Portia, the wife of Brutus?

LUCULLUS. Yes; show her in.

Enter PORTIA

PORTIA. It's such a beautiful morning that I thought a nice brisk walk would do me good, and as I was passing your door I couldn't help just looking in.

LUCULLUS. I'm delighted.

PORTIA (*sitting down*). I wanted to ask you whether you would mind giving your patronage to the Old Slaves' Pensions Fund? Cicero has helped us a great deal, and Cæsar has promised. By the way, is Cæsar dining with you to-night?

LUCULLUS. Yes, I believe he is.

PORTIA. Well, he particularly wants to see Brutus, and he said something about meeting us here to-night, and as I had heard nothing from you I thought I would just ask. The slaves are so stupid about letters—not that I want very much to dine out. You see, I'm very busy just at this moment, and there's a Committee Meeting to-night for the O.S.P.F. (*She sighs.*) But one can't always think of oneself, and Brutus has been so depressed lately. He sleeps badly, and we've tried everything. The new Greek doctor has done him no good, and we've tried fomented eucalyptus and poppy soup, and the cold-water cure; but it all seems to make him worse, and the doctors say that what he wants is *society*, and we so seldom see any one.

LUCULLUS. I shall be quite delighted if you both could come to-night. (*He calls out*) Lucius. (*Enter* SLAVE.) Tell Æmilius at once we shall be two extra to dinner to-night; and tell him to get some more hoopoes' eggs.

PORTIA. Of course, I didn't mean to propose myself (*she laughs nervously*)—you mustn't think that; and have you really got room for us?

LUCULLUS. Oh, there's plenty of room. (*Pensively*) Do you like hoopoes' eggs?

PORTIA (*simpering*). Well, they're dreadfully indigestible, but I must say I never can resist a good hoopoe's egg. (*Getting up*) Then I can count on your patronage?

LUCULLUS. Certainly; is there a subscription?

PORTIO. Not for the patrons. You see——

LUCULLUS. Yes, I see.

PORTIA. Good-bye. Thank you so much.

Exit PORTIA. LUCULLUS *sees her to the door and returns.*

LUCULLUS (*pensively*). Brutus never drinks wine.

Enter SLAVE

THE SLAVE. The Queen of Egypt is here. Æmilius says it's too late to cook dinner for twelve now without spoiling it; he says we're one too many as it is, and that he can't get any more hoopoes' eggs, and that there won't be enough to go round.

LUCULLUS. Show the Queen in.

[*Exit* SLAVE.

Enter CLEOPATRA

CLEOPATRA. Don't get up, Lucullus; I'm not going to keep you a minute. I want to know if you could possibly dine with me to-night. I've got some dancing; a little Persian girl—so clever—she does a parakeet dance with live birds.

LUCULLUS. There's nothing I should like so much, dear Egypt; but I've got a dinner of my own. Do you want a man?

CLEOPATRA. I want *two* men, dreadfully.

LUCULLUS. I'll tell you who are coming—Mark Antony.

CLEOPATRA. I don't know him.

LUCULLUS. Cicero.

CLEOPATRA. I'm afraid he wouldn't do.

LUCULLUS. Brutus and his wife.

CLEOPATRA (*laughing*). They don't know me.

LUCULLUS. Catullus. Oh, I forgot Cæsar and his wife.

CLEOPATRA. Of course Cæsar would do beautifully, but I suppose you couldn't spare him.

LUCULLUS. To tell you the truth, I've got too many guests and not enough hoopoes' eggs to go round, but——

CLEOPATRA. Well, I happened to meet Cæsar quite by chance this morning, and he said that poor Calpurnia had got one of her headaches and was dying not to dine out, but you know how dear and unselfish she is. So if you should put them off, I think it would be rather a relief to *her*, and then Cæsar could just run in for a moment to my dinner.

LUCULLUS. Certainly; I'll say I've mistaken the date.

CLEOPATRA. That is charming of you; thank you so much. And you must come and dine quite quietly with me one night, and you might bring Mark Antony; I want to know him so much.

LUCULLUS. He's not interesting; he bolts his food.

CLEOPATRA. How funny! Just like Cæsar. Good-bye; I must fly. [*Exit* CLEOPATRA.

Enter SLAVE

THE SLAVE. Clodia, the wife of Metellus Celer, wishes to see you.

LUCULLUS. Show her in, and tell Æmilius we shan't be two extra.

Enter CLODIA

CLODIA. It's too bad of me, Lucullus, to disturb you so early in the morning.

LUCULLUS. On the contrary——

CLODIA. What a charming room. (*Pointing to a statue of Hermes*) That's a Praxiteles, isn't it?

LUCULLUS. No; it's only a copy I had made by a little man at Puteoli.

CLODIA. I think it is wonderful.

LUCULLUS. It is clever.

CLODIA. You got my note?

LUCULLUS. Yes; I'm delighted you can come.

CLODIA. Well, that's just what I wanted to explain. Metellus says you've asked Catullus, and last night we were all dining with Pollio, and Catullus was there. Of course, I don't know him very well, but I've always been civil to him because of Metellus, who happens to like him. Well, last night he was so rude to my father-in-law that I don't feel as if I could meet him again to-night. I mean I don't think it would be right. Couldn't you put him off and say he made you thirteen?—otherwise I don't think I can come, and I wouldn't miss your dinner for worlds.

LUCULLUS (*enchanted*). Quite delighted, I assure you, to render you the smallest service. I will write at once. (*He scribbles two notes.*) Lucius! (*Enter a* SLAVE.) Take this note to Caius Valerius Catullus at once, and this one to the Queen of Egypt, and tell Æmilius we shall only be nine. (*To* CLODIA) I assure you it won't matter to him, as Cleopatra is giving a dinner to-night and is looking out for a man. I have written to tell her.

CLODIA. Cleopatra! Oh!

LUCULLUS. Yes; don't you like her?

CLODIA. Metellus hates Greeks; and I only just know her, but I do admire her. Metellus thinks she's so second-rate. I don't see it.

LUCULLUS. She's cultivated.

CLODIA. Yes; Greeks always are.

Enter a SLAVE *with a letter, which he gives to* LUCULLUS

THE SLAVE. Waiting for an answer.

LUCULLUS. May I read this?

CLODIA. Please.

[LUCULLUS *opens the letter and looks at the signature.*

LUCULLUS. It's from one of my guests—Cynthia. I can't read it; I'm so short-sighted and I left my emerald upstairs.

CLODIA. Shall I read it for you?

LUCULLUS. That would be very kind.

CLODIA (*reads*). "DEAR LUCULLUS—I find I can come to dinner after all. I have just found a letter which has been going all over Rome for me for the last week, from the King of Nubia, who had asked me to-night (and of course it was a command), saying that his dinner is put off. So I shall be delighted to come to-night if I may.—CYNTHIA." That will just make you a woman over, won't it; but it will be all right if I don't come.

LUCULLUS. On the contrary——

CLODIA. Of course it will. You see, I may just as well come another night, and Metellus will come without me—husbands are always so much nicer without their wives. As a matter of fact, Metellus didn't much want me to come, because my throat's been rather bad lately, and he thinks I oughtn't to go out at night; so it all fits in. Good-bye, Lucullus.

LUCULLUS. Good-bye. (*Exit* CLODIA.) She'll go to Cleopatra's—after all, food is wasted on women. Lucius!

Enter the SLAVE

THE SLAVE. If you please, sir, Æmilius has killed himself!

LUCULLUS. Then who's going to cook the dinner?

THE SLAVE. The head sauceman says he can manage the nightingales' tongues and the fish, but he's no experience of peacock.

LUCULLUS. Peacock! I should think not. He's not to touch the peacock. (*He walks up and down in great agitation, thinking.*) Tell the head sauceman —who is it—Balbus?

THE SLAVE. Yes, sir.

LUCULLUS. Tell Balbus I will have dinner in my room an hour and a half before the other dinner. He can give soup, fish, pheasant, nightingales' tongues, the cold boar pie which was left from yesterday, and some hoopoes' eggs—and as for the dinner, you can send out for it. Send now to Varro's shop and order dinner for nine—eight courses—anything you like. Go at once. They may not be able to do it in time.

THE SLAVE. If you please, sir, one of the slaves was over at Varro's this morning about the extra slaves to wait, and they said they had a dinner ordered and countermanded by Calpurnia on their hands.

LUCULLUS. That will do. But tell Balbus if my nightingales are not satisfactory he shall be impaled.

CURTAIN.

XV

THE STOIC'S DAUGHTER

SCENE.—*A room in the house of* BURRUS, *Prefect of the Prætorian Guards of Nero.* BURRUS *is discovered in an attitude of despondency.*

Enter a SLAVE

BURRUS. Well?

SLAVE. Caius Petronius would like to speak to you.

BURRUS. I will see him.

Enter C. PETRONIUS—PETRONIUS ARBITER, *middle-aged, but very elegant.*

PETRONIUS. Good morning. I've come about that dinner. The Emperor quite approves of the list of guests.

BURRUS. I don't suppose you wish me to come now.

PETRONIUS. Why not?

BURRUS. Well, after Lucius's—er—unfortunate escapade——

PETRONIUS. My dear fellow, I assure you that's not of the slightest consequence. If we had to be responsible for our sons' misdeeds life would become impossible. As it is, the Emperor, while sympathising with your feelings——

BURRUS. Please don't talk about it. You can understand how inexpressibly painful it is to me.

PETRONIUS. It might have been worse. He might have gone on the stage.

BURRUS. The gods spared us that. That would have killed Æmilia.

PETRONIUS. I suppose she feels it dreadfully.

BURRUS. It's not so much the thing she minds, but the family name being dragged into publicity —people making bets——

PETRONIUS. Yes, yes—but there's nothing to be done. After all, when all's said and done it is much less degrading to be a gladiator than an actor —or a charioteer. Piso's nephew is a charioteer, and Tigellinus's brother appeared on the stage for some charity.

BURRUS. I don't know what the world is coming to.

PETRONIUS. I suppose he'll drop it immediately. Then I should send him abroad for a little, and the world will forget all about it. These things are forgotten so quickly. After all, boys will be boys. Believe me, young men must sow their wild oats, and the sooner they get it over the better. Well, please give my respects to Æmilia, and I can count on you for certain for the fifteenth?

BURRUS. I shall come without fail.

[*Exit* PETRONIUS.

Enter ÆMILIA—BURRUS'S *wife*

ÆMILIA. Well? What did he say?

BURRUS. Nothing, practically. The Emperor doesn't seem to have said anything.

ÆMILIA. But do you mean to say you haven't arranged anything?

BURRUS. What about? The dinner-party?

ÆMILIA. Dinner-party, indeed! I mean about Lucius not appearing at the Games again.

BURRUS. No, I haven't. What is there to arrange?

ÆMILIA. You really are too helpless. You must get him banished, of course—just for a short time.

BURRUS. I didn't like to—but I'll write to Seneca.

ÆMILIA. Seneca's no use. Write to Petronius. He'll arrange it without any fuss.

BURRUS. I hardly like——

ÆMILIA. If Lucius appears once more in the circus as a gladiator I shall open my veins in my bath.

BURRUS. Oh, well, of course, if you insist——

ÆMILIA. Yes, I do insist.

Enter a SLAVE

SLAVE. Lucius Annæus Seneca, and Annæus Serenus wish to see you.

BURRUS. Show them in.

Enter LUCIUS A. SENECA, *and* A. SERENUS

[*Exit* SLAVE.

SENECA. I've only just heard the news, or else I would have come sooner.

SERENUS. And I had no idea until Seneca told me.

BURRUS. I suppose it's all over Rome by now.

SENECA. You mustn't take these things to heart.

ÆMILIA. It's all very well for you to talk, Seneca; you haven't got a son.

SENECA. I would esteem it a privilege to be

visited by troubles of this nature. It is only the noblest souls that the gods plague with such disasters in order that, tempered by affliction, the true steel, emerging triumphant from the trial, may serve as an example to mankind.

SERENUS. Not being a stoic, Burrus, I take a different view of the incident. I consider that man is born to enjoy himself, and that the opportunities of enjoyment are rare and far between. Life is monotonous. If your son finds a relaxation from the tediousness of existence in fighting as a gladiator, by all means let him continue to do so. It is a profession which calls forth many of the noblest qualities of man.

ÆMILIA. But think of the family, Serenus. Think of us, of my sisters, my sisters-in-law, my cousins; think of my husband and the harm that it may do him professionally.

SENECA. Vain thoughts, I assure you, Æmilia. A man's merit depends on the aspirations of his soul and not on the idle gossip of his relations.

SERENUS. All one's relations are liars. It is much better that they should say your son is a gladiator who fights in public—which is true—than that they should say he is a drunkard who drinks in secret, which would be untrue. They would no doubt say that, had they no other food for gossip.

ÆMILIA. But Lucius never drinks. He had never given us a day's anxiety until this.

BURRUS. He got all the prizes at school.

ÆMILIA. He was working so hard to become an officer.

SERENUS. Ah! Over-education, I see. I assure you the whole matter does not signify.

ÆMILIA. It is breaking his father's heart.

BURRUS. I shall never hold up my head in public.

SENECA. Come, Burrus, think of Brutus, and what he had to endure from his son.

SERENUS. Yes, and think of the many Roman sons who have killed their fathers.

SENECA. In every evil, in every misfortune there is always a seed of consolation. You must, of course, deal kindly with him, but firmly, and I am convinced he will listen to reason.

ÆMILIA. He wouldn't listen to us at all. We all tried our best to dissuade him—except his cousin Lesbia. Heartless woman! It was entirely her fault.

BURRUS. He shall never cross this threshold again as long as I live.

SENECA. Set a noble example of forgiveness, Burrus, and the world will be grateful to you.

BURRUS. I will never set eyes upon him again. He has disgraced himself and his family for ever. There are certain stains of dishonour which can never be effaced.

Enter a SLAVE

SLAVE. Paulina, the wife of Seneca, is here. She wishes to speak to you.

SENECA. My wife! What can she want?

BURRUS. Show her in

[*Exit* SLAVE.

Enter PAULINA

PAULINA. Forgive me, Burrus, for forcing my way in—they said you were not at home to any visitors—but it is a matter of life and death—and

I must speak to Seneca. (*To* SENECA) I have been hunting for you the whole morning, and it's by the merest chance I found out you had come here.

SENECA. What is it?

PAULINA. A terrible catastrophe has befallen us.

SENECA. My Greek vases!

PAULINA. No, it's nothing to do with your horrible collections.

SENECA. Then don't you think we had better go home and discuss the matter in private?

PAULINA. No, I want Burrus's help.

SENECA. What can have happened?

PAULINA. It's Julia.

SENECA. I suppose she's run away with some one.

PAULINA. Oh no; it's far worse than that.

SENECA. You mean——

PAULINA. I don't mean anything. I mean she has disgraced us all.

SERENUS. These little affairs blow over so quickly.

PAULINA. But you don't understand—you will never believe it. The girl has become a Christian.

SENECA. A Christian!

BURRUS. No!

ÆMILIA. My poor Paulina!

SERENUS. Curious!

BURRUS. She must have been got hold of by the Jews.

ÆMILIA. They are terribly cunning; and people say they're everywhere, and yet one doesn't see them.

SERENUS. But surely there is nothing irretrievable about this. As long as nobody knows about it, what does it signify?

SENECA. You don't understand. It's a matter of principle; I could not possibly harbour a daughter under my roof whom I knew to be a traitor to the State.

SERENUS. It is annoying.

PAULINA. But you don't know the worst: she has gone to prison.

SENECA (*very angry*). Well, I hope you will let her know that she shall never come back to our home as long as she lives. Her conduct is not only immoral, but it is immodest. It is inspired solely and simply by a passion for self-advertisement. It is this modern craze for publicity which is the ruin of our children; she is bitten by this same passion for notoriety which—you will excuse me saying so, Burrus—led your son to be a gladiator. I call it vulgar, tawdry, Byzantine, hysterical, and essentially un-Roman.

SERENUS. But surely, my dear Seneca, nobody can think it amusing to go to prison? Think of the risk.

SENECA. I beg your pardon. People of her class risk nothing. They have got a morbid craze for new sensations.

SERENUS. Rather disagreeable sensations, aren't they? To be eaten by a tiger, for instance?

SENECA. There's no question of that. It's only the worst criminals who are treated like that. Am I not right, Burrus?

BURRUS. Perfectly. A purely religious offender is immediately released on making the mere outward sign of allegiance to the State. An oath is not even required.

PAULINA. Well, that's just what I've come

about. The child is in prison, and it appears—it is very foolish and obstinate of her, but Julia always was an obstinate child—that she refuses to fulfil the necessary formality, sacrifice, or whatever it is. So I thought I would come to you, Burrus, and ask you just to say a word to the prison authorities, and then she could be let out—quite quietly, of course. Nobody need know about it.

BURRUS. My dear lady, you know how gladly I would do anything in the world to be of use to you. But in this case—and I am sure you will understand—I cannot see my way; indeed it is quite impossible for me to take any action. You see, Petronius's cousin was released three weeks ago, and smuggled out of the country, and the demagogues got hold of it and complained to the Emperor, who—courting popularity as usual—said it was not to occur again. So you see in what an awkward position we are placed. We can't make these distinctions simply between people of position and others——

PAULINA. But it's always done.

BURRUS. That's just why it can't be done this time. The Emperor is extremely annoyed at people of good family having anything to do with those horrible Christians, and he's determined to stamp this mania out. But all she has got to do is to sacrifice——

PAULINA. But you don't realise how obstinate the girl is.

Enter LESBIA, *a lovely gay woman, about twenty-five.*

LESBIA. Good morning, good morning. I've

got some places for the Games, and Lucius comes on at three. You *must* see him fight. He's too wonderful. And it's horrible of you not to go and see him, and then they're going to throw *all* the Christians to the lions directly afterwards, so you must come.

CURTAIN.

XVI

AFTER EURIPIDES' "ELECTRA"

SCENE.—*A room in the house of* CINYRAS, *at Athens. Reclining on couches round the tables are* SOCRATES, ALCANDER (*a man about Athens*), DEMETRIUS (*a critic*), XENOCLES (*a playwright*), ANTAGORAS (*an important official*), NAUCYDES (*a soldier*), HELIODORE (*wife of* CINYRAS), *and her friends*, LYCORIS, TIMARETA, NICYLLA, *and* HEGESO.

HELIODORE. Euripides has promised to come; but we won't wait for him. I don't know what you feel, but I'm very hungry.

NAUCYDES. So am I. Makes one hungry, don't you know—that kind of thing. Splendid show.

LYCORIS. What I say is, it's too long. It lasted nearly all day. If he had made it about half as long, it would be just as beautiful, and much more enjoyable for us. Of course, I don't pretend to be a judge, but I do say it's too long.

CINYRAS. Much the best thing is to do as I do and not go to the play at all.

LYCORIS. No, I like a *good* play. But I don't care for Diophantus' acting. It's just the same with Tityus. What I say is, Diophantus is always Diophantus and Tityus is always Tityus.

DEMETRIUS. But surely the business of the actor is never to let his personality change?

NICYLLA. What did you think of the play, Demetrius?

DEMETRIUS. I am afraid I must not tell you that until my opinions are published. It wouldn't be fair on the author.

NICYLLA. And what did you think, Socrates?

SOCRATES. I admired it immensely.

HEGESO. I thought it wonderful. I loved the story. I loved Clytæmnestra's clothes, that wonderful, dirty, wine-stained dress, and Electra's pale, shivering, stone-cold mask; and Orestes was such a darling. So mad, and distraught, and rebellious.

HELIODORE. I thought it was marvellous.

NICYLLA. I think it's so much better than Sophocles' *Electra.*

ALCANDER. It's very clever, of course; brilliantly clever; but it's not a play. It's really only a discussion.

HEGESO. But I was thrilled by the story and so frightened.

TIMARETA. You know, it's not the story. It's the acting. Apollodorus told me it's the acting. It's wonderful. It's felt. I felt it.

LYCORIS. I must say, I don't like that sort of play. I think it leaves a nasty taste in one's mouth and one doesn't quite know why. I know it's very clever.

NICYLLA. Oh, Lycoris, how old-fashioned of you! Now don't you think Electra was right, Socrates, to kill her mother?

SOCRATES. We'll ask Euripides that when he comes. My business is to ask questions——

NAUCYDES (*aside to* HELIODORE). And a great nuisance he is, too, with his questions.

SOCRATES. And not to answer them.

NAUCYDES (*aside to* HELIODORE). I don't believe he knows what the answers are.

NICYLLA. But don't you think, Demetrius, that a girl is justified in taking the law into her hands in such very exceptional circumstances; or do you think a girl's first duty is to her mother?

ANTAGORAS. I think she deserved a good whipping, if you ask me. However, it's not the story I object to. I mean, we all know the story, and we're quite ready to see a new play on the subject, as long as it's treated reverently and decently; but one never knows with Euripides when he's serious, or whether he's laughing in his sleeve the whole time or not. Now I like Æschylus.

XENOCLES. Poor Euripides! He's shot his bolt.

NICYLLA. Do you think he's played out?

LYCORIS. What I say is this, that Clytæmnestra thoroughly deserved to die, but Electra wasn't the person to kill her, and that as she did kill her mother she ought to have been punished.

TIMARETA. It was Fate, that's what it was. Apollodorus told me it was all Fate.

HEGESO. Yes, and she was so sad, so miserable; she couldn't bear doing it. She *loved* her mother, although her mother had been so unkind, and turned her out of that beautiful house into a cold cruel hut, and only a herdsman to talk to. Don't you agree, Naucydes, with me, that Electra was cruelly treated? She couldn't help it, could she?

NAUCYDES. Rather an awkward case, don't you

know. Sort of fix when everything you do's wrong. (*He laughs loudly.*)

HEGESO. And wasn't the music too heavenly?

ALCANDER. It's like the play—clever; but it isn't music, any more than the play's a play.

ANTAGORAS. I couldn't make head or tail of it—but then I'm not musical.

HEGESO. Didn't you love those divine little screams, like a saw cutting ice, and the noise the cymbals made, like slippery sandals rushing down a marble mountain?

NICYLLA. What did you think of the music, Demetrius?

DEMETRIUS. There are no ideas in it, and it's very thin; there's no colour in it either, but a certain amount of clever arabesque work.

NICYLLA. Don't you think music acts on one's sub-conscious superself without one's noticing it? When I hear certain kinds of music I go quite mad, and sometimes when I hear music I feel as if I could understand everything. I am sure you agree with me, Socrates. And now, *do* tell me: Does music have an Apolline or a Dionysic effect on you? Sometimes it has a Dionysic effect on me and sometimes an Apolline.

SOCRATES. What is music, Nicylla? If you can answer me that, I will tell you the nature of its effect on me.

NICYLLA. Music is the language of the soul. It is to man what the perfume is to the flower.

ANTAGORAS. Music's a nuisance.

DEMETRIUS. Not necessarily; but it is often an interruption.

ALCANDER. And sometimes an accompaniment.

LYCORIS. Yes, as in the play to-day. What I say is, all this new music isn't music, but noise.

ANTAGORAS. I agree with you; it oughtn't to be allowed.

DEMETRIUS. But isn't all music noise?

HEGESO. Yes; delicious, heavenly noises, all caught like tame mice and put in chains and made to be obedient.

HELIODORE. Don't let's discuss the music till we've finished talking about the play. Now, Xenocles thinks that Euripides is played out.

XENOCLES. Euripides has talent, but he is essentially mediocre; his verses are vulgar and facile. However, I've no doubt the sausage-sellers enjoy his plays. It is the kind of thing which would appeal to them. And they say the Barbarians find them extraordinarily profound.

NICYLLA. Now, that's one of your paradoxes, Xenocles. How brilliant he is, isn't he?

TIMARETA. Apollodorus says his characters are too natural. They are just what one sees every day.

ANTAGORAS. Good gracious! I hope not.

NICYLLA. Now, Socrates, I know you admire Euripides, and I always have admired him. I always said from the first that he was far the greatest playwright we'd ever had. I want to know what Xenocles admires.

XENOCLES. Well, there's Agathon, but no one else.

NICYLLA. And I'm sure you don't admire Sophocles?

XENOCLES. The gods forbid.

DEMETRIUS. His work is quite dead. I believe his plays are still admired in Thrace.

NAUCYDES. I saw one the other day, and I'm afraid I liked it.

NICYLLA. Oh, Naucydes, how can you say such a thing? They're so empty. There's no soul in them. No world-sympathy. No atmospheric intuition. Nothing cosmic. And then they say his verses are all wrong. Aren't they, Xenocles?

XENOCLES. Sophocles undoubtedly wrote some good lines, but his philosophy is childish. It is essentially Mid-Athenian.

HEGESO. Oh, I adore Mid-Athenian things. I've had a room furnished in the Mid-Athenian style with archaic busts; you can't think how quaint and charming it looks.

HELIODORE. Won't you have a little more partridge, Hegeso?

HEGESO. No, thank you, dear. I never touch food at this time in the evening. I can only eat a little parsley and mint in the morning.

HELIODORE. I'm sure you must be hungry after all we've gone through. I confess I cried like a child.

TIMARETA. That's what it is—Euripides is so pathetic. He's not great and he's not mystic, but he's pathetic. He touches one just here. (*She points to her throat.*) Apollodorus told me he's pathetic. He's got bathos.

HEGESO. I felt so sorry for Clytæmnestra. I was miserable when she screamed. I jumped up in my seat and cried: "I can't bear it, I can't bear it; they're killing Clytæmnestra." And Callias, who was sitting next to me, was so cross. (*She helps herself to a quail.*) It has been a wonderful day.

HELIODORE. Wonderful! I've never been through anything like it before.

NICYLLA. I felt as if my soul had escaped and was just floating in mid-ether between one world and another; between the two gates, don't you know.

TIMARETA. I was moved, that's what it was—moved. I felt like—as if I were at a funeral—a State funeral, with music and torches.

ALCANDER. Yes, it was certainly a fine performance.

NAUCYDES. By Zeus, yes!

DEMETRIUS. I don't mind saying that I was interested.

HEGESO. I shall never get over it, never. I feel as if it had all happened to me. (*She helps herself to another quail.*)

Enter a SLAVE

THE SLAVE. Euripides has sent to say he is very sorry he can't come to supper. He is too tired.

SOCRATES. I am afraid I must leave you. I have some pupils waiting for me at home.

HELIODORE. Oh, don't go, Socrates. I haven't spoken to you at all, and I have got so many things to say to you.

SOCRATES. I'm afraid I must go. Farewell, and a thousand thanks for your kind hospitality.

DEMETRIUS. And I'm afraid I must go. I've got to write about the play.

[*Exeunt* SOCRATES *and* DEMETRIUS.

HELIODORE. I must say I do think it's rather thoughtless of Euripides to throw me over at the last minute. I do think he might have let me know.

You see, Socrates only came because of Euripides. And you see what happens the moment he hears he's not coming—he goes.

XENOCLES. He always does that. He's spoilt. I told you he was overrated.

HELIODORE. I don't mind personally a bit. I don't happen to care for him; but I have asked thirty people to come in afterwards to meet him, and I do think it's selfish.

LYCORIS. I could tell from his play he was selfish.

TIMARETA. He's no heart, that's what it is. He's heartless. Just like Electra—heartless.

HELIODORE. But I do think Socrates might have stayed.

XENOCLES. Don't you understand why he's gone? He didn't want to tell Euripides how bad he thought the play was!

NICYLLA. Do you mean he really thinks it bad?

XENOCLES. I'm convinced of it.

ANTAGORAS. It's much worse than bad; it's undermining.

ALCANDER. Yes, I'm afraid it's a failure.

HEGESO. Oh no, don't say that, because I did so love it.

HELIODORE. I never liked Euripides.

NICYLLA. I told you he was finished. I'm never wrong. I knew it was all a mistake.

XENOCLES. He means well.

ANTAGORAS. No, he doesn't; that's just it.

LYCORIS. What I say is, that those kinds of plays do harm.

ANTAGORAS. The man's an atheist.

LYCORIS. He's a scoffer.

ANTAGORAS. But Socrates is far worse than he is.

NICYLLA. Oh, he's such a bore.

HEGESO. I love his little snub nose.

HELIODORE. I shall never ask them again.

ALCANDER. Tiresome people.

LYCORIS. What I say is, people like Socrates and Euripides ought to be put in prison.

NICYLLA. Especially Socrates.

ANTAGORAS. So he will be, or else my name's not Antagoras. He only deserves one thing, and that's capital punishment.

HEGESO. Poor little Socrates! But I hope you'll let Euripides off.

ANTAGORAS. He doesn't count; he's only a playwright.

CURTAIN.

XVII

JASON AND MEDEA

SCENE.—*A room in the house of* JASON, *looking on to garden, at Corinth. Discovered:* JASON *ana* GLAUCE.

JASON. I think you really had better go. She may be in any minute now.

GLAUCE. Very well; but you promise to tell her to-day?

JASON. I swear.

GLAUCE. It's all very well, but you said that yesterday.

JASON. Yes, and I would have told her yesterday, only I was interrupted——

GLAUCE. I know; the only thing I say is, you must tell her to-day and do it nicely, because I shouldn't like poor little Medea to be hurt.

JASON. No, of course not. Good-bye.

GLAUCE. Good-bye. Then to-morrow at eleven, at the Creon Institute.

JASON. Very well, at eleven.

GLAUCE. And then we might—no.

JASON. What?

GLAUCE. Nothing. I was only thinking we might have some food at the "Golden Fleece," *downstairs.*

JASON. The whole of Corinth would see us.

GLAUCE. There is never a soul downstairs, and I don't see now that it much matters.

JASON. It's a pity to make oneself conspicuous; your father——

GLAUCE. You know best, but I should have thought——

JASON. That's Medea coming through the garden.

GLAUCE. To-morrow, at eleven.

JASON. Yes — yes — to-morrow. (GLAUCE *goes out L.*)

Enter MEDEA *from the garden*

MEDEA. I can't get any one for dinner to-morrow night. We want somebody amusing.

JASON (*wearily*). Would Orpheus do?

MEDEA. We've got too many heroes as it is. And then, if Orpheus comes, we shall be obliged to ask him to play.

JASON. What about Castor and Pollux?

MEDEA. Heroes again—and I think it's a mistake to ask brothers together.

JASON. Heracles is staying at Corinth.

MEDEA. He would do beautifully.

JASON. I'm not sure he would do. He doesn't get on with Admetus.

MEDEA. Why not? Admetus ought to be very grateful.

JASON. For bringing back his wife from the grave?

MEDEA. Yes, of course.

JASON. Of course. (JASON *looks pensive.*)

MEDEA. Then we shall want another woman.

JASON. How would Ariadne do?

MEDEA. What are you thinking of? Theseus is coming.

JASON. I thought all that had entirely blown over.

MEDEA. We want an unmarried woman, if possible.

JASON. I don't know any one.

MEDEA. Do you think we could get King Creon's daughter by herself? She's so pretty. I mean Glauce.

JASON (*blushing scarlet*). I don't think—er—no—you see—we can't very well.

MEDEA. Why not?

JASON. She's a girl.

MEDEA. She goes everywhere. She doesn't count as a girl.

JASON. Then we should have to ask King Creon.

MEDEA. No, Alcestis will bring her. That will do beautifully. I'll send a message at once.

JASON. For the sake of the gods, do nothing of the kind.

MEDEA. But she'll do beautifully.

JASON. You don't understand. You see, King Creon has—he's—well, I don't quite know how to say it.

MEDEA. What *do* you mean?

JASON. Well, it's very awkward. The fact is, King Creon has approached me politically—about something——

MEDEA. What has that got to do with asking Glauce?

JASON. No, nothing, of course, except that we should have to ask him.

MEDEA. I've already told you that it's unnecessary.

JASON (*firmly*). I shouldn't dream of asking her without her father, and we can't ask him.

MEDEA. Why not?

JASON. Oh, because he never does dine out.

MEDEA. I'm sure he would come here.

JASON. It's impossible. You see, to tell you the truth—I've been meaning to tell you this for some time, only I've never had the opportunity—the King is rather severe about you.

MEDEA. Severe! How?

JASON. Well, you see, he's old-fashioned, and he doesn't consider our marriage is a marriage.

MEDEA. We were married in the temple of Aphrodite What more does he want?

JASON. He doesn't consider that a girl's marriage is valid when it is made without the consent of her parents; and your poor dear father, you know, was most unreasonable.

MEDEA. Papa being silly has got nothing to do with it. When a man and a woman are married in a temple, with the proper rites, they are man and wife. Nothing can ever alter the fact.

JASON. Yes, but it's not only that. Creon goes much farther than that. He made me certain revelations concerning some family business which, I must say, surprised me immensely.

MEDEA. What family business?

JASON. Well, it appears that soon after I started for Colchis my father entered into secret negotiations with King Creon, and signed an offensive and defensive alliance with him, with the object of safeguarding himself against Pelias. The word-alliance remained secret. But at a State banquet Creon laid great stress on the friendship between himself and the Æolidæ, and brought in the words "friendly understanding" several times. Now in the treaty, which was drawn up and published, to mask the alliance, there were several secret clauses. One of them concerned the Sardine Fisheries in the Isthmus of Corinth, and the other—well—er, my marriage.

MEDEA. Your marriage.

JASON. Yes, it is extraordinary, isn't it? It appears that during my absence, and without my being consulted in any way whatsoever, I was formally married, by proxy, of course, to Creon's daughter Glauce—who was at that time a mere child. It was further settled that as soon as she was grown up, the marriage should be announced and the King should publicly adopt me as his heir.

MEDEA. No wonder he was annoyed at your having married me.

JASON. Well, you see, he isn't annoyed at that, because he says our marriage wasn't valid.

MEDEA. Not in the eyes of the law, perhaps; but I am sure Aphrodite would not only be pained, but extremely angry if we cancelled vows which were made in her temple.

JASON. No, that's just it. It appears he consulted all the oracles and the priestesses, and the Pythonesses, and they all say that our marriage is not only illegal, but positively criminal, and that my lawful wife, both in the eyes of man and of the gods, is Glauce.

MEDEA. And my children?

JASON. Well, about the children, opinion was

slightly divided; but they inclined to think that, if I adopted them, they would be considered legitimate.

MEDEA. Legitimate! I should hope so. But what did you say to Creon? I suppose you told him you were very sorry, but that it couldn't be helped. (*She laughs.*) Poor Glauce! It's a shame to make a girl so ridiculous.

JASON. I don't think you quite realise how seriously Creon regards the matter.

MEDEA. I don't care an obol what he thinks. What I want to be told is how you told him what you think.

JASON. Of course, I said that I felt highly flattered.

MEDEA. But that you were married already.

JASON. No, it was no use saying that, because —as I've already said twice—he does not think our marriage counts.

MEDEA. Then what did you say?

JASON. Oh, I said I would lay the matter before you, and trust to your great good sense.

MEDEA. Do you mean to say that you did not give him to understand that the whole thing was altogether mad, absurd, and utterly preposterous?

JASON. How could I? After all, he is the King; and, moreover, he is backed up by all the legal and hieratic authorities. I could do nothing. I was quite helpless, quite defenceless. I simply had to incline myself before his higher authority.

MEDEA. Oh, I see; you accepted, in fact.

[*She reflects a moment.*

JASON. I didn't exactly accept. But what else could I do?

MEDEA. No, of course, it's quite simple. You said that our marriage didn't count; you would be delighted to marry Glauce.

JASON. I didn't use the word "delighted."

MEDEA. "Highly honoured," perhaps?

JASON. Something like that.

MEDEA. So you are engaged to be married? (*Without any irony in her voice*) Well, I congratulate you.

JASON. Not engaged. You see, the King——

MEDEA (*cheerfully*). I know. You mean you are married to Glauce theoretically, and now you are going to make the marriage a reality.

JASON (*intensely relieved at there not being a scene*). How clearly you put things!

MEDEA. I'm delighted for your sake. She's a charming girl, and I am sure she will make you very happy.

JASON. But, Medea, what about you? You quite understand that I am ready to give up the whole thing unless you are quite sure you don't mind?

MEDEA. My dear Jason, why should I mind? My only wish is that you should be happy.

JASON. I'm afraid that's impossible. I need hardly say I am not in the least in love with Glauce.

MEDEA. Of course not. But what about my children?

JASON. Ah, there's the difficulty. The King says they will have to remain with me. But you will be able to come and see them whenever you like.

MEDEA. Oh, I see.

JASON. The King is very particular about children being brought up by their father. He thinks women make them into mollycoddles.

MEDEA. Yes, of course. I suppose, since the marriage ceremony has already been performed, you won't have to go through it again.

JASON. It's unnecessary; but I'm sorry to say the King wishes it.

MEDEA. Then I suppose it will be soon. I shall leave Corinth as soon as my things can be packed.

JASON. The King wants the ceremony to be this week; but you mustn't inconvenience yourself in any way.

MEDEA (*smiling*). No, I won't. Good-bye for the moment. I am going out to buy Glauce a present. [*She goes out.*

JASON *walks up to a flower-pot and takes a lily from it. He speaks into the lily:* Is that oooo Corinth Wall? Darling, is that you? Yes, it's all over. She's taken it wonderfully. No. Yes, certainly ask her to stay later. Creon Institute to-morrow at eleven. Good-bye, darling.

CURTAIN.

XVIII

MEDEA GOES SHOPPING

SCENE.—*A Shop in Corinth. Discovered* GLAUCE *looking at some models and* MEDEA *looking at something else.*

MEDEA (*to* GLAUCE). Is there nobody in this shop who can attend to me? I've been waiting a quarter of an hour. (GLAUCE *stares at her icily.*) Oh, I beg your pardon! Oh, it's darling Glauce. How funny! You know how shortsighted I am. You are just the person I wanted to see. Jason has been telling me. I do congratulate you. I think it's such an excellent plan. You see I never could have left the poor old thing. It would have been too great a shame. You must be kind to him and see that he has his cup of goat's milk, *boiled*, you know, *every* night, and only a pint of Chian wine in the evening. All the doctors say that for his age he's wonderfully well preserved. But he *must* be careful.

GLAUCE. I'm afraid I must go.

MEDEA. You mustn't let me be in the way. I can come any time.

GLAUCE. Thank you very much. I have seen everything I wanted to see.

MEDEA. Of course, darling, you get everything from Carthage. What a lovely frock that is! So Punic.

GLAUCE. It's very old. My maid just threw it together. Good-bye.

MEDEA. Good-bye, darling.

[*Exit* GLAUCE.

Enter a SALESMAN

MEDEA. I want something for a wedding present for a friend. Something she can wear in the evening. Not too expensive. But something that will look nice and make an effect.

SALESMAN. Certainly, Madam. We have some very nice Carthage models.

MEDEA. I'm afraid I can't run to that.

SALESMAN. Is it a dress you want, Madam?

MEDEA. No, not a dress, a cloak. Something to wear for going out to a feast, a "Terpsichore" Exodos.

SALESMAN. Yes, Madam. An amphitheatre cloak. (*Showing a cloak.*) This is very much worn now. Halcyon feathers and petals of asphodel. Quite a novelty. The Queen of Crete ordered six of them yesterday. Just the thing for Olympia. Stylish without being loud. And a real bargain, thirteen talents. Can be worn in the daytime or in the evening, and suitable for half mourning.

MEDEA. I don't want mourning. It's for a wedding present.

SALESMAN. I quite understand, Madam. We've a very nice peplos in orange pungee. Indian silk is very fashionable just now.

MEDEA. It's too young-looking.

SALESMAN. Yes, Madam. A second marriage, perhaps. We've the very thing. Here's a chiton. Our own model. Persian muslin. We call it the Amazon.

MEDEA. I don't want a riding habit.

SALESMAN. We've a very nice chlamys, Madam; cerulean silk, trimmed with imitation pearls.

MEDEA. How much is that?

SALESMAN. Eleven talents, Madam. It's reduced. We were asking twelve for it.

MEDEA. It doesn't seem very fresh.

SALESMAN. It's slightly shop-soiled, and on account of that I could take something off. I could let you have it, Madam, for ten talents, thirty drachmas, and seventy-five obols.

MEDEA. I'm afraid all these models are too expensive. I think I'll buy the stuff and run it up at home. Can I see some stuff?

SALESMAN. For a peplos or a chiton, Madam?

MEDEA. I think it had better be a chiton.

SALESMAN. Quite so, Madam. Stockinette or crêpe?

MEDEA. Not stockinette.

SALESMAN. This, Madam, is a beautiful material, just come in, called Golden Fleece taffetas.

MEDEA. That wouldn't do at all.

SALESMAN. We've some very nice Etrurian muslin.

MEDEA. Can I see it?

SALESMAN. Certainly, Madam (*throws out the stuff on the counter*).

MEDEA. How much is that?

SALESMAN. It's really given away, Madam, ten drachmas a yard.

MEDEA. It's too flimsy.

SALESMAN. Perhaps, Madam. Not quite important enough for an occasion. Now, here's a new material, just in from Athens. Georgette, called after the Gorgon sisters. We have it in mauve, pink, and grey. The Medusa shade is very much sought after.

MEDEA. That would do all right for the day, but I don't think it would show by lamplight.

SALESMAN. We can see in a moment, Madam. I will darken the room.

[*The room is darkened but for one small lamp. The* SALESMAN *waves the material in front of the lamp.*

MEDEA. It's flat by lamplight. The wedding torches would kill it.

SALESMAN. Here's something from Africa, Madam Moorish kraipnos, it's called. Just the thing for a wedding, not too young, and yet quite bridal.

MEDEA. How much is it?

SALESMAN. That would be *for you*, Madam, as you're an old customer, fifty drachmas a yard.

MEDEA. Double width?

SALESMAN. Thirty-one inches, Madam.

MEDEA. It's very dear.

SALESMAN. We have some cheap organdies, Madam. White and crushed arbutus.

MEDEA. That would be too light.

SALESMAN. We've some beautiful "charmatodes" satin, or some cream tussore, or a saffron bombychine, very hymeneal.

MEDEA. I suppose the "Sphinx" kraipnos is very expensive?

SALESMAN (*showing some*). Not at all, Madam. This only runs to thirty drachmas a yard, double width.

MEDEA. That would do, but I don't like the colour.

SALESMAN. We could do it you in magenta and golden—I mean in *silver* fleece shades.

MEDEA. I think I'll have it dyed. I'll send you the dye. I've an excellent precious dye at home, made of Centaur's blood, by a little man. Could you use that?

SALESMAN. Certainly, Madam. The "Nessus" preparation, I suppose? It is, of course, Madam, as you know, highly inflammable.

MEDEA. But I suppose it wouldn't be very dangerous unless worn next to the skin?

SALESMAN. No, Madam, not unless worn next to the skin. But if it was worn next to the skin it would certainly blister—as it's for a jumper—I mean a chiton——

MEDEA. I'm not sure I shall make it into a jumper, and it's for a chilly person.

SALESMAN. Quite so, Madam. How many yards may I put up for you, Madam?

MEDEA. Three and a half, please.

SALESMAN. I'll just measure it for you, Madam. (*He measures it.*) Very nice weather we've been having lately.

MEDEA. The climate's so changeable, one never knows what to wear.

SALESMAN. That was a dreadful thing about poor Mr. Phæthon.

MEDEA. Dreadful, but if inexperienced whips will drive the sun——

SALESMAN. Exactly so, Madam. Nothing seems to get any safer. Is it to be entered to account, or shall I send it?

MEDEA. Yes, please enter it, and send it, as soon as you have dyed it, to Queen Medea, the Palace.

SALESMAN. Yes, Your Majesty. (*Writes down and reads as he writes*), Her Majesty, the Queen of Corinth.

MEDEA. No, no, no. Queen Medea, the Palace, Corinth.

CURTAIN.

XIX

KING ALFRED AND THE NEAT-HERD

SCENE.—*Interior of a* NEAT-HERD'S *hut, near the river Parret, in Somersetshire.*

Enter a NEAT-HERD, *followed by* KING ALFRED, *who is miserably clad and shivering from cold; he carries a bow and a few broken arrows. A log fire is burning smokily in a corner of the hut.*

THE NEAT-HERD (*scratching the back of his head*). Reckon t' old 'ooman 'ull be baack zoon.

THE KING. We are very hungry.

THE NEAT-HERD. Reckon t' old 'ooman 'ull be baack zoon. She be a baaking.

[*The* KING *sits down by the fire and warms himself. Enter the* NEAT-HERD'S WIFE *with much noise and bustle; she carries a batch of newly-kneaded loaves on a tray, which she puts down in front of the fire. The* NEAT-HERD *says something to her in an undertone; she mutters something in answer about "strange folk." Then she goes up to the* KING.

THE NEAT-HERD'S WIFE. If ye be a-staying here ye must make yournself useful.

THE KING (*rising and bowing politely*). We should be delighted to do anything in our power.

THE NEAT-HERD'S WIFE (*looking at the* KING *with distrust, and talking very quickly*). I'ze warrant ye be strange in these parts. (*To her husband*) I reckon we've no time to see after strange folk. We all be hungry, and it's a mercy we've still got a morsel of bread in the house to keep the children from ztark ztarving, and that's zo. But if he'll look to t' baatch whiles I zee to t' cows, maybe ee'll get a morsel for his pains. (*To the* KING) Now do ee be zure, stranger, ye turn the baatch when they're done a one side.

THE KING (*who has only partially understood what she has said*). We shall be delighted. (*He bows.*)

THE NEAT-HERD'S WIFE (*to her husband*). I reckon he do be daaft.

THE NEAT-HERD. He's no daaft; he be strange.

THE NEAT-HERD'S WIFE. See ee turn the baatch.

THE NEAT-HERD. Oo! AR!

[*The* NEAT-HERD'S WIFE *goes out and slams the door.*

[*The* KING *sits again by the fire and begins to mend his broken arrows; after a pause:*

THE KING. Do you care for verse?—poetry?

[*The* NEAT-HERD *scratches the back of his head, and after reflecting for some time:*

THE NEAT-HERD. Oo! AR!

THE KING. Then we will repeat to you a few little things—mere trifles—we composed in the marshes during our leisure hours. (*He looks pensively upwards.*)

There are clouds in the sky,
  I'm afraid it will rain.
I cannot think why
There are clouds in the sky.
Had I wings, I would fly
  To the deserts of Spain.
There are clouds in the sky,
  I'm afraid it will rain.

THE KING. That is a triolet.

THE NEAT-HERD. Oo! AR!

THE KING. Here is another. It was written in dejection.

I've had nothing to eat
  For nearly two days.
It's beginning to sleet,
I've had nothing to eat;
Neither oatmeal nor wheat,
  Nor millet nor maize.
I've had nothing to eat
  For nearly two days.

That is also a triolet—perhaps not quite so successful. (*He looks at the* NEAT-HERD *inquiringly.*)

THE NEAT-HERD. Oo! AR!

THE KING. We will now repeat to you a sonnet. It is adapted from Boethius. It is called "Suspiria."

[*He passes his hand through his hair and looks upward towards the right.*

I used to sit upon an ivory chair,
And wear a jewelled crown upon my head;
Fine linen draped in folds my carven bed,
With myrrh I used to smooth and scent my hair.

I used to play upon a golden harp,
And every one agreed I played it well;
The servants bounded when I rang the bell;
I used to feed on immemorial carp.

But now I wander in a pathless fen,
Unkinged, forsook, discredited, discrowned;
I who was born to be the King of Men,
I who made armies tremble when I frowned,

I—in a neat-herd's damp and draughty hut—
Perform the menial duties of a slut.

Do you think the last rhyme weak? (*The* NEAT-HERD *does not answer.*) We have also written a ballad, but we cannot remember all of it. It is addressed to Guthrum, King of the Danes. The *Envoi*, however, runs like this.

Prince, you are having the time of your life,
From the Straits of Dover to Glaston Tor,
And writing it home to your Danish wife;—
But where are the bones and the hammer of Thor?

If we had a harp with us we would sing you the music, but we are sorry to say we lost it in the marsh yesterday.

THE NEAT-HERD. Oo! AR!

Enter the NEAT-HERD'S WIFE

THE NEAT-HERD'S WIFE. Be the baatch ready?

THE KING. Oh yes, of course. We shall be delighted.

[*He hurriedly lifts the tray with the loaves from the hearth and places it on the table.*

THE NEAT-HERD'S WIFE. Drat th' man! If they bain't all burnt! Ye take strange folk to house, and aask un to mind the baatch and turn't, and draat un if they doan't forget to turn when they be burning. Ize warrant ye be ready enough to eat un when they be done! Drat the man if I haven't half a mind to give un a beating with th' rolling-pin! Not a morsel shall ee get; good-for-nothing, idle, vagabond, wastrel, ramscullion, thief, robber.

THE NEAT-HERD. Easy, old woman, ee be th' *King!*

THE NEAT-HERD'S WIFE. Well, and if that bain't like a man, to let me tongue run on not knowing nothing neither! (*Curtsying.*) I'm zure I beg your Majesty's humble pardon, and I'm zure I knew nothing and meant no harm; and my man be that foolish not to tell a body that the King's self be here, so homelike and all, taking pity on us poor folk. I'm zure as I meant no harm, and I do for to beg your Majesty's pardon, and that I do, an' right humbly.

THE KING. Do not mention it. We assure you it is not of the slightest consequence. It was exceedingly careless of us to burn your loaves—your admirably kneaded loaves. And we most humbly and sincerely apologise. We are, we are afraid, given to these fits, these sudden and unwarrantable fits of absent-mindedness.

THE NEAT-HERD'S WIFE. And me always a-wanting to see a real Dane, too! Only yesterday I zaid t' Mary, "Mary," I do zay, "the Danes be all over the country." "Lord-amercy," she zay, "who be they!" "I bain't zet eyes on one on un yet," zay I, "but folks do zay as they be mighty pleasant folk," zav I: and now to have the

King of the Danes himself in my hut. . . . Well, who'd a thought as zuch a thing would coom to me an' mine!

THE NEAT-HERD. Ye be mistaken, ye be. He bain't the Danish King, he be t'other, he that wur th' King of England—bor! Alfred as was——

THE NEAT-HERD'S WIFE. What?

THE NEAT-HERD. Th' King o' England as was till th' Danes coom ower! Alfred they called 'un!

THE NEAT-HERD'S WIFE. He as be driven away, like?

THE NEAT-HERD. Oo! AR!

THE NEAT-HERD'S WIFE (*to the* KING). Oh, you be he, be you? Then ye ought to be ashamed of yoursel', that ye ought, coming into strange folk's houses at this time o' day, and begging for bread; and then when they've pity on ye for your misery, and give ye the chance of turning an honest penny by a piece of work as mony a man'd be glad to get, and any child could ha' done better, forgetting to turn th' loaves and spoiling th' whole baatch; an' ye know well enow I can't baake again this week—not that I mind th' baatch; but I can't have ye here, nohow! Ye'd best be a-going, and that quick! Bor!

THE KING. But cannot you possibly let us remain here until to-morrow? We are in need of shelter for the night.

THE NEAT-HERD. Don't be too 'ard on him, old 'ooman.

THE NEAT-HERD'S WIFE. Be ye daaft? We'd ha' the Danish soldiers, th' archers, and th' whole Danish army here in no time for a-sheltering a traitor like, and a rubbul. I reckon we're honest folk, and loyal servants of the King, and we bain't be going to shelter any gurt rubbul here. I'ze brought up to be loyal; I'ze warrant I'm a loyal servant till I do die. No rubbuls here. Out ye go, ye scurvy traitor, and that quick, ye knave, or else I'll bring my rolling-pin to ye! Not that I grudge ye a morsel. There, ye may take one of them burnt cakes with ye, that ye may, and enjoy it, too. And now out with ye, avoor one o' th' neighbours caatch a sight on ye. Out, do ye 'ear me! out!

THE KING (*sighing*). Very well, we are going. (*To himself*) Nothing fails like failure, but perhaps a time will come. (*He goes out peevishly, biting his nails.*)

CURTAIN.

XX

ROSAMUND AND ELEANOR

SCENE.—*A room in* ROSAMUND'S *house, "The Labyrinth," Woodstock. Discovered:* ROSAMUND (*playing a harp*) *and* MARGERY. *It is night.*

MARGERY. There's a lady wishes to see you, milady.

ROSAMUND. A lady! How can she have found her way through the Labyrinth? You know that I'm not at home to any visitors. (*She throws down her harp.*)

MARGERY. She said she wished to see your ladyship very particular.

ROSAMUND. Who is she?

MARGERY. She didn't give any name, but she said it was something about fortune-telling.

ROSAMUND. Oh! she's the fortune-teller I heard about—the gipsy.

MARGERY. She's not that sort, milady.

ROSAMUND. Do you mean she's a lady?

MARGERY. She's dressed poor—but——

ROSAMUND. What?

MARGERY. Well, milady, I thought she had come to beg, what with her poor clothes; but when I said as you were not at home to visitors, she ordered me about like, so rough, that I saw at once she was a real lady; and then her shoes are beautiful, I'm sure, the best red velvet.

ROSAMUND (*pensively*). I promised Henry not to see any one—but then once can't matter—and I do so want to have my fortune told. (*Abruptly*) Show her in. (*Exit* MARGERY.) After all, Henry never need know. And I don't see why I should never see a soul. I am becoming quite rusty for want of human society. Besides, Henry promised to let me have my fortune told.

Enter MARGERY *and* QUEEN ELEANOR. QUEEN ELEANOR *is a commanding-looking woman, shabbily dressed.* MARGERY *withdraws.*

ROSAMUND (*rising shyly*). How do you do?

ELEANOR. Please sit down. I will sit down too. (*They both sit down.*) You have got a beautiful house.

ROSAMUND. Yes, isn't it nice? Mavis built it.

ELEANOR. Mavis! Really? I've always considered him too extravagant for me.

ROSAMUND. You ought to come in the day time and see the garden. The roses are beautiful this year. I beg your pardon, but I didn't quite catch your name.

ELEANOR. Never mind about my name. I've come to talk business. How long have you been living here?

ROSAMUND. Let me see, we—I mean I—go in on Lady Day. But aren't you going to tell my fortune?

ELEANOR. So you do wish your fortune told?

ROSAMUND. Oh yes, please tell it me if you can.

ELEANOR. All in good time.

ROSAMUND. But before you do so, you won't be offended, I'm sure, if I ask you how you found your way through the Labyrinth?

ELEANOR. Fortune-tellers know that kind of thing by instinct.

ROSAMUND (*greatly interested*). Really? Then you must tell me who is going to be champion at the Winchester Tournament, and whether (*she hesitates*)——

ELEANOR. What?

ROSAMUND. Oh! Nothing. How do you tell one's fortune? By looking at the hand or in a crystal?

ELEANOR. I will look at your hand first. Show it me. No; the left hand first, please. (ROSAMUND *gives her her left hand.*) Yours is a most interesting hand. The Mountain of the Moon is strongly developed.

ROSAMUND. Oh! How interesting! What does that mean?

ELEANOR. It means that you have a warm, affectionate nature.

ROSAMUND. That's true.

ELEANOR. You had several illnesses when you were a child.

ROSAMUND. Yes; I had whooping-cough when I was four, measles when I was seven, and scarlatina when I was nine.

ELEANOR. Exactly. You have more intuition than judgment; your first instincts are true, but you are inclined to let them be overruled by your second thoughts.

ROSAMUND. That's perfectly true.

ELEANOR. You are very generous, but inclined to be extravagant in dress. You are fond of luxury, devoted to flowers, and you like soft stuffs. You are fond of music, but you have more taste than actual skill. You are quick-tempered, but not resentful; you are gentle, modest, and unassuming, but inclined to be obstinate, if you are driven beyond a certain point.

ROSAMUND. It's too wonderful!

ELEANOR. The Mountain of Jupiter is highly developed; Saturn fair, and Mercury almost imperceptible. That means you are ambitious but easy-going, rather lazy, and most careless about money matters.

ROSAMUND. It's like second sight.

ELEANOR. You have had one great love affair in your life. (*She pauses.*)

ROSAMUND. Do go on.

ELEANOR. The man you love is tall; he has red hair, almost the colour of a ruby, and a violent temper. He is impulsive, and often does things on the spur of the moment which he regrets bitterly afterwards.

ROSAMUND. Yes, yes.

ELEANOR. He is a powerful man. He holds a position of great importance in the State.

ROSAMUND. And will he love me for ever and ever?

ELEANOR. You have a double line of life, and it is marked with a star.

ROSAMUND. What does that mean?

ELEANOR. It means that the man you love is threatened with a great disaster.

ROSAMUND. Oh! How dreadful! Is there no means by which it can be averted?

ELEANOR. There is one way.

ROSAMUND. What is it? Tell me quickly.

ELEANOR (*solemnly*). By an act of willing self-sacrifice on your part. That is to say, by your death —self-inflicted, of course. If you give up your life you will save your lover's.

ROSAMUND. Oh!

ELEANOR. And you will go down to posterity as a devoted woman—a heroine.

ROSAMUND. Oh!

ELEANOR. But unless you perform this act of self-sacrifice at once, it will be too late. The danger is imminent.

ROSAMUND. What kind of danger is it?

ELEANOR. On that point the stars are reticent.

ROSAMUND. But tell me more about the—about him.

ELEANOR. About whom?

ROSAMUND. The man with ruby hair. Is he married?

ELEANOR. Yes, and hence the trouble. He is married to a high-born, noble, unselfish, generous, gifted, and beautiful woman—a paragon. But I am sorry to say, he has for a brief moment proved faithless to her in thought—it is only a temporary whim, of course; but even a passing infidelity—even though it be only an infidelity in thought—is at once visited with a just retribution. It is because of the infidelity that he is now meditating, that the vengeance of the stars pursues him, and that danger threatens.

ROSAMUND. It's not true! His wife is horrible. She has driven him away by her cold, callous conduct. She's a scold. She bullies him. She nags at him from morning till night. Besides which she's very, very ugly, and dresses like a scarecrow.

ELEANOR. How dare you talk like that to me! On your knees, wretched minx!

ROSAMUND. I don't believe you're a fortune-teller at all. I don't believe you know anything about it.

ELEANOR. You are right. I am no fortune-teller. I am the Queen. My name is Eleanor.

ROSAMUND. Oh dear! You've no business to come here. This is my house.

ELEANOR. Your house, indeed! However, I have not come here to waste my time. I have come, as I said before, on business. Here is a dagger, and here in this vial is an effective but entirely painless poison. I give you two minutes to choose which way you will take it.

[*She places the vial and the dagger on a small table.*

ROSAMUND (*crying*). Oh! Go! You frighten me.

ELEANOR. Now, do you hear what I say? Two minutes.

ROSAMUND (*kneeling and sobbing*). I can't. Oh, please spare me! I will do anything; I will go away—anywhere—to a nunnery; but please spare me.

ELEANOR (*with tragic grimness*). One minute and a half.

ROSAMUND. Oh, I'm so young! I'm sure I never meant any harm. Spare my life. Have mercy!

ELEANOR. One minute.

ROSAMUND. Oh, you are cruel. I'm so young. Think what it is to be young.

ELEANOR. The time has elapsed. Now, which is it to be?

ROSAMUND (*rising and drying her eyes*). After all, why should I? (*She takes the dagger and the vial and throws them on to the floor.*) I won't take either. So there! You can do your worst. (*She calls*) Here, Margery! Rosalie! Topaz! Anselm! Richard! Thomas! Quick! Help! Murder! (*Margery and a bevy of servants rush into the room with torches and staves.*) This fortune-teller has insulted me! Turn her out of the house at once!

ELEANOR. How dare you! I'm the——

ROSAMUND. Quick! Quick! Turn her out. She's tried to poison me! If you don't turn her out at once I'll tell the King——

[*The servants turn out* QUEEN ELEANOR, *who struggles violently.*

ROSAMUND. Mind, Margery, if there should be *any* other visitors, I'm not at home.

CURTAIN.

XXI

ARIADNE IN NAXOS

SCENE.—*A room in* ARIADNE'S *house at Naxos. Discovered:* ARIADNE *and* ŒNONE, *her attendant.*

ARIADNE. When Theseus comes, show him in here directly. I am expecting Dionysus in half an hour. If he comes sooner, which he probably will do, don't announce him, but show him into the dining-room, and then come in here and make up the fire so that I may know he's there. You quite understand?

ŒNONE. Yes, perfectly.

ARIADNE. There is Theseus walking up the drive. Go and let him in quickly.

[ŒNONE *goes out.*

[ARIADNE *arranges herself by a spinning-wheel, near a fire where myrtle-twigs are burning, in an attitude of simple, brave, and unaffected dejection. She rubs her eyes with a silken scarf to make them appear red.*

Enter THESEUS

ARIADNE (*smiling bravely*). It's wonderful of you to be so punctual.

THESEUS. Yes, I——

ARIADNE. Sit down here. Or do you mind the fire?

THESEUS. No, I assure you.

ARIADNE. Are you quite sure you don't mind the fire?

THESEUS. I like it, really.

ARIADNE. Perhaps you would like a screen?

THESEUS. No, I promise you.

[ARIADNE *rings a small silver hand-bell.*

No, please don't ring.

Enter ŒNONE

ARIADNE. You may just as well have the screen. It's there. Œnone, will you please bring a screen for the Duke? The fire's so hot.

[ŒNONE *goes out.*

ARIADNE. Would you like a little wine?

THESEUS. No, thank you, really; I never drink wine in the morning.

ARIADNE. There's some in the next room, if you would like to have some.

Enter ŒNONE, *bringing a screen, which she puts in front of* THESEUS

THESEUS. Oh, thank you so much!

[ŒNONE *goes out.*

ARIADNE. Is that right for you?

THESEUS. That's perfect! (*With nervous decision*) I've come to tell you that I'm so sorry I was rude yesterday, and that of course I didn't mean——

ARIADNE. When you get to Athens I want you to do something for me. Do you think you will have time? Do you think you could possibly remember it? It would be too heroic of you if you would.

THESEUS. Of course I would; but——

ARIADNE. It's the most tiresome commission . . . I want you to send me two pounds of Hymettus honey.

THESEUS. But I really wasn't thinking of——

ARIADNE. Will you have it sent by the next messenger, care of the King, to Crete, and then I shan't have to pay the duty?

THESEUS. But really, Ariadne——

ARIADNE. And you won't forget to give your father a hundred messages from me, will you? I hope they've packed the Minotaur's head properly. It would be a terrible tragedy if the horns were broken.

THESEUS. I haven't had anything packed yet. I really——

ARIADNE. Œnone will help to pack for you. She's a wonderful packer. (*She rings the bell.*) She packs like an angel.

THESEUS. But my slave can do it; besides, I really want——

Enter ŒNONE

ARIADNE. Oh, Œnone, I want you to go round to the Duke's house later—when the doctor comes —and help to pack the Duke's things; and at the same time you might see that the slaves pack the Minotaur's head properly.

ŒNONE. Yes. [*She goes out.*

THESEUS. Ariadne, I must really tell you——

ARIADNE. Let me think: you will get to Athens the day after to-morrow. You won't forget to let me hear what kind of a crossing you have. And you must take warm enough things with you. It's always quite bitter on board that ship. But of course you're a good sailor, aren't you?

THESEUS. I don't mind a long voyage, but sometimes just crossing the isthmus upsets me.

ARIADNE. I have got some wonderful stuff Æsculapius gave me. It's quite harmless. You take one dose two hours before starting and one dose when you get on board; then you lie down; but you must eat nothing. It's wonderful. It's called *Asphodol*. I like the name so much, don't you? You had better have the Minotaur registered straight through to the Piræus. Then you won't have any bother at the other ports with the Customs. If you do have any tiresome bother, you can use my father's name; I will give you the passport he had made out for us. I have scratched my name out, but that will not matter. I have always found them very civil in Greece. They let me bring in bushels of silk from Tyre. You must give my love to Hippolyta, if you see her. She's not been well lately.

THESEUS. Really?

ARIADNE. No, poor darling! I've been rather worried and anxious about her. She's been having that horrible neuritis again. I had a letter yesterday from Athens, saying that she had lost her buoyancy and had had to give up riding altogether! Isn't it too terrible? She was such an inspired rider, wasn't she, with those hands and that unerring judgment? I can't imagine anything more ironical and more tragic; and they say she's so brave about it. She would be, of course. Don't you think people like that always surprise one by being a little better than their best in an emergency?

THESEUS. Yes.

ARIADNE. Don't you think Hippolyta is the most straight and true character we have ever known?

THESEUS (*uncomfortable*). Yes, yes——

ARIADNE. And almost more beautiful than anybody?

THESEUS. Yes, she is beautiful.

ARIADNE. I love her straightness of line, and her strong capable hands, and that *magic* cast in her left eye, which gives a kind of strangeness to her face, doesn't it?

THESEUS. She is very good-looking.

ARIADNE. But don't you think much more than that? Don't you put her almost higher than anybody for charm?

THESEUS. I'd never thought about her like that.

ARIADNE. And then isn't she quite unlike any one else? Doesn't one feel absolutely certain with her, like one does with a perfect chariot-driver?

THESEUS. Yes, she has a very fine character.

ARIADNE. Almost more than fine, isn't it? Something rare?

THESEUS. But, Ariadne, I really must——

ARIADNE. You needn't go yet. You've lots of time to pack. Œnone will help with the packing. You don't sail till sunset, do you? Because of the tide. I hope you've got the right pilot. The old man with one eye. He's too charming. He's my greatest friend.

THESEUS. Ariadne——

ARIADNE. I shall watch you from the hill. I shan't come down to the quay because of the crowd —you might wave from the ship. You will be able to see me. I shall stand next to the clump of cypress-trees and watch the ship till she's out of sight. There's a new moon to-night, just as there was the first night you arrived at Crete. Do you remember how papa bored you by talking about astrology? And you were so angelically kind to him and patient. You bore it so well. It was like you. I don't think you know how devoted papa is to you, and how much he will miss you.

THESEUS. Ariadne—please——

ARIADNE. You won't forget to write and say whether the Minotaur arrives safely, will you? Because papa will simply be longing to know, and he'd be miserable if anything went wrong.

THESEUS (*getting up and knocking down the screen in his agitation*). Ariadne, I simply can't bear this any longer. I must speak. You must and shall hear me. The whole thing's a mistake—a nightmare. I swear I didn't mean a thing yesterday. It was too stupid of me to—to say—I mean I didn't mean—I mean I lost my temper—just like any one. Of course I didn't mean, really.

Enter ŒNONE. *She brings in a large bundle of firewood, which she throws on to the hearth*

ARIADNE (*getting up*). I'm afraid you oughtn't to stay another minute now, or else you will miss the ship—Œnone will go with you and help you to pack. Good-bye, Theseus. It's been too perfect, hasn't it? I have loved it all so. You won't forget the honey, will you? Two pounds. Now you'll really have to run—and I have got the doctor coming in one second. Good-bye, Theseus, and my best love to your father and to dear Hippolyta if you see her. Œnone, please go with the Duke.

[ARIADNE *shakes hands with* THESEUS.

THESEUS. But, really——

ARIADNE. I'm afraid I must fly. I hope you'll have a perfect crossing.

THESEUS (*hopelessly*). Good-bye, Ariadne——

[*He goes out very sadly with* ŒNONE *L. As soon as they are gone,* ARIADNE *gently opens a door R. and calls:* Dionysus!

Enter DIONYSUS

DIONYSUS. Has he gone?

ARIADNE. Yes, at last, I think. Haven't I managed it too beautifully? He was longing not to go away at all.

DIONYSUS. When does he sail?

ARIADNE. At sunset. Sit down. We've got millions of things to say, haven't we? Do you mind the fire? There's the screen there on the floor—if you do——

DIONYSUS. No, I love it.

CURTAIN.

XXII

VELASQUEZ AND THE "VENUS"

SCENE.—VELASQUEZ'S *studio.* DONA SOL, *a beautiful dark-haired lady, elaborately dressed in stiff farthingale, is sitting for her portrait.* VELASQUEZ *is standing in front of an easel, vehemently throwing paint on to the canvas with a large, long brush. In the corner of the studio is an open virginal.*

VELASQUEZ. Are you getting tired?

DONA SOL. No, I never get tired of sitting; I'm so used to standing up at Court.

VELASQUEZ. Would you mind turning your head a shade to the left? Yes, that's right.

DONA SOL. You will be careful about the nose, won't you?

VELASQUEZ. Ah! you've a very wonderful nose from the painter's point of view.

DONA SOL. They always exaggerate my nose—and I do so hate exaggeration, don't you?

VELASQUEZ (*absently*). Yes.

DONA SOL. Shall I be able to see the picture to-day?

VELASQUEZ. I think so. It's practically finished now. I have only got to finish that piece of lace on your left wrist.

DONA SOL. Shan't you want another sitting?

VELASQUEZ. No—I——

DONA SOL. But Dona Anna had a dozen sittings.

VELASQUEZ. But she's fair—I find fair people more difficult to paint.

DONA SOL. I can't see what there was to paint in her at all. She's all bones.

VELASQUEZ. That's just it. I can't get that lace right. Do you mind if I play a tune on the virginal?

DONA SOL. No, please do.

[VELASQUEZ *goes to the virginal and plays a wild, rhythmic dance.*

DONA SOL. Is that Moorish?

VELASQUEZ. No. English. Quaint, isn't it? It's what they call a Morris-dance. Isn't it charming?

DONA SOL. Yes. I love English music. It's so uncivilised and fresh.

VELASQUEZ. Yes, they are a wonderfully musical people. (*He breaks off in the middle of the tune.*) I've got it. (*He runs to the canvas and flings a piece of white paint on to it.*) Ah, that's it. It's finished.

DONA SOL. What, the whole picture?

VELASQUEZ (*with a sigh of relief*). Yes, the whole picture.

DONA SOL. May I look?

VELASQUEZ. Certainly.

[DONA SOL *gets down from the platform and walks to the easel.*

DONA SOL. It's wonderful, Velasquez; quite wonderful. I like it enormously. You haven't quite finished the hands yet, have you?

VELASQUEZ. Yes, I think the hands will do like that. You don't quite get the light where you're standing. If you come here you'll see better.

DONA SOL (*moving*). I think its wonderful. Only I should like the hands to be a little more distinct. The dress is beautiful, and so is the necklace. But you've made my blue ribbon look green.

VELASQUEZ. That's the sun on it.

DONA SOL. But it isn't green. It's blue. Look at it. No amount of sun will make this blue into green.

VELASQUEZ. You see, the sun was full on it yesterday.

DONA SOL. I think it's all perfect, except the nose. My nose is tip-tilted, and you've given me a nose like a potato. You *must* alter that. I know my nose is difficult.

VELASQUEZ (*slightly darkening a shadow on the face*). Is that better?

DONA SOL. Yes, that's better. But it's still a little too heavy. You see, my nose is my best feature. I don't mind what you do to my hair and my mouth. I don't want to criticise. I never do criticise my own portraits. In fact, I think it's quite absurd for the sitter to criticise a picture. But I do think I'm a rather good judge of noses. Couldn't you make it just a shade more delicate?

VELASQUEZ (*giving the nose a touch with the brush.*) Is that better?

DONA SOL. Yes, that's better. I think that really is better. (*A pause.*) Don't you think you could make the eyebrows a little darker? You've made them so faint. And then I think the hair ought to be a little brighter, and the expression a shade less severe. I don't think you've quite got my smile. I look cross. Of course I suppose I look like that sometimes—when everything goes wrong. Every one does look cross sometimes—but that's not what I usually look like.

VELASQUEZ (*making a few imperceptible alterations*). Is that better?

DONA SOL. Yes, that's much better. I think it's perfect. May I look at some of the other pictures?

[*She walks round the studio till she finds several canvases turned face backwards against a heavy piece of furniture.*

VELASQUEZ. Let me help you. (*He turns several pictures round.*)

DONA SOL. Ah, that's the King. It's quite excellent. And that's the dear old Admiral. It's exactly like him. Oh, and that's Dona Elvira—*how* like, but *how* cruel!—How could you do that? Didn't she mind dreadfully? And what a dear little girl! That's not finished, I suppose? Oh, and I do love that seapiece. It's a storm, I suppose?

VELASQUEZ. I'm afraid it's meant to be a man riding in a field. It's just a study.

DONA SOL. Of course it is. How stupid of me. I couldn't see properly. It's wonderful—quite wonderful. And what's that large picture on an easel over there with a curtain over it?

VELASQUEZ. Oh, that's nothing. It's only a sketch—it's not finished.

DONA SOL. Do let me see it.

VELASQUEZ. I'm afraid I can't, really.

DONA SOL. But I insist on seeing it. I've been such a good sitter. Now I'm going to pull the curtain off.

VELASQUEZ. It's not my picture at all. It's not by me. It's by one of my pupils. It's by Mazo.

DONA SOL. Then of course I can see it. (*She pulls away the curtain, revealing a picture of Venus looking into a glass.*) Oh, but that's my head! How dared you do such a thing? No wonder you didn't want me to see it. Oh, how could you do such a thing?

VELASQUEZ. But I assure you you're mistaken. In the first place, I never painted the picture. I never touched it. It's Mazo's work. And he did it out of his head. At least, he did it from a model. It's meant to be Eros and Psyche or Venus, I've forgotten which.

DONA SOL. How could you put my head on such a hideous body? I call it mean, odious, and cowardly, and quite unpardonable. I shall burn my picture.

VELASQUEZ. But, my dear lady, do listen to me for one moment. The picture's not my work. I flatter myself really that I can draw a little better than that. That's mere apprentice work. Just compare it with my pictures. I never use those hot reds and those dull, lifeless greys. Just compare it with the other pictures.

DONA SOL (*crying*). How can I compare it with the others? You've never dared paint any one else like that.

VELASQUEZ. And then the face in the glass is no more your face than it is mine. It's not the least like you. It's a model's face. Mazo may have got a hint, a suggestion, quite unconsciously from seeing my picture, but nothing more. He's never set eyes on you.

DONA SOL. I don't believe it's by Mazo. I believe it's by you—or else you wouldn't have been so anxious for me not to see it.

VELASQUEZ. Well, I promise you that Mazo painted that picture from a model—a flower girl. I saw him do it. But to satisfy you, he shall get another model and paint in a different face.

DONA SOL. That's the least you can do.

VELASQUEZ. It shall be done to-day. Mazo's coming here this morning.

DONA SOL. Will you promise me that the face will be *quite, quite* different?

VELASQUEZ. On my word of honour as a Spaniard and as a painter.

DONA SOL (*drying her eyes*). Very well, I will forgive you—on one condition.

VELASQUEZ. What is it?

DONA SOL. That you will change the nose in *my* picture and make it less like a potato.

VELASQUEZ. Of course I will.

DONA SOL. Very well then. Good-bye. I shall come back to-morrow morning and see,—but oh! what a shame!

[VELASQUEZ *makes a low bow and leads her out. He comes back and, opening a door into a room adjoining the studio, he calls:* Mazo!

Enter MAZO

VELASQUEZ. The "Venus" is by you. Do you

hear me? You painted it. And you must change the face.

MAZO. I don't understand—change it in what way?

VELASQUEZ. You must change it altogether. Paint in any face you like. And you must say you painted the whole picture. Do it at once, and put your signature somewhere in the picture too.

MAZO. But, master, it's one of your greatest triumphs.

VELASQUEZ. I know that as well as you do—nevertheless, that picture must go to the King and be known to all the world as a Mazo, and not as a Velasquez.

CURTAIN.

XXIII

XANTIPPE AND SOCRATES

SCENE.—*A room in* SOCRATES' *house.* XANTIPPE *is seated at a table, on which an unappetising meal, consisting of figs, parsley, and some hashed goat's meat, is spread.*

Enter SOCRATES

XANTIPPE. You're twenty minutes late.

SOCRATES. I'm sorry, I was kept——

XANTIPPE. Wasting your time as usual, I suppose, and bothering people with questions who have got something better to do than to listen to you. You can't think what a mistake you make by going on like that. You can't think how much people dislike it. If people enjoyed it, or admired it, I could understand the waste of time—but they don't. It only makes them angry. Everybody's saying so.

SOCRATES. Who's everybody?

XANTIPPE. There you are with your questions again. Please don't try to catch me out with those kind of tricks. I'm not a philosopher. I'm not a sophist. I know I'm not clever—I'm only a woman. But I do know the difference between right and wrong and black and white, and I don't think it's very kind of you, or very generous either, to be always pointing out my ignorance, and perpetually making me the butt of your sarcasm.

SOCRATES. But I never said a word.

XANTIPPE. Oh, please, don't try to wriggle out of it. We all know you're very good at that. I do hate that shuffling so. It's so cowardly. I do like a man one can trust—and depend on—who when he says Yes means Yes, and when he says No means No.

SOCRATES. I'm sorry I spoke.

XANTIPPE. I suppose that's what's called irony. I've no doubt it's very clever, but I'm afraid it's wasted on me. I should keep those remarks for the market-place and the gymnasia and the workshops. I've no doubt they'd be highly appreciated there by that clique of young men who do nothing but admire each other. I'm afraid I'm old-fashioned. I was brought up to think a man should treat his wife with decent civility, and try, even if he did think her stupid, not to be always showing it.

SOCRATES. Have I by a word or hint ever suggested that you were stupid?

XANTIPPE. Oh, of course not—never. However, we won't discuss that. We will change the subject, if you don't mind.

SOCRATES. But really——

XANTIPPE (*ignoring the interruption*). Please give me your plate. I will help you to the goat.

SOCRATES. None for me, thank you, to-day.

XANTIPPE. Why not? I suppose it's not good enough. I'm afraid I can't provide the food you get at your grand friends' houses, but I do think it's rather cruel of you to sneer at my poor humble efforts.

SOCRATES. I promise you, Xantippe, nothing was farther from my thoughts. I'm not hungry. I've really got no appetite for meat to-day. I'll have some figs, if you don't mind.

XANTIPPE. I suppose that's a new fad, not to eat meat. I assure you people talk quite enough about you as it is without your making yourself more peculiar. Only yesterday Chrysilla was talking about your clothes. She asked if you made them dirty on purpose. She said the spots on the back couldn't have got there by accident. Every one notices it—every one says the same thing. Of course they think it's my fault. No doubt it's very amusing for people who don't mind attracting attention and who like being notorious; but it *is* rather hard on me. And when I hear people saying "Poor Socrates! it is such a shame that his wife looks after him so badly and doesn't even mend his sandals"—I admit I do feel rather hurt. However, that would never enter into your head. A philosopher hasn't time to think of other people. I suppose unselfishness doesn't form part of a sophist's training, does it?

[SOCRATES *says nothing, but eats first one fig and then another.*

XANTIPPE. I think you might at least answer when you're spoken to. I am far from expecting you to treat me with consideration or respect; but I do expect ordinary civility.

[SOCRATES *goes on eating figs in silence.*

XANTIPPE. Oh, I see, you're going to sulk. First you browbeat, then you're satirical. Then you sneer at the food, and then you sulk.

SOCRATES. I never said a word against the food.

XANTIPPE. You never said a word against the food. You only kept me waiting nearly half an hour for dinner—not that that was anything new—I'm sure I ought to be used to that by now—and you only refused to look at the dish which I had taken pains to cook with my own hands for you.

SOCRATES. All I said was I wasn't hungry—that I had no appetite for meat.

XANTIPPE. You've eaten all the figs. You've got quite an appetite for those.

SOCRATES. That's different.

XANTIPPE. Oh, that's different, is it? One can be hungry enough to eat all the fruit there is in the house, which I was especially keeping for this evening, but not hungry enough to touch a piece of meat. I suppose that's algebra.

SOCRATES. You know I very rarely eat meat.

XANTIPPE. Really? I hadn't noticed it. I always hear of your eating meat in other people's houses; but my poor cooking is not good enough for you. I'm sorry, but I can't afford those spicy, messy dishes. If I had a husband who had a *real* profession, and worked, and did something useful to earn his living and support his house and home, it would be different; only I think the least you could do is not to sneer at one when one is only trying to do one's best.

SOCRATES. I very rarely eat meat anywhere now.

XANTIPPE. That's why you're looking so ill. All the doctors say it's a mistake. Some people can do without meat They don't need it—but a man who works with his brain like you do *ought* to eat nourishing food. You ought to force yourself to eat meat, even if you don't feel inclined to.

SOCRATES. I thought you said just now that I did nothing.

XANTIPPE. There you are, cross-examining me like a lawyer, and tripping me up. I've no doubt it's very amusing for a professional philosopher to catch out a poor ignorant woman like me. It's a pity your audience isn't here. They *would* enjoy it. However, I'm afraid I'm not impressed. You can twist my words into anything you like. You can prove I meant black when I said white, but you know perfectly well what I mean. You know as well as I do that your eccentricity has made you thoroughly unpopular. And what I say is, it's just these little things that matter. Now do put all that nonsense away and have some goat.

SOCRATES. No, thank you. I really can't.

XANTIPPE. It's excellent goat, and there's some garlic in the sauce. I hate garlic, and it's there on purpose for you——

SOCRATES. Oh!

XANTIPPE. Give me your plate.

SOCRATES. I'd really rather not.

XANTIPPE. It would do you all the good in the world.

SOCRATES. But I've had quite enough. I've finished.

XANTIPPE. I suppose you had dinner before you came here, or you're going to have dinner somewhere else presently.

SOCRATES. I haven't touched food since I left the house.

XANTIPPE. Then it's quite ridiculous your not eating. Let me give you some goat at once.

SOCRATES. I couldn't, really. Besides, I must go in a minute.

XANTIPPE. There! I knew it! You're going out to dinner.

SOCRATES. You are mistaken, Xantippe.

XANTIPPE. You'd far better tell me the truth at once. I'm quite certain to find it out sooner or later. You can't think how foolish it is to tell lies and then be found out afterwards. You can't think how much a woman despises a man for that—you couldn't do anything more foolish.

SOCRATES. I promise you by all the gods that I'm not going to dine elsewhere.

XANTIPPE. I suppose you don't expect me to fall into that trap! Swearing by all the gods, when every one in Athens knows you are a professed atheist—when you do nothing but mock the gods from morning till night—and, what's far worse, make other people mock them too; when I scarcely like to have a slave in the house because of your impiety—and your blasphemy.

SOCRATES. I really think you are rather unfair, Xantippe. You will be sorry for this some day.

XANTIPPE. Then may I ask where you are going?

SOCRATES. I've got an important engagement.

XANTIPPE. And with whom?

SOCRATES. I would rather not say, for your sake.

XANTIPPE. That's very clever and ingenious to put it on me. But I'm tired of being bullied. Even a worm will turn, and I demand to be treated just for once like a human being, and with the minimum of courtesy and frankness. I don't ask for your confidence, I know that would be useless. But I do ask to be treated with a grain of straightforwardness and honesty. I insist upon it. I have borne your sneers, your sarcasm, and your sulkiness, your irritability, your withering silence, quite long enough. I will not put up with it any longer.

SOCRATES. Very well. Since you will have it, I have been impeached by Lycon, Meletus, and Anytus on some ridiculous charge, the result of which, however, may be extremely serious—in fact it may be a matter of life or death—and I am obliged to appear before them at once.

XANTIPPE. Oh dear, oh dear! I always said so. I knew it would come to this! This is what comes of not eating meat like a decent citizen!

[XANTIPPE *bursts into tears.*

CURTAIN.

XXIV

CALYPSO

First performed by Officers of H.M.S. Calypso at Gibraltar, March 1928; performed at the Adelphi Theatre, May 6th 1928.

SCENE.—*A Grotto in the Island of Ogygia.* CALYPSO *discovered, looking languid. Enter* STEWARD.

STEWARD. There is *one* god outside for you.
CALYPSO. One what ?
STEWARD. One god from Olympus.
CALYPSO. Which one ?
STEWARD. One very nice god with wings on his feet.
CALYPSO. It's Mercury. Show him in.

[CALYPSO *arranges her face and hair with a hand mirror and lip-stick.*

Enter STEWARD *and* MERCURY.

MERCURY. Calypso !
CALYPSO. Mercury ! Well, this is a surprise !
MERCURY. I haven't seen you for ages.
CALYPSO. Not for two centuries. How did you come ?
MERCURY. I flew.
CALYPSO. Of course. . . . A drop of nectar ?
MERCURY. No, no, thank you ; it's much too early.

CALYPSO (*through the curtain*). Steward! Two Calypso's. No, two Circe's. (*To* MERCURY.) Well, what's the news?

Enter STEWARD *with two cups. He gives one to* CALYPSO *and one to* MERCURY.

MERCURY. Happy days!

CALYPSO (*wearily*). Happy centuries.

[*They drink.*

MERCURY (*dazed*). That's good. (*He wipes his forehead.*) *Very* good. What is it made of?

CALYPSO. Only honey, mint, juniper, and a dash of wormwood. My sister Circe invented it. I like it because it's not too strong.

MERCURY. No.

Whenever I drink with you, Calypso,
I feel that I might grow to be a dypso.

CALYPSO (*looking at* MERCURY *with satisfaction*). Steward, bring the god an olive.

Enter STEWARD *with snacks on a tray.* MERCURY *eats an olive.*

You have only drunk half of it.

MERCURY (*recovering control and smiling in triumph at her*). Don't be silly! (*Quite sober and businesslike.*) By the way, isn't Ulysses staying here?

CALYPSO. Yes. He's asleep. He sleeps a great deal. It's the sea air.

MERCURY. Of course, let me see, how long has he been here? Seven years, isn't it?

CALYPSO. No, not quite seven. Six and a half.

MERCURY. Don't you think it's time——

CALYPSO. He went home? I do indeed. Every

day for the last six and a half years I've said to him: You know, Ulysses, I love having you here, but I do think you ought to go home. After all, you are a married man, and I shouldn't like to vex darling Penelope; she must be getting anxious—but he won't hear of going.

MERCURY. Well, they are rather worried about it at Olympus. In fact I have been sent by Jupiter to beg you to let him go.

CALYPSO. *Let* him go! As if I wanted him to stay! He's always drunk before dinner, and after dinner he goes to sleep. And then he's a bore—a Trojan War bore. He's beginning to believe it all really happened. I'm longing for him to go, but——

MERCURY. What?

CALYPSO. How could I send him home without a boat? You know, I've asked for a boat for centuries.

MERCURY. What about the *Argo?*

CALYPSO. They won't let her be used.

MERCURY. Economy?

CALYPSO. Yes. And considering what Venus spends on clothes——

MERCURY (*pensively*). Clothes?

CALYPSO. My dear Mercury, you know perfectly well there's nothing so costly as simplicity. Golden hair is very expensive, and even leaves——

MERCURY. Yes. Couldn't Ulysses make a raft?

CALYPSO. What with?

MERCURY. The pine trees round this grotto.

CALYPSO. What! Cut down the trees in my garden—the only trees in the island? Never!

MERCURY. I'd willingly give him a passage, but I'm not allowed to carry mortals.

Calypso. Well, you see it's impossible. Please tell Jupiter, with my compliments, that I'm very, very sorry, but it's impossible.

Mercury. It's no good, Calypso. You've got to let him go. It's an order.

Calypso. Very well. But I call it murder, with these currents, and the sea infested with Sirens. Of course, if they want him to be drowned——

Mercury. Shall I tell him?

Calypso. No, I will. Goddesses understand these things better than gods.

Mercury. Very well. I must take advantage of the visibility. Good-bye, Calypso. I'm sure to be looking in again soon.

Calypso. Good-bye, Mercury. Remember me to all of them.

Mercury. Good-bye. I'm sure to be looking in again soon.

[*Exit* Mercury. *He leaves his winged cap behind him on the floor.*

Steward! Show the god out, and ask Ulysses to speak to me, if he is up.

[*Exeunt* Steward *and* Mercury. Calypso *pulls down her hair, tears her clothes, and sits on the floor weeping.*

Enter Ulysses, *looking sleepy and tired.*

Ulysses (*wearily*). What's the matter now, darling?

Calypso. You're leaving me!

Ulysses. What on earth put that into your little head, your lovely little head?

Calypso. Nobody. But I thought by what you said last night that you wanted to go.

ULYSSES. Nonsense!

CALYPSO. Then you don't want to go?

ULYSSES. Of course not. How *could* I?

CALYPSO. And nothing would make you go?

ULYSSES. Nothing in the whole world.

[*He walks up and down in agitation.*

I swear by all the gods (*he trips up over* MERCURY'S *flying cap.*) What's this? (*He picks it up.*) A winged cap? Has Mercury been here?

CALYPSO. He did just look in.

ULYSSES. With a message?

CALYPSO. Nothing of importance. He was flying over the island, and he landed here to oil his sandals.

ULYSSES. Did he mention me?

CALYPSO. Yes, he said that they thought at Olympus that you were perhaps fretting to get home, but I told him that we were *very, very* happy.

ULYSSES. I see.

CALYPSO. And then I said that even if you did want to go, there was the boat difficulty.

ULYSSES. Oh, that's no difficulty. I could easily make a raft. I prefer small ships to large ones. I served in rafts for years.

CALYPSO. Then you do want to go?

ULYSSES. No, I don't *want* to go, but of course an order is an order.

CALYPSO. Who said it was an order?

ULYSSES. I thought you said that Mercury brought an order from Olympus. He certainly didn't come here for nothing. He never flies unless he can help it. It makes him sick.

CALYPSO. But they can't make you go if you don't want to——

ULYSSES. I shouldn't like you to incur the wrath of Jove.

CALYPSO. Don't bother about me, please.

ULYSSES. And the Grotto isn't thunderbolt-proof.

CALYPSO. I don't mind thunderbolts.

ULYSSES. But I do. I'm not immortal.

CALYPSO. But if you marry me, you will be immortal.

ULYSSES. Mixed marriages are always a mistake. And then, there's Penelope.

CALYPSO. I see. You're going.

ULYSSES. Of course, if it hadn't been an order——

CALYPSO. It wasn't an order, darling. I was only joking. Mercury never even mentioned you. Let's forget all about it.

ULYSSES (*intensely disappointed*). Very well, darling, let's forget all about it.

[*A pause.* ULYSSES *sits looking gloomily in front of him.*

CALYPSO. Will you have a Calypso, darling?

ULYSSES. Yes, please, a Circe. A double one.

Enter MERCURY.

MERCURY. I'm sorry, Calypso, but I think I left my flying cap behind.

CALYPSO. Yes, there it is.

MERCURY. Thank you. Good morning, Ulysses. I suppose Calypso gave you my message?

ULYSSES. No.

MERCURY. You are to proceed forthwith to Ithaca, reporting to the swineherd on arrival. You must find your own transport. They can't give you a boat.

You had better make a raft. A raft is far the safest craft in these waters.

ULYSSES (*joyfully*). Far the safest. The only craft.

MERCURY. Very well. That's understood. I must go at once. It's blowing up. So long, Calypso. (*To* ULYSSES, *smiling and half aside.*) Good luck!

CALYPSO. Mercury always lets one down.

CURTAIN.

XXV

THREE MINUTES

OR

THE DEATH OF CÆSAR*

SCENE I

The stage is divided into three sections. L. CLEOPATRA *is lying on a couch. Centre is a telephone exchange in which a female operator is seated, wearing head-pieces, facing the stage and reading the poems of Ovid. R.* CÆSAR *in his study at a table. Night.*

CÆSAR (*taking off a receiver from a telephone*). Tibur, fifty-fifty. No, not Tiger, Tibur. (*Spelling.* T-I-B-U-R. T for Toga, I for Ida, Princess Ida, B) for Balbus, U for Urbs—no, not 'Erb—*Urbs,* R for Rex.

The bell rings

CLEOPATRA. Hullo, who is that, please ?

CÆSAR. Is that you, Cleopatra ?

CLEOPATRA. Yes, is that you, Cæsar ?

CÆSAR. Yes, it's me, Cæsar.

CLEOPATRA. Well ?

CÆSAR. I've just been dining with Lepidus.

CLEOPATRA. Yes.

CÆSAR. They want me to go to the Senate to-morrow morning.

CLEOPATRA. Yes.

* At the time of Cæsar's death Cleopatra was living in Rome and fled the country as soon as he was killed.

CÆSAR. To arrange about the campaign.

CLEOPATRA. Yes.

CÆSAR. And they say I shall be offered the Crown.

CLEOPATRA. What, again ?

CÆSAR. Yes, again.

CLEOPATRA. By Mark Antony ?

CÆSAR. No, by the whole Senate.

CLEOPATRA. And you will refuse it again.

CÆSAR. I wanted to refuse it but they want me *not* to.

CLEOPATRA. Of course they do.

CÆSAR. Why ?

CLEOPATRA. They know it would be fatal for you to take the title of King. You are quite unpopular enough as it is.

CÆSAR. I can't see why it should make very much difference.

CLEOPATRA. It would make *all* the difference.

CÆSAR. Well, I told them I would accept.

CLEOPATRA. You must tell them you've changed your mind.

CÆSAR. It's too late to let them know now.

CLEOPATRA. You can just *not* go.

CÆSAR. To the Senate ?

CLEOPATRA. Yes.

CÆSAR. I must. It's important.

CLEOPATRA. You can put off going till the day after to-morrow and that will give you time to think it over.

CÆSAR. I don't like going back on my word.

CLEOPATRA. You want to be called King.

CÆSAR. I don't but the people want it.

CLEOPATRA. I wonder. Who would be Queen ?

CÆSAR. Calpurnia, of course.

CLEOPATRA. Would she be called Queen ?

CÆSAR. Not Queen regnant—Queen consort.

CLEOPATRA. It sounds too ridiculous, doesn't it? Poor Calpurnia! You wouldn't inflict that on her? Have you told her?

CÆSAR. Not yet.

CLEOPATRA. I shouldn't.

CÆSAR. On the contrary, I mean to tell her at once. I'm sure she'll agree with me.

CLEOPATRA. I'm sure she won't. She's far too sensible. She won't want to look ridiculous and to make you look ridiculous.

CÆSAR. Why should it be ridiculous?

CLEOPATRA. Anyone in the world will tell you that to be called Cæsar is dignified, but to be called King Cæsar is silly. It sounds like the name of a pet dog.

CÆSAR. People will soon get used to it.

CLEOPATRA. Then you are quite determined.

CÆSAR. On what?

CLEOPATRA. To go to the Senate to-morrow.

CÆSAR. Quite.

CLEOPATRA. And to accept the Crown?

CÆSAR. Yes.

CLEOPATRA. Why not put it off twenty-four hours?

CÆSAR. Because when I make up my mind I make it up. . . .

CLEOPATRA. King Cæsar and Queen Calpurnia! My poor child! Really!

CÆSAR. Well, it's going to be!

CLEOPATRA. I know the real reason.

CÆSAR. What?

CLEOPATRA. You want to wear a crown to hide your baldness. That laurel wreath you wear doesn't hide it enough.

TELEPHONE OPERATOR. Three minutes.

CÆSAR *rings off*

SCENE II

The same. Morning.

CÆSAR. Tibur, fifty-fifty.

CLEOPATRA (*sleepily*). Hullo.

CÆSAR. Is that you, Cleopatra ?

CLEOPATRA (*only half-awake*). Yes, but I've only just been called. Well, what's your day ?

CÆSAR. It's very cold.

CLEOPATRA (*sleepily*). I couldn't sleep a wink. What *is* your day ? Oh ! I remember. Are you just starting ?

CÆSAR. What for ?

CLEOPATRA. The Senate.

CÆSAR. Well, as a matter of fact I'm not sure I'm going to the Senate.

CLEOPATRA. Oh ! really ! Why not ?

CÆSAR. Calpurnia is rather upset.

CLEOPATRA. Why ?

CÆSAR. Well, she had a bad night.

CLEOPATRA. Of course she did with that thunder-storm. We all had bad nights. My shutters were blown off the wall. . . .

CÆSAR. Yes, but it was not only that. Her maid said a lioness had whelped in the yard.

CLEOPATRA. Why shouldn't it ?

CÆSAR. It's said to be unlucky. I, of course, am not superstitious. But the slaves saw ghosts walking about the streets and signs in the sky.

CLEOPATRA. It was just the storm.

CÆSAR. Well, just to pacify Calpurnia, I made the priests do sacrifice at once. The augurers have just sent in their report and they say I had better stay at home to-day as they couldn't find a heart in the beast.

CLEOPATRA. What sort of beast ?

CÆSAR. I don't know. Just an ordinary beast.

CLEOPATRA. The augurers are idiotic. I call that silly.

CÆSAR. It *is* silly, but after all if Calpurnia is nervous—and she is nervous—and begs me not to go to the Senate to-day, the least thing I can do is to put off going till to-morrow.

CLEOPATRA. You are very careful to respect *her* feelings.

CÆSAR. I try to be. She is my wife, after all.

CLEOPATRA. Yes . . . after all. But I think it's silly all the same.

CÆSAR. What ?

CLEOPATRA. Not to go to the Senate.

CÆSAR. Why ?

CLEOPATRA. They'll think you are afraid.

CÆSAR. Of omens ? Ha ! Ha ! they can if they like. I can rise above that.

CLEOPATRA. They'll think it all the same.

CÆSAR. You think I ought to go ?

CLEOPATRA. Yes, of course I do.

CÆSAR. Well, I don't.

CLEOPATRA. I've no doubt you know best.

CÆSAR. I think in this case I *do* know best.

CLEOPATRA. Perhaps it is better you should do as Calpurnia tells you.

CÆSAR. That's nothing to do with it. It's silly to talk like that. I wasn't going anyhow. You persuaded me not to last night.

CLEOPATRA. I did ?

CÆSAR. Yes, you, of course.

CLEOPATRA. I persuaded you not to go to the Senate ?

CÆSAR. You said it would be ridiculous for me to accept the Crown.

CLEOPATRA. Really, Cæsar, may the gods forgive

you! I never said any such thing! I said it would be ridiculous for a Queen to be called Queen Consort, that's all. I was in favour of your being King and I am all for your going to the Senate to-day because if you go to-day they will offer you the Crown, but if you put it off till to-morrow, who knows?

CÆSAR. I have quite made up my mind to refuse it. I hate the sight of a crown.

CLEOPATRA. Well, I think it's very childish not to go to the Senate.

CÆSAR. Possibly I'm childish, but I've made up my mind.

CLEOPATRA. Not to go?

CÆSAR. Yes; once my mind's made up it's made up.

CLEOPATRA. Oh, very well.

CÆSAR. Shall I see you to-night?

CLEOPATRA. I'm afraid not. I've got Mark Antony dining with me.

CÆSAR. But. . . .

OPERATOR. Three minutes.

CLEOPATRA *rings off*

SCENE III

The same as before. A little later.

CLEOPATRA (*taking off the receiver*). Palatine, one four. No, not Palestine, Palatine. P for Pons, A for Asinorum, L for Lesbia, A for Aspasia, I for idiot, N for Numa, E for Egypt.

CÆSAR. Hullo.

CLEOPATRA. Is that you, Cæsar?

CÆSAR. Yes, it's me, but I haven't a moment to spare. It's eight o'clock and I am late already.

CLEOPATRA. What have you settled?

CÆSAR. What about?

CLEOPATRA. About going to the Senate.

CÆSAR. Well, I thought over what you said and I came to the conclusion you are right and I *am* going after all.

CLEOPATRA. But, Cæsar, I particularly told you I thought it was a mistake.

CÆSAR. What?

CLEOPATRA. To go to the Senate to-day.

CÆSAR. You really have a very short memory.

CLEOPATRA. And you have no memory at all. I implored you to put it off for twenty-four hours.

CÆSAR. That was last night.

CLEOPATRA. What does it matter *when* it was? I beg you to put it off now.

CÆSAR. It's too late.

CLEOPATRA. Why?

CÆSAR. They are all downstairs waiting for me at this moment in the hall.

CLEOPATRA. Who?

CÆSAR. Brutus and Cassius and the lot. And between you and me, only you mustn't repeat it yet, they *are* going to offer me the Crown *to-day*.

CLEOPATRA. And you?

CÆSAR. I shall refuse it to-day and then see. Wait and see. That is my motto. I came. I waited. I saw.

CLEOPATRA. I ask you as a special favour *not* to go to the Senate to-day.

CÆSAR. Why?

CLEOPATRA. Because I asked my maid the date and she said it was the Ides of March and we were both told to beware of that date and I spilt the salt when I was having breakfast, and whenever I do that something always happens. The last time I did it, I went out with a hole in my stocking.

CÆSAR. You should have thrown it three times over your left shoulder.

CLEOPATRA. I did.

CÆSAR. Then it's all right.

CLEOPATRA. No, it isn't, because as I did so I saw a single magpie in the garden and the gardener walked under a ladder and I noticed there were three lamps burning in the room.

CÆSAR. All right, I won't go.

CLEOPATRA. That's perfect.

CÆSAR. But on one condition.

CLEOPATRA. What is it ?

CÆSAR. That you put off Mark Antony to-night and dine with me instead.

CLEOPATRA. But, my dear Cæsar, it's impossible.

CÆSAR. Why ?

CLEOPATRA. Because I can't put off Mark Antony.

CÆSAR. Why not ?

CLEOPATRA. Well, because I never do put off people. Wait a second.

A slave brings in a letter

Someone has sent me an urgent letter. It's from Artemidorus. He says there's a plot. Wait——

OPERATOR. Three minutes.

CÆSAR *rings off and goes out*

CLEOPATRA *rings :*

CLEOPATRA. Is that the exchange ? Please put me on to Palatine, one four. We've been cut off ; no, not Palestine, Palatine. No, not a trunk call, *toll.* Palatine, Cæsar's house. Private line. . . .

OPERATOR. Sorry, there's no reply from Palatine one four.

CURTAIN

DEAD LETTERS

"To most people of time past and present, at least, history is a pageant, no less and no more. It is a vast procession of human lives, fascinating to us because of the likeness underlying all the differences and because of the differences through which we see the likeness."

J. W. ALLEN (*The Place of History in Education*).

"Il n'y a pas de lettres ennuyeuses."

The Man in the Iron Mask.

DEDICATION
TO LORD LUCAS

My dear Bron,

I wish to begin this bundle of "Dead Letters," collected from the Dead Letter Office of the World, with a living letter to you.

These letters are in no wise meant to be either historical documents or historical studies or aids to the understanding of history, or learning of any kind with or without tears. They are the fruits of imagination rather than of research. The word research is not even remotely applicable here, for in my case it means the hazy memories of a distant education indolently received, a few hurried references to Smith's "Classical Dictionary," a map of Rome which is in the London Library, and Bouillet's "Biographie Universelle." So that if you tell me that my account of the Carthaginian fleet is full of inaccuracies, or that the psychology of my Lesbia conflicts with the historical evidence, I shall be constrained to answer that I do not care. Yet amidst this chaff of fancy there are a few grains of historical truth. By historical truth I mean the recorded impressions (they may be false, of course, and the persons who recorded them may have been liars, in which case it is historical falsehood) of men on events which were contemporary with them. One of the letters is entirely composed of such grains. I will not tell you which one it is until some of our common friends, who are historical experts, have singled it out as being the one letter which oversteps all bounds of historical possibility and probability. (It is not the letter on Heine, part of the substance of which was taken from Memoirs and freely blended with fiction.) Such singling out has already occurred with regard to certain details of the letters as they appeared week by week in the *Morning Post.* But I confess that I have so far suffered more from the credulity than from the scepticism of my readers, and I was tempted at one moment rather to insert the impossible than to make the possible appear probable. For correspondents wrote to me, asking me to give them from my secret store further details with regard to Lady Macbeth's housekeeping, Lord Bacon's business affairs, and the table talk of the Emperor Claudius.

On the other hand, a sceptic asked to be supplied with the historical evidence for Guinevere's extravagance in dress. I am conscious that in some of these letters I may have laid myself open to the charge of irreverence towards certain themes which are hallowed by romance and overshadowed by the wings of the great poets. I plead "Not guilty." I am sure that you, of all people, will acquit me; for those (such as you) whose enjoyment of the great poets is vital and whose belief in the permanence of Romance is robust are seldom offended at a levity which they have no difficulty in recognizing to be the familiarity, not breeding contempt but begotten of awe, of the True Believer, nor have they any difficulty in distinguishing such laughter from the scoff of the Infidel.

To end on a less pompous note, let me add that if you like this book that is enough for me; and the blame of the rest of the world, although it will ultimately affect my purse—and a purse, as Shakespeare says, is trash—will disturb neither my peace of mind nor my digestion and will therefore not vex me.

On the other hand there is no amount of praise which man and an author cannot endure with equanimity. Some authors can even stand flattery. I hope, therefore, to earn a certain measure both of your approval and others'; while theirs will be the more profitable, yours will be the more prized.

Maurice Baring.

Sosnofka, Tambov, Russia.
October 19th, 1909.

FROM THE MYCENAE PAPERS

Clytaemnestra to Aegisthus

MYCENAE.

Honoured Sir,

I am sorry I was out when you came yesterday. I never thought that you seriously meant to come. I shall be very busy all next week, as Helen and Menelaus are arriving and I must get everything ready. Orestes was quite delighted with the cup and ball. You spoil him.

Yours sincerely,
CLYTAEMNESTRA.

Clytaemnestra to Aegisthus

Most honoured Aegisthus,

One line to say that I have received your letter and *loved* it all except the last sentence. Please do not say that kind of thing again as it will quite ruin our friendship, which I thought was going to be so *real*.

Yours very sincerely,
CLYTAEMNESTRA.

Clytaemnestra to Aegisthus

Most honoured Aegisthus,

The flowers are beautiful, and it was kind of you to remember my birthday. But your letter is really too naughty. . . .

(The rest of the letter is missing)

Clytaemnestra to Aegisthus

MYCENAE.

Most honoured Sir,

This is to say that since you persist in misunderstanding me and refuse to listen to what I say, our correspondence must end. It is extraordinary to me that you should wish to debase what might have been so great and so wonderful.

Yours truly,
CLYTAEMNESTRA.

Clytaemnestra to Aegisthus

MYCENAE.

Most honoured Aegisthus,

I was much touched by your letter and I will give you the one more trial you ask for so humbly and so touchingly.

Paris has arrived. I don't know if you know him. He is the second son of the King of Troy. He made an unfortunate marriage with a girl called Œnone, the daughter of a rather disreputable river-person. They were *miserable* about it. He is very good-looking—if one admires those kind of looks, which I don't. He dresses in an absurd way and he looks theatrical. Besides, I hate men with curly hair. He has a few accomplishments. He shoots well and plays on the double flute quite remarkably well for a man who is not a professional; but he is totally uninteresting, and, what is more, impossible. But Helen likes him. Isn't it extraordinary that she always has liked impossible men? They sit for hours together saying nothing at all. I don't in the least mind his paying no attention to me—in fact, I am too thankful not to have to talk to him; but I do think it's bad manners, as I am his hostess.

Helen is certainly looking better this year than she has ever looked; but she still dresses in that affectedly over-simple way, which is a pity. I don't know how long he is going to stay. I don't mind his being here, but Helen and he are really most inconsiderate. They use my sitting-room as though it were theirs, and they never seem to think that I may have things to do of my own, and they expect me to go out with them, which ends in their walking on ahead and my being left with Menelaus, whom I am very fond of indeed, but who bores me. He talks of nothing but horses and quoits. It is a great lesson to Queen Hecuba for having brought up her son so badly. Paris was educated entirely by a shepherd, you know, on Mount Ida. The result is his manners are shocking. Helen doesn't see it. Isn't it odd? I must say he's nice with children, and Orestes likes him.

I am your sincere friend,
CLYTAEMNESTRA.

Clytaemnestra to Aegisthus

MYCENAE.

Most honoured Aegisthus,

We are in great trouble. I told you Helen was attracted by Paris. We of course thought nothing of it, because Helen always has flirted with rather vulgar men, and her flirtations were, we thought, the harmless distractions of a woman who has remained, and always will remain, a sentimental girl.

Imagine our surprise and dismay! Paris and Helen

have run away together, and they have gone to Troy! Helen left a note behind for Menelaus saying she realized that she had made a mistake, that she hated hypocrisy, and thought it more honest to leave him. She said she would always think of him with affection. Poor Menelaus is distracted, but he is behaving beautifully.

Agamemnon is furious. He is overcome by the disgrace to his family, and he is so cross. We are all *very* miserable. Agamemnon says that the family honour must be redeemed at all costs, and that they will have to make an expedition against Troy to fetch Helen back. I think this is quite ridiculous. No amount of expeditions and wars can undo what has been done. I am sure you will sympathize with us in our trouble. I shouldn't have minded so much if Iphigenia wasn't grown up.

Electra has got whooping-cough, but she is going on as well as can be expected. I have no patience with Helen. She always was utterly thoughtless!

Your sincere friend,

CLYTAEMNESTRA.

Clytaemnestra to Aegisthus

MYCENAE.

Most honoured Aegisthus,

There is no end of worry and fuss going on. Odysseus, the King of Ithaca, has arrived here with his wife, Penelope. They discuss the prospects of the expedition from morning till night, and I am left alone with Penelope. She has borrowed my only embroidery frame, and is working some slippers for her husband. They are at least two sizes too small. She talks of nothing but her boy, her dog, her dairy, and her garden, and I can't tell you how weary I am of it. She made me very angry yesterday by saying that I spoilt Orestes, and that I should be sorry for it some day. She is always casting her boy Telemachus in my teeth. Whenever Helen is mentioned she puts on a face as much as to say: "Do not defile me."

Your sincere friend,

CLYTAEMNESTRA.

Clytaemnestra to Aegisthus

MYCENAE.

Most honoured Aegisthus,

My worst fears have been realized. They are going to make an expedition against Troy on a large scale. Odysseus is at the bottom of it. I cannot say how much I dislike it. All the Kings have volunteered to go, but the Fleet will not be ready for two years, so I am in hopes that something may happen in the meantime to prevent it.

Iphigenia is learning to make bandages, and says she will go to the front to look after the wounded. I am, of course, against this, and think it's absurd, but unfortunately she can make her father do what she likes. My only consolation is that the war cannot possibly last more than a week. The Trojans have no regular army. They are a handful of untrained farmers, and the town cannot stand a siege. It is all too silly. It is too bad of Helen to have caused all this fuss.

Your sincere friend,

CLYTAEMNESTRA.

P.S.—No, of course I haven't written to Helen. She is as good as dead to me.

Clytaemnestra to Aegisthus

(*Two years later*)

MYCENAE.

My dear Aegisthus,

We have at last got some news. The Fleet has arrived at Aulis, and they are waiting for a favourable wind to be able to go on. At present they are becalmed. They are all well. Iphigenia writes that she is enjoying herself immensely. She has the decency to add that she misses me! I have not had a good night's rest since they have started.

Your most sincere friend,

CLYTAEMNESTRA.

Clytaemnestra to Aegisthus

My dear friend,

Please come here at once. I am in dreadful trouble. From the last letter I received from Agamemnon I understood there was something wrong and that he was hiding something. To-day I got a letter from Calchas, breaking to me in the most brutal manner an appalling tragedy and a savage, horrible, and impious crime! They have sacrificed my darling Iphigenia—to Artemis, of all goddesses! to get a propitious wind for their horrible Fleet! I am heartbroken. I cannot write another word. Please come directly.

Your friend,

CLYTAEMNESTRA.

Clytaemnestra to Aegisthus

(*Two months later*)

I see no reason why you should not come back; I have a right to ask whom I like to stay here. Do come as soon as possible; I am very lonely without you. Now that I no longer communicate with Agamemnon, in order to get news, I have written to Helen, and sent the letter by a very clever silk merchant, who is certain to be able to worm his way into Troy. Come as soon as you get this.

C.

P.S.—Agamemnon still writes, but I do not take the slightest notice of his letters. I trust the Trojans will be victorious. They have at any rate determined to make a fight for it. Our generals are certain to quarrel, Achilles and Agamemnon never get on well. And Achilles' temper is dreadful.

Clytaemnestra to Aegisthus

(*Three months later*)

I can no longer bear these short visits and these long absences. I have arranged for you to stay here permanently.

I wrote to Agamemnon last month a cold and dignified *business* letter, in which I pointed out that unless some man came here to look after things, everything would go to pieces. I suggested you. I have now got his answer. He agrees, and thinks it an excellent plan.

Odysseus wrote me, I must say, a most amusing letter. He says everything is at sixes and sevens, and that Priam's eldest son is far the most capable soldier on either side. He expects to win, but says it will be a far longer business than they thought it would be at first. Come as quickly as you can. Best and most beloved.

Your C.

Helen to Clytaemnestra

(*Ten years later*)

TROY

Dearest Clytaemnestra,

Your letters are a great comfort to me when I get them, which is very seldom. Everything is going on just the same. It is now the tenth year of the siege, and I see no reason why it should ever end. I am dreadfully afraid the Greeks will never take Troy.

I can give you no idea of how dull everything is here. We do the same thing and see the same people every day. We know exactly what is going on in the Greek camp, and most of the time is spent is discussing the gossip, which bores me to death. You are quite right in what you say about Paris. I made a fatal mistake. It is all Aphrodite's fault. He has become too dreadful now. He is still very good-looking, but even compared with Menelaus he is pitiable in every way and every bit as cross. Hector is very nice, but painfully dull. The King and the Queen are both very kind, but as for Cassandra, she is intolerable. She is always prophesying dreadful calamities which never come off. She said, for instance, that I would lose my looks and make a long journey in Egypt. As if I would go to Egypt from here! As to my looks, you know, darling, I never was vain, was I? But I can honestly tell you that, if anything, I have rather *improved* than otherwise, and among the Trojan women, who are absolute frights and have no more idea of dressing than sheep, I look magnificent. Andromache has got quite a nice face, and I really like her; but you should see her figure—it's like an elephant's, and her feet are enormous, and her hands red and sore from needlework. She won't even use a thimble! Cassandra always dresses in deep mourning. Why, we cannot conceive, because none of her relatives have been killed.

There is really only one person in the palace I can talk to—and that is Aeneas, who is one of the commanders. He is quite nice. What I specially like about him is the nice way in which he talks about his parents.

The Greeks are quarrelling more than ever. Achilles won't fight at all because Agamemnon insisted on taking away Briseis (who is lovely) from him. Wasn't that exactly like Agamemnon? I hope this won't make you jealous, darling, but I don't expect it will, because you have never forgiven Agamemnon, have you?

Everybody tries to be kind to me, and I have nothing to complain of. They all mean well, and in a way this makes it worse. For instance, every morning, when we meet for the midday meal, Priam comes into the room saying to me: "Well, how's the little runaway to-day?" He has made this joke every day for the last ten years. And then they always talk about the cowardice and incompetence of the Greeks, taking for granted that as I have married into a Trojan family I must have become a Trojan myself. It is most tactless of them not to understand what I must be feeling.

I suppose I am inconsistent, but the pro-Greek party irritate me still more. They are headed by Pandarus, and are simply longing for their own side to be beaten, because they say that I ought to have been given up directly, and that the war was brought about entirely owing to Priam having got into the hands of the Egyptian merchants.

I manage to get some Greek stuffs smuggled into the town, and the merchants tell me vaguely what people are wearing at Mycenae; but one can't get anything properly made here. Andromache has all her clothes made at home by her women—to save expense. She says that in times of war one ought to sacrifice oneself. Of course, I can't do this, however much I should like to, as the Trojans expect me to look nice, and would be very angry if I wasn't properly dressed.

I feel if I could only meet Odysseus we might arrange some plan for getting the Greeks into the town.

How is everything going on at home? There is a very strict censorship about letters, and we are all supposed to show our letters to Antenor before they go. I don't, of course. I daresay, however, many of your letters have been intercepted, because I have only heard from you five times since the siege began, and not once this year. Kiss the dear children from me.

Shall I ever see you again? I shall try my best to come home.

Your loving sister,
HELEN.

Clytaemnestra to Helen

MYCENAE.

Dearest Helen,

Your last letter has reached me. I must implore you to be very careful about what you do. I hope with all my heart that the siege will be over soon; but if it is I don't think it would be quite wise for you to come back directly. You see everybody here is extremely unreasonable. Instead of understanding that Agamemnon and Odysseus were entirely responsible for this absurd war, Agamemnon has got his friends to put the blame entirely on you, and they have excited the people against you. It's so like a man, that, isn't it? I have been very lonely, because all our friends are away. Aegisthus is staying here just to look after the household and the affairs of the city. But he hardly counts, and he is so busy that I hardly ever see him now. There is a strong pro-Trojan party here, too. They say we had absolutely no right to go to war, and that it was simply an expedition of pirates and freebooters, and I must say it is very difficult to disprove it. If there is any talk of the siege ending, please let me know *at once.* Electra has grown into a fine girl; but she is not as lovely as poor darling Iphigenia.

Your loving sister,
CLYTAEMNESTRA.

Penelope to Odysseus

ITHACA.

My darling Husband,

I wish you would write a little more distinctly; we have the greatest difficulty in reading your letters.

When will this horrid siege be over? I think it is disgraceful of you all to be so long about it. To think that when you started you said that it would only last a month! Mind you come back the moment it is over, and come back *straight*, by Aulis.

The country is looking lovely. I have built a new house for the swineherd, as he complained about the roof letting the rain in. Next year, we must really have a new paling round the garden, as the children get in and steal the apples. We can't afford it *this* year. The people have no sense of honesty; they steal everything. Telemachus is very well. He can read and write nicely, but is most backward about his sums. He takes a great interest in the war, and has made up a map on which he marks the position of the troops with little flags.

I am surprised to hear of Achilles' *disgraceful* conduct. If I were there I would give him a piece of my mind. I hope Ajax has not had any more of his attacks. Has he tried cinnamon with fomented myrtle leaves? It ought to be taken three times a day *after* meals. The news from Mycenae is deplorable. Clytaemnestra appears to be quite shameless and callous. Aegisthus is now openly living in the house. All decent people have ceased to go near them. I have had a few visitors, but nobody of any importance.

I am working you a piece of tapestry for your bedroom. I hope to get it finished by the time you come back. I hope that when the city is taken Helen will be *severely* punished.

We have taught Argus to growl whenever Hector is mentioned. I don't, of course, allow any one to mention Helen in this house. Telemachus sends you his loving duty. He is writing to you himself, but the letter isn't finished.

Your devoted wife

PENELOPE.

Helen to Clytaemnestra

SUNIUM.

Dearest Clytaemnestra,

Since I last wrote to you several important things have happened. Hector was killed yesterday by

Achilles. I am, of course, very sorry for them all. All Cassandra said was, "I told you so!" She is so heartless. I have at last managed to communicate with Odysseus; we have thought of a very good plan for letting the Greeks into the city. Please do not repeat this. I shall come home at once with Menelaus. He is my husband, after all. I shall come straight to Mycenae. I doubt if I shall have time to write again. I am sending this through Aenida, who is most useful in getting letters brought and sent.

Please have some patterns for me to choose from. I hope to be back in a month. Your loving sister,

HELEN.

Agamemnon to Clytaemnestra

SUNIUM.

Dear Clytaemnestra,

We have had a very good journey, and I shall reach Mycenae the day after to-morrow in the morning. Please have a hot bath ready for me. I am bringing Cassandra with me. She had better have the room looking north, as she hates the sun. She is very nervous and upset, and you must be kind to her.

Your loving husband,

AGAMEMNON.

Odysseus to Penelope

THE ISLAND OF OGYGIA.

Dearest Penelope,

We arrived here after a very tiresome voyage. I will not tire you with the details, which are numerous and technical. The net result is that the local physician says I cannot proceed with my journey until I am thoroughly rested. This spot is pleasant, but the only society I have is that of poor dear Calypso. She means well and is most hospitable, but you can imagine how vexed I am by this delay and the intolerable tedium of this enforced repose. Kiss Telemachus from me.

Your loving husband,
ODYSSEUS.

Clytaemnestra to Aegisthus

I am sending this by runner. Come back directly. I expect Agamemnon any moment. The bonfires are already visible. Please bring a good strong net and a sharp axe with you. I will explain when you arrive. I have quite decided that half measures are out of the question.

C.

WITH THE CARTHAGINIAN FLEET, 216 B.C.

Letter from a Carthaginian Civilian to a Friend in Carthage

On Board the *Hamilcar Barca*,
SARDINIA.

My dear Gisco,

IT is now five weeks that we have been in this place, and we shall have to stay here until the "battering practice" is over. We have already got through our "rammers' test." I do not think it is a bad place myself, and most of the people seem to prefer it to Thule, where they spent the whole summer, except Mago our physician, who cannot endure either the Romans or the Sardinians, and who is longing to get back to the glittering quays and the broad market-places of Carthage. It is true that the Sardinians are a thievish race, and they seldom, if ever, speak the truth; moreover, they trade on the honesty and the good nature of our people, and our unfamiliarity with their various and uncouth jargons. For instance, a favourite plan of theirs is this: many of them gain their living by the catching of lobsters, which they send by Ostia to Rome to supply the banquets of the rich patricians of that city. One such fisherman came to the captain of our vessel with the following complaint: He professed that for many weeks he had toiled and caught a great number of lobsters; these lobsters he said, he was keeping against the feasts of the Saturnalia at Rome, in a large wicker basket not far from the shore; and that some of our men having gone ashore in one of our swift and brass-prowed boats, had in the darkness of twilight collided with his wicker basket and caused the escape of many hundreds of live lobsters, for which loss he demanded a compensation amounting to two hundred talents. On consulting the Roman Magistrate of the place we learnt that this fisherman made a similar demand from every ship which visited the bay; moreover, that he had caught but one lobster. So although he reduced his demand to the eighth of one talent, it was refused to him.

Another stratagem of the Sardinian native is to demand money for the poultry destroyed by the sailors of our ship. Every family in the village complained that their poultry had been annihilated by our unprincipled mariners, but little credence was lent to the tale, because at the moment when the complaint was made there was only one hen in the village, a dead one that had just perished of old age.

Life on board this vessel is full of variety and interest to the stranger. Long before sunrise one is wakened by the sound of a brazen trumpet. This is followed by much whistling and a deep, but not unmusical, call from some elder sailor, who exhorts and finally persuades those over whom he is put in authority to rise from their narrow couches and to taste the morning air. They then set about to wash the upper part of the ship, an occupation which is pursued more from a disinterested love of cleaning than from any practical purpose, as by evening the ship is as dirty as it was before it was washed. But the men enjoy this work, and indeed the only people who suffer from it are such men as myself who are on board ship by chance, and who are used to sleeping uninterruptedly until some time after the sun has arisen. Some people have been known to sleep unconcernedly through all this noise, but such men are rare.

An hour or two after this process of washing is accomplished, food is served to the officers and men of the ship. The officers rarely partake of more than one olive in the early morning; such is their endurance and their self-denial. This they wash down with a small glass of red native wine, which is singularly pleasant and exhilarating. As soon as this light repast is over the real business of the day begins.

First of all the men are inspected on deck, and it is carefully noted whether they are in a state of cleanliness and order, and further whether they are sober enough to perform their daily duties. Any man who is found twice running to be in a state of absolute intoxication is drowned, and the ship is thereby disembarrassed of superfluous cargo. The greater part of the forenoon is spent in teaching the young their duties, and in teaching the lads who have lately arrived from Carthage the full duties of a seaman. This task is carried out with patience and persistence by the instructors, who are never known to raise their voice in anger, or to use a harsh word. Indeed the nearest approach to harshness which I observed was when one day I heard one of the elder mariners say to a lad who was slow to perform his duty, " Take care lest I should observe thee to bend." This is a nautical expression which means, so I am told, " be strenuous in all things."

H*

At noon the second repast of the day is taken, the food consisting of black bread, herbs, preserved olives, and a small fish which is caught in great quantities in the bay by such as are skilful. When the meal is over the officers retire to a small cabin, where they aid their digestion by playful gambols, such as wrestling and beating each other with their fists, until they are weary. After this they fall into a profound slumber on the benches of the cabin, with the exception of one officer who needs must always remain on deck to observe the weather and the omens, and make note thereof, for the captain of the vessel is inquisitive with regard to such matters.

The younger officers are respectful to their seniors and address them as "Suffetes"; but this outward form of respect when duty is concerned does not prevent the more youthful of the juniors from expressing the innate exuberance and impertinence which are natural to youth. Moreover, they call each other by familiar names, such as "Sheep," "Hog," "Little Hog," "Little Pig," "Canary," "Cat," "Little Cat."

Later in the afternoon there is a further inspection on the deck, which takes place to the sound of many trumpets. At sunset, after a still louder blast of the trumpet, the third repast is held. The officers attend this in state, wearing silken togas, jewelled helmets, and golden chains, and during all the meal a hundred slaves make music on silver cymbals, harps, and drums. This they do with great skill, knowing that should they be unskilful in their art, they risk being hurled into the sea. All the officers dine together, with the exception of the Captain, who feeds in a small turret by himself and partakes of especial dainties due to his rank, such as nightingales' tongues and the livers of peacocks.

At the end of the repast the eldest of the officers fills a golden bowl full of wine and water and drinks to the health of the "Gerusia." Immediately before he does so the goblet of every officer present is filled with wine and water, but should any one taste of his wine before the Elder of the assembly rises to his feet, he is constrained to empty one after another every goblet at the board and to refill them at his own expense. And this proves a tax both on his moral courage, his physical endurance, and his material resources.

When this ceremony has been accomplished such officers who are skilled in the art make music on the flute or the tom-tom, while others sing plaintive Carthaginian ditties about the dark-eyed lasses they have left behind them. Sometimes others, still more skilful, give a display of dancing. After this has continued for about an hour another deafening blast on the trumpet announces that all must seek their cabins for the night, save those unhappy officers who take it by turn for a space of four hours at a time to observe the features of the landscape, the aspect of the heavens, the position of the stars, and the nature of the omens. According as these omens are favourable, or unfavourable, the nature of the following day's work is determined.

There are in the ship a particular race of men who are neither soldiers nor sailors; these are called by the Latin name "Legio Classica." Their duties consist in maintaining discipline amongst the company of the ship and in dealing out retribution when it is necessary; they are well known for the unerring accuracy of their statements, so much so that if anyone in the ship makes a statement or relates a tale that bears in it the signs of improbability, he will be ordered to go and tell it to the men of this legion, for it is known that should the statement be untruthful or inaccurate they would be swift to detect it and to laugh the man to scorn.

The monotony of life on board ship, and the rigour of the discipline enforced, are relieved by many pleasant occupations. Thus the officers throw dice on a place of the ship specially appointed for the purpose, which is called the "bridge," and often in the evening the sailors sing together in soft and tuneful chorus. With regard to the "ramming" and the "battering practice"—both of them most interesting spectacles—I will write to you another time. In the meantime, farewell.

HANNO.

P.S.—The Roman Fleet is expected here to-morrow. It is said they intend to build eight *Hamilcar Barcas.*

LESBIA ILLA

> . . . Lesbia illa,
> Illa Lesbia, quam Catullus unam
> Plus quam se atque suos amavit omnes.

Extract from a letter written by Clodia, the wife of Metellus Celer, to her friend Portia in Athens

We arrived at Baiae yesterday evening. I am most thankful the journey is over, because Metellus is a most trying traveller. He started, of course, by making a scene directly he saw my luggage. I had scarcely taken anything, only what was absolutely indispensable, and I got it all into eight boxes; but men never know how much room clothes take up. As it is, I have got nothing to wear at all. But as soon as Metellus saw the litters with my poor luggage in them he lost his temper, and during the whole journey he complained of my extravagance. Needless to say, he took more things than I did. Men think because their clothes are cheap and cost nothing, and because a toga lasts them four or five years, we ought to be able to do the same! But it's no use discussing that with a husband. No husband in the world has ever understood, or ever will understand, how expensive our clothes are.

We found the villa looking very clean and fresh; and it is a great blessing to get away from Rome. I never mean to go back there as long as I live; especially after what has happened. I suppose you have heard all about it, but I want you to know the truth, as everybody in Rome is telling horrible lies about me and giving a wrong complexion to the whole story, especially Lalage, who is a spiteful cat, and is sure to write and tell you all about it.

Well, of course I've known Catullus for years. We were almost brought up together. He was always in and out of the house. He used to amuse me; Metellus liked him, and we were both very kind to him. I used to think he was thoroughly nice. He was so sympathetic when my sparrow died, and quite understood what a shock that was, and what a state of despair I was in. By the way, I've got a new sparrow now. It's quite tame. I've called it Julius. We used, in fact, to see a great deal of Catullus. We were useful to him, too, because he met a great many clever and important people at our house; and when we first knew him nobody had ever heard of him. It only shows what a mistake it is to be kind to people. After a time he began to give himself airs, and treated the house as if it belonged to him. He complained of the food and the wine. He insisted upon my sending away Balbus, the best slave I have ever had. He made Metellus buy some old Falernian from a cousin of his (that disreputable Rufinus who lost all his money at Capua last year). The fact was, his head was turned. People flattered him (Lalage, of course, told him he was wonderful), and he began really to think he was a real poet, a genius, and I don't know what, and he became quite insufferable. He began to meddle with my affairs, and to dictate to me about my friends. But it was when I got to know Julius Cæsar that the crisis came.

Of course you know as well as I do that nobody

could possibly be *in love* with Julius Cæsar. He is *quite* bald now, and I think—in fact, I always did think—most tiresome. I never could understand what people saw in him. And, oh, what a bore he used to be when he told me about his campaigns, and drew imaginary plans on the table with his finger! But of course I was *obliged* to be civil to him because of Metellus and my brother Clodius, to whom he has been useful. Directly he began coming to our house—and he came very often, he had to see Metellus on business constantly—Catullus became quite mad. He lost his head, and I had to arrange for them not to meet, which was most annoying and inconvenient, as they both came every day, and sometimes twice a day. I know I ought to have taken steps at once to put an end to all that nonsense. But I was foolishly kind-hearted for a time, and gave way weakly. It was a great mistake.

The crisis came the other day. I had arranged a supper party, really a divine party. Just Pollio, Julius Cæsar, Marcus Tullius, Cicero, Lavinia, Lalage, and a few others. I didn't tell Catullus, as I thought he wouldn't quite do (apart from Julius Cæsar being there), as I had invited Bassianus, who is a *real* professional poet, and writes the most beautiful things about the moonlight, memory, and broken hearts. His verses quite make me cry sometimes. They are far better than Catullus's, which I confess I can't read at all. But Metellus says it's unfair to compare an amateur like Catullus with a *real* writer like Bassianus.

Somebody told Catullus about the supper, I suspect it was Lalage—she is jealous of me, and Catullus made up to her years ago and then left her. He came to me and made a scene, and said he was coming too. Then he tried to find out who else was coming, and I refused to tell him. He said : " Of course, you have asked Julius Cæsar," and I said : " It is not your business; I shall ask the people I choose to my own house without consulting you." Then he said a lot of horribly unfair things about Julius Cæsar, and a lot of absurd things about me; only I managed to calm him more or less. All this happened in the afternoon, and he went away really quite repentant and meek. He always was easy to manage if one had time, and I told him Cicero had praised his verses, which soothed him, although it wasn't true. He never could resist flattery.

The supper began very well. Julius Cæsar was, I must say, brilliant. He can be really clever and pleasant sometimes, and he talked to me the whole time, and this made Lalage very angry; she was between Metellus and Bassianus, and she bored them. Then suddenly in the middle of supper, just as I was beginning to feel more or less happy about it all, Catullus walked in, very flushed and excited. I saw at once he had been drinking. He was given a place between Cicero and Lavinia, and opposite me and Julius Cæsar; and no sooner had he settled himself on his couch than he began to monopolize the conversation. He talked at the top of his voice. He was rather amusing at first, and Cicero answered him back, and for a time everything went well; but I was dreadfully uneasy, as I felt certain something would happen, and there was a dangerous look in his eye. Besides which he drank off a great bowl of wine and water (with very little water in it), and grew more and more flushed and excited. He didn't pay any attention to

Julius Cæsar at all, and talked across to me as though Julius Cæsar hadn't been there. But Julius Cæsar didn't seem to notice that Catullus was being rude, and he turned to me and really was charming. He said, among other things, that the only woman he had ever seen who could compare with me for wearing clothes *properly* was Cleopatra, but that she was dowdy in comparison with me. He said, too, that I was the only woman he had ever met who had any real grasp of the fiscal question. This made Catullus mad; and he asked Lavinia in a loud whisper, which we all heard, who the slightly bald gentleman sitting opposite might be. I was dreadfully uncomfortable, because Julius Cæsar can't bear any allusions to his baldness (it's so silly, as if it mattered to us!) and he turned red in the face.

Then Catullus began to chaff Cicero about his verses, but as Cicero knows him very well it didn't much matter, he knew he didn't mean it, really. To make a diversion, I proposed that Bassianus should sing us a song. But Catullus broke in and said: "Rather than that I will recite a poem."

I was very angry, and spoke my mind. I said I thought it was most rash and daring for an amateur to recite before professionals like Cicero and Bassianus. I was really frightened, because Catullus's verses are either terribly long and serious—I have never been able to listen when he reads them out; in fact, I always used to ask him to read to me when I wanted to add up my bills mentally—or else they are short and quite *impossible*.

He then turned scarlet, and said something about drawing-room poetasters who wrote stuff fit for women, and, looking at Cæsar, he recited a short poem which was *dreadful.* I didn't understand it all, but I felt—and I am sure every one else felt—that he meant to be rude. I sent him a small note by a slave, telling him that if he did not know how to behave he had better leave the house. But I looked as if I hadn't noticed anything, and tried to treat it all as a joke. But every one felt hot and uncomfortable.

I then ignored Catullus altogether, and devoted my whole attention to Julius Cæsar. I suppose it was that which really made him lose all his self-control. He entirely forgot himself. He got up and said that, as the company did not like comic verse, he had written a serious poem, which he was quite certain would interest them. He had no wish, he said (and for once in his life he was modest !), to rival such great writers of verse, such masters of music and passion, as were Cicero and Bassianus, but his verse, although it could not rival theirs in art and inspiration, had at least the merit of truth and sincerity. He said (and he almost shouted this) he was a plain man, who expressed in the simplest possible words what were the common experiences of every one, from the Senator to the man in the street. (So vulgar !) He said his verses were about a woman (how could I ever have thought he was a gentleman !) who was far-famed for her beauty, and still better known for her heartlessness. She heightened her wickedness by the supreme coquetry of pretending to be virtuous. She professed virtue and practised vice. (He always was coarse !) He would not name her; he would call her by a name which was colourless, namely, Lesbia. (Of course every one knew he had written verses to me under that name !)

Then, looking me straight in the face, he recited a poem which was *quite, quite* impossible, with a *horrible* word in it (at least Lalage said it was horrible). Pollio came to the rescue, and said that Catullus was ill, and dragged him out of the room. And in a way it was true, for he was quite tipsy, and tears were rolling down his cheeks; and I do hate drunken men, but, above all, I hate coarseness.

The next day all Rome knew the poem by heart. And it was a cowardly, blackguard thing to do, and I shall *never* speak to him again as long as I live, and I shall *never, never* let him come into my house again. Not being a gentleman he can't know what one feels about those kind of things. He is thoroughly second-rate and coarse to the core, although he oughtn't to be. Of course, I really don't care a bit. Only if Lalage writes and tells you about it, don't believe a word she says. I hate Catullus. I must stop now.

Your loving
CLODIA.

P.S.—Lalage had the impertinence to say that I ought to make allowance for men of genius. As if Catullus was a genius! I asked Cicero (who likes him) if his poetry was really good, and he said that, to be honest, it was a *bad* imitation of Calvus's and his own, only that it was very good for an amateur.

P.P.S.—Julius Cæsar is coming to stay with us next Saturday, if he can get away. Don't forget the Persian silk, the palest shade, six and a half yards.

CLEOPATRA AT ROME

Letter from Charmian, at Alexandria, to her friend Chloe, at Baiae, 44 B.C.

It all came so suddenly. I never thought that I should leave Rome without seeing you again and without being able to say farewell. Even now I cannot believe that it is true and that the whole thing is not a dream. I keep on thinking that I shall wake up and find myself once more by the banks of the Tiber, sitting in the shade of the terebinths, listening to the amusing discussions of Atticus, Cicero, and Cæsar.

The suddenness with which everything happened was terrible. It all began with the dinner party which Cleopatra had arranged on the eve of the great event which was to happen on the Feast of the Lupercalia, when Cæsar was to be offered the Crown. Cleopatra was in the highest spirits. Some months before this Cicero had asked her to get him from Alexandria some manuscripts and some Canopian vases, of which he had need, as such things are rare in your barbarous cities. Cleopatra had promised to do this, and she told him that she had done it. As a matter of fact, she had forgotten all about it. He was invited to the dinner, and had sent her a note saying that he would be delighted to come, and reminding her of her promise with regard to the manuscripts and the vases. He had already reminded her two or three times before. As she read the note she was convulsed with laughter, and when I asked her what she would say to Cicero she answered that she would of course tell him what she had already said before, that the vases and the manuscripts were on the way. I asked her if she was going to send for them, and she answered firmly: "No, it is a great mistake to lend books to men of letters. They never give them back, or if they do there are always a lot of thumb marks on them, or notes in the margin, which are worse. I like my books to be clean."

She took immense pains to dress herself that night for the dinner, according to the very latest Greek fashion, that is to say, in the austerest simplicity. She wore a grey silk robe made absolutely plain, and one wild flower in her fair hair. The curious thing is—which I have noticed since we got back to Alexandria—that here she is considered a real beauty, but we had not been back a week before she realized that what suited Rome does not suit Alexandria. So she has entirely changed her style of dress and of demeanour. She has had her hair dyed a dark bronzed red; she wears gold tissue, golden bracelets and chains, and she goes about fanned by Cupids with huge peacock feathers, and wearing a stiff gold train. Of course in Rome or in Greece this would be thought vulgar, but it is quite right here, and she is so clever that she divined this at once.

Well, to go on with the dinner party. It was not quite a success. Cæsar, who had been anxious about politics during the last week, and in a frightfully bad temper, was preoccupied and absent-minded. When Cicero arrived he was very civil and did not mention he Greek vases directly, but we all saw he was thinking of nothing else, and he managed to get the conversation first on to Alexandria, then on to the library, and finally he said: "By the way, I can't quite remember, but I think you were kind enough once to say that you were going to have a manuscript sent me from the library."

Cleopatra clapped her hands together and said: "Of course! I think they must have arrived this morning. We had a messenger from Alexandria, but the things have not yet been unpacked, as everybody in the house has been busy. But I will let you know to-morrow morning without fail."

Cicero kissed her hand and told her she was the divinest and most thoughtful of women.

There were quite a lot of people at dinner, and several came afterwards, among others a man called Mark Antony, who is a well-known gambler, and who is still in the Army. Cleopatra had once or twice asked Cæsar to bring him, but Cæsar had always said that he was not the kind of man she would like, as he was boisterous, uneducated, and rather common. Cæsar was perfectly right about this, because Cleopatra would not look at him. He made several attempts to speak to her, and paid her one or two extravagant but badly-turned compliments, and she said to me afterwards that it was astonishing how tiresome these Roman soldiers were. During dinner she made signs to me as though to point out that Antony was drinking a great deal more than was good for him—which he did do, and his conversation and his jokes were in the worst possible taste. Cleopatra herself was at her very best, so modest, so quiet, so delicately witty, so highly distinguished and refined.

They talked of mathematics and astronomy, and Cleopatra astounded Atticus by her knowledge of these sciences. Mark Antony took no part in this conversation. He was frankly bored. From astronomy the talk went on to music, and from music to dancing. Here Mark Antony brightened up and monopolized the whole conversation by describing a dancer from Asia he had seen two or three days before. The play of the muscles on her arms, he said, was quite unparalleled, and she managed to execute a rippling movement which started from her shoulders and went to the tips of her fingers.

In the middle of dinner Cæsar received a note. I guessed at once it was from his wife, whose jealousy lately had been something quite frightening. Cæsar read the note and was visibly disturbed and irritated. Cleopatra pretended not to notice the incident. The moment dinner was over Cæsar said that he would have to go home for a moment in order to attend to a business matter, but that he would be back shortly. He was still living, you know, in the public offices in the Via Sacra. Cleopatra did not make the slightest objection to his going; she only said that she hoped he would be back soon, and that as for herself she would be well occupied talking to Cicero, whom she had not seen for some time.

Cæsar was just making ready to go, and the flute-players had been sent for, when Casca (who, I think, is the best-looking young man in Rome) walked up to Cleopatra and occupied the empty seat next to her. Cæsar suddenly changed his mind, and said he would not go home after all. This was typical of his behaviour during these days: he had been constantly changing his mind about small matters and never seemed able to come to any decision. Besides this, he was always jealous of any one younger than himself, especially of Casca, who has got such thick hair.

Mark Antony tried to lure Cleopatra into conversation with him, paying her still more fulsome and still more crude compliments than before. And she, with perfect civility but with icy determination, ignored the compliments and took no notice of him.

After the flute-players had ceased we all had our fortunes told by an Asiatic soothsayer. He told Cleopatra and myself that we would be very lucky, but that we should beware of figs and the worms inside them. We laughed a great deal at this, because neither Cleopatra nor myself ever eat raw fruit. He told Mark Antony that he would love and be loved by the most wonderful woman in the world; upon which Mark Antony bent on one knee before Cleopatra and did mock homage. You should have seen her face! He did not feel inclined to do it twice, and there is no doubt that he knew he had made a grotesque exhibition of himself; in fact it was rather painful, and we were all sorry for him.

The soothsayer told Cæsar that all would be well with him should he follow the advice of those who loved him most. When the soothsayer said this, Cæsar looked at Cleopatra with infinite tenderness, and she smiled at him very sweetly. It was all I could do to keep from laughing. The vanity of men is extraordinary! I thought to myself—How can that conceited old politician think that a woman as young, as clever, and as pretty as Cleopatra could possibly care for him, or feel anything else but disgust at his attentions!

The soothsayer then told Cicero's fortune. He said

that his worst enemy was his tongue, but that if he went through life without offending any of the present company he would have a fortunate and successful career. We laughed a great deal at this, as every one in the room happened to be a great friend of his.

Cæsar was not satisfied with what the soothsayer had told him, and asked further details; but the soothsayer said that it was unlucky to tell a person's fortune twice in one evening, upon which Cæsar desisted, since he is intensely superstitious.

The guests went away, leaving Cæsar and Cleopatra alone. I was in the next room and could hear what they said through the silken curtain. I listened attentively. Cæsar began by calling her the sun of his life, and she complained of headache. Then he turned the conversation on to serious topics, and said he was greatly in need of her advice with regard to the events of the next day. Should he or should he not receive the Crown which was to be offered him by Mark Antony in the Forum?

Cleopatra said that if he did not accept it he would be a fool and a coward, and she for her part would never speak to him again. This seemed to satisfy him, and he went away.

The next morning he did not appear at the villa. We heard the noise of cheering, but we first learnt what had happened from one of the slaves who had been in the crowd. He told us that Cæsar had refused the Crown. Cleopatra was frightfully put out and really angry, for she had determined that if Cæsar accepted the Crown she would make him divorce Calphurnia, and marry him herself. It was her great ambition to be Queen, though nobody knew of this at the time of course, because ever since she had lived in Rome, Cleopatra had been a model not only of Roman economy but of Greek moderation, and her household books had been a lesson to the strictest of Roman matrons. That is all changed now, and I must say it is rather a relief.

To go on with my story: Cæsar himself came to see us before supper. He said that he had refused the Crown for the moment because he did not think the occasion was opportune, but that he firmly intended to accept it on a later occasion. "I am only drawing back," he said, "in order to take a greater leap." Cleopatra said sarcastically that no doubt he knew best and that he had been right to climb down. He told her, among other things, that a soothsayer—not the same one we had seen—had told him to beware of the Ides of March, when he intended to go to the Senate, and he asked Cleopatra whether she thought it would be wise for him to go.

She laughed at the superstition and told him that if he paid attention to such trifles people would begin to say that he was an old woman; in fact they were already saying it, and she was beginning to think it was true. This annoyed him so much that he banged the door, and went away in a huff. We expected him, however, to come to us the next day, as these sort of quarrels had often happened before.

But Cæsar did not come the next day, and a week passed without our seeing him. I suggested to Cleopatra she had better write, but she was quite obdurate. The days passed, and it was fully three weeks before we had further news of him. That was on the Ides of March, when a slave rushed into the house and told us that Cæsar had been murdered, and that we had better escape as soon as possible, since all friends of his were in danger.

Cleopatra showed great presence of mind. She packed her jewels and nothing else; she stained her face with walnut-juice, and put on a coarse peasant's garment, bidding myself and Iras do likewise; then, taking plenty of money with us, we went out through the back gate, crossed the river, and quite unobserved reached the Gate of Ostia. There we took a litter and started for Ostia, whence we embarked for Alexandria.

We have now been here a week, and Cleopatra, as I have already told you, is completely changed. But the change as far as we are concerned is for the better, for I can give you no idea of the fun we are having. Please come here as soon as you can. Alexandria is far more amusing than either Rome or Athens, and there is no tiresome Cæsar to interfere with us. Farewell.

CHARMIAN.

OVID'S BANISHMENT

Letter from Diogenes, a Sculptor, to a friend in Athens

My work, or rather the business which called me to Rome, is now accomplished, and the Caryatids which I was commissioned to make for the Pantheon of Agrippa are now in their place. But in what a place! Alas, they have been set up so high that their whole effect is lost, and the work might just as well be that of any Roman bungler. The Romans are indeed barbarians. They consider that as long as a thing is big and expensive it is beautiful; they take luxury for comfort, notoriety for fame, eccentricity for genius, and riches for wisdom; or rather they deem that wealth is the only thing which counts in the modern world, and here at Rome this is true. Their attempts at art are in the highest degree ludicrous. Yesterday I visited the studio of Ludius, who is renowned in this city for his decorative work. He paints walls and ceilings, and the Emperor has employed him to decorate his villa at Naples.

His work, which is not devoid of a certain talent, is disciplined by no sense of proportion. It would not be tolerated in Greece for a moment owing to an extravagance and an exaggeration which, so far from displaying any originality, merely form the futile mask of a fundamental banality. The man himself wears his hair yards long like a Persian, and favours a pea-green toga. I could not help saying to him that in Greece artists took pains to dress like everybody; it was their art that was exceptional.

Last night I supped with Maecenas at his house on the Esquiline. Let me do justice to my host and give praise where praise is due; here are no jarring notes and no foolish display. Maecenas has exquisite taste; his house is not overcrowded with ornaments nor overwhelmed by useless decoration. By a cunning instinct he has realized that art should be the servant of necessity. Everything in his house has a use and a purpose; but where a vase, a bowl, a cup, a chair, or seat is needed, there you will find a beautiful vase, a beautiful bowl, and so forth.

Maecenas himself is bald, genial, and cultivated; he looks older than he is, and dresses with a very slight affectation of coxcombry; his manner is a triumph of the art which conceals art. He talks to you as though you were the one person in the world he had been anxious to see, and as if the topic you were discussing were the preponderating interest of his life. As I entered his hall I found him pacing up and down in eager conversation with Agrippa, the famous admiral; my ears are sharp, and I just caught a fragment of their conversation, which happened to concern the new drains of Rome. Yet as Maecenas approached me he greeted me with effusion, and turning to Agrippa he said: "Ah, here he is!" as if their whole talk had been of me.

We reclined almost immediately. The fare was delicious, and distinguished by the same supreme simplicity and excellence as the architecture and the ornamentation of his dwelling. There were many celebrities present besides Agrippa—Ludius the painter, most grotesquely clothed, several officials and politicians, Cinna, Grosphus, three minor poets, Horatius Flaccus, Propertius and Crassus; Ovidius Naso, the fashionable writer; Virgilius, the poet, and many young men whose names escape me. Naso is by far the most prominent figure in the Roman literary world at present. He is the arbiter of taste, and sets the criterion of what is to be admired or not. Heaven forbid that I should read his verse, but there is no doubt about the flavour of his conversation, which is more interesting than his work.

The literary world despises Virgilius (the only Roman poet at present living worthy of the name!); on the other hand they admire this Crassus, who writes perfectly unintelligible odes about topics barren of interest. He has invented a novel style of writing, which is called symbolism. It consists of doing this: If you are writing about a tree and the tree seems to you to have the shape of an elephant you call it an elephant. Hence a certain chaos is produced in the mind of the reader, which these young men seem to find delectable. If you mention Virgilius to them they say: "If he only knew how to write. His ideas are good, but he has no sense of form, no ear for melody, and no power of expression."

This, of course, is ridiculous; for although Virgilius is a writer who has no originality, his style is felicitous, delicate, and lofty, and often musical. In fact he writes really well. With regard to the other poets, they are of little or no account. Horatius Flaccus has a happy knack of translation; Propertius writes amiable, sentimental stuff, and Tibullus babbles of pastures; but they are all of them decadent in that they, none of them, have anything to say. And they either display a false simplicity and a false archaism, or else they are slavishly imitative or hopelessly obscure.

At first the conversation turned on naval matters. It was debated at some length whether the Romans needed a fleet at all, and, if they did, whether it should be a small fleet composed of huge triremes or a large fleet of smaller and swifter vessels. Agrippa, who has the great advantage of practical experience in naval warfare, was in favour of the former type of vessel. But another sailor, a friend of Cinna's, who was present, and who was also experienced, said that the day of large vessels was over. The conversation then veered to literary matters.

Ovidius—a little man with twinkling eyes, carefully curled hair, and elaborately elegant clothes—he has his linen washed at Athens—excelled himself in affable courtesy and compliment to Crassus, whom he had never met hitherto. He had always been so anxious, he said, to meet the author of odes that were so interesting, although they were to him a little difficult.

"I'm afraid you must be deeply disappointed," said Crassus, blushing—he is a shy, overgrown youth with an immense tuft of tangled hair and a desperately earnest face.

"No," said Ovidius, "I am never disappointed in men of letters. I always think they are the most charming people in the world. It is their works which I find so disappointing. Everybody writes too much," he continued, "and, what is worse still, everybody writes. Even the dear Emperor writes hexameters; they do not always scan, but they are hexameters for all that. It has even been hinted that he has written a tragedy. Of course it doesn't matter how much verse a young man writes as long as he burns it all, but our dear Master's hexameters are preserved by the Empress. She told me herself with pride that she often 'mends' his verses for him. And they need mending sadly, because so many stitches in them are dropped. But how delightful it is to have a literary Emperor. He was good enough to ask me to read him a little poetry the other day. I did so. I chose the passage from the 'Iliad' where Hector says farewell to Andromache. He said it was very fine but a little old-fashioned. I then recited an ode of Sappho's, perhaps the loveliest of all of them. He seemed to enjoy it, but said that it was not nearly as good as the original, and that he preferred that kind of song when it was set to music. What the 'original' might be to which he alluded I did not ask, as I have always held that a monarch's business is to have a superficial knowledge of everything but a thorough knowledge of nothing. And therefore I say it is an excellent thing, Virgilius, that our dear Emperor is aware that you and Crassus and myself all write verse. But it would be in the highest degree undesirable that he should know so much about the business as to command you to write verses of society, and myself to write a Georgic.

"But, you will say, he is a poet himself, and the Empress mends his verses. It is true she mends his verses, but she also mends his socks, and a sensible monarch no more bothers to write his own verse than he bothers to make his own socks, or else what would be the use of being a monarch? But, again, you will object: if they are written for him, why don't they scan? The answer is simple. The man who makes them knows his business, and he knows that if they did scan nobody would believe that our dear Master had written them.

" And in having his verse written for him by a professional, and a bad professional—I hope, Horatius, it is not you, by the way—the Emperor displays not only sense but a rare wisdom. For a gentleman should never bother to acquire technical skill. If he loves music let him hire professional flute-players, but do not let him waste his time in practising ineffectual scales; and if he wants poetry let him order of Virgilius an epic, and if he wishes to pose as a literary monarch let him employ our friend Horatius to write him a few verses without sense or scansion —although I am afraid Horatius would find this difficult. You are too correct, Horatius. That is your fault and mine. We write verse so correctly that I sometimes think that in the far distant future, when the barbarians shall have conquered us, we shall be held up as models somewhere in Scythia or Thule by pedagogues to the barbarian children of future generations! Horrible thought! When Rome falls may our language and our literature perish with us. May we be utterly forgotten! My verse at least shall escape the pedagogues, for it is licentious; and yours, Crassus, I fear they will scarcely understand across the centuries. But, O Virgilius, the spirit of your poetry, so noble and so pure, is the very thing to be turned into a bed of Procrustes for little Dacians!"

" You are unfair on the Emperor," said Virgilius, " he has excellent taste."

" In poets certainly," said Ovidius, " but not in poetry."

The conversation then turned to other topics; the games, the new drains, the theatre of Balbus, the Naumachia, and the debated question whether the Emperor was right in having caused Vedius Pollio's crystal beakers to be broken because the latter had condemned a slave, who had accidentally dropped one of them, to be thrown into his pond of lampreys and eaten. The sentence would have been carried out had not the Emperor interfered and caused the slave to be released. Horatius said that Vedius Pollio deserved to be eaten by lampreys himself, but Ovidius and Ludius considered the punishment to be out of all proportion to the crime. Agrippa could not understand his minding the goblet being broken, as there were plenty of goblets in the world. Virgilius thought that Pollio's act was monstrous. Cinna said that the slave was his own. Maecenas considered that although it was a reprehensible act (and such deeds created dangerous precedents) nobody but a collector knew how terribly severe the punishment was.

We sat talking till late in the night. I cannot write any more, but I have just heard a piece of startling news. Ovidius Naso has been banished *for life* to some barbarous spot near Tauris. The reason of his disgrace is unknown. Hail!

THE CAPREAE REGATTA,

A.D. 27

Letter from Sabina to Chloe

CAPREAE, *August.*

We arrived late the night before last from Rome, and never have I seen Capreae so crowded. There are hundreds of yachts here, and many from Egypt, Greece, and Asia, and the whole fleet has arrived, and is drawn up ready for inspection. Clothes are, of course, a difficulty, because one is expected to be elegant, and if one wears anything beautiful it is certain to be spoilt when one gets in and out of boats. Clodia looks too absurd in Egyptian silks and gold chains, just as if she were going to the Games, and Lesbia looks sillier still dressed up as a Greek sailor boy. I have tried to steer a middle course between the two extremes, and I have got a plain white peplum with brown sandals; this all looks cool and summer-like, but it is really substantial enough for the fickle, breezy weather.

Yesterday we went with Sejanus to be shown over one of the ships, the *Servius Tullius*. It was one of the new kind, with three decks and four of what they call turrets. The officers on board were very proud of themselves because in their "battering practice," which they had just been doing in some outlandish place, they had successfully destroyed the *boom* (which is a kind of mast sticking out from the ship) of the dummy ship on which they practise. Julius says that these experiments are a waste of money, because each of these dummy ships costs I don't know how much money. But then Julius is a Little Roman, and I always tell him that if everybody thought as he did, we should have the barbarians in Rome in no time.

The officers have such a hard life on board. They have to get up before sunrise, and if any of them is at all disobedient he is told to climb up the mast and sit in a kind of basket for several hours with nothing to do. As for the sailors, they live in a dark hole with scarcely any light in it and no air at all. I asked one of them whether this didn't give them a headache, and he said that some clever mathematician had invented a kind of fan which buzzed round and round so as to ventilate their cabin. He said this was a horrible invention, and made such a draught that nobody could sleep. If you live at sea, he told me, you want to be warm in your cabin. You have quite enough fresh air on deck. Julius said this showed how perverse and conservative sailors are. If he was the captain of a ship he would make the sailors sleep on deck in hammocks without any blankets. The sailor said they were all thankful Julius was a politician and not a sailor. And Julius, who has no sense of humour, thought it was meant as a compliment.

There have been heaps of visitors on board all the ships. The captain of the *Servius Tullius* said it was wonderful what an interest people took in the fleet now, and what intelligent questions they asked, especially the women. I was rather flattered by this, as I have always taken an intelligent interest in naval things, and I had only just said to him (to show I wasn't ignorant) that my favourite boat was a *spinnaker*.

To-morrow there are going to be some races. I am going to try to get Lucius Aemilius to take me on board his schooner, the *Hirundo*. I always think a schooner is a safer boat than a cutter. I don't really like racing, because nobody will talk to one, and the men are all so rude and absent-minded while the race is going on, and whatever one does one is always in the way and in the wrong place, but I shall get rid of Julius for a whole day, because he is a very bad sailor and nothing would drag him on board a racing yacht.

Capreae is terribly crowded. I was invited upon Sejanus' yacht, but I think it much more comfortable to live in the most uncomfortable villa than in the most comfortable yacht. There is no privacy in a yacht, and salt water ruins my skin. Our villa, which we have hired for the week, is quite clean, only there is only one bath in it, so that we all have to use it by turn.

Vitellius, the admiral, has put one of the little pinnaces belonging to his ship, the *Remus*, at our disposal. So we can go backwards and forwards whenever we like. The pinnace is managed by one of the quite young officers—such a nice little boy, and so willing! He doesn't mind how long I keep him waiting at the pier. It seems extraordinary that such young boys should be able to manage a whole boat full of men, doesn't it? Ours looks about fifteen years old, but I suppose he is really much older. I asked him to come and dine with us, and Julius was cross about it, and said I was making myself ridiculous by talking to children. But I promise you this boy has much more assurance than many grown-up men. In fact, once or twice I have had to speak severely to him because he was on the point of going too far. As it was, I treated it all as a joke, and told him I was old enough to be his mother.

There have been a lot of the "Lysistratists" here—you know, the women who are in favour of senators being all women. Of course, I have nothing against their principles. If a man is a senator why shouldn't a woman be? Any woman is cleverer than any man. But I do think their methods are silly and so *unwomanly*. One of them took a piece of chalk and wrote "Women and Freedom" on Sejanus' carpet. And another dressed herself up as a Numidian slave, and shouted "Justice for Women" just as he was in the middle of a serious speech at his banquet. But the sailors like them very much, because they are so graceful, and on board one of the ships of the fleet—I think it was the *Scipio*—one of the chief "Lysistratists," Camilla, entirely converted one of the men of the "Legio classica"—those kind of half-soldiers, half-sailors, who keep order on board the ships—and he is now a fervent "Lysistratist" himself. The other sailors say this is very curious, as the man in question had such a stern character. But then, you see, Camilla is quite charming. Sejanus is horribly put out about it, and his house has to be guarded day and night by soldiers. It is most inconvenient, because the other day his own daughter Lydia was arrested as she was going into the house. They had mistaken her for a "Lysistratist."

Last night all the ships were illuminated with oil lamps, and ten thousand Egyptian slaves danced and sang in the gardens. The result was I did not get a wink of sleep, and the worst of it is that these songs and dances go on all day as well as all night. On the beach, too, there is every kind of acrobat, gipsy tumblers, and fortune-tellers. There is a woman here who tells one marvellous things by looking at one's hand, only Julius, who, like all husbands, is now and then quite unaccountably obstinate about little things, absolutely forbade me to consult her and so I had to give it up. She told Clodia she would be married three times.

The Persian fleet arrives here to-morrow on a visit. Julius and I are invited to dine at the Emperor's villa, and Julius has to wear a Persian uniform as a compliment to the Persians. It is made of scarlet silk with orange sleeves, and a long green train fringed with silver; he also has to wear a high tiara of steel and gold covered with jewels, and extraordinary sandals laced up the leg with little bells. He tried it on last night, and I can't tell you what he looked like. (Julius has grown to look much older since you saw him, and only the soberest togas suit him.) I couldn't help telling him he looked like a circus-rider, and he was so offended that I have not been able to mention the dinner since. Men are so funny. Julius is ashamed of being thought a clever politician, which he is, and wants to be thought an excellent quoit-player, and he can't throw a quoit a yard. He stoops and he is flabby, and yet he wants everybody to take him for an athlete!

How different from those nice sailors, who are so modest, and who are pleased because they are sailors, and wouldn't be anything else for the world.

I must stop now, because the pinnace is "awaiting my pleasure," and I don't want to keep my little sailor boy waiting. Farewell. I will write again soon.

P.S.—Whenever Julius is bad-tempered now I say I wish I had married a sailor, because they are never, never, never rude to their wives. It is true, of course, that they seldom see them, but I did not say that.

P.P.S.—Later. We dined at the Emperor's villa last night. It appears that this morning a tiresome incident occurred. A fisherman brought the Emperor some lobsters, and it turned out that one of them was not quite fresh. So the Emperor had the fisherman hurled from the cliff into the sea. He is subject every now and then to these fits of petulance; but I must say he was charming last night, and most agreeable. Of course he is self-conscious and he makes some people feel shy; but I get on with him beautifully. He knows so much about everybody. We fancy he already knew that Metellus has quite given up Clodia, and is now desperately in love with Irene. He was most tactful with me, and never alluded either to Sejanus or to Julius.

MESSALINA

Letter from Pallas, Librarian to the Emperor Claudius, to a Friend

THE PALATINE, ROME.

A slave brought your letters this morning from Antium, and since the Emperor is sending one back to-morrow I take advantage of the opportunity to obey your behest and to give you the news which you ask for.

You demand a full account of my new life, and although it is now only three weeks ago that I arrived, I feel as if many years had passed, so crowded have they been with incident, experience, and even tragedy. I will not anticipate, but will begin at the beginning.

As soon as my appointment was settled I was commanded to come to the Palace and to take up my new duties at once. I arrived early one morning about three weeks ago. I was shown the room I was to occupy, and the library where I was to work—which is magnificent—and briefly instructed in my duties, which are not heavy. I was to have my meals with the Emperor's Secretaries.

The first day of my arrival I saw no one, but the second morning, just after I had settled down to my work—I have two assistants—a man walked into the library and asked in a hesitating manner for a Greek dictionary.

"I am sorry to trouble you," he added, apologetically, "but I am a wretched speller."

I became aware—why exactly I cannot tell, since he was dressed in a loose robe and slippers--that it was the Emperor. He looked at me furtively, fixing his glance on the edge of my toga, so much so that I began to think it must be dirty. He is badly made, his head looks as if it might fall off his shoulders, his features are too big for his face, and his hand shakes. In spite of all this there is about him a mournful dignity—an air of intelligence, melancholy, and authority. I gave him the dictionary and he looked out the word he wanted, but my presence seemed to embarrass him, and he fumbled, and was a long time before he could find what he was seeking. At last he found it and returned me the book with a nervous cough. As he left the room he asked me to dine with him that night. It would be quite informal, he said, only himself and the Empress.

I looked forward to the evening with fear and curiosity, and when at the appointed hour I found myself in the ante-room I was trembling with nervousness. Presently the Emperor entered the room and said the Empress would be down directly. He seemed to be as shy as I was myself. After a prolonged silence he remarked that the month of October, which had just begun, was the pleasantest month in the year. After this he bade me be seated, relapsed into silence, and did not seem to notice my presence. He stared at the ceiling and seemed to be engrossed in his thoughts. Nearly twenty minutes passed in uncomfortable silence, and then the Empress entered with a jingle of chains and bangles. She smiled on me graciously, and we went into the dining-room.

I had heard much about the beauty of the Empress, and the accounts were scarcely exaggerated. Her face was childish and flower-like, her hair and complexion dazzlingly fair, her smile radiant, her expression guileless and innocent, and in her brown eyes there danced a bright and delightful mischief.

We reclined, and course after course of rich and spicy dishes were brought. We began with sturgeon and fried eels, followed by roast sucking-pig, wild boar, calf, wild peacock, turkey, and various kinds of game. The Emperor helped himself copiously and partook twice of every course. The Empress toyed with her food and sipped a little boiling water out of a cup. The Emperor did not speak at all, but the Empress kept up a running conversation on the topics of the day--the games, the new port of Ostia, the Emperor's new improved alphabet, and the progress of the History of Etruria, which he is writing in Greek.

"You will be a great help to him," she said, talking as if he were not present. "There is nobody at all literary at Court just now, and he loves talking about literature. I am so anxious he should go on with his writing—you must encourage him. I do what I can, but I am not up to his scholarship and science; I am only an ignorant woman."

Towards the end of dinner, Britain having been mentioned, the Emperor discoursed at length on the native religion of that insignificant island. The people there, he said, held the oak tree in great reverence and sacrificed to a god who had certain affinities with the Etrurian Moon-god; he intended to devote a chapter of his Etrurian history to a comparison between the two religions; and he explained at enormous length, and with a wealth of illustration which revealed untold erudition, their likenesses and differences.

The Empress sat in rapt attention, drinking in every word, and when he had finished she said : " Isn't he wonderful? " He looked at her and blushed, as pleased as a child at the praise.

When at last the long meal came to an end the Emperor took us to his private study and showed me his books, almost all of which dealt with history and philosophy. He pulled down many of them from their shelves, and discoursed learnedly about them, but the Empress always brought the conversation back to his own writings, and insisted on his reading out passages of the History of Carthage. (This I had to fetch from the library.)

" You must read us my favourite bit about the death of Hannibal," she said.

The Emperor complied with her wishes, and read out in an expressionless voice a narrative of the death of the Carthaginian hero, which I confess was not distinguished either by originality of thought or elegance of diction. It was, to tell the truth, tedious and interlarded with many moral reflections of a somewhat trite order on the vanity of human achievement. But during all the time he read, the Empress sat opposite him with an expression of rapt interest, and at the more pathetic passages tears came into her eyes. By the peroration on Hannibal's character, which said that he was a great man but a victim of ambition, and that in contemplating so great an elevation and so miserable an end man could not fail to be impressed, she was especjally moved. When it was finished she made him repeat some verses which he had written about the death of Dido. The

Emperor showed reluctance to do this, but she finally persuaded him, saying that people might say what they liked, but that she greatly preferred his verse to that of Virgil. It was more human and more manly. In Virgil, she said, there was always a note of effeminacy. I could not agree with her there, but her admiration for her husband's work was deeply touching in its sincerity.

"If only he had more time to himself," she said wistfully, "he would write a magnificent epic—but he is a slave to his duty."

The Emperor then mentioned that he was starting for Ostia in a few days. The Empress put on a pained expression, and said it was too cruel of him not to take her with him. He explained that he would willingly have done so, but as his time there would be entirely devoted to formal business he was sure she would be more happy at Rome. She then asked him if he had any objection to her organizing a little ceremony for the Festival of Bacchus during his absence. Silius had promised to help her. They had even thought of performing a little play, quite privately, of course, in the gardens, just for a few friends.

The Emperor smiled and said he had no objection, only he begged her to see that etiquette was observed and that the guests should not be allowed to take any liberties. "The Empress is so good-nautred," he said, "and people take advantage of her good nature and her high spirits, and the Romans, especially the matrons, are so spiteful." He had, of course, no objection to a little fun, and he wanted her above all things to enjoy herself.

At that moment Narcissus, the freedman, entered with some papers for the Emperor to sign. The

Emperor glanced through them, signed most of them, but paused at one.

"I thought," he said, and then hesitated and coughed, "that we had settled to pardon them."

"There was an idea of it at first," said Narcissus, "but you afterwards, if you remember, agreed that it was necessary to make an example in this case."

"Yes, yes," answered the Emperor.

"Are you talking of Verus and Antonius?" the Empress broke in. "You promised me that they would be pardoned."

"So I did," said the Emperor, and then, turning to Narcissus, he said: "I think in this case, in view of the rather exceptional circumstances, we might strain a point."

"But they are quite undeserving," began Narcissus.

"The Emperor has pardoned them," broke in the Empress, "he told me so yesterday; let us scratch out their names," and bending over the Emperor with a kind and lovely smile, she suited the action to the word. The Emperor smiled lovingly at her, and Narcissus withdrew, biting his lips. Soon after that I withdrew also.

The next morning the Emperor started for Ostia. During the week that followed the Empress visited me frequently in the library, and was extremely kind; she took an extraordinary interest in my work, and revealed a wide knowledge of literature. Her criticisms were always acute. She evidently missed the Emperor very much. The more I saw of her the more I admired her beauty, her kindness, and her wit, and the more readily I understood the jealousy she inspired at Rome, a jealousy which found vent in spiteful gossip and malicious scandal.

The Empress, I at once understood, was a creature compact of kindness, gaiety, and impulse; she could not understand nor brook the conventions and the hypocrisy of the world. She was a child of nature, unsophisticated and unspoilt by the artifices of society. This is the one thing the world can never forgive. When she was pleased she showed it. Her spirits were unbounded, and she delighted in every kind of frolic and fun, and was sometimes imprudent in giving rein to her happy disposition and to the charming gaiety of her nature in public. This did her harm and gave her enemies a pretext for inventing the wildest and most absurd calumnies. But when she heard of this she only laughed and said that the malice of her enemies would only recoil on their own heads.

Alas! she was grievously mistaken. Her enemies were far more numerous and more bitter than she supposed; moreover, they resented the influence she exerted over her husband, just because this influence was gentle and good. Here are the bare facts of what happened. The Emperor was still at Ostia. The Empress was celebrating the Festival of Bacchus in the Palatine Gardens according to the Emperor's wish. The feast lasted several days. Silius and Veltius Valens, who are both skilled at that sort of thing, had arranged an effective amphitheatre, and there were dances, music, and a whole pageant in honour of Bacchus. It was a lovely sight.

On the last day of the festival a procession of Bacchanals, clad in leopard skins and crowned with vine leaves, danced round the altar playing the double flute. One day on the stage in the amphitheatre a wine-press was revealed, and a chorus of wine harvesters, led by the Empress herself, trod the grapes.

Never had the Empress looked so beautiful as in this Bacchanal's dress, and she joined in the fun with a wild, irresponsible gaiety and enjoyed herself like a child. During the whole festival, which had lasted a week, she had played a thousand pranks, and on the first day of the merry-makings Silius had dressed up as Bacchus, and the Empress as Ariadne, and they acted a play in which a mock marriage ceremony had been performed—all this in fun, of course.

But there were spies among us, and Narcissus, who was at Ostia, received daily accounts of what was happening. Skilfully he distorted the facts and represented what had been a piece of harmless fun as a scandalous orgy. He said the Empress, clad only in a vine-wreath, had danced before all Rome, and that she had publicly wedded Silius. He added a whole list of infamous details which were the fruits of his jealousy fancy; but, worst of all, he accused Silius and the Empress of conspiracy, and said that they had attempted to bribe the Praetorian Guards, that they were plotting to kill Claudius and usurp the Throne. The festival was not over when a slave arrived breathless, and told us what Narcissus had done. The Emperor, he said, was on his way home. The Empress knew she must meet him face to face. She also knew that Narcissus would do everything in his power to prevent it. The courtiers, scenting the Empress's overthrow, deserted her, and she set out on foot to meet the Emperor. But Narcissus prevented the meeting, and the Empress fled to Lucullus' Villa, which Valerius Asiaticus had bequeathed to her.

The Emperor arrived in time for dinner. I was summoned to his table. He partook heartily of eight courses almost in silence, but seemed gloomy and depressed. After dinner his spirits rose and he asked whether I considered that Silius and the Empress had really plotted against him. I told him the whole truth, and he expressed great annoyance at Narcissus' perfidy. He sent a message to say that the Empress was to return at once—to be judged, he added cunningly, for he did not wish Narcissus to know that he knew the truth. But Narcissus divined his peril. He knew that as soon as the Empress returned his doom would be sealed, and he told the tribune on duty that the Emperor had ordered Messalina to be killed.

That evening I was bidden to supper; and before we had finished the Emperor asked why Messalina had not come.

"Messalina," said Narcissus, "is no more. She perished by her own hand."

The Emperor made no comment, but told the slave to fill his goblet. He finished supper in silence.

The next morning the Emperor came into the library. He asked for his own Carthaginian history, and sat by the window, looking at it without reading. Then he beckoned to me, and finding the passage on the death of Hannibal, he pointed to it and tried to say something.

"She"—he began, but two large tears rolled down his cheeks, and he choked. Since then he has never mentioned Messalina; he works, eats, and talks like a man whose spirit is elsewhere, or a person who is walking in his sleep.

Farewell, I can write no more, for I am shattered by this tragedy and the dreadful end of one of the few really good women I have ever seen.

MASTER NERO

Express despatch by special courier from Cn. Domitius Ahenobarbus to Gaius Caesar (Caligula) Antium, 37 A.D.

ANTIUM, *December* 15.

Humble Duty. Thanks to favour of Jove and Venus and to your Majesty's auspicious intercession, fine boy born this morning. Agrippina doing very well. Sends dutiful love.

Letter from Drusilla (nurse to L. Domitius Ahenobarbus, son of Cn. Domitius Ahenobarbus and Agrippina, daughter of Germanicus Caesar) to Euryclea, a maid in the Imperial Household at Rome, 39 A.D.

December 15.

Dear Miss Euryclea,

To-day was our darling boy's second birthday. The little man had a tea-party in the nursery. His father gave him a beautiful woolly lamb with a blue ribbon round its neck, and his mother gave him a stuffed eagle, which he had fancied for some time. His father said this wasn't a suitable present and might be *misunderstood,* and told our darling that he should have something else instead, but the little precious took on dreadfully, and his mother took his part, so it was settled that he should have the eagle to play with in the *nursery,* but not *downstairs,* or at any rate not when there is company.

He had his cousins to tea, Master Balbus and Master Æmilius; and little Miss Octavia. He had a beautiful cake with two candles on it, and all went off very well, except that Miss Octavia teased him, and he pulled her hair, but, as I said at the time, *she* began it and was to blame. He's a beautiful boy and has his mother's spirit. He says "ta-ta," and "me want more" and "shan't" very nicely.

Virginia, the new nursery maid, is not to be trusted. I can't leave her alone with the baby for a moment. She left him all alone in the night nursery while I was getting ready to bath him and the poor darling set fire to his cot with one of the birthday candles, and luckily I came back just in the nick of time. I heard the pet calling "Nanna, 'ook at fire" (Fancy his being able to say all that!), otherwise the house would have been set on fire and we should all have been burnt.

I shall have to get him some new shoes soon. We all go to Rome next week.

Letter from Drusilla to Euryclea, 40 *A.D.*

December 15.

Dear Miss Euryclea,

The little boy was three years old to-day. We had prepared a treat for him, and his cousins were coming to tea, but everything had to be put off at the last moment. The poor darling child, owing entirely to Virginia's carelessness, got hold of a bottle of his mother's drops of henbane which she takes for her insomnia, and he poured some of it, when we weren't looking, into Virginia's wine, just before her dinner.

The girl, who has weak nerves and is full of fancies,

took it upon herself to feel queer and faint directly he said he had done this, although she felt quite well up till then, and we had to send for a doctor, and we had quite a job to bring her to. The doctor said it was quite a harmless dose she had taken and that she would be all the better for the nap, but she gave us all a turn, and I had my hands so full that I couldn't have company to tea, and our little darling's birthday was spoilt.

His mother said he might keep his birthday another day. He was so brave about it, and not at all frightened. When I asked him why he had poured the medicine into the silly girl's wine he said, "I wanted to see what she would be like when she was deaded." He is a real cure sometimes. He's growing fast. Her Ladyship is calling me, so I must stop.

Letter from Drusilla to Euryclea, 41 *A.D.*

December 15.

Dear Miss Euryclea,

It seems only yesterday that our little jewel was three, and to-day he was four years old, and he's getting almost too big for the nursery. He wore his new "Toga" suit for the first time to-day. Last night his father came to kiss him good-night and prodding his plump little arms he said "What are you made of?" What do you think the little darling answered? "Dust." Did you ever hear of such an old-fashioned child?

What do you think he asked for for his birthday? A harp, a pineapple, and a yard of purple silk. He lost his first tooth yesterday and gave it to me to be made into a ring. He is still very fanciful about his food and won't touch his fish till he's had his meat first. He is to begin lessons next year, poor darling. I'm sure he learns quick enough already without their plaguing his poor little head with lessons. When his father asked him the other day what he was going to be when he grew up he said "An artist." He's certainly one for drawing. He drew a beautiful picture for his mother of a lion eating a naughty slave.

His cousins and little Miss Octavia came to tea, but I won't have them in my nursery another time unless they can learn how to behave. They tease him so dreadfully. As for Octavia, I've no patience with her. They were playing quietly at the Siege of Troy, and the little man was being Achilles, when Octavia suddenly said: "I'm Paris and I wound you in the heel, and now you're dead." The precious child was dreadfully upset. He said it wasn't fair, as she couldn't be Paris because she was a girl; and he said "If you're Paris I am the avenging Greek Army, and you shall perish in the flames," and he set fire to her hair, which was always far too long. He meant no harm, the poor child. I told her she had brought it on herself. She screamed enough to bring the house down, although we put the flame out at once, but that child's so vain that she couldn't bear to think that her hair had been even singed.

I hope we may be moving to Rome soon, as the child is outgrowing all his winter vests.

Agrippina to her Uncle Claudius, 44 *A.D.*

BAIAE, *December* 15.

Dearest Claudius,

To-day was my darling's birthday; in writing to you I don't mind calling him by his name that is to be Nero. We all went for a picnic on the bay. It was beautiful. Little Nero did a sketch of Mount Vesuvius and said he wished the mountain were a volcano, as it would look so picturesque with smoke coming out of it.

He recited a Greek poem for his father. Seneca was annoyed because he had chosen a passage for him to learn from Pindar, but the dear little child learnt something else all by himself as a surprise, a piece of Sappho's. Very pretty. He said it so nicely. Seneca would have liked to scold him, and he said it wasn't suitable, but I wouldn't have my little one scolded on his birthday. He sang the words and played the harp. I think he has quite a remarkable ear for music, and they all say that he would be good enough to go on the stage if he had to earn his living.

On the way back we had rather an annoying accident. Somebody loosened the cork in the bottom of the boat and it began to leak, and we did not notice it till the boat was half full of water. Little Nero showed the greatest presence of mind and found out the place where it was leaking, and the missing cork, and we baled out the water. I was glad to see how he could behave in an *emergency*. Even Seneca was obliged to admit that the child had surprised him by his promptness and coolness. Farewell.

AGRIPPINA.

Letter from Seneca to Claudius Caesar, 46 *A.D.*

Confidential.

Most Illustrious Master,

I present my humble duty and hasten to offer you my respectful congratulations on your marriage with my august benefactress, your most noble niece, Agrippina. I am highly honoured by being the first recipient of this interesting and confidential information, and I lose no time in answering your inquiries as to the nature and progress of your great-nephew. I note that he is in future to be called Nero.

Ever since Master Nero has been under my tuition, I have had every cause for satisfaction. He is an uncommonly sharp and thoughtful lad, and if he exerts the necessary application, should develop into a fine scholar. He is at present somewhat averse to drudgery of any form. He talks Greek fluently, and his knowledge of literature, and especially poetry, is astonishing, but he is weak in geography and arithmetic, and takes no interest in political economy. He is fond of music and has a good ear and an eye for colour, but I cannot get him to apply himself to free-hand drawing.

He is fond of reading, but prefers mythology to history, and shows little aptitude or inclination to study the natural sciences, and takes little interest in political questions. As to his character and disposition, I cannot speak too highly. I think your Majesty could not do better than to adopt him, as your Majesty suggests, and I can imagine no one more likely to develop into a wise, just, and beneficent ruler.

I should recommend a suitable wife being found for him as soon as he is of an age to marry. This would perhaps tide over what might otherwise be a difficult period and give him a guide and a helpmate at an age when he is liable to be easily influenced.

He is extremely warm-hearted and kind, and only yesterday, knowing that I was suffering from rheumatism, took the trouble to ride five miles in order to procure for me a particular kind of ointment which he knew was prepared by a poor Greek dancing girl (whom

Master Nero appears to have befriended) in one of the neighbouring villages.

I am, with humble duty,
Your Majesty's most obedient humble servant,
SENECA.

From Drusilla to Euryclea, 53 *A.D.*

PRIVATE.

December 15.

Dear Miss Euryclea,

I am sending this by the slave, who will smuggle it to you somehow. There is great news. Master Nero is engaged to be married to Miss Octavia. I could have wished a better match for our pet lamb, as I never did like Miss Octavia, and I feel she may *nag* our precious child. I shall tell her to her face that hers will be a position of great responsibility, to be wife of the Emperor that is to be, and that if all does not go well we shall know whom to blame.

Master Nero is very well and had tea in the nursery only last night. He ate two lobsters, a crab, a boiled chicken with rice, six Saffron buns, and some sweetmeats, and some bread and honey. I told him it reminded me of old times, and when he finished his tea he said: "Nanny, may I get down?"

NERO INTERVIEWED

ROME, A.D. 64

Letter from a Greek Traveller to his Friend in Athens

It is fifteen years since I was last in Rome, and although I was prepared to find a change in everything, I had not expected this complete transformation. The Rome I knew, the Rome of the straggly, narrow streets and rotting wooden houses, has disappeared, and in its place there is a kind of Corinth on a huge scale, marred of course by the usual want of taste of the Romans, but imposing nevertheless and extraordinarily gay and brilliant. The fault of the whole thing is that it is too big: the houses are too high, the streets too broad, everything is planned on too large a scale. From the artist's point of view the effect is deplorable; from the point of view of the casual observer it is amusing in the highest degree. The broad streets—a blaze of coloured marble and fresh paint—are now crowded with brilliant shops where you see all that is new from Greece and the East together with curiosities from the North and the barbarian countries. Everybody seems to be spending money. The shops are crowded from morning till night. The display of gold trinkets, glass vases, carpets, rugs, silks, gold and silver tissues, embroideries, all glittering in the sunlight, dazzles the eye and imposes by the mass and glare of colour and gaudiness.

There is no doubt that the Emperor is extraordinarily popular, and whenever he shows himself in public he is greeted with frantic enthusiasm. Of course there are some malcontents among the old-fashioned Liberals, but they have no influence whatever and count practically for nothing, for what are their grumblings and their eternal lamentations about the good old times and the Empire going to the dogs, in the scale with the hard, solid fact that ever since Nero came to the throne the prosperity of the Empire has increased in every possible respect? For the first time for years the individual has been able to breathe freely, and owing to the splendid reforms which he has carried through in the matter of taxation, an intolerable load of oppression has been lifted from the shoulders of the poor, and I can assure you they are grateful.

A few nights ago I had dinner with Seneca, to meet some of the leading literary lights. He is somewhat aged. Discussing various differences between our people and his, Seneca said that it is all very well for us to talk of our intellectual superiority, our artistic taste, our wit, our sense of proportion, but we had no idea either of liberty of trade on the one side, or liberty of thought on the other. "That kind of liberty," said Seneca, "always fares better under a King or a Prince of some kind than under a jealous democracy. We should never tolerate the religious tyranny of Athens." I could not help pointing out that what struck me at Rome to-day was that whereas almost everybody had "literary" pretensions, and discussed nothing but eloquence, form, style, and "artistry," nearly everybody wrote badly, with the exception of Petronius Arbiter, whom the literary world does not recognize. The Romans talk a great deal of "art for art's sake," and language, instead of being the simple and perfect vesture of thought, is cultivated for its own sake. "This seems to us Greeks," I said, "the cardinal principle of decadence, and the contrary of our ideal, which is that everything should serve to adorn, but all that is dragged in merely for the sake of ornament is bad." I think Seneca agreed, but the younger literary men present smiled with pitying condescension on me and said patronizingly: "We've got beyond all that."

After that dinner I made up my mind that I had seen enough of the literary set. Seneca was kind enough to get me an audience with the Emperor. I was received yesterday afternoon in the new gold palace which Nero has built for himself. It is a sumptuous building, to our taste vulgar, but not unimposing, and suits its purpose very well, though all his *suite* complain of the insufficient accommodation and the discomfort of the arrangements. I was taken into a kind of ante-room where a number of Court officials, both civil and military, were waiting, and I was told that the Emperor would probably see me in about a quarter of an hour. They all talked for some time in subdued tones as if they were in a temple; as far as I could see there was no reason for this, as the Emperor's room was at the other end of a long passage, and the doors were shut. At the end of a quarter of an hour a young officer fetched me and ushered me into the Emperor's presence.

He was seated at a large table covered with documents and parchments of every description, and had evidently been dictating to his secretary, who left the room on the other side as I entered. He is very like his pictures, which, however, do not give one any idea of his short-sighted, dreamy eyes, nor of his intensely good-humoured and humorous expression. He has a kind of way of looking up at one in a half-appealing fashion, as much as to say " For Heaven's sake don't think that I take all this business seriously." His movements are quick but not jerky. He held in his hand a chain of amber beads which he kept on absent-mindedly fingering during the whole interview. His fingers are short, square, and rather fat. He spoke Greek, which he speaks very purely indeed and without any Latin accent. Indeed, he speaks it too well. He asked me whether I was enjoying my visit to Rome, how long it was since I had been here, what I thought of the improvements, and if I had been to the new theatre. I said I had not been to the theatre, but that I was told the games in the Circus were extremely well worth seeing. The Emperor laughed and shrugged his shoulders, and said that it was very civil of me to say so, since I knew quite well that those spectacles, although hugely enjoyed by the ignorant rabble, were singularly tedious to people of taste and education like myself. I bowed as he made this compliment. As for himself, he continued, the games frankly bored him to death, but, of course, it was a State duty for him to attend them. " It is part of my profession," he said, " but if I had my own way I should witness nothing but Greek plays acted by my own company in my own house." He asked after several of my relatives whom he had met in Greece, remembering their exact names and occupations. He asked me if I had been writing anything lately, and when I said that I was sick of books and intended henceforth to devote all my leisure to seeing people and studying them, he laughed. "Nothing is so discouraging," he said, "as trying to improve the literary taste in this city. We are an admirable people; we do a great many things much better than other people—I do not mean only our colonization"—he said, smiling—"and our foreign trade, but our portrait painting and our popular farce. But as a general rule directly we touch Art we seem to go altogether wrong, and the result is nauseous. Therefore, if you want to find a Roman who will be thoroughly sympathetic, capable and intelligent, and decent, choose one who knows nothing about Art and does not want to. With you it is different," he added. "Athens is a city of artists." He then changed the subject and referred to the rather bitter criticisms published at Athens about his policy with regard to the Jews, especially that new sect among them who called themselves Christians.

"Of course," he said, "your sense of proportion is shocked when any extreme measures are adopted, but, believe me, in this case it is necessary. The Jews are everywhere, and everywhere they claim the rights of citizenship. But they do not live as citizens: they retain their peculiar status; they claim the rights of the citizen and exceptional privileges of their own—in fact, their own laws. They wish to have the advantages of nationality without being a nation, without taking part in the functions of the State. We cannot tolerate this. The whole matter has been brought to the fore by the attitude of these so-called Christians, who are, I am obliged to say, extremely difficult to deal with: In the first place because they adopt the policy of passive resistance, against which it is so difficult to act, and in the second place because they are getting the women on their side—and you know what that means. I have no personal objection either to Jews or Christians. What one can't tolerate is a secret society within the State which advocates and preaches neglect of the citizen's duty to the State, the worthlessness of patriotism, and the utter non-existence of citizenship."

I said I quite understood this, but did not his Majesty agree with me in thinking that penal oppression was rarely successful, and frequently defeated its own object.

The Emperor replied that there was a great deal in what I said, but that he did not consider he was dealing with a national or universal movement, which had any element of duration in it, but with a particular fad which would soon pass out of fashion, as the majority of all sensible people were opposed to it.

"The unfortunate part is," he said, "the women have got it into their heads that it is a fine thing, and of course the more they see it is opposed to the wishes of all sensible men the more obstinate they will be in sticking to it. The whole matter has been grossly exaggerated both as regards the nature of the movement and the nature of the measures taken against it; but that one cannot help. They have represented me as gloating over the sufferings of innocent victims. That is all stuff and nonsense. Great care has been taken to investigate all the cases which have arisen, so that the innocent should not suffer with the guilty. Besides which, any Jew or Christian who is willing to make a purely formal acknowledgement of the state authorities is entirely exempt from any possibility of persecution. But this is precisely what they often obstinately refuse to do—why, I cannot conceive. There is also a great deal of hysteria in the matter, and a large amount of self-advertisement, but one cannot get over the fact that the movement is a revolutionary one in itself, and can only be dealt with as such. I doubt whether in any country a revolutionary movement which has taken so uncompromising an attitude has ever been dealt with in so merciful a manner. So you see," the Emperor concluded, "how grossly unfair is the manner in which I have been treated in this matter. However, I suppose I can't complain: whatever one does it is sure to be wrong."

He then rose from his table and said that the Empress wished to see me before I went away, and he led me into her apartment, which was next door.

The Empress Sabina Poppaea is the perfection of grace; she is more like a Greek than a Roman, and speaks Greek better than the Emperor, using the language not only with purity but with elegance. All the stories we were told of her extravagance in dress and of how she powdered her head with gold, are of course absurd. She was dressed with the utmost simplicity and did not wear a single ornament. She was absolutely natural, put one at one's ease, talking continuously herself on various topics without ever dwelling long on one, till she had said all she had got to say, and then by a gesture delicately shadowed, she gave me the sign that it was time for me to go.

The Emperor said that the Empress Mother would have seen me only she was suffering from one of her bad attacks of indigestion. He told me to be sure to let him know should I visit Rome again, that he hoped himself to be able to spend some months in Greece next year, but he did not think the pressure of affairs would allow him to. Farewell.

P.S.—Later. The gossips say that the Empress Mother is being poisoned.

MARCUS AURELIUS AT LANUVIUM

Letter from Celsus to Lucian

I arrived at Lanuvium last night. The Court are here for the summer; that is to say, the Emperor, the Empress, the Heir Apparent, and the Emperor's nephew, Ummidius Quadratus, and the Senator who is on duty. As soon as I arrived I was taken by Eclectus, the Chamberlain, to my apartments, which are small, but from which one obtains a beautiful view of the Alban Hills. I was told that I would be expected to come to supper, and that I must take care not to be late, as the Emperor was punctual to a minute, and the water clocks in the villa were purposely an hour fast according to ordinary time.

A few minutes before the hour of supper a slave was sent to fetch me, and I was ushered into a large room, opening on to a portico from whence you have a gorgeous view of the whole country, where the Emperor and his family meet before going into the dining-room.

I had never seen the Emperor before. He is short and looks delicate and a great deal older than he really is. His eyes have a weary expression, and the general impression of the man would be one of great benevolence and dignity were it not marred by a certain stiffness and primness in his demeanour. When he greets you with great affability, you say to yourself, "What a charming man!" Then he stops short, and it is

K

difficult, nay, impossible, to continue the conversation. After a prolonged pause he asks you a question or makes some remarks on the weather or the topics of the day. But he does not pursue the subject, and the result is a succession of awkward pauses and a general atmosphere of discomfort.

Whether it be from the reserve which at once strikes you as being the most salient feature of his character, or whether it be from the primness and the slight touch of pedantry which are the result of the peculiar way in which he was brought up, there is a certain lack, not of dignity, indeed, but of impressiveness in the man. He strikes you more as a dignified man than as a dignified monarch. Indeed, were I to meet Marcus Aurelius in the streets of Rome or Athens, dressed as a simple mortal, I should be inclined to take him for a barber who catered for the aristocracy. As it was, when I was first introduced into that ante-room and saw the Emperor for the first time, a wild longing rose in me to say to him, "I will be shaved at half-past eight to-morrow morning."

The Empress Faustina is quite unlike what I had expected. There is no trace of Imperial or any other kind of dignity about her. She is not very tall; she has a delicate nose, slightly turned up, laughing eyes which will surely remain eternally young, and masses of thick, curly fair hair. I had imagined from the pictures and effigies of her that she was dark; possibly she may have dyed it lately, but I do not think so. She is restless in her movements; she is never still, but is always on the move, and one has the impression that she is longing to skip and jump about the room like a child, and would if she dared. As it is, her arms, and especially her hands, are never for a moment still, and her eyes shift quickly from one person to another, smiling and laughing. She made one feel that she was trying the whole time to be on her best behaviour, to curb her spirits, and not to overstep the bounds in any way, nor to do anything which would displease the Emperor or offend his sense of etiquette and decorum.

We waited four or five minutes for the Heir Apparent, who was late. The Emperor remarked with some acidity to the Empress that if Commodus could not learn to be punctual he had better have his meals in his own villa with his tutor. The Empress said that the poor boy was given such long lessons and so many of them that he scarcely had time even to dress; that he was overworked and a martyr to discipline.

At that moment the "poor boy" entered the room. For a boy of sixteen he is enormous: very tall, large, and fat. He has dark hair, a low forehead, with a thick and rebellious tuft of hair growing over it, rather coarse features, and thick lips. He must be immensely strong, but although you could not find a greater contrast to his pale, prim, and dapper father, there is a strong family likeness, nevertheless. You see at once that he is a son of Marcus Aurelius. It is as though the gods had wished to play a huge joke, and had made in the son a caricature, on a large scale, of the father. It is as if one saw the caricature of the most delicate ivory statuette made in coarse clay. He was told to salute me, which he did somewhat awkwardly.

The Empress said: "You must excuse him; he is very shy."

Upon which I saw that he with difficulty suppressed

a shout of laughter by stuffing his fist into his mouth, while his whole body was shaking.

The Emperor did not notice this. He led the way into the dining-room, and we all reclined.

At first there was a dead silence, and then Ummidius Quadratus, who seems to me far the most lively member of the family, said that the quails this year were much fatter than he had ever remembered them.

" Is that so ? " said the Emperor. " The best quails I ever ate," he added, " were those we got near the Danube. Unfortunately, my physician does not allow me to touch meat."

After this, there was a prolonged silence, which was broken by the Empress saying she did not believe in doctors. " Whenever they are at a loss as to what to prescribe, they ask you what you are fond of eating, and tell you to stop eating it."

Commodus, as if to show his agreement with his mother's ideas, at that moment put almost an entire quail into his mouth, and choked in the process. His mother hit him on the back, and told him to look up towards the ceiling. A slave brought him some water. The Emperor frowned, and told him not to eat so fast.

" It is my habit," he said, " and a habit which you would do well to imitate, to count twenty-six between each mouthful."

But Commodus, who had turned purple in the face, merely went on choking, and this lasted several minutes.

The Emperor asked me a few questions about Athens, and what was being done and said and written in our city. I answered him as best I could, but he did not seem to take notice of my replies, and went on, as though he were a machine, to other topics and other questions. I spoke of you, and I mentioned your latest book, but he changed the subject as though it were distasteful to him. I suspect that your ideas are too frivolous for him, and may even shock him.

Then Commodus, having recovered from his choking fit, began to talk of a pugilistic match which was to take place in a neighbouring village. He described at great length the champions who were to take part in it, the chances and the odds, and entered into many technical details which were tedious, and indeed quite incomprehensible to me. But the Emperor and the Empress listened with smiling and patronizing approval, and with obvious admiration of their son's knowledge. The Emperor is extremely conservative, and does all he can to encourage national sports and pastimes. He never misses a single event of importance at the Games, and even when he is in a country retreat like this, he patronizes the local efforts, in which his son seems to play so prominent a part.

After this dissertation on pugilism, which seemed to me interminable, had come to an end, Commodus related how he had played a practical joke on one of the freedmen who had been looking on at the sports. It appears that the man, who was old and rather fat, had been on the point of sitting down, and Commodus had pulled the chair from under him and he had come heavily to the ground, much to the amusement of the bystanders.

The Emperor thought this extremely funny, and indeed I was not a little bewildered by the mixture of severity and lenience with which the boy seems to be treated, for when a little later he asked if he might have a new toga to wear during the daytime, as his present one was getting worn out, the Emperor said, in a tone which admitted of no discussion, that it was quite out of the question; that boys should learn to be economical, and, as it was, he was a great deal too extravagant for his age, and already thought too much of such trifles. The Emperor said that his own toga was older than his son's, and yet he did not complain. It was certainly true that the Emperor seemed the perfection of neatness and tidiness, although it was obvious that his clothes were by no means new.

It was arranged that we should all go for a picnic on the lake next day and that I should be shown the country.

The Empress clapped her hands at the idea, and said there was nothing she enjoyed so much as a picnic. We should take our food with us and cook it ourselves. Commodus should catch us some fish and perhaps kill some game.

Commodus, for his part, looked sulky and sullen when this was mentioned; he evidently had some other plan in his mind. The Emperor said that he also found picnics a very pleasant relaxation; but a dismal expression came over the faces of the Chamberlain and of the few Court attendants who were present.

As I was most anxious to ascertain what was going on in the political world at this moment, I hazarded a remark with regard to the recent disturbances at Lyons which have been caused by the Christians. The Emperor at once became chillingly formal, but did not decline to discuss the matter; in fact, he was evidently anxious that I should be in no doubt with regard to his ideas on the subject. He said that it had become necessary to take extreme measures, that the attitude of these fanatics was intolerable; that they were in the highest degree unpatriotic and were a positive danger to the State. He was, however, not going to tolerate this any longer; he had no patience with stubbornness, and had determined, once and for all, to put his foot down. Conciliatory measures had been tried and had proved a failure. There was not the slightest use in pandering to sentimentalism and hysteria. He said he had just drafted an edict ordering the authorities to take the very severest measures to overcome the obstinacy of the rebels, and that should these prove ineffectual they were to resort to wholesale capital punishment without further discrimination or delay.

The Empress said that the Christians were disgusting, and that such vermin ought to be stamped upon. I said that I could not conceive the attitude of the Christians. Personally I had taken some trouble to ascertain what their doctrines were, and had interviewed several of the leading Christians in Greece and Asia. I agreed that Christianity was the national religion of no one; it was a religion adopted as a protest against the national religion by men who were infected by the spirit of all secret societies; that if the Christians refused to observe public ceremonies and to render homage to those who presided over them they should also, logically, give up wearing the *toga virilis*. But if they wished to share the benefit of civil life they should then pay the necessary honours to those who are charged with administration. But I added that should they do this I could not understand why their religion should not be tolerated on the same footing as other religions, such as that of the Egyptians, since nothing was required of them which was contrary to their principles.

The Emperor said that the Christians had already made such a thing impossible. "It is not," he said, "as if we had ever forced a pious man to commit an impious action or to say a shameful thing. He would be quite right in that case to endure any tortures rather than do so. But it is quite a different thing when a man is ordered to celebrate the Sun or to sing a beautiful hymn in honour of Athene. These are merely outward forms of piety, and one cannot have too much piety."

Here Ummidius Quadratus broke in and said that the Christians argued that it was a matter which concerned their conscience, which was no business of the State, and that they were perfectly ready to fulfil any duties, either civil or military, which had no religious character.

The Empress said she did not know anything about the ideas of the Christians, but she did think it was a disgraceful thing that in the present enlightened age people should be allowed to cover children with flour, to massacre them, and eat them.

I said I did not think the Christians did this. But the Empress said she knew it was true; she had heard it on the best authority; in fact, her maid knew some one who had seen them do it.

Here Ummidius Quadratus observed that some people in the best society had become Christians, and that he had even heard that—and here he mentioned the niece of a well-known patrician whose name I have forgotten—was one of them.

The Emperor drew himself up as though some dreadful solecism had been committed, and told his nephew that he had no right to say so shocking and so monstrous a thing at his table, especially before a stranger and a guest.

I will go on with my letter this evening, for a slave has just told me that we are to start for the picnic at once.

THE CAMELOT JOUSTS

Guinevere to King Arthur

CAMELOT, *Monday*.

Dearest Arthur,

I am feeling a little better. Merlin, who came over the other day from Broceliande, advised me to drink a glass of tepid water before breakfast every day and not to eat *brown* bread. This treatment has really done me good. I will see that everything is ready for the Jousts. They are getting on with the lists, but they have painted the outside paling red instead of green, which is very provoking. I think we must send the Under Seneschal away at Lady Day. He forgets everything.

I have asked Yniol to stay at the castle for the Jousts, and the Lord of Astolat and one of his sons. (We can't be expected to ask the whole family.) I thought it was no use asking poor little Elaine because she never goes anywhere now and hates the Jousts. Do you think we *must* ask Merlin this year? We asked him last year and I don't see that we need ask him *every* year. He has become so cross and crotchety, and Vivien complained that when he was here last year he behaved disgracefully to her and was quite impossible. Of course, I will do exactly as you like. I have asked Sir Valence, Sir Sagramore, Sir Percevale, Sir Pelleas, and Sir Modred. I won't have Melissande, she is so peevish and complaining.

Then there is King Mark. Shall I ask him? Without Iseult, of course. He can't expect us to ask her after all that has happened. I hear the King of Orkney asked them both and that he now expects her to be asked, but nothing shall induce me to receive her. If you think it is impossible to ask him alone we had better leave it, and ask neither of them.

Oh! I quite forgot. There's Lancelot. Shall we ask him to stay? He's been so often, so if you would rather not have him we can quite well leave him out this time. I don't want him to think he's indispensable to you.

The weather has been fine and the hedges are a mass of primroses. Vivi the cat (I christened her after dear Vivien) caught a mouse yesterday. Do come back quickly.

Your loving
GUINEVERE.

King Arthur to Guinevere

CARLEON, *March* 20.

My dearest Guinevere,

I was delighted to hear from you. I am glad you are recovering, but I must beg you to take care of yourself. These east winds are very trying and the March sun is most treacherous. We shall arrive two or three days before Whitsuntide. I will let you know the exact day. We have had a most successful and satisfactory time in every way. We rescued six damsels and captured two wizards and one heathen King. The knights behaved admirably.

With regard to the Jousts I do not wish to seem

inhospitable, but are you sure there is room for every one you mention? Merlin must, of course, be asked. He would be very much hurt if we left him out.

As to King Mark, we must ask him also with the Queen. They are now completely and officially reconciled, and Tristram is engaged to be married to a Princess in Brittany. Therefore, since King Mark has magnanimously forgiven and forgotten, it would not be seemly for us to cast any insidious slight upon them. To ask neither of them would be a slight, but to ask the King without the Queen would be a deliberate outrage. Besides, apart from our private feelings, the public good must be considered. We cannot afford to risk a war with Tintagel at this moment. I shall, of course, ask Lancelot. He is with me now. I cannot see any possible objection to his coming, and I have the greatest regard for him.

Please wrap up well when you go out. I am, with much love,

Your devoted husband,

ARTHUR.

Sir Lancelot to Guinevere

March 21.

The King has asked me to stay for the Jousts. From what he said about your health I gather you do not want me to come, so I said my old wound would not allow me to take part in the Jousts. Perhaps it is better that I should stay away. People are beginning to talk. Burn.

L.

Guinevere to King Arthur

CAMELOT, *Friday*.

Dearest Arthur,

Of course you know best. I entirely give in about Merlin and Lancelot, although I do think Merlin is trying, and that it makes the others jealous to ask him so often. But it is rather hard on me to be obliged to receive Iseult.

Of course with your noble nature you only see the good side of everything and everybody, but in Iseult's case the scandal was so public and the things they did so extraordinary that it is difficult to behave to her just as if it had never happened.

I like Iseult personally. I always liked her, but I do think it is trying that she should put on airs of virtue and insist on being respected. However, I have asked her *and* Mark. If they have any sense of decency they will refuse. I am quite well now. Merlin really did me good. We are having delicious weather, and I miss you all very much. Sir Galahad stopped here on his way West yesterday, but never said a word. I have ordered a new gown for the Jousts, but it is not finished yet. The weavers are too tiresome. The lists are getting on. If possible, bring me back six-and-a-half yards of the best green Samite, double width, from Carleon. The same shade as I had before. They can't match the shade here. I am so glad everything went off well. It seems centuries to Whitsuntide.

Your loving

GUINEVERE.

Guinevere to Lancelot

CAMELOT.

I am sending this by P——, who is entirely to be trusted. You were wrong. It is most necessary that you should come to the Jousts. Your absence would be far more noticed than your presence. It is a pity you told that foolish lie. It is a great mistake ever to tell unnecessary lies. However, now it's done, the best thing you can do is to come disguised as an unknown knight. Then when you reveal yourself at the end—for I suppose there is no chance of your not winning?—you can say you thought your name gave you an unfair advantage, and that you wished to meet the knights on equal terms. The King will be pleased at this. It is an idea after his own heart.

Iseult is coming with King Mark. At first I thought this dangerous, but there was nothing to be done, and she will be quite safe, as her one idea now is to be thought respectable, only we must be most careful. Iseult is a cat.

I dare not write more. G.

Guinevere to Iseult

CAMELOT, *April* 21.

Darling Iseult,

I am overjoyed that you can both come. It will be too delightful to see you again. It is ages since we have met, isn't it? I do hope that the King is quite well and that his lumbago is not troubling him. Merlin will be here, and he will be sure to do him good. He might also do something for his deafness.

Arthur will be delighted to hear you are coming,

He is devoted to the King. It will be a tiny party, of course—only Merlin, Yniol, Orkneys, Astolats, and a few of the knights. We will try to make you comfortable; but Camelot isn't Tintagel, and we have nothing to compare with your wonderful woods.

Good-bye, darling, give my best regards to the King.

Your loving
GUINEVERE.

P.S.—Sir Kay Hedius has just come back from Brittany. He was at our old friend Sir Tristram's wedding. He said it was glorious, and that she—Iseult the Lily-handed—was a dream of beauty. Tristram was looking very well and in tearing spirits. He's grown quite fat. Isn't it funny?

Iseult to Guinevere

TINTAGEL.

Darling Guinevere,

Thank you so much for your most kind letter. I am afraid that after all I shall not be able to come to the Jousts. It is too tiresome. But I have not been at all well lately and the physicians say I must have change of air. I am ordered to the French coast and the King has got some cousins who live in a charming little house on the coast of Normandy. I am starting to-morrow, and I shall probably stay there during the whole month of May. It is too tiresome to miss the Jousts, and you cannot imagine how disappointed I am. The King will, of course, come without me.

I hear that Sir Lancelot of the Lake is not going to compete this year for the Diamond on account of his health. I am so sorry. The people here say he is afraid of being beaten, and that there is a wonderful new knight called Lamorack who is better than everybody. Isn't it absurd? People are so spiteful. How you must miss the dear King, and you must be so lonely at Camelot without any of the knights.

By the way, is it true that Sir Lancelot is engaged to Elaine, the daughter of the Lord of Astolat? She is quite lovely, but I never thought that Lancelot cared for young girls. I think she is only sixteen.

Your loving

ISEULT OF CORNWALL.

Guinevere to Lancelot

Whit-Sunday.

The King has just told me whose sleeve it was you wore to-day. I now understand everything, and I must say I did not suspect you of playing this kind of double game. I do hate lies and liars, and, above all, stupid liars. It is, of course, very humiliating to make such a mistake about a man. But I hope you will be happy with Elaine, and I pray Heaven she may never find you out.

GUINEVERE.

KING LEAR'S DAUGHTER

Letter from Goneril, daughter of King Lear, to her sister Regan

I have writ my sister.
King Lear, Act I, Scene iv.

THE PALACE, *November*.

Dearest Regan,

I am sending you this letter by Oswald. We have been having the most trying time lately with Papa, and it ended to-day in one of those scenes which are so painful to people like you and me, who *hate* scenes. I am writing now to tell you all about it, so that you may be prepared. This is what has happened.

When Papa came here he brought a hundred knights with him, which is a great deal more than we could put up, and some of them had to live in the village. The first thing that happened was that they quarrelled with our people and refused to take orders from them, and whenever one told any one to do anything it was either—if it was one of Papa's men—"not his place to do it"; or if it was one of our men, they said that Papa's people made work impossible. For instance, only the day before yesterday I found that blue vase which you brought back from Dover for me on my last birthday broken to bits. Of course I made a fuss, and Oswald declared that one of Papa's knights had knocked it over in a drunken brawl. I complained to Papa, who flew into a passion and said that his knights, and in fact all his retainers, were the most peaceful and courteous people in the world, and that it was my fault, as I was not treating him or them with the respect which they deserved. He even said that I was lacking in filial duty. I was determined to keep my temper, so I said nothing.

The day after this the chief steward and the housekeeper and both my maids came to me and said that they wished to give notice. I asked them why. They said they couldn't possibly live in a house where there were such "goings-on." I asked them what they meant. They refused to say, but they hinted that Papa's men were behaving not only in an insolent but in a positively outrageous manner to them. The steward said that Papa's knights were never sober, that they had entirely demoralized the household, and that life was simply not worth living in the house; it was *impossible* to get anything done, and they couldn't sleep at night for the noise.

I went to Papa and talked to him about it quite quietly, but no sooner had I mentioned the subject than he lost all self-control, and began to abuse me. I kept my temper as long as I could, but of course one is only human, and after I had borne his revilings for some time, which were monstrously unfair and untrue, I at last turned and said something about people of his age being trying. Upon which he said that I was mocking him in his old age, that I was a monster of ingratitude—and he began to cry. I cannot tell you how painful all this was to me. I did everything I could to soothe him and quiet him, but the truth is, ever since Papa has been here he has lost control of his wits. He suffers from the oddest kind of delusions. He thinks that for some reason he is being treated like a beggar; and although he has a hundred knights—a hundred, mind you! (a great deal more than we have)—in the house, who do nothing but eat and drink all day long, he says he is not being treated like a King! I do hate unfairness.

When he gave up the crown he said he was tired of affairs, and meant to have a long rest; but from the very moment that he handed over the management of affairs to us he never stopped interfering, and was cross if he was not consulted about everything, and if his advice was not taken.

And what is still worse: ever since his last illness he has lost not only his memory but his control over language, so that often when he wants to say one thing he says just the opposite, and sometimes when he wishes to say some quite simple thing he uses *bad* language quite unconsciously. Of course we are used to this, and *we* don't mind, but I must say it is very awkward when strangers are here. For instance, the other day before quite a lot of people, quite unconsciously, he called me a dreadful name. Everybody was uncomfortable and tried not to laugh, but some people could not contain themselves. This sort of thing is constantly happening. So you will understand that Papa needs perpetual looking after and management. At the same time, the moment one suggests the slightest thing to him he boils over with rage.

But perhaps the most annoying thing which happened lately, or, at least, the thing which happens to annoy me most, is Papa's Fool. You know, darling, that I have always hated that kind of humour. He comes in just as one is sitting down to dinner, and beats one on the head with a hard, empty bladder, and sings utterly idiotic songs, which make me feel inclined to cry. The other day, when we had a lot of people here, just as we were sitting down in the banqueting-hall, Papa's Fool pulled my chair from behind me so that I fell sharply down on the floor. Papa shook with laughter, and said: "Well done, little Fool," and all the courtiers who were there, out of pure snobbishness, of course, laughed too. I call this not only very humiliating for me, but undignified in an old man and a king; of course Albany refused to interfere. Like all men and all husbands, he is an arrant coward.

However, the crisis came yesterday. I had got a bad headache, and was lying down in my room, when Papa came in from the hunt and sent Oswald to me, saying that he wished to speak to me. I said that I wasn't well, and that I was lying down—which was perfectly true—but that I would be down to dinner. When Oswald went to give my message Papa beat him, and one of his men threw him about the room and really hurt him, so that he has now got a large bruise on his forehead and a sprained ankle.

This was the climax. All our knights came to Albany and myself, and said that they would not stay with us a moment longer unless Papa exercised some sort of control over his men. I did not know what to do, but I knew the situation would have to be cleared up sooner or later. So I went to Papa and told him frankly that the situation was intolerable; that he must send away some of his people, and choose for the remainder men fitting to his age. The words were scarcely out of my mouth than he called me the most terrible names, ordered his horses to be saddled, and said that he would shake the dust from his feet and not stay a moment longer in this house. Albany tried to calm him, and begged him to stay, but he would not listen to a word, and said he would go and live with you.

So I am sending this by Oswald, that you may get it before Papa arrives and know how the matter stands. All I did was to suggest he should send away fifty of his men. Even fifty is a great deal, and puts us to any amount of inconvenience, and is a source of waste and extravagance—two things which I cannot bear. I am perfectly certain you will not be able to put up with his hundred knights any more than I was. And I beg you, my dearest Regan, to do your best to make Papa listen to sense. No one is fonder of him than I am. I think it would have been difficult to find a more dutiful daughter than I have always been. But there is a limit to all things, and one cannot have one's whole household turned into a pandemonium, and one's whole life into a series of wrangles, complaints, and brawls, simply because Papa in his old age is losing the control of his faculties. At the same time, I own that although I kept my temper for a long time, when it finally gave way I was perhaps a little sharp. I am not a saint, nor an angel, nor a lamb, but I do hate unfairness and injustice. It makes my blood boil. But I hope that you, with your angelic nature and your tact and your gentleness, will put everything right and make poor Papa listen to reason.

Let me hear at once what happens.

Your loving

GONERIL.

P.S.—Another thing Papa does which is most exasperating is to quote Cordelia to one every moment. He keeps on saying: "If only Cordelia were here," or "How unlike Cordelia!" And you will remember, darling, that when Cordelia was here Papa could not endure the sight of her. Her irritating trick of mumbling and never speaking up used to get terribly on his nerves. Of course, I thought he was even rather unfair on her, trying as she is. We had a letter from the French Court yesterday, saying that she is driving the poor King of France almost mad.

P.P.S.—It is wretched weather. The poor little ponies on the heath will have to be brought in.

LADY MACBETH'S TROUBLE

Letter from Lady Macbeth to Lady Macduff

Most Private.

THE PALACE, FORRES,

October 10.

My dearest Flora,

I am sending this letter by Ross, who is starting for Fife to-morrow morning. I wonder if you could possibly come here for a few days. You would bring Jeamie, of course. Macbeth is devoted to children. I think we could make you quite comfortable, although of course palaces are never very comfortable, and it's all so different from dear Inverness. And there is the tiresome Court etiquette and the people, especially the Heads of the Clans, who are so touchy, and insist on one's observing every tradition. For instance, the bagpipes begin in the early morning; the pipers walk round the castle a little after sunrise, and this I find very trying, as you know what a bad sleeper I am. Only two nights ago I nearly fell out of the window walking in my sleep. The doctor, who I must say is a charming man (he was the late King's doctor, and King Duncan always used to say he was the only man who really understood his constitution), is giving me mandragora mixed with poppy and syrup; but so far it has not done me any good; but then I always was a wretched sleeper and now I am worse, because

—well, I am coming at last to what I really want to say.

I am in very great trouble and I beg you to come here if you can, because you would be the greatest help. You shall have a bedroom facing south, and Jeamie shall be next to you, and my maid can look after you both, and as Macduff is going to England I think it would really be wiser and *safer* for you to come here than to stay all alone in that lonely castle of yours in these troublesome times, when there are so many robbers about and one never knows what may not happen.

I confess I have been very much put about lately. (You quite understand if you come we shall have plenty of opportunities of seeing each other alone in spite of all the tiresome etiquette and ceremonies, and of course you must treat me just the same as before; only in *public* you must just throw in a "Majesty" now and then and curtchey and call me "Ma'am" so as not to shock the people.) I am sorry to say Macbeth is not at all in good case. He is really not at all well, and the fact is he has never got over the terrible tragedy that happened at Inverness. At first I thought it was quite natural he should be upset. Of course very few people know how fond he was of his cousin. King Duncan was his favourite cousin. They had travelled together in England, and they were much more like brothers than cousins, although the King was so much older than he is. I shall never forget the evening when the King arrived after the battle against those horrid Norwegians. I was very nervous as it was, after having gone through all the anxiety of knowing that Macbeth was in danger. Then on the top of that, just after I heard that he was alive and well, the messenger arrived telling me that the King was on his way to Inverness. Of course I had got nothing ready, and Elspeth our housekeeper put on a face as much as to say that we could not possibly manage in the time. However, I said she *must* manage. I knew our cousin wouldn't expect too much, and I spent the whole day making those drop scones he used to be so fond of.

I was already worried then because Macbeth, who is superstitious, said he had met three witches on the way (he said something about it in his letter) and they had apparently been uncivil to him. I thought they were gipsies and that he had not crossed their palm with silver, but when he arrived he was still brooding over this, and was quite *odd* in his way of speaking about it. I didn't think much of this at the time, as I put it down to the strain of what he had gone through, and the reaction, which must always be great after such a time; but now it all comes back to me, and now that I think over it in view of what has happened since, I cannot help owning to myself that he was not himself, and if I had not known what a sober man he was, I should almost have thought the 1030 (Hildebrand) whisky had gone to his head—because when he talked of the old women he was quite incoherent: just like a man who has had an hallucination. But I did not think of all this till afterwards, as I put it down to the strain, as I have just told you.

But now! Well, I must go back a little way so as to make everything clear to you. Duncan arrived, and nothing could be more civil than he was. He went out of his way to be nice to everybody and praised the castle, the situation, the view, and even the birds' nests on the walls! (All this, of course, went straight to my heart.) Donalbain and Malcolm were with him. They, I thought at the time, were not at all well brought up. They had not got their father's manners, and they talked in a loud voice and gave themselves airs.

Duncan had supper by himself, and before he went to bed he sent me a most beautiful diamond ring, which I shall always wear. Then we all went to bed. Macbeth was not himself that evening, and he frightened me out of my wits by talking of ghosts and witches and daggers. I did not, however, think anything serious was the matter and I still put it down to the strain and excitement. However, I took the precaution of pouring a drop or two of my sleeping draught into the glass of water which he always drinks before going to bed, so that at least he might have a good night's rest. I suppose I did not give him a strong enough dose. (But one cannot be too careful with drugs, especially mandragora, which is bad for the heart.) At any rate, whether it was that or the awful weather we had that night (nearly all the trees in the park were blown down, and it will never be quite the same again) or whether it was that the hall porter got tipsy (why they choose the one day in the year to drink when one has guests, and it really matters, I never could understand!) and made the most dreadful noise and used really disgraceful language at the front door about five o'clock in the morning, I don't know. At any rate, we were all disturbed long before I had meant that we should be called (breakfast wasn't nearly ready and Elspeth was only just raking out the fires). But, as I say, we were all woken up, and Macduff went to call the King, and came back with the terrible news.

Macbeth turned quite white, and at first my only thought was for him. I thought he was going to have a stroke or a fit. You know he has a very nervous, high-strung constitution, and nothing could be worse for him than a shock like this. I confess that I myself felt as though I wished the earth would open and swallow me up. To think of such a thing happening in our house!

Banquo, too, was as white as a sheet; but the only people who behaved badly (of course this is strictly between ourselves, and I do implore you not to repeat it, as it would really do harm if it got about that I had said this, but you are safe, aren't you, Flora?) were Donalbain and Malcolm. Donalbain said nothing at all, and all Malcolm said when he was told that his father had been murdered was: "Oh! by whom?" I could not understand how he could behave in such a heartless way before so many people; but I must say in fairness that all the Duncans have a very odd way of showing grief.

Of course the first thing I thought was "Who can have done it?" and I suppose in a way it will always remain a mystery. There is no doubt that the chamber grooms actually did the deed; but whether they had any accomplices, whether it was just the act of drunkards (it turned out that the whole household had been drinking that night and not only the hall porter) or whether they were *instigated* by any one else (of course don't quote me as having suggested such a thing) we shall never know. Much as I dislike Malcolm and Donalbain, and shocking as I think their behaviour has been, and not only shocking but *suspicious,* I should not like any one to think that I suspected them of so awful a crime. It is one thing to be bad-mannered, it is another to be a parricide. However, there is no getting over the fact that by their conduct, by their extraordinary behaviour and flight to England, they made people suspect them.

I have only just now come to the real subject of my letter. At first Macbeth bore up pretty well in spite of the blow, the shock, and the extra worry of the coronation following immediately on all this; but no sooner had we settled down at Forres than I soon saw he was far from being himself.

His appetite was bad; he slept badly, and was cross to the servants, making scenes about nothing. When I tried to ask him about his health he lost his temper. At last one day it all came out and I realized that another tragedy was in store for us. Macbeth is suffering from hallucinations; this whole terrible business has unhinged his mind. The doctor always said he was highly strung, and the fact is he has had another attack, or whatever it is, the same as he had after the battle, when he thought he had seen three witches. (I afterwards found out from Banquo, who was with him at the time, that the matter was even worse than I suspected.) He is suffering from a terrible delusion. He thinks (of course you will never breathe this to a soul) that he killed Duncan! You can imagine what I am going through. Fortunately, nobody has noticed it.

Only last night another calamity happened. Banquo had a fall out riding and was killed. That night we had a banquet we could not possibly put off. On purpose I gave strict orders that Macbeth was not to be told of the accident until the banquet was over, but Lennox (who has no more discretion than a parrot) told him, and in the middle of dinner he had another attack, and I had only just time to get every one to go away before he began to rave. As it was, it must have been noticed that he wasn't himself.

I am in a terrible position. I never know when these fits are coming on, and I am afraid of people talking, because if it once gets about, people are so spiteful that somebody is sure to start the rumour that it's true. Imagine our position, then! So I beg you, dear Flora, to keep all this to yourself, and if possible to come here as soon as possible.

I am, your affectionate,

HARRIET R.

P.S.—Don't forget to bring Jeamie. It will do Macbeth good to see a child in the house.

AT THE COURT OF KING CLAUDIUS

From a Player's Letter

We arrived at Elsinore in the morning. We were at once let into the presence of the Prince. He received us with the courtesy and kindliness which were native to him, and he seemed but little changed since his student days when he was as much our companion as our patron. It is true that his face and his expression have grown older and more serious, just as his body has grown more portly, but in so far as his conduct and demeanour are concerned he is the same. No words can picture the dreariness and monotony of the life which he leads here in the Court. He is virtually a prisoner, for should he in any way transgress the fixed limits of the tradition and etiquette which govern this place, the courtiers and the officials of the Court do not hesitate to say that he is deranged in his mind. As soon as he greeted us he recalled a thousand memories of those freer and happier days, and he seemed to take as great a delight in our art and our trade as in days gone by. His love for the stage, for well-turned verse, and the nice declamation of noble lines is as ardent as ever, and he bade me recall to him a speech from a tragedy on which his sure taste had alighted, although it escaped the notice and the applause of the populace.

It was arranged that on the night following the morning of our arrival we should play before the

King and the Court. The piece chosen by the Prince was entitled "The Murder of Gonzago," a somewhat old-fashioned bit of fustian, chosen no doubt to suit the taste of the King and his courtiers. The Prince himself wrote a speech of some sixteen lines which he bade me insert in my part. We spent the day in study and rehearsal, which were sorely needed, since we had not played the piece for many years. In the evening a banquet was held in the castle. The King and Queen, the Chamberlain and all the Court dignitaries were present, and the Prince, although he did not grace the feast with his presence, insisted that we, the players, should take part in it. The Court dignitaries were averse to this, but the Prince overruled their objections by saying that unless we took part in the banquet he would not be present at the performance.

The feast was in the banqueting-hall; the King and the Queen together with all the Court took their places before a high, raised table at the end of the banqueting-hall. We players sat at a separate table at the further end of the hall. The feast began long before sunset and lasted far into the night. There was much deep drinking, but an atmosphere of ceremony and gloom hung over the festivity; the mirth rang hollow and the hilarity was false and strained.

Towards the end of the banquet the King rose to his feet and in pompous phrase spoke of the pleasure that he felt in seeing so many loyal friends gathered about him and that he looked forward to the day when the Prince, his nephew, would once more join heart and soul in the festivities of the Court, and then looking towards us he was pleased to say that he trusted to the skill, the well-known skill, and the widely-famed art of the players who were now visiting his capital to have a salutary influence and to be successful in distracting the mind and in raising the spirits of the Prince, which had been so sadly affected ever since the demise of his much-to-be-regretted brother. These words elicited loud cheers from the assembly, and it was pointed out to us by the Chamberlain that the speech of the King was a further sign of his Majesty's unerring tact and never-failing condescenion.

As we left the banqueting-hall, after the King and Queen had retired, I noticed that the Prince was pacing up and down the terrace of the castle, lost as it were in abstraction. During the whole of the next day we were busy in study and rehearsal. The Lord Chamberlain was somewhat concerned as to the nature of the performance we were to give. He desired to be present at a rehearsal, but here again the Prince intervened with impetuous authority. The Lord Chamberlain then sought me out in person and said that he earnestly trusted there would be nothing either in the words of the play or in the manner in which it should be played that would give offence to the illustrious audience. I replied that the play had been chosen by the Prince and that it would be well if he would address any suggestions he had to make directly to His Royal Highness. The Lord Chamberlain said that the Prince was in so irritable a frame of mind that he could ill brook any interference, but that he relied on our good sense and inherent tact to omit any word or phrase which, in the present circumstances (for he pointed out that the Court was in half-mourning) might be likely to give offence. He said that for instance any too exuberant display of buffoonery, any too great an insistence on broad jokes would be out of place at the present time. I assured him that so far from the Prince having instigated us towards clowning he had begged us to suppress all buffoonery of any kind, which had ever been distasteful to him, and this none knew so well as I.

Elsinore, like all courts, was rife with gossip, the common talk being that the Prince was courting the daughter of the Chamberlain, who, owing to the position she occupied, they professed to find beautiful, and who in reality is but an insipid minx and likely to develop on the lines of her doddering old father, while they say that she will not hear of his suit, being secretly but passionately enamoured of one of the minor courtiers, by name Osric.

Others say that the Prince's passion for the Chamberlain's daughter is a mere pretence and that it is his friend Horatio who is in reality plighted to her. But we, who know the Prince well, know that he has no thought of such things. He is an artist, and had he not had the misfortune to be born a Prince he would have been a player of first-rate excellence. Being gifted with the artistic temperament and the histrionic nature, the mode of existence which he is forced to lead amidst the conventions, the formalities, the rules, and the unvarying tediousness of stiff and stately Court decorum, is to him intolerable. He is thinking the whole time of modes of expression, pictures, phrases, situations, conceits, and his mind lives in the world of dream and holds office at the court of Art. That is why, in this nest of officials, he is like a cuckoo among a brood of respectable blackbirds.

The performance took place after the banquet on the second evening of our stay. The stage was appointed in a long, low room adjoining the banqueting-hall. Slightly raised seats for the King and the Queen were erected in the centre of the room in front of the stage, and the Court were assembled in line with them and behind them. The Chamberlain and his daughter sat in the front row, and the gossip of the place seemed to be in some way substantiated by the fact that she never took her eyes off Osric the courtier (a handsome lad) during the whole of the performance. He was standing next to the Queen's throne.

The Prince, before the trumpets sounded for the performance to begin, came to us and gave us his final instructions which bore, as ever, the stamp of his fine taste and nice discrimination, and he proved to us once more that he was by nature a professional player. When the performance began he strolled into the hall and reclined on the floor at the feet of the Chamberlain's daughter. We played as well as might be expected considering the chilling effect which cannot fail to be produced by the presence of exalted personages, for the Court had their eyes fixed on the throne and only dared to murmur approval when approval had already been expressed from that quarter. During all the first part of the play such moments were rare and indeed the audience seemed to have some difficulty in comprehending the words and the still plainer action which we suited to the words. But the Prince came to our aid, whispering audibly to his uncle and his mother and elucidating for them the passages which proved perplexing. He also made various comments to the Chamberlain's daughter, and was quick to apprehend the slightest play of feature, gesture, or intonation which struck him as being successful and true.

The Chamberlain's daughter was listless throughout and seemed to take no interest in the play, and her father was too enfeebled in mind to catch the drift of it at all, but the manifest interest which the Prince took in it, seemed, nevertheless, to cause him uneasiness, and he never ceased furtively to glance at the King and the Queen. The Queen, on the other hand, seemed much pleased, and indeed they say that she has ever been fond of spectacles and stage-playing. By the time the play had reached its climax, with the entry of Lucianus who spoke the lines which had been inserted by the Prince, the King, who had been growing more and more fretful (for he has no taste for letters) rose from his seat and gave the signal for departure, and the Chamberlain immediately gave orders that the play should cease. The King remarked that the heat in the hall was oppressive and he withdrew, followed by the Court, and the Prince, who was in an ecstasy of joy at the beautiful performance, clapped his hands loudly and congratulated us warmly, saying that he had seldom enjoyed a play so much.

So tedious is the routine at these courts that this little incident was much discussed and debated, and the Prince's conduct in so loudly applauding a play after His Majesty had signified that the performance was tedious has been severely commented on. Tomorrow we sail for Hamburg.

"THE BALLIOL TOSHER"

Letter from Professor Roger Bacon to Signor Alighieri

OXFORD, *February*, 1283.

Most illustrious Signor Alighieri,—

It is now four weeks since your son, Dante, arrived at the University, and I am able to do what I was not able to do before, to write you a short report of his progress. I greatly regret to inform you that he still persists in his obstinate determination not to enter his name on the books of any college.

As I have already told you, I consider the decision to be an unfortunate one. What it means is practically this: your son is living the life and enjoying the privileges of an undergraduate without sharing the responsibilities of the corporate life of a college; and by not being subject to the regulations of any one college he avoids to a great extent the discipline which I cannot help thinking would, in his case, be salutary. He consorts mostly with the undergraduates of Balliol College; but not, I regret to say, wholly with the scholars of that not altogether enlightened and in some ways retrograde college, but with a set of undergraduates, remarkable neither at work nor play, who are disinclined even to take athletics seriously, and who are constantly giving trouble by organizing pranks and escapades, such as climbing on the roofs, scaling the walls, and other childish pranks of the same kind.

The undergraduates of Merton and other of the older colleges of the University call your son "The Balliol Tosher," which is their way of designating a student who belongs to no particular college; and while the joke is meant in good part, I hardly think that the scion of so illustrious a family as yours, Signor Alighieri, should be known by so undignified an appellation.

With regard to your son's studies, I regret to inform you that he did not do well in responsions. He barely managed to scrape through in mathematics. On the other hand, his French and colloquial Italian carried him through, but he narrowly escaped shipwreck, curiously enough, in Latin. Your son, as you know, has a fluent, an extremely fluent knowledge, and easy familiarity with the Latin language. Whether the examiners were ruffled by what they thought a display of over-confidence, or whether, as it was said, they were nettled at being caught out by your son's quotation of an obscure classical passage, which the Latin professors criticized and corrected as if it had been of his own invention, whereas it was in reality a recently discovered fragment of Cicero, I cannot say.

It is certain they made a great deal of fuss about his pronunciation in the *viva voce* examination, alleging that your son spoke with an uncouth Tuscan accent! They complained, too, that when this peculiarity was civilly commented on (they pointed out to your son—so they said afterwards—that full allowance was being made for him, as it was appreciated he had not had time to learn to pronounce Latin *correctly*), he apparently fired up and answered back, saying that the

Italian method of pronouncing Latin, which had been good enough for Virgil, was good enough for him. Whether this trivial (!) charge (*Querelle de Latinistes !*) is well founded, I really don't know.

My own opinion, which I do not mind mentioning confidentially to you, illustrious Signor, is that your son knows Latin a great deal better than any of the *monks* and professors here; and that his use of the Latin language is classical and theirs is comparatively barbarous. But not being a classical scholar (thank Heaven !) I have really no right to any opinion.

However, one of the examiners was fortunately a man of the world, who had once had the honour of being entertained by His Holiness at the Vatican, and he treated your son's remarks as a joke.

The Latin professors now say that your son is making considerable progress in Latin conversation, and that his pronunciation is improving every day, and indeed they hold out hopes of his being entirely cured of his Tuscan accent by the end of the month.

I cannot help thinking it regrettable that he should have made great friends with a certain Sir Michael Scott, who, although he is a Knight and comes from a respectable family, has a deplorable leaning towards a charlatan form of necromancy and other doubtful practices.

I have no fault to find with Dante in the practice of his religion, except that he resolutely refuses to abstain on Fridays. It appears he obtained a dispensation from his Confessor (an ingenious Benedictine monk) on the grounds that, having done his military service in Italy and being liable to be called to the colours, he is still technically a soldier.

He attends lectures, but not as regularly as I could

wish, and, indeed, during one lecture, delivered by the Master of Merton, he was discovered, I regret to say, writing a sonnet in his notebook. The poem in question was written in Italian.

I will write again, most illustrious Signor, before long, and report further progress.

I remain,
Your most obedient, humble Servant,
ROGER BACON.

From Roger Bacon to Messire Thibaut, Professor of Science at the University of Paris

OXFORD, *March*, 1283.

My dear Colleague,—

Many thanks for your letter of February 1st, which has only just reached me. The almost indescribable inconvenience caused not only by the delays in the post, but also by the extreme carelessness of the postal authorities, and the disorder of their arrangements, has led me to wonder whether one might not devise some means of communication with persons at a distance which would not be at the mercy of our deplorable roads and unreliable couriers.

I think I have found out what is needed. I have devised an extremely simple and practical method for propagating electric waves over long distances. The vibrations passed through a wire are used to set up similar vibrations in the ether. These waves vibrate in every direction; and I have devised a simple receiving instrument, which I transmit herewith, and which will enable you to receive the messages I send you. (I enclose the transmitter also with full directions on the wrapper.) I think by means of this simple device we shall be able to correspond easily, not only with distant countries, but also with the neighbouring planets, Mars and Venus.

Be careful, however, to send nothing confidential in this way, as it is impossible to believe that many other students in other countries will not have thought of the same idea; and I need not point out to a scientist of your calibre that the vibrations which pass through the ether can be tapped by anyone who is in possession of a receiver, wherever he may be.

I have made no mention of this device to the College authorities so far, because I have no doubt it would arouse their conservative and reactionary prejudice.

Only the other day I dropped a hint to the Master of Balliol about my long-distance speaking tube, by which I daily communicate with my next-door neighbour, Dr. Celsius of Wittenberg, and the Master sniffed and said he did not like *hasty* things.

So we must be careful. Care is all the more necessary at this moment, because an undergraduate named Michael Scott has been the means of discrediting the cause of science by indulging in grossly unscientific charlatanry, such as devil-raising, instantaneous solar portraiture, ventriloquism and magnetic suggestion. It is a scandal that he is not sent down; but his father, who is a Patron of the University, has exerted powerful pressure, and so far Scott's practices have been hushed up.

I am sending this letter and parcel in the care of a trusty friend, and I shall know when they reach you by receiving an electrical vibratory message in the manner I have indicated.

The Italian student to whom you gave a letter of introduction to me, D. Alighieri, has not a scientific mind. He is inattentive, hot-tempered, and obstinate, and were it not for his connexions and the friendship I have for his respected father, I should recommend his transfer to the sister University.

Believe me, my dear Colleague,

Your sincere friend,

ROGER BACON.

Letter from Sir Michael Scott, Oxford (non-Collegiate), to Bertold Schwarz, Student of the University of Wittenberg

OXFORD, *March*, 1283.

Dear Bertold,

I hope you will find this letter, carefully hidden as it is in the tome of the preposterous would-be scientific volume, I am sending you. It is safest so. I find Oxford more and more tedious. The Professors are hide-bound pedants, and the students most of them are overgrown children. I despair of finding a single disciple. I had hopes of one, a newcomer, called Alighieri. He showed glimmerings of intelligence, but I soon found that the only things that interest him really are books, anecdotes, personal questions and verse, and that he takes no interest whatever in science. He was present in my rooms a few nights ago when I was about to raise the devil. We were all sitting at a round table. Crosses had been taken off and holy images removed, and the sitting gave every promise of being unusually successful and interesting, when this Italian youth, who was holding a pencil in his hand for the sake of spirit-writing, pressed too hard on it, and breaking the point, exclaimed, "Santo Diavolo," in a loud voice. Of course the Devil was offended and refused to appear for the rest of the evening. Nobody except you and I realize how dreadfully touchy the Devil is, let alone the minor demons, and how careful one has to be in dealing with him.

I attend the lectures of Professor Bacon. He is terribly behind the times, and still persists in thinking that the earth moves round the sun. This is the last new fad of the Professors (they teach us that privately, of course) and of course we have to pretend to believe it—*they* think it very daring! Some of the students think that he trots out all these would-be paradoxes with his tongue in his cheek, but I do not agree. I think Bacon is *really* ignorant. He has forbidden me to point out the whereabouts of water, in spite of the great shortage just at this moment, as if that were a trick instead of a purely scientific experiment.

It is all very disheartening and I am seriously thinking of giving up science altogether, and taking to the Schoolmen or to modern languages. The modern languages set for Greats are Assyrian, Basque and Irish.

Please let me hear from you soon.

Your affectionate friend,

MICHAEL SCOTT.

P.S.—I forgot to tell you that the experiments that I carried out of throwing a small bridge across the Tweed, and setting the bells of Notre Dame ringing from Salamanca, where I happened to be staying in the vacation, were both completely successful.

Letter from Stephen de Cossington, undergraduate at Balliol College, to Thomas Felton, of the University of Cambridge

Vincent's Hostel,
OXFORD, *March*, 1283.

Dear Tom,

We expect you next Saturday morning, and we are sending horses to meet you at Abingdon. On Saturday afternoon we have a supper at the Mitre Hostel, and on Sunday we will dine in College after High Mass, and sup at Gloucester with the Benedictines, who have an excellent after-supper cordial.

I am not able to give you any interesting river news, as an instrument called a watch, which a chap called Scott made for me to compare the times with, was broken to pieces by my scout. I foolishly left it on my table when I was changing, so I can only give you a little general criticism.

Merton are good in the stem, as far back as five, but after that not up to much. They have an excellent stroke and seven, both of them first-rate College oars, if not up to 'Varsity form. Five, three and four seem to be chiefly engaged in testing the strength of their front stops. However, we all know how Merton can race when it comes to the pinch. In the Gloucester boat you can see a fine example of what first-class coaching can do with a poor lot of men. If they had a real tearer to row five they would be well able to keep their place, but five is, I think, a weak point, a *very weak* point in their boat.

Branson is stroking badly, he washes out so, and *bustles* his men.

I think we shall go up, we are short and ugly, but we all *plug*.

Don't forget to bring a rattle and a speaking tube.

Good-bye, vieux Harricot,

Yrs. etc.

STEVE.

P.S.—I quite forget to tell you that the little Dago at bow, Allagers, we call him, his real name is something like Alligeary, is an honest worker, although his body form is not quite so good as that of—say Nickals.

Letter from Guy de Faryngdon, of Balliol College, Oxford, to William Beauchamp, of Grays Inn Court, London

AT THE SIGN OF ST. SIMON OF THE GRIDIRON,

OXFORD, *March*, 1283.

Dear Bill,

John Chandos has been sent down; all owing to that fool of an Italian, Daggers Allagers, or, if you prefer it, Dante Alighieri. This is what happened. We have to write an essay about the Greek Tragedians, Aeschylus, Sophocles and Euripides, and read it out to the Master. We all did something. The Master whistled like a bullfinch while I read mine, but said nothing. We all got through all right, except John. This is what happened. He had been out hawking all the day before, and he came back utterly fagged. He couldn't sit down and write an essay. He's not a fluent writer, as you know, at any time.

We had all done ours and read them, so we were of no use to him. So he asked Allagers to write an essay for him. The Dago had already written and read his in Latin, and it made the Master scratch, it was so difficult. So he wrote another for John, on his head, in English, and John took it and read it out to the Master. Of course it was much too good, but all went well till he came to a sentence which John read like this:—

"Thus midway between the elemental fire and superhuman energy of Aeschylus, and the speculative courage and subtle sympathy of Euripides, we have the ideal serenity, the marvellous music, and the large untroubled wisdom of Bofocles." Here the Master stopped him and said, "Surely, Mr. Chandos, you mean 'Sophocles'?" John went to the window and held up Allagers' crabbed script to the light, scrutinised it carefully, and said, "No, Master, it's *Bofocles.*" The result is that John has been sent down for a term, and Allagers has been gated for a week.

I hear you are going to read a paper to the Beowolf Society. I shall be there.

Yours, etc.,
GUY.

Letter from Roger Bacon to Signor Alighieri

OXFORD, *April*, 1283.

Most illustrious Signor Alighieri,

Please accept my most respectful thanks for your truly amiable and interesting letter. The news you send me from Italy and the information on the subject of the new gas discovered by Fra Bartolomeo is exactly what I needed. I am delighted to hear that Signora Alighieri and yourself are enjoying good health. I am myself very tolerably well, and would have nothing to complain of were it not for the spring winds. However,

> Non semper imbres nubibus hispidos
> Manant in agros, aut mare Caspium
> Vexant inaequales procellae,

as I believe one of the Latin poets says. Please do not let any of the Latinists see my quotation. I am certain they would detect in it some inaccuracy, besides which they despise Horace, the only readable Latin author. There is no doubt that all the professors here and all the University authorities are deplorably behind the times. They are hide-bound and fundamentally hostile to progress, and, if they only knew it, to all research and to the cause of learning. This leads me to a topic which I am afraid will be as painful to you as it is unpleasant and vexatious to myself. It is with regard to your son, Dante.

I have myself since his residence at the University found him extremely amiable, and he has never given me the slightest cause for complaint. I must impress upon you at once that I am in no way responsible for what I am about to relate to you. Last Saturday evening the undergraduates of Balliol College held what they call a "Bump Supper," a festivity celebrating certain aquatic contests and feats on the water, which I need not trouble you with in detail.

When the festivity was ended, the young undergraduates, who, I think, had unwisely been regaled in the College Hall with copious draughts of a particularly heady beverage which is made by the Benedictine monks, not unnaturally indulged in dance, song, and various frolics. Michael Scott, whom I have already told you about, was, of course, the ringleader in this business, and to my great annoyance he took from my rooms a provision of a new powder which I have been experimenting with lately and which is in reality only a new form of a very old thing, namely, "Greek Fire."

The boys made a bonfire in the quadrangle, and, when they had set it alight, threw into the flames a quantity of the powder. This produced a small explosion. Some of the trees were damaged, and the coat-of-arms over the Master's house was injured and scorched. The Master came out of the Lodge and sent the undergraduates to bed. They departed quietly enough, but when all was still two of them (who they were is not known, but it is suspected that Scott was one of them) emerged from their rooms later, and with some paints that they procured, I do not know how, climbed up to the escutcheon over the arch of the Master's Lodge and painted a bar sinister across the handsome coat-of-arms.

The next day the culprits refused to come forward. It was known what boys had taken part in the bonfire escapade, as their names had been taken down, and the two most prominent figures in this really quite harmless prank were said to be Michael Scott and your son Dante. Had your son consented to belong to a college this would not have occurred; it would simply have been a question of a college meeting.

As it was, Scott, who is also a non-collegiate, and your son were summoned before the Vice-Chancellor of the University. They both admitted that they had had a hand in lighting the bonfire, but they both denied having had anything to do with the defacing of the escutcheon, and also denied all knowledge of the identity of the culprits. The Vice-Chancellor waived the accusation of defacing the escutcheon as far as Scott and your son were concerned, but they were both asked to apologize to the Master for the damage done originally to the escutcheon, which was the cause of the second and more wounding insult. It was pointed out to them that, as the Master's sister was staying, and was known to be staying, at the Lodge at the time, and that as she is in poor health and a martyr to insomnia (the Master will not let her take any of the harmless drugs I have prescribed), it would be only civil on their part if they apologized, if only for the noise and disturbance they had made.

Scott consented to apologize, but your son looked upon the matter differently. He said he had nothing to do either with the damage done to the escutcheon or with the painting of it subsequently, and that it was impossible for him to apologize since he had committed no offence. It was pointed out that he had been seen in the quadrangle with a group of undergraduates, who were dancing round the bonfire. Your son pointed out that it was his custom to walk in the quadrangle every night before going to bed, and he was not to blame for the presence of a bonfire at the moment he was taking his daily walk.

The Master, anxious to meet him half-way, said they would be quite satisfied if your son were to express regret that the Master and his sister had been disturbed, leaving on one side the origin and authorship of the disturbance. Your son said he regretted not being able to apologize, but that with him it was a point of honour and a sacred principle *never* to apologize. He appears here to have spoken somewhat vehemently and perhaps rashly. He reminded the Vice-Chancellor that the Master of Balliol had once said in a lecture, "Never apologize." No words and no arguments, neither persuasion nor threats, had the slightest effect on your son's attitude. He resolutely refused to budge from the position he had adopted, and when pressed by the Board, and reminded by them that they had the right to ask him to leave the University, he is reported to have used fiery and perhaps intemperate expressions, and to have said (though I do not quite credit it) that he would be only too glad to shake the dust of Oxford from his feet.

The result was that the Vice-Chancellor had no course open to him but to request your son to leave the University, and he has just been to take leave of me.

I need hardly tell you that it is with unfeigned regret that I part with him. All this lamentable incident proves once more that what we need at Oxford is a radical change in the curriculum. Greek should no longer be compulsory, and astrology and alchemy should be made a *sine qua non* for responsions. As it is, the authorities are so wrapped up in the literature of a dead and forgotten age, so blind to the present and so deaf to the clarion call of the future (with all its possibilities), that no progress is possible. New discoveries are being made every day, and they, the teachers of the young, not only pass them heedlessly by, but they actually put obstacles in the way of pioneers and spokes in the wheels of research.

However, I fear there is nothing to be done. I am sorry to see your son leave Oxford so prematurely. He is not a man of science, and never will be, but in spite of that I seem to see in him the promise of a vigorous mind. The vitality of his temperament, as this last episode shows, is only too marked, but in our personal relations I never found him anything but civil and respectful.

I should not recommend his going to Cambridge.

I am, with many regrets, once more your obedient servant,

ROGER BACON.

ROMEO AND ROSALINE

One fairer than my love! the all-seeing sun
Ne'er saw her match since first the world begun.

ROMEO ON ROSALINE.
Romeo and Juliet, Act I, Scene ii.

Is Rosaline, whom thou didst love so dear,
So soon forsaken? Young men's love then lies
Not truly in their hearts but in their eyes.
Jesu Maria! what a deal of brine
Hath wash'd thy sallow cheeks for Rosaline!

Romeo and Juliet, Act II, Scene ii.

Letter from Rosaline to her Friend Olivia

VERONA.

My dear Olivia,

Thank you very much for your kind letter. I am only just beginning to be able to write letters, as you may well imagine after all that we have gone through, and I am still in half-mourning, although *they* say this is ridiculous. As a matter of fact, nobody has a better right to be in mourning for Romeo than I, considering that he would certainly have married me had it not been for a series of quite extraordinary accidents. Mamma says that I was to blame, but I will tell you exactly what happened, and you can judge for yourself.

I made Romeo's acquaintance two years ago. We at once got on well together, and I never minded his childishness, which used to get on some people's nerves. He was the kind of person whom it was really impossible to dislike, because he was so impetuous, so full of high spirits and good humour. Some people thought he was good looking; I never did. It was never his looks that attracted me, but I liked him for *himself.* Wherever I went he used to be there, and whenever we met he always talked to me the whole time and never looked at any one else, so that we were *practically* engaged although nothing was announced.

After this had gone on for some time Mamma became annoyed; she said we must do one thing or the other; we must either be engaged and announce our engagement or else that I must give up seeing Romeo altogether. This of course I refused to do. At last we made a compromise: in our own house I was allowed to see Romeo as much as I liked, but if I went out to banquets or masques I was to talk to other people and not to Romeo. Papa and Mamma had nothing against my marrying Romeo, because Mamma never liked the Capulets, although they are Papa's relations. The result of this compromise, which was only arranged quite lately, was quite disastrous. Romeo could not understand it at all. He thought it was my fault, and that I was growing tired of him. It was then that he begged me to let our engagement be publicly announced. I did not want the announcement to be made public until the winter, because one never really has such fun once an engagement is known. However, I would no doubt have given in in the end. As it was, Romeo was annoyed, and just before the Capulets' banquet we had a scene. I told him quite plainly that he had no business to treat me as if I belonged to him. I had given him to understand, however, that I would be at the Capulets' banquet, and I fully expected him to come and to beg for a reconciliation.

He came to the banquet, and it so happened that Lady Capulet's daughter, who was far too young for that kind of thing, was allowed to come down that night. A child of that age is of course allowed to do anything, as it is supposed not to matter what they do. And as she had been told that the one thing she was not to do was to speak to a Montague, out of sheer naughtiness and perverseness she went to Romeo and made the most outrageous advances to him. Romeo, out of *pique* and simply to annoy me, kept up the farce, and they say that he even climbed over a wall that night, right into the house of the Capulets, and spoke to Juliet! All this time Juliet was betrothed to her cousin, the County Paris, and it was arranged that their marriage was to take place shortly.

What exactly happened we none of us know, but it is quite certain that Lady Capulet had found out what was going on, and having heard that Romeo had been climbing her garden wall and serenading Juliet under her very nose, she thought it would be an excellent opportunity to settle the old family quarrel and reconcile the two families by an alliance. So she forced Romeo to *promise* her he would marry Juliet, and some people say that the marriage ceremony was actually performed in secret, but this is *not true*, as I will tell you later. Of course, Lady Capulet did not dare tell her husband; on the contrary, every arrangement was made for Juliet's marriage with Paris; but the day before it was to come off a put-up quarrel was brought about between Romeo and one of the Capulets, which ended in Romeo's being banished to Mantua. He wrote to me every day, saying how miserable he was that all this tiresome business had happened, and how he was longing to see me again, and how it was not his fault.

Lady Capulet then gave Juliet a strong sleeping draught, which was to have the effect of making her like a corpse for forty-two hours. Every one was to think she was dead. She was to be taken to the vault of the Capulets and Romeo was to fetch her after the forty-two hours were over, when she should come to from her sleep. This was Lady Capulet's plan, and Romeo of course could do nothing but accept it, much as he must have hated that kind of thing. Romeo had many faults, but I must say he was never deceitful. I did not know anything about it at the time. All we knew was that, owing to a street brawl which had ended unfortunately, Romeo had been banished to Mantua. He wrote from there every day. He said over and over again in his letters that he was in great difficulties, but that he hoped to be back soon and see me again. I did not answer his letters because I was annoyed at the way in which he had spoken to Juliet at the ball. I had not then heard about the incident of the orchard, otherwise I should have been angrier still.

While things were in this state the whole matter took a tragic turn by the stupidity of Lady Capulet's nurse, who gave Juliet the wrong sleeping draught. Instead of giving her a potion which made her sleep for forty-two hours, they gave her some very strong rat poison which happened to be lying about. She drank it, poor thing, and never woke again.

Romeo came back from Mantua to meet Juliet at the vault, where he no doubt intended to have a final explanation with her and her family, to explain the whole thing: his engagement to me, and the impossibility of his contracting any alliance with the Capulet family, especially as he had very strong principles on this point. But when he got to the tomb he found the County Paris, who was nominally engaged to Juliet, and of course extremely angry to find a Montague in such a place. They fought and Paris killed Romeo, thus putting an end to all Lady Capulet's intrigues. But she was not to be defeated thus. She had already bribed an old Franciscan monk, called Friar Laurence, to say that he had secretly *married* Juliet and Romeo, and her nurse (a horrible old woman) corroborated the friar's evidence. And so, with very much solemnity and fuss, a reconciliation was brought about between the two families, and they say that Benvolio, Montague's nephew, is to marry Katherine, Lady Capulet's niece by marriage, and thus the quarrel between the families has finally been settled and Lady Capulet has got her way.

I don't mind the two families being reconciled in the least; in fact we are all very glad of it, as life in Verona was made quite intolerable by their constant brawling and quarrelling. But what I do think is unfair, and what is particularly irritating to *me*, is that everybody, even Papa and Mamma, take it for granted that Romeo was really in love with Juliet, and had given up all thoughts of me. Nobody knows the truth except me, and I cannot tell it without making myself appear conceited and ridiculous. You can imagine how irritating this is. Of course, when all this happened I was so overcome by the shock that I was very ill and did not care what was said, one way or the other. Papa and Mamma had to take me to Venice for a few days, as I was in such a state of nerves. Now, the change of air has done me good, and I am slowly getting better again. I am told that everybody believes that Romeo and Juliet were married by Friar Laurence. Of course, once such a legend gets about nothing will ever make people think the contrary. But even if they *were* married it would not really affect me, for it was a sheer case of coercion. If Romeo did marry Juliet he did it because he could not help himself, after having been discovered in her garden by that old cat Lady Capulet, who is a very, very wicked woman, and capable of anything. In fact I am not at all sure that she did not poison her daughter on purpose, and so bring about the reconciliation between the two families without having all the trouble of facing and defeating her husband's opposition to the match.

When you next come to see me I will show you Romeo's letters. Fortunately I have kept them all. They are very beautiful, and some of them are in rhyme; and you will see for yourself whether he loved me or not. I cannot read them without crying. You have no idea what lovely things he says in them. For instance, one day he sent me a pair of silk gloves, and with them, written on a small scroll:

> Oh that I were a glove upon thy hand,
> That I might touch thy cheek.

His letters were full of lovely things like that, and I cannot think of them without crying.

Your loving
ROSALINE.

THE DUCHESS OF FERRARA

Letter from Sir Antony Wodeville, travelling in Italy for pleasure, to his father

FERRARA, *March* 14, 1517.

Sir,

We arrived at Ferrara last Saturday after a tedious journey and found spacious, if rather chilly, rooms in the Hotel Royal York, which was named after our King while his elder brother was still alive, and is kept by a charming host, Signor Presto. The food is delicious, and as soon as we arrived, Signor Presto gave us each a glass of an Italian cordial which he calls *Prestissimo.* It was most invigorating. We lost no time in writing our names on the Duke and the Duchess, and on the following day, we received an invitation to a *banquet intime.* The Duchess receives her more intimate friends on Monday evenings. The manner in which the invitation was sent is worthy of note. We received no card, but a slip was left in our room, at the Hotel, saying that the clothes which would be worn at the Duchess's collation on Monday evening were short doublets, black sashes, daggers, but no swords, and only the order of the Golden Fleece, which neither I nor Cousin Charles have got. We presented ourselves at the Palace, and we were received by the Lords in Waiting. We were offered some coffee, but I thought it might spoil our appetite to drink coffee *before* dinner, so I left mine untouched and cousin Charles did the same. We were then ushered into a magnificent apartment, where, after we had waited a few minutes, doors were thrown open, clarions were sounded, and the Duke and the Duchess entered.

The Duke looked pale and rather worn. He is said to suffer from insomnia, but I was told in confidence that the real cause of his ill-health is that he never ceases taking quack medicines as a preventive against the food served at his table, which, in obedience to family tradition, and the etiquette of the Court, is sumptuous and highly spiced.

After we had made our obeisance we followed the Duke and Duchess into the dining-hall, and I had the honour of sitting on the Duchess's right.

The Duchess has a noble presence. She was simply dressed in black, with no other jewels or ornaments than one large and exquisitely wrought enamel ring. During the repast, a band of minstrels in the gallery played some Italian ditties, one of which, called *Addio Napoli*, particularly took my fancy.

There were not many guests. The Duchess told me she had invited all the chief representatives of the nobility to meet me, but that the prevailing epidemic of indigestion brought on by the fatal habit prevalent in Ferrara of eating oysters in May had compelled many of them to decline. There were, however, some distinguished and eminent men present, nearly all of them doctors and men of science, one or two Cardinals, the Chief of the Secret Police and the Commander-in-Chief of the Army, who in Ferrara ranks below the Field-Marshal, several dowagers, and a young artist only just seventeen, called Cellini. He was on a visit from Rome, and the Duchess told me he is really a clever jeweller—for an amateur, and had made her the ring she was wearing. It was an ingenious ring, she said, and contained a pastille for the throat. She finds the north winds at Ferrara most trying. Cellini seemed a youth of spirit and wit, and his sallies, which were sometimes audacious, were much relished by the Duke and Duchess, who seemed to allow him a great deal of licence, but cousin Jack and I thought that when he, with the help of an orange, gave an imitation of a lady being seasick, he was going too far. The Duke laughed heartily. But the Duchess said she had no patience with people who imagined they were ill. One of the doctors present, Signor Colombo, said that seasickness, like all other diseases, was only due to the imagination, and that one only had to say to oneself that one was quite well and one was quite well. The Duchess heartily concurred with this statement, but the Duke said that if that were true there would be no more use for doctors or drugs. He had himself, he said, derived great benefit from a medicine called Antitoxin, upon which the Duchess laughed amiably and changed the conversation. The Duchess is deservedly popular at Ferrara. She is not only a patroness of learning and of the arts, but a great supporter of all charitable institutions and she spends much time and takes endless trouble in the performance of private charities. Her face reflects the virtues of her character and the strength of her intelligence. It is a pity that no adequate portrait of her exists. She sat to Leonardo da Vinci, but the painter, she told me, was not successful in her case. He gave her such a peevish expression that the Duke had the portrait destroyed. She deplored the lack of portrait painters in Italy, and she was kind enough to say that, in respect of the arts, Italy was far behind England. I told her that this could hardly be said to be true, although I admitted that the English were the most musical people in the world. She agreed, and the minstrels were asked to play, and performed with masterly skill, one of the most recent compositions of the King. The Duchess asked a great deal after the King and Queen Katharine, and Cardinal Wolsey, who, she said, corresponded with her regularly. She said she was sure the Scottish and the Irish problems gave the King much anxiety, but she felt certain that the Cardinal would end by solving them both. He was a man of such infinite resource and so persuasive in argument. He had so much personal charm and was so quick.

At this moment the Duke interrupted her and said that Cardinal Wolsey had no sense of humour. He had tested this the first time he had ever met his Eminence. " He came to see me," said the Duke, " and as he walked into my library I threw a cushion at his head. It was an accurate shot, although I say it who shouldn't. Would you believe it, his Eminence never even smiled."

We all agreed that this betrayed a distorted sense of humour on the part of his Eminence, except the Duchess, who said that the cushions in the Palace Library were too heavy. " Alphonso throws so hard," she added to me.

The talk then veered on to the prevailing epidemic caused by oysters. All the various men of science present offered different explanations to account for the mortality among oyster eaters, but Cellini laughed at them and said that he believed the recent increase of mortality among the aristocracy of Ferrara had nothing to do with oysters at all. When asked to what he attributed the number of regrettable deaths in high places he answered quietly : " Weed killer."

"Yes," said the Duchess—"*amateur* gardeners are very careless."

She was, she explained, an assiduous gardener. The worst of Italy was one could only have a spring garden. Everything was burnt up in summer and the Italians took no trouble with their gardens. They preferred flowers in pots. It was only foreigners, in reality only the English, who had gardens in Ferrara. The English were so clever at gardening.

"But still," said Cellini, taking no notice of the conversation on gardening, "you will admit that it is rather a strange coincidence that last Monday Countess Strozzi dined at the Palazzo Alberti and died as soon as she reached home, that the day after the Marquis of Guidarelli after dining at the same house was taken violently ill and died in the same night, and that two days later the great singer Dorio after having sung at the place took some slight refreshment at the buffet and immediately complained of pains. He was dead within an hour."

"But think," said the Duke with a chuckle, "of the numbers that survived."

"If people will eat oysters in May, what can you expect?" said the Duchess.

"It's the pearls, not the oysters that are dangerous," said Cellini.

At that moment a man called Michelotto entered the dining-room. He is treated at Court with the highest respect, and spiteful people say he is the Duke's bravo. He apparently knew all the guests except Doctor Colombo. He walked up to him. He was wearing long, gauntleted, buckskin gloves.

"Excuse my glove," he said to the doctor.

The doctor, who was feeling the heat, turned pale.

They shook hands. Shortly afterwards the Duke and Duchess retired, then went home. Half an hour after we had returned from the banquet, Signor Presto came into our room in great agitation and announced that Doctor Colombo had died suddenly from eating oysters.

A FIRST NIGHT

Letter from Jean-Antoine de Binet to a Friend in Paris, July 20, 1602

Yesterday I went to the theatre to see a Tragedy played by the Lord Chamberlain, his servants, called "*The Revenge of Hamlet, Prince of Denmark.*" I was taken thither by Guasconi, who is attached to the Italian Ambassador, and who desired that I should not miss any of the curiosities of the city. The play was new, and the theatre was crowded with people, many of whom were of high rank, since noblemen in this country are fond of visiting the playhouse. They sit in places kept for them on the stage, and encourage the players by applause, and they express their approval and their blame.

The play is written partly in a kind of verse, which is pleasing to the ear and not without a certain happy fancy; but Guasconi told me that the English, who have learnt our science and make sonnets and madrigals after the pattern of our masters, do not consider this kind of writing to be either poetry or literature; these rough and unpolished rhythms are used to tickle the popular ear and to please the taste of the common people.

There were in the theatre many well-known faces. Sir Bacon was sitting in the front, but he went to sleep shortly after the beginning of the play, and slept right until the end, none daring to disturb him. At the end of the play his servants woke him up by shaking him. He is a busy man, and goes to the theatre for repose, liking well the music, the high screeching of the players, and the buzz of tongues, and finding them conducive to repose. In one of the boxes Guasconi pointed me out the beautiful Countess of Nottingham, who, he said, is considered to be by the English one of their most beautiful countrywomen. She has the marks of race, and was richly and elegantly dressed in black and crimson colours. With her was a young nobleman whom I took to be her son, but Guasconi told me that this was not so. He was her second husband. One nobleman, the Earl of Essex, arrived in the middle of the performance, and talked loudly to his friends, paying but little attention to the players. Since his father was beheaded not long ago it was considered a lapse in taste on his part to visit the theatre so soon. In the theatre were several well-known players from other theatres, who were much clapped by the populace when they entered. The crowd was good-humoured, and pleased with the show: but they made a great noise, eating oranges and nuts, and throwing shells and peel right and left. There were also in the audience some men of letters, scholars and noblemen, whose fame as writers of verse is the talk of the town. For instance, Lord Southampton, who has written over a hundred sonnets; Sir Iger and the Countess of Pembrock, the author of "The Fall of Troy," which those who know say is the finest epic which has been written since the death of Virgil. There were also many students, who were tempestuous and unruly in the expression of their enjoyment, and among these many vagabond writers and ballad-mongers.

The show was not displeasing, being full of much excellent clowning and fine dresses. It is a tale of murder and revenge such as have been brought into the fashion by the Italian story-tellers. It is brutal, and therefore suits the English taste, for Guasconi tells me the English will not go to the playhouse unless they can see tales of battle and murder with plenty of fighting on the stage, mixed with grotesque episodes and rough horseplay. The players declaimed their words nicely, and the utterance of the verse, especially that which was spoken by the young boy who played the part of the mad heroine of the play, struck me as being not unmelodious poetry, but when I said this to the young literary noblemen with whom we supped after the performance, they split their sides with laughter, and said how impossible it was for a foreigner to judge the literature of a country which was not his own.

The author of the play, whose name I have forgotten, but which was something like John or James Shockper or Shicksperry, was himself, they told me, one of the players, which proved that he could neither be a man of education nor capable of writing his own tongue. In the play, they told me, he had played the part of the ghost. If this really be so, he cannot be a man of talent, for he spoke his lines so feebly and so haltingly that the vagabonds in the body of the theatre laughed and interrupted him several times, shouting such things as "Speak louder!" and "Go back to your grave." The stage plays are, I was told, almost always written by players, for they best know what suits the popular taste, being of the populace, and vagabonds themselves.

The scene which pleased the audience most was

that of a fight in which the players fought bravely, more after the Italian style than the French, and the audience was greatly delighted by the close of the play, and laughed heartily when all the characters were killed and rolled about on the stage. The actor who played the King was especially popular; he had a jovial face, so that whenever he spoke, and sometimes even before he spoke, the audience laughed, heartily enjoying his comic talent.

There is no intelligible story in the play, nor is it possible to follow the sequence of events that happen on the stage; but it is rather the aim of the performance to present the public with a series of varied pictures, pleasant to the eye owing to the finery, the brave dresses, the glint of steel rapiers, the tinselled cloaks, and pleasing to the ear owing to the interludes of viol and hautboy playing.

At the end of the performance there was loud clapping, and the chief actor, who is famous in this country—so famous, indeed, that there is talk of emancipating him from his position as a vagabond and making him equal to a soldier of the Queen—was called on to the stage; nor would the public let him depart until he had spoken to them, which he did. He thanked them for their warm welcome, and for expressing their pleasure at the performance of the fine play which John or James Shicksperry had written. He said he had felt sure that this play would not disappoint them, and he intended before long to give them another of the same kind, in which there would be still more murders, still more fighting, many more ghosts, and yet finer dresses. What the name of that play was, he said, was as yet a secret: who had written it was a secret. Here the audience shouted out: "We all know who has written it, it is old John or James." (Now I come to think of it: I remember his name was Bill or Billy or Ben.) Since they had guessed, he said, he would not conceal it any longer: it *was* Billy, and the play, which he knew they would enjoy, and in which there was plenty of clowning, was called *King Lear*.

The audience was pleased at this, and cheered for several minutes. They shouted for the author, for old Ben, and went on shouting while people hurried backward and forward across the stage. The author did not come forward, and the shouting continued. At last the chief actor returned, and bowing to the audience, said that old Ben was no longer in the house: he had gone to the tavern. After this there was more cheering, and the actor, kissing his hand to the audience, left the stage.

Guasconi took me to the Mermaid Tavern, a low place where the actors go after such performances, and where some of the nobles and the learned repair also, for the sake of change and to enjoy the spectacle. Here we were obliged to drink a great deal of a hot and nauseous mixture called sack, which is made of good wines spoilt by the admixture of much sugar and spice. I hate these English mixtures; their sweetmeats are made of sugared cake mixed with meat, and with their meat they eat sugared fruits. You can imagine how nauseous is this system, and indeed it reminds me of their plays. Their plays are like their plum puddings, full of great lumps of suet in which little sweet plums and currants are imbedded, but difficult to find. I said this to Guasconi, but he told me I must not judge of the English either by their food or their plays, but that if I wished to judge of their literature I should read the Sonnets of the Countess of Rutland, and he quoted one which begins:

Shall I compare thee to a summer's day?

Moreover, he said, the English were not a literary but a musical nation. Their music was unequalled in all Europe; it was the art (and the only art) in which they excelled; witness the divine melodies of Orlando Gibbons, Morley, and Dowland, which, indeed, I had heard performed at the Court, and had greatly enjoyed, for we have nothing like it in France.

The author of the play, Ben Shicksperry, arrived at the Mermaid late, and a learned man who was there, and whose name they told me was Will Johnson, condescended not only to speak but to drink with him. The players made a great noise, toasting each other, likewise the noblemen, who spent the time in violent disputes on the merits and demerits of this writer and that writer. After a time everybody began to talk of public affairs, of the policy of Spain, and of a party of English politicians whom they called pro-Spaniards: and they all agreed that these latter deserved to be immersed in a horse-trough, and so, late in the night, they set out to accomplish this unrefined joke. The English, in spite of their great culture, and their learning, their wonderful power of speaking foreign languages—for every one of the noblemen speaks perfectly not only Greek and Latin, but five or six other languages, and is well versed in astrology, music, and chess-playing—the English, I repeat, in spite of all this, have something barbarous at heart, which is awakened after they have partaken much of that nauseous potion called sack.

THE POET, THE PLAYER, AND THE LITERARY AGENT

Letter from Mr. Nichols, Literary Agent, to Lord Bacon

My Lord,

I have now submitted the plays which your lordship forwarded to me to seven publishers : Messrs. Butter, Mr. Blount, Mr. Thorpe, Mr. Waterson, Mr. Andrew Wise, Mr. Steevens, and Mr. G. Eld; and I very much regret to inform your lordship that I have not been able to persuade any of these publishers to make an offer for the publication of any of the plays, although Mr. Thorpe would be willing to print them at your lordship's expense, provided that they appeared under your lordship's name. The cost, however, would be very great. No one of these publishers is willing to publish the plays anonymously, and they agree in saying that while the plays contain passages of exceptional merit, there is, unfortunately, at the present moment no demand in the market for the literary play. This form of literature is in fact at present a drug on the market; and they suggest that your lordship, whose anonymity I have of course respected, should convert these plays into essays, epics, masques, or any other form which is at present popular with the reading public. There is certainly very little chance at present of my being able to find a publisher for work of this description. Therefore I await your lordship's instructions before sending them to any other publishers.

At the same time I would suggest, should your lordship not consider such a course to be derogatory, that I should submit the plays in question to one or two of the best known theatrical managers with a view to performance. I would of course keep the authorship of the plays a secret.

Awaiting your lordship's commands in this matter,

I am,

Your lordship's most humble and obedient servant,

J. J. Nichols.

Letter from Mr. Nichols to Lord Bacon

My Lord,

I am in receipt of a communication from Mr. Fletcher, the chief of the Lord Chamberlain's servants, now playing at the Globe Theatre. Mr. Fletcher informs me that he has read the plays with considerable interest. He considers that they are not only promising but contain passages of positive merit.

Mr. Fletcher, however, adds that your lordship is no doubt fully aware that such plays are totally unsuited to the stage; indeed it would be impossible to produce them for many reasons. With regard to the first batch, namely, the Biblical series, the *David and Saul* trilogy, *Joseph and Potiphar*, and *King Nebuchadnezzar*, there could of course be no question of their production, however much they might be altered or adapted for the stage; for it would be impossible to obtain a licence, not only on account of the religious subject matter, which of necessity must prove shocking to the greater part of the audience, but also owing to the boldness of the treatment. Mr. Fletcher begs me to tell your lordship that he is far from suggesting that your lordship has handled these solemn themes in any but the most reverent manner; but at the same time he is anxious to point out that the public, being but insufficiently educated, is likely to misunderstand your lordship's intentions, and to regard your lordship's imaginative realization of these sacred figures as sacrilegious.

With regard to the second series, the tragedies, Mr. Fletcher states that the play entitled *Hamlet* might, if about three-quarters of the whole play were omitted, be made fit for stage presentation, but even then the matter would be extremely hazardous. Even if enough of the play were left in order to render the story coherent, the performance would still last several hours and be likely to try the patience of any but a special audience. Such a play would doubtless appeal to a limited and cultivated public, but, as your lordship is aware, the public which frequents the Globe Theatre is neither chosen nor cultivated, and it is doubtful whether a public of this kind would sit through a play many of the speeches in which are over a hundred lines long. Mr. Fletcher adds that a play of this kind is far more suited for the closet than for the stage, and suggests that your lordship should publish it as a historical chronicle. With regard to these tragedies, Mr. Fletcher further points out that there are already in existence several plays on the themes which your lordship has treated, which have not only been produced but enjoyed considerable success.

With regard to the third series, the comedies, Mr. Fletcher states that these plays, although not without considerable charm and while containing many passages of graceful and melodious writing, are far more in the nature of lyrical poems than of plays. Mr. Fletcher adds that if these were also considerably reduced in length and rendered even still more lyrical and accompanied by music, they might be performed as masques or else in dumb show.

Finally, Mr. Fletcher suggests, if the author of these plays is anxious that they should be performed, that your lordship should send the plays to an experienced actor who should alter and arrange them for stage presentation. Mr. Fletcher suggests that should your lordship see your way to agree to this, he has in his company a player named William Shakespeare who is admirably fitted for the undertaking, and who has already had much experience in adapting and altering plays for the stage.

I am,
Your lordship's most obedient
and humble servant,
J. J. NICHOLS.

Letter from Mr. Nichols to Lord Bacon

My Lord,

In accordance with your lordship's instructions I submitted the plays to Mr. William Shakespeare. I am now in receipt of Mr. Shakespeare's full report on the plays.

Mr. Shakespeare confirms Mr. Fletcher's opinion that the plays in their present state are far too long for production. The religious series he does not discuss, as being by their nature precluded from performance. With regard to the historical tragedies, *Edward III*, *Mary Tudor*, *Lady Jane Grey*, and *Katherine Parr*, Mr. Shakespeare points out that none of these plays would be passed by the Censor because they contain many allusions which would be considered to touch too nearly, and give possible offence to, certain exalted personages.

With regard to the tragedies, Mr. Shakespeare is quite willing to arrange *Hamlet, Prince of Denmark*, for the stage. More than half of the play will have to be omitted : the whole of the first act, dealing with Hamlet's student days at Wittenberg, Mr. Shakespeare considers to be totally irrelevant to the subsequent action of the play, although the long scene between the young prince and Dr. Faustus contains many passages which are not only poetical but dramatic. Mr. Shakespeare regrets to have to sacrifice these passages, but maintains that if this act be allowed to stand as it is at present, the play would be condemned to failure. Mr. Shakespeare is also anxious to cut out the whole of the penultimate act, which deals entirely with Ophelia's love affair with Horatio. This act, though containing much that is subtle and original, would be likely, Mr. Shakespeare says, to confuse, and possibly to shock, the audience. As to the soliloquies, Mr. Shakespeare says that it is impossible to get an audience at the present day to listen to a soliloquy of one hundred lines. Mr. Shakespeare suggests that if possible they should all be cut down to a quarter of their present length.

Out of the remaining plays, Mr. Shakespeare selects the following as being fit for the stage : *Macbeth*, *Romeo and Juliet*, *Mephistophelis*, *Paris and Helen*,

Alexander the Great, and *Titus Andronicus*. Of all these Mr. Shakespeare says that by far the finest from a stage point of view is the last. It is true that the action of this play is at present a little slow and lacking in incident, but Mr. Shakespeare says that he sees a way, by a few trifling additions, of increasing its vitality; and he is certain that, should this play be well produced and competently played, it would prove successful. The tragedy of *Macbeth* might also be adapted to the popular taste, but here again Mr. Shakespeare says the play is at least four times too long.

I would be glad if your lordship would inform me what reply I am to make to Mr. Shakespeare.

I am,

Your lordship's obedient and
humble servant,

J. J. NICHOLS.

Letter from Lord Bacon to Mr. Nichols

Sir,

I am quite willing that Mr. Shakespeare should try his hand on *Hamlet*, *Macbeth*, *Romeo and Juliet*, and *Titus Andronicus*, but I cannot consent to let him shorten my *Mephistophelis*, my *Alexander the Great*, or my *Paris and Helen*. I should of course wish to see a printed copy of the play as arranged by Mr. Shakespeare before it is produced.

I am,

Your obedient servant,

BACON.

Letter from Lord Bacon to Mr. Nichols

Sir,

I received the printed copies of my four plays as arranged by Mr. Shakespeare. I would be much obliged if you would communicate to him the following instructions: (1) *Hamlet* may stand as it is. The whole nature of the play is altered, and the chief character is at present quite unintelligible, but if Mr. Shakespeare thinks that in its present form it will please the audience, he is at liberty to produce it, as it is not a piece of work for which I have any special regard, and it was written more as a exercise than anything else. (2) I cannot allow *Romeo and Juliet* to appear with the changed ending made by Mr. Shakespeare. Mr. Shakespeare is perhaps right in thinking that his version of the play, ending as it does with the marriage of Juliet and Paris and the reconciliation of Romeo and Rosaline, is more subtle and truc to life, but in this matter I regard my knowledge of the public as being more sound than that of Mr. Shakespeare. As a member of the public myself, I am convinced that the public is sentimental, and would be better pleased by the more tragic and romantic ending which I originally wrote. (3) With regard to Mr. Shakespeare's suggestion that in *Macbeth* the sleep-walking scene should fall to Macbeth, instead of to Lady Macbeth, I will not hear of any such change. (Confidential: The reason of my refusal is that this change seems to me merely dictated by the vanity of the actor, and his desire that the man's part may predominate over the woman's.) (4) *Titus Andronicus*. I have no objection to Mr. Shakespeare's alterations.

Your obedient servant,

BACON.

Letter from Lord Bacon to Mr. Nichols

Sir,

I was present last night at the Globe Theatre at the performance of my play *Macbeth,* as produced by Mr. Shakespeare. I confess that I was much disgusted by the liberties which Mr. Shakespeare has taken with my work, which I am certain far exceed the changes and alterations which were originally presented to me, and which I myself revised and approved. For instance, Mr. Shakespeare has made a great many more omissions than he originally suggested. And at the end of many of the scenes he has introduced many totally unwarranted tags, such as, for instance :

I'll see it done,
What he hath lost noble Macbeth hath won.

And, worst of all :

It is concluded :—Banquo, thy soul's flight,
If it find Heaven, must find it out to-night.

The whole play is riddled with such additions, not to speak of several incidents of an altogether barbarous and outrageous character, and of certain other interpolations of coarse buffoonery, inserted in the most serious parts of the play to raise a laugh among the more ignorant portions of the rabble. Of course I cannot now withdraw them from the stage without risking the discovery of their authorship. Mr. Shakespeare is at liberty to produce and perform in any of the plays written by me which are now in his possession, provided that they appear under his name, and that the authorship is attributed to him.

Your obedient servant,

BACON.

THE CLOAK

Letter from Sir Walter Raleigh to the aunt of his half-brother, Mrs. Katharine Ashley

Dear Aunt Kat,

So far everything has passed off favourably, but the one pressing, pinching need still remains, namely, the need of money. Pole, the tailor, is patient indeed, but his patience is not inexhaustible, and I have been compelled by the force of hard necessity to strain it to the breaking point. It is needless to say that I am living far above my means; at this initial stage of my career it is all-important to make an effect, and to strike hard.

For this purpose, in view of the recent festivities at Greenwich, I ordered from Pole a costume of rare splendour, to wit, a brown satin doublet sewn with pearls, a hose of crimson velvet, a ruff of Venetian point lace, shoes adorned with imitation emeralds, but so skilfully counterfeited as to deceive the experts themselves, and a cloak of crimson plush fringed with silver lace, but lined, for the sake of economy, since it is ever the linings that weigh the tailor's bill, with Italian cloth, and as the lining does not show, who is the wiser? And of what profit is it to spend double the sum on a lining, which nobody sees, as on the gorgeous exterior itself? But, as it chanced, the goddess of finery all but played me a scurvy trick. I arrived in Greenwich in good time so as to be able to encounter her Majesty on her daily walk. The weather was fine; and my attire, when I reached the gay crowd of expectant courtiers, all as gorgeous as butterflies and as futile, was such, I say it without shame, as to outshine them all and to cause them to murmur with envious astonishment.

"Who is this gallant," they whispered one to another, "who is dressed like a comedian and walks like a peacock?" But I could see well that they envied me; for my attire, chiefly owing to the manner in which it was worn, eclipsed theirs, although the lining of my cloak was but of Italian cloth, and the emeralds on my feet and in my waistband imitation instead of real. Burleigh indeed scrutinised the flat emerald in my waistband narrowly (it was made of glass and loaned from Tarleton the comedian for the sum of 1*s.* 8*d.*), and inquired with feigned interest whether it were an emerald. "It is a shamrock turned to stone," I replied, "from the grave of an Irish King," and the courtiers praised my ready wit, and Burleigh, if you will overlook the play of words, became surly.

We waited for some time, and just as her Majesty was about to set forth on her Royal progress a heavy shower of rain fell, and we were obliged to seek shelter in a summer-house. The shower passed, and the sun shone out once more brightly, but the garden paths were wet, although the hot sun presently absorbed the damp, save in a few patches. As soon as the sun began to shine, the Queen, attended by her Maids of Honour, her Ladies in Waiting, and her Officers of State, set out from the Palace. We, the courtiers, were lined up, in double file on either side of the Royal progress. As fortune would have it, on the pathway directly opposite me there was a muddy patch, albeit nothing to speak of. When the Queen approached this spot, not because it was in any way damper or more muddy than the rest of the pathway, along which she had walked with the greatest unconcern, but because she wished to call the attention of Burleigh and others to the neat trimmings of her dainty shoes, she halted, and first she coughed, and sighed; and then she swore, and spat, as is her so charming habit, and cried, " Ods Bodikins, how can I avoid the filing of my, Byrlady! feet?" I at once pressed forward, and taking off my cloak, being careful to hold the lining downwards, so that the inferior texture should escape the notice of the courtiers, made as though I would fling it on to the ground, so as to spread a carpet and a footcloth for her feet; I naturally waited for her to cry out against the ruining of so fair and so costly a cloak; but no, instead she cried out: " Here is a footcloth that indeed pleaseth me, Ods Bodikins!" and other words to that effect, and out of an excess of coquetry she expressed her Royal wish to tread rather on the lining than on the exterior; I was constrained, therefore, to spread the cloak before her, with the plush downwards and the lining showing, but at the same time I grasped her Royal hand firmly, and led her over the dangerous spot rapidly, and no sooner had she crossed it, than I seized the cloak, and flinging it once more swiftly over my shoulders, I said to the Court: " This floorcloth is now Royal, and therefore for her Majesty alone." And the Queen was pleased to laugh loudly, and, after a few elegant oaths, she proceeded on her Royal progress. Thus what had threatened to be a misfortune ended well, for no one, so swift was the gesture and so unexpected, noticed the inferior material of the lining; but in spite of this, the cloak is, needless to say, ruined for ever.

I sent it at once to the tailor for repair, but he has reported that the damage is irreparable, and I shall have to order a new cloak, although this one is not yet paid for, and Pole is clamouring for payment, or for some payment on what he is pleased to call *account*, and I do not know where to turn for the money. I am not, I need hardly say, suggesting, or even hinting in the remotest way, that you should lend me the necessary sum, my dear Aunt Kat—you have always been far too generous in the past, and the sum needed far exceeds that which a lady of your slender means can afford. The price of the cloak was 400 golden crowns—and the price of the new cloak will be 400 golden crowns, which makes 800 golden crowns. Would that you and I enjoyed the wealth which is necessary to our station in life !

However, as I have already pointed out to my tailor with some emphasis, the present loss in actual estate may be amply compensated for in the future by the increased favour in the Queen's eyes which this incident has lent me. Her Majesty's notice at least has been assured, and more than assured. I am bidden to all the banquets and festivities (more money, more expense !), and her Majesty even confided to me in confidence last night that she had penned a few sonnets on which she would be so glad to have the opinion of a professional poet before sending them to a publisher, which, of course, she would only do anonymously. I received this intelligence with some misgivings, as my experience so far has led me to believe that the writing of verse—with some notable exceptions, such as Sappho, Mary Stuart, and yourself, dear Aunt Kat—is not a woman's strongest point, and also that Royal personages are, as a rule, strangely susceptible as to their literary gifts, and that while no flattery is too gross for them, unless it be administered with subtle skill, they are inclined to suspect its genuineness. I, of course, feigned the utmost rapture at being initiated into the secrets of the Royal muse; and the Queen, blushing and bashful, and with many a shy oath, produced from a small casket a small MS. bearing the inscription "To W.H.," and casting her eyes down she said, "I did not dare to write to W.R.," and then she quoted Greek, to the effect that "those who had ears to hear might hear," which, in truth, she might just as well have said in English. The sonnets, which are addressed to me, are affectionate in tone, and subtly complimentary, in that they urge me to marry, which, of course, is the last thing the Queen desires. They are, for a woman, well writ, although I need hardly say, freely plagiarised, from the French, the Italian, and from our modern poets Spenser, Sydney, and even myself. The incident of the cloak she has versified pleasantly enough in a sonnet, which begins:

> Why didst thou promise such a beauteous day,
> And make me travel forth without my cloak?

and there are some pleasing lines, beginning

> Being your slave . . . .

So far she has only written twenty or so, but she threatens to write and publish a whole century. I am strongly averse to the publication, for although she names me Will instead of Walter throughout, the disguise is thin and they will make people talk. And now, Aunt Kat, I must make end, and remain your assured and impoverished (where can one turn for money in these hard times?) friend and nephew,

WALTER.

BATH, 1663

Letter from a Frenchman to a Friend in Paris

BATH, *August* 20, 1663.

We arrived here with the Court last week, the physician having decided that the hot waters of this far-off and desolate spot would prove more beneficial to the Queen's health than the cold waters of beautiful Tunbridge Wells. Bath has not the sunny elegance of the latter place, but the Court are doing their best to enliven this otherwise dreary resort. One of their chief occupations is to play at bowls, but you must not think that this game is confined, as in France, to artisans and lackeys. On the contrary, it is here a game of gentlefolk, and there is both skill in it and a certain art, and the places where these games are played are singularly charming and elegant. They are called "boulingrins." They consist of small meadows, of which the grass is as smooth as a billiard table. As soon as the heat of the day is over everybody meets here, and many heavy wagers are made. I confess that I have lost considerable sums at this sport, but have been more successful at cock-fighting.

There is dancing every night at the King's. Often a comedy is played, which is followed by a supper. As for music, it never ceases. The English are above all things a musical nation; their skill both in the art of singing and dancing far excelling that of our courtiers. For instance, the Chevalier de Grammont, who is reckoned one of our most accomplished dancers, is not sufficiently skilful to take part in the Royal dance.

The fashionable instrument is now the guitar, which was introduced here by an Italian, whose compositions so pleased the King that everybody became mad about this instrument, so that you see no one at the Court who does not play the guitar, whether or no they possess a talent for so doing. Some, such as the Earl of Arran, play as well as the Italian himself. Others extract but futile discord from this difficult instrument. It is a curious thing that the English, who have obtained an unexampled liberty in political matters, show themselves curiously slavish and lacking in initiative and independence in matters of thought, pleasure and recreation. Their political liberty is extraordinary; for instance, in their Parliament the members are not only allowed to speak their minds freely, but also to do a number of astonishing things, such as call the most important members of the State to the Bar! The Earl of Bristol remained free in the town after he had accused the Lord Chancellor of high treason! And even the populace considers that it has the right to speak of public affairs.

Not long ago, at the Stock Exchange, I heard a political speech quoted on every side, and even the boatmen in the barges discuss matters of State with the noble Lords whom they convey to the Houses of Parliament. On the other hand, in matters of pleasure and pastime the English are slaves of convention; everybody wishes to do what every one else is doing. The matter of the guitar-playing is an instance of this. As soon as some high personage makes a sport, an occupation, or a manner of dress fashionable, the crowd follow in abject obedience and perfect uniformity, like sheep.

Indeed, we not long ago had a narrow escape from having a peculiarly tedious occupation forced upon us: the Duke of York fell in love with a Scotch game called *goff*, which is played, so they say, in the more sterile regions of the extreme north of Scotland, where the inhabitants still feed on oats and wear scarcely any clothes. This game consists in hitting a hard ball about the size of a turkey's egg into the dense heath with a kind of stick. Several hours are then spent in looking for the ball, and when, after much difficulty and discomfort, it has been found, the player immediately hits it as hard as he can into the distance and resumes the laborious search. This game would no doubt have become the fashion had not the King, who has a horror of introducing an element of seriousness into pastimes which are designed exclusively for recreation, remarked that such a game was fit only for very small children or for men who were so old that they had reached their second childhood. After that we heard no more of this intolerable sport.

Again, Prince Rupert, who is distinguished by his studious habits, his love of chemistry and mathematics and his awkward manners, attempted to introduce a game of cards called "Trump" or "Whist." The most notable feature of this game is that it must be played in complete silence. It is not surprising, therefore, that it failed to find favour at Court, for the English love conversation above all things, and excel in repartee, apt quotation, and madrigal-making. But it is curious that although the Court is highly cultivated, and although the courtiers speak elegantly both in English and Latin, and make verses and madrigals in these languages, there appears at the present time to be no English literature at all. Our Ambassador tells me that among learned circles in London, although there are certain philosophers of merit, such as Hobbes, there remain but few traces of the art of letters for which England was once famous. The only writers whose memory still subsists to a certain degree are Bacon, Morus, Buchanan, and in the last century a certain Miltonius who acquired an evil notoriety by his scurrilous and seditious pamphlets. Letters have deserted England and given way to music and painting. The art of madrigal-making, which is cultivated at Court with assiduity and exquisite skill, belongs, of course, to music.

What has struck me most since I have been here is the beauty of the English women; they are all being painted at this moment by a painter called Lely; he is an accomplished artist, but he does not succeed in rendering the personality of the people he paints, and his pictures are all alike. Most of these ladies speak French not only with correctness but with elegance; some of them, such as Miss Stewart, for instance, speak French better than their own language. Others, on the other hand, are so unfamiliar with our manners and customs that they seem to imagine that a Frenchman must necessarily be half-witted, and address him in a kind of broken language such as nurses and mothers use to their babies.

Lady Hyde is remarkable, even in England, for her grace and her wit. Her hands are delicate and her feet astonishing. She is surrounded by the wits of the Court, and one evening after supper she organized a kind of tournament of wit. It was thus: we all sat round the gaming table, but instead of playing we had set before us counters made of mother-of-pearl, on each one of which a letter of the alphabet was worked in gold. These were placed face downwards and turned up in turn; each player who turned up a letter was obliged to compose a line of a sonnet beginning with the letter in question. The game would have proved highly successful had not Lord Rochester caused some annoyance by ending the sonnet, which had up till then been delicate and tender, with an unexpectedly crude and uncourtly expression, which, while it tickled the mirth of some of the company, offended our sensitive hostess.

Miss Stewart is childish and frivolous. She laughs at everything and everybody. She has a passion for those games which are usually played only by children of twelve and thirteen, such as, for instance, Blind Man's Buff; and even when at cards the play is at its highest, she builds houses and castles with the cards, and forces everybody to join in the pastime. She is encouraged in her gaiety and her frivolity by the Duke of Buckingham, who sings agreeably, and has a wonderful talent for mimicking, not without a certain spice of malice, the voices and the tricks of his friends.

Play is everywhere high, and at every "boulingrin" there is a pavilion where refreshments are sold —liquors such as cyder, hydromel, sparkling ale, and Spanish wine. There is a race of men called "Rooks" who meet together to smoke and to drink. They are what we should call grooms in France, and they always have about them enough money to lend to those who have lost at play; they are themselves so skilful at games of hazard, especially at one particular game which is played with three cards, that no one who plays with them wins. The Chevalier de Grammont once tried his luck with them at dice, and, strange to say, the first time he played he won. They begged him to continue the game. This he refused to do, in spite of the many well-turned compliments they paid to his prowess.

The English are somewhat concerned at this moment at the state of their Navy, which they say leaves much to be desired. There are many politicians who are in favour of building an increased number of ships, but it appears that this cannot be done without grievously taxing the rich, who are already overtaxed. The Duke of Buckingham told me yesterday that if the taxes were to be in any way increased he would be obliged to dismiss his third gardener and his Groom of the Chambers. He assured me that this agitation in favour of an increased Navy was entirely due to a foolish fear of the Dutch, a fear which he said was utterly groundless, for it was inconceivable that the Dutch could wish to invade England; moreover, if they did so they would be defeated by the English Navy, such as it was.

PETER THE GREAT

Letter from an English Architect

St. Petersburg, *July*, 1715.

Dear Sir,

Although it is almost six weeks ago that I arrived at St. Petersburg, I have not until this moment had leisure to write you my impressions. And now before I impart these to you I must advert to a conversation which I had in Berlin with X——, who, as you know, spent many years in Russia, before the accession of the present Czar, and who is an eminent Russian scholar. He assured me that in entering the Russian service at the present moment I was doing a foolish and perilous thing. Russia, he said, was on the eve of a grave crisis, which might very probably lead to the dismemberment of the nation. This was owing to the character of the present Sovereign. The Czar was inspired with inordinate ambition and blind obstinacy; he was, moreover, pursued by a demon of restlessness, and a desire to change and reform everything that was old. This love of improvement was no doubt in itself a laudable ambition; yet in view of the peculiar circumstances of the case, the ignorance of the great mass of Russians, the fundamental conservatism of the educated class, the deficiency and the inadequacy of all necessary material and instruments, the designs of the Czar were akin to madness.

He was attempting to make bricks without straw, and this could only have one result—the disruption of the kingdom of Russia and the consequent rise of a large and powerful Poland. Poland would once again reduce Russia to servitude, and all civilized Europe would once more be revolted by the spectacle of civil and religious tyranny. Moreover, a powerful Poland was, as far as all European countries were concerned, far less to be desired than a powerful Russia. I will comment on these remarks in due time. At present I must resume my narrative.

On arriving at St. Petersburg I went straight to the Summer Palace. I was told that the Czar had gone to Cronstot. He had left orders that I was to follow him thither as soon as I arrived, in a snow which was waiting to convey the Dutch Minister. It was a fine, sultry day when we started from St. Petersburg. I was much impressed by the sight of the city, which possesses already many thousands of houses and some fine churches and palaces. We started with a fair wind, but soon a storm arose, and our condition was the more perilous owing to the lack of experience of the captain and the mate. The Dutch Minister was prostrate with sea-sickness, and upon his asking whether there was any chance of escape—and he seemed, such were his pains, to hope for a negative answer—the captain, who was facing the emergency by doing nothing at all, kept on repeating in a soothing voice the word *Nichevo* (which means "all is well") "we shall arrive." All seemed to be very far from well. The mate, when consulted, folded his hands together and said *Bog Znaet*, which means "God knows." At last, after two days and three nights, which we spent without fire or provisions, we arrived at Cronstot. We were forthwith bidden to the Czar's pleasure-house, Peterhof, on the coast of Ingria, whither a fair wind took us without further mishap.

We were at once taken into the Czar's presence. Anything less like the state and formal etiquette of Paris, Berlin, or Madrid, it would be difficult to imagine. To speak of the simplicity of the Czar would be to understate my meaning. He seemed to be divested not only of the formality of sovereigns, but of the ordinary convention and reserve which unwittingly hang over every human being like a cloak. He greeted us as if he had known us all his life, and as if he were continuing a conversation but lately interrupted. His dress—which was dark, plain, and sober—his demeanour, his manner, were not only free from all trace of pomp but would have struck one as simple in a common sailor. And yet the overwhelming mastery and intelligence and power of the man were instantly apparent in the swiftness of his look and the stamp of his countenance. It was clear from the first moment that he was a man who went straight to the point and had the knack of eliminating and casting aside the unessential and the superfluous with the quick decision with which a skilful gardener removes dead flowers from a tree with his garden knife.

This was evident when speaking of the concern he had felt for us owing to the storm. The Dutch Minister launched out into a diffuse narrative. The Czar at once seized on the essential fact that the skipper was incapable and deftly changed the subject, keeping the garrulous Minister charmed all the while. He welcomed me to Russia and said that he had been awaiting my arrival with impatience, as he had much work for me to do. "But we will talk of that later," he said; "at present you must be hungry."

We then followed him into another room, where we were presented to the Czarina. The Czarina, who is of humble origin, has that peculiar grace, that intangible beauty and charm, which baffle verbal description and cause the painter to burn his canvas. She is the embodiment of spontaneous and untaught refinement, and her manner, like that art which consists in concealing all art, proceeds from the certain instinct which bids her make the right gestures and say the right word without either effort or forethought.

We proceeded to dinner, which was served punctually at noon. The first course consisted of many cold meats, followed by a second hot course, and then by a third course of fruits. During dinner we were all of us plied with Tockay wine. His Majesty himself partook of it freely but forebore drinking too much; but we by the end of the meal could scarcely stand, and the Dutch Minister was obliged nevertheless to empty a bowl holding a full quart of brandy which he received at the Czarina's hand. The result was he rolled under the table, and was carried away by two men to a quiet place where he could sleep.

The Czar laughed and talked without ceasing, and asked many pertinent questions concerning England and Scotland, and was thoroughly posted in all the latest news. Talking of the Stuarts, he said they would never return, because, apart from their talent for mismanagement, the English people did not feel strongly enough on the subject to make a rising in their favour, however popular such a restoration would be if it could be effected by a *Deus ex machina*. The Stuarts, he said, had always had the people on their side and the oligarchy against them. He blamed the English people with regard to Ireland, saying the English had neither annihilated the Irish nor made them happy. He compared this to the action of the Poles in Russia in the past, and pointed to the result.

After dinner I retired to sleep, but at four o'clock we were awakened and brought back to the Czar's presence. He gave us each a hatchet and orders to follow him. He led us into a wood of young trees, where he marked a walk of a hundred yards to be cut to the seashore. He fell to work, and we (there were seven of us) followed; (the Dutch Minister found such a work in his half-dazed condition hard) and in three hours' time the path was cut. At supper, to which we were bidden, more Tockay was consumed, and the Czar joked with the Dutch Minister about the violent exercise he had caused him to take. We retired early, but about eight the next morning, I was bidden to Court to partake of breakfast, which consisted, instead of coffee or tea, of large cups of brandy and pickled cucumbers.

After dinner we were taken on board the Czar's vessel. The Czarina and her ladies sought the cabin, but the Czar remained with us in the open air, laughing and joking. A strong wind was blowing, which in two hours became a gale, and the Czar himself took the helm and showed the utmost skill in working a ship as well as huge strength of body. After being tossed about for seven hours we at last reached the port of Cronstot, where the Czar left us with the words: "Good-night, gentlemen. I fear I have carried the jest too far."

The next day I returned to St. Petersburg, and was lodged in the Summer Palace so as to be near the Czar. The Czar sent for me early in the morning, and discoursed for two hours on various buildings he wished me to design. He went into every detail, and soon showed me that he was as skilled an architect as he was a sailor. He also talked on various other subjects, including theology, mechanics, music, painting, the English Navy, and the German Army. England, he said, was his model as far as the Navy was concerned, Germany for the Army, and France for architecture. At the same time he was not disposed slavishly to follow any particular models, and force on his people those details of any system which might not be in concord with the genius of the Russian character. It is undeniable that the Germans have far the best system of military discipline, he said, but it would be quite impossible to get Russian soldiers to act with the mathematical precision of the Prussians.

"I adopt the system as far as I can, and adapt it to my material. That is why I get Scottish officers when I can, and English architects, because it is difficult to make a Frenchman understand that Russia isn't France, and that a Russian workman must work in his own way."

I had not been in St. Petersburg long before I realized that X——'s forebodings are baseless. He is right in saying that the Czar is ambitious. He is right in saying that he is actuated by restlessness, if by restlessness he means a ceaseless and indefatigable energy. He is right in saying that the Czar's materials are bad and scanty and that the Czar thus had to make bricks without straw. He is right in saying that the Russians are fundamentally conservative and regard all reforms with distrust.

But what he has not realized is this, that a man of genius can make bricks without straw. The Czar has proved it. He has built St. Petersburg on a marsh. He has built a fleet and organized an army. He has made palaces, schools, academies, factories, and dockyards, and he has inspired others with his fever for work. Like all great workers, he never gives one an impression of hurry. He seems always to have leisure to see whom he wants, to have his say out, and to indulge in recreation when he feels so inclined. He rises every morning at four o'clock. From eleven to twelve he receives petitions from all ranks of his subjects, who have access to him during that hour. He dines at twelve o'clock. At one he sleeps for an hour; the afternoon and evening he spends in diversions, and at ten he goes to bed.

He seems to delight in finding out a project which appears to be impossible, and in achieving it forthwith. No scheme is too large for him to devise, and no detail of it too small for him to attend to. He has the gift of discovering any useful scrap of knowledge either in men or books. At his balls and entertainments, which he now gives at the Summer Palace, or, on extraordinary occasions, at the Senate House, all degrees of persons are invited. Different tables are arranged in separate rooms for the clergy, the officers of the Army, those of the Navy, the merchants, the shipbuilders, the foreign skippers. After dinner the Czar goes from room to room and talks to everybody, especially with the masters of foreign trading vessels. The Dutch and English skippers treat him with familiarity, and call him by no other name than Skipper Peter. He is followed by a lettered serf, who carries a small book, and whenever the Czar finds a point which interests him he calls to the serf, "Make a note of that, Ivan."

He never appears to court popularity or to fence with subjects of which he is ignorant. On the contrary, he makes it manifest that he is talking on a subject because it interests him and because he is thoroughly acquainted with it. And any man who is an expert at any trade or profession cannot converse with him for a few moments without realizing that he knows what he is talking about and that his knowledge is the result of practical experience. He has a hatred of baseless theory, a contempt for convention, and an insatiable passion for fact and reality. He has no respect for inherited rank or for the glory of lineage; merit is to him the only rank. He will at a moment's notice, should he think it necessary, degrade a nobleman into a peasant or make a pastry-cook into a Minister. Indeed he had done this in the case of Prince Menzikoff.

It is useless to pretend that he is as popular with the Russian people as he is with foreigners. Many of the ignorant peasantry regard him as the Antichrist, and they worship his utterly worthless son, the Czarevitch, because they consider that he respects and embodies their ancient customs. In spite of this there is no danger that what the Czar has accomplished will be overturned in the immediate future. He has done something which cannot be undone, like putting salt into a pudding. Moreover, his genius and his versatility, his extraordinary varied talents, are based on a soundness of judgment, a level-headedness and a sanity of instinct which, while they lead him to do things which are seemingly impossible, justify him, in that success is achieved, and prevent him from undertaking what, owing either to the backwardness of the population or the temper of popular feeling, would in reality and of necessity end in failure. He knows exactly where to draw the line. In a speech he made to the Senate some time ago he said that the ancient seat of all sciences was Greece, whence they were expelled and dispersed throughout Europe but hindered from penetrating further than Poland. The transmigration of sciences was like the circulation of the blood, and he prognosticated that they would some time or other quit their abode in Western Europe and settle for some centuries in Russia, and afterwards perhaps return to their original home in Greece. In the meantime he recommended to their practice the Latin saying *ora et labora*.

Now what the Czar has already achieved is that he has made such a circulation possible. He has broken down the barrier which was between Russia and Western Europe, and let in to the great veins of his country a new drop of blood which nothing can either expel or destroy.

I am, sir,

Your obedient servant,

DETMAR LUTYENS.

P.S.—The Czar has a horror of wasps.

HAMLET AND DR. DODD

Letter from a Frenchman, translated from the French

LONDON, *June* 28, 1777.

Sir,

It is now three days since I arrived in London. I am still bewildered by the noise of the carriages and overwhelmed by an admiration which any foreigner must feel when for the first time he beholds the streets, the lanterns, and the pavements of London. Nothing could be better than these three things. The streets are wide; the manner in which they are lit up at night, and the commodity of the ways made for foot-passengers so that they may be safe from vehicles in the most dangerous thoroughfares are astonishing. There is nothing to compare with it in Europe. It is only in London that such thoroughfares and such superb nightly illumination are to be found, and where so careful an attention is paid to the safety of the public. And all this decoration, and indeed half of the city, are not more than twenty years old!

I have already become an adopted Englishman. I drink my tea twice a day, I eat my "tostes" well buttered. I read my Gazette scrupulously every morning and every evening. I have been waiting with impatience for one of those plays to be performed which have obtained universal applause, such as those, for instance, of the " divine " Shakespeare. I have at last been rewarded. Yesterday I read on the playbill (*affiche*), *Hamlet, Prince of Denmark.* So I said to my sister, who is with me, We must go and see *Hamlet.* We set out, therefore, for Covent Garden.

We had intended to take tickets for the boxes, but there were none left. We tried to get into the first gallery (our *premières loges*), but there were no seats to be had there. I proposed then that we should try the upper gallery, but we were advised not to. There remained the pit. This was also full. I must needs stand, and my sister obtained half a seat at the end of a crowded bench. It was all most brilliant. The house, which is square and partly gray and partly glided, without harmony of ornament or design, is not imposing in itself. But the crowd of spectators, the quantity of lights, the rapt attention of the coloured crowd, make a striking *ensemble.*

No sooner had we seated ourselves than to my extreme astonishment something fell on to my sister's hat. It turned out to be a piece of orange peel. Here I must mention that an essential part of a lady's *coiffure* in London is a flat round hat, which is a most ingenious device of coquetry. It heightens beauty and diminishes ugliness; it confers grace and play to the features. It is impossible to tell you all the varied effects an Englishwoman can derive from her hat. Curiously enough, the hat is not worn on State occasions, and neither at Court nor at assemblies, nor even in the *premières loges* of the theatre, and its place is taken by French feathers. I was just wondering whence the piece of orange peel had proceeded when I saw a man come from behind the scenes with a large broom in his hand. Knowing that Shakespeare makes use of everything that pertains to human life, I thought that *Hamlet* was going to begin by a sweeping scene. I was mistaken. It was only a servant who was cleaning the front of the stage, which I now noticed was covered with the remains of the feast of oranges and apples which was taking place in the upper gallery. My sister received a small sample on her hat.

At last the play began. Not having the good fortune to understand the English language, I could not follow one word of the dialogue. But I am told that the play gains rather than loses by being translated, though our Anglomaniacs say it is untranslatable. But I have now read the play in M. Letourneur's translation. The play is sheer madness—nay, more, it is the wildest and most extravagant thing that a madman could devise in a fit of delirium. Towards the end of the play only six characters remain alive, and they all die a violent death. The King and the Queen are poisoned on the stage. Hamlet, after having assassinated the Lord Chamberlain and his son, dies himself of a poisoned wound. His lady-love throws herself out of the window and is drowned; the Ghost, who enlivens this farrago of horrors, was poisoned himself (in the ear).

Lest the spectators should be overcome by so many murders, the " divine " Shakespeare has given them moments of relief in the person of the Lord Chamberlain, who is a coarse buffoon, and the conversation of the grave-diggers, who, while they crack their insipid jests, dig a real grave, throw real black earth on to the stage, of the same colour and substance as that which is found in churchyards, full of real bones and real skulls. In order to give an effect of reality, there are some large skulls and some small ones. Hamlet recognizes one as having belonged to a clown whom he knew. He seems to caress it, and to moralize over it. And these horrors, and the still more disgusting pleasantry, seemed vastly to please the upper gallery, the pit, and even the boxes. The people who were near me and behind me stood up on their seats and craned forward to look, and one man, in order to see better, lifted himself up by pulling my hair.

What strikes me most in thinking of this performance is the contrast that exists in England between the mildness and the leniency of the English customs and legislation in criminal matters, and the barbarity and savagery of the entertainments in their playhouses. On the same morning that *Hamlet* was performed, the execution of Dr. Dodd was carried out at Tyburn. Doctor Dodd was a minister of the Church, highly respected for his eloquence. He had been *Aumonier* to the King, and cherished the ambition of becoming a bishop. With this object, he had, through his wife, offered the sum of a thousand guineas to the wife of a Minister. The transaction was discovered and Dr. Dodd was dismissed from his post, but still retained a living. He had been the tutor of a son of a man who is well known here, Lord Chesterfield, and in the name of the young lord he signed a bond of four thousand guineas. This was also discovered, and it constitutes what they here call the crime of forgery, for which Dr. Dodd was condemned to death. In spite of many petitions the sentence was carried out yesterday, June 27. I assisted at the execution. A stranger accustomed to the terror-inspiring machinery, to the noise and fuss with which, in the rest of Europe, the decrees of justice are executed, and all that is designed to serve as an example, would be astonished at the manner in which it is done here. Here there are no soldiers, no representatives of the army, no outward signs of ferocity, no preliminary torture. Here that humanity, which the law seems to forget from the moment the judge has uttered the word guilty—by letting a long delay elapse between the pronouncement of the sentence and the execution—reappears as soon as the prison opens its doors and delivers the prisoner to the sheriffs, who are charged with carrying out the sentence. The sheriffs are not military men; they have no mercenaries under them, but merely a certain number of constables, ordinary *bourgeois,* whose only uniform consists in a long stick painted and partially gilded.

The victim, bound, without constraint, by the cord which is to hang him, is seated on a cart draped in black, or he may obtain leave to use a carriage, and this is what was done yesterday. The carriage passed slowly up Oxford Street, one of the longest and broadest streets of London. The prisoner had no escort, save a small number of constables on foot, and some sheriffs on horseback. He is condemned by the law; it is the law which leads him to death. The officers show no signs, either of threatening or fear, lest the people should oppose themselves to a severity which has their safety for object.

The immense crowd which fills the streets, especially in a *cause célèbre* of this nature, maintains a respectful silence. When they arrived at Tyburn Dr. Dodd left his carriage and mounted on a cart which stopped under the horizontal beam of the gallows. The executioner then appeared, untied the rope, and attached it to the transverse beam. The victim conversed with a minister of the Church, who recalled his crime, and spoke of the necessity of expiation. After a short pause, the executioner covered the victim's head with a handkerchief, which he drew down to his chin. The first sheriff made a sign; the executioner touched the horse, the cart went on, and the work of execution was thus almost imperceptibly accomplished. After the body has remained hanging for an hour it is cut down and restored to the relatives of the deceased. He is then no longer a culprit, but a citizen in possession of the rights he had forfeited. His memory is not held in obloquy; for instance, the brother of Dr. Dodd succeeded to his living on the recommendation of Lord Chesterfield.

Now to return to the playhouse and *Hamlet*. How is it that a people which abhors bloodshed in general, which fears murder, to whom poison and assassination are unknown, and which carries regard even towards the criminal to the extent I have described, can take pleasure in theatrical spectacles as barbarous and revolting as their own? The executions at London seem but games. The tragedies of the playhouse, on the other hand, are butcheries, causing even such spectators as are familiar with bloodshed to shudder.

It is only fair to say that those Englishmen who have read and travelled are slightly embarrassed when a foreigner, who has heard the extravagant praises paid to the "divine" Shakespeare, comes to London to see for himself the works of this genius.

They tell us that the populace are the lords of the English stage, and that they must needs be pleased. It is their depraved taste, we are told, which maintains these spectacles which would empty the theatres in any other country. I am quite ready to believe it; but then it is only drunken sailors who should be asked to admire Shakespeare, since it is only by drunken sailors that his altars are supported.

On the other hand, I cannot help adding that educated society shares to a certain extent the prejudice of the rabble, since it shares their pleasures. The boxes are always full when Shakespeare is on the bill, and last night the play was well received; the disgusting jokes and the extravagant ravings duly listened to and applauded by men, women, lawyers, merchants, lords, and sailors. One and all they seemed to breathe with delight the obnoxious vapours of that earth which is made up of the remains of corpses. Compare this deliberate brutality, which educated men have tried to justify in books, with the mildness of the penal laws and the real executions, and explain it if you can! As for me, I will not visit the playhouse again until the question is solved.

HERR MÜLLER

Letter from Sir Richard C—— to his Cousin

ROME, *January* 4, 1787.

I have been here a fortnight and have been able more or less to look round. I wrote a long letter to Horace yesterday in which I described at great length the journey from Venice, so I will not repeat to you what I have already written to him.

Rome is a great deal altered since I was here last ten years ago. It is being spoilt, and such damage as the Goths and Vandals left undone is now being accomplished by the modern architects. I am afraid that by the time the next generation is grown up the beautiful Rome that we have known and loved will have entirely disappeared, and that when our sons and daughters make the pilgrimage which we looked upon as the reward of our studies and the greatest privilege of our youth, they will find a new city, elegant, no doubt, and not without grandeur, but devoid of that special charm, that rare and solemn dignity, which clothed the city as we knew it. Of course, certain of the monuments and works of art will always remain, and nothing can prevent Nature from performing her careless miracles. No defacing hand will be allowed to touch the trees that grow in the Coliseum, the vegetation which runs riot in the baths of Caracalla, or to desecrate the divinely elegant fountain of Tivoli. Again, no modern artist will be allowed to lay hands on the grassy Forum, or to intrude upon the Gardens of the Borghese Palace which remind one of the fabled meadows and parterres of Elysium. But it is in the body of the city that the barbarians of the present day are allowed to commit their impious sacrilege, and it is not only a melancholy and bitter task to trace the remains of antiquity in the Rome of to-day, but it is even difficult to recognize in what now exists the city as she was when we were last here together.

The weather has so far not been very favourable. The *sirocco* is blowing, and daily brings with it a quantity of rain, but it is warm, warmer than it ever is in London. Rome is, I need scarcely tell you, very full of visitors at this moment, and it is especially crowded with our dear countrymen, whom I sedulously try to avoid, for I have not come to Rome, as do so many of our friends, for the purpose of continuing London life, and of hearing and helping to increase the scandal and the tittle-tattle which we are only too familiar with. It is for this reason that I have thus far shunned society, and the only people I have seen are artists and students, of whom there are many. Most of them are Germans, and several of these have received me with great civility and kindness, and afforded me much useful assistance in visiting the museums and conducting my trifling researches.

So far I have not seen much. The new museum is a fine institution, and possesses many treasures. I have visited the ruins of the palace of the Cæsars, the Coliseum, which impressed me more than ever by its size and solemnity, the Sistine Chapel, and St. Peter's, on to the roof of which I climbed in order to enjoy the view.

The theatres are opened once more, and a few nights ago I went to the opera. Anfossi is here, and they gave *Alessandro nel Indie* (which is tedious), followed by a ballet representing the Siege and Fall of Troy, which I greatly enjoyed. I have also seen, since I have been here, Goldoni's *Locandiera*. As you know, all parts here are played by men; and all the dancers in the ballet are men also. They act with ease and naturalness, and their facial play is especially remarkable.

From the moment I arrived in Rome until yesterday I was oppressed and somewhat saddened by the feeling —whether this was the result of the *sirocco* or of the shock of seeing so many unexpected changes I do not know—that I was not in any way in touch with Rome. I never seemed to say to myself "This is Rome indeed!" nor to experience that peculiar charm which I remember feeling so acutely when I was here last. It was in vain that I brooded over the ruins, admired the monuments of antiquity, and the masterpieces of Salvator Rosa and Dolci; in vain I lingered on the Palatine at twilight, or roamed in the Baths of Diocletian. I admired with my reason, but I did not feel with my heart as before. Something was wanting. But yesterday the magic returned.

I went for a walk by myself along the Appian Way to the tomb of Metella. It was a gray day; it had been raining nearly all the morning, but by the time I started the rain had ceased, though a layer of high, piled-up clouds remained; the air was mild and almost sultry.

I walked along the Appian Way, and the desolation of the Campagna, with its fragments of broken arches, its ruined aqueducts and the distant hills, which on a day like this seem curiously near and distinct, came over me. In the distance, above Rome itself, the clouds had slightly lifted, and St. Peter's was lit up by a watery gleam of light. I cannot describe to you the beauty and the melancholy of the scene.

All at once, while I was standing by the grassy plain and looking towards Rome, I became aware of a plaintive sound: a Roman shepherd boy dressed in sheepskins was fluting one or two monotonous notes on a wooden pipe. His music seemed to complete the landscape, and to express the very spirit of the Campagna, which brings home to me the Rome of ancient days more poignantly and more nearly than all monuments and museums.

The veil which had hung over me during all these days was abruptly lifted. The old spell and the old charm returned, and I could say to myself: "This is Rome! I have at last found what I was seeking."

I had remained for some time musing, when I suddenly noticed that a man was seated not far from me, on a portable stool and making a sketch in water-colour of a broken archway. He had been there the whole time, but I had not noticed him. I do not know why, but I felt a desire to speak to some one, and I approached him and asked in French if he could tell me the time. He answered me civilly, and by his accent I perceived that he was a German, one of the artists no doubt who are here so numerous, although I did not remember having seen him before. He was extremely handsome—I should say between thirty and forty—and though his face was young, his eyes had a searching sadness about them, a piercing expression, as though they had sounded unexplored depths of experience.

We fell into conversation, and he told me that he was a German, that his name was Müller, and that he was spending some months in Rome. I said that I presumed he was an artist; he replied that he was only now learning the rudiments of the art of drawing, but that he had begun too late, and that he would never be anything but a dilettante.

As he spoke he folded up his sketching-book, for it was already too dark to draw, and we walked towards the city together. He said he had never been to Rome before, but that he had been steeped ever since his youth in the culture of antiquity, and the monuments and the pictures which he had seen since his arrival were to him like old friends with whom he had frequently corresponded, but whom he had never seen in the flesh. But all previous study, he said, as far as Rome was concerned, struck him as being ineffectual as soon as he arrived in the city, because he was sure that it is only in Rome itself that one can prepare oneself to study Rome. He had not been here many weeks, but so far, the three things which had impressed him most were the Rotunda, which he considered the thing most *spiritually* great he had seen, St. Peter's, and the Apollo Belvidere, which he thought, as a work of genius, was the greatest of all; for although he had seen innumerable casts of this work, and indeed possessed one himself, it was as though he had never seen the statue before.

I told him that he was to be congratulated on never having seen Rome before, since his impressions would not be marred by the memories of a Rome more unspoiled and more charming. He said that he was only too keenly aware of the havoc which the modern architects had wrought, and that he feared that in twenty years' time Rome would be unrecognizable.

"But perhaps," he added, "we are mistaken. Rome has an assimilative power so great that it is able to suffer any amount of alteration, vandalism, superstructure, and addition, without losing anything of its eternal character and divinity. In Rome there is a continuity with which nothing can interfere." And he added that he thought there was something in the atmosphere, the vegetation, the very grass and the weeds of the place which acted like a spell and softened what was ugly and modern, reconciled all differences, and reduced all discords into an eternal harmony which was the genius of the city.

We talked of other matters also, and I found that he was well versed in ancient and modern literature, and had an intimate knowledge of English. He admired the plays of Shakespeare; with Dryden he was less well acquainted, but he possessed a knowledge very striking in a foreigner of the untrodden byways of our literature. For instance, he told me that he had read the plays of Marlowe with great interest, especially the tragical history of Dr. Faustus. This, he told me, was a favourite theme for German writers; in the last few years there had been almost a hundred plays written on the subject.

I asked him if he wrote himself. He said he had done so, and had begun many books, but that he found it difficult to finish them.

"I have dabbled," he said, "in art, in science, and in literature; they all interest me equally. But I am affected by the malady of our age, which is dilettantism, and I fear I shall be nothing but a dilettante all my life."

I asked him if he was engaged on any literary labour at present. He said he was thinking of writing a poem on the subject of Dr. Faustus, and that he had indeed already written fragments of it. I expressed my surprise that he should choose a subject which he had himself told me had already been used by a multitude of writers. He then smiled, and said :

" Everything has been thought and everything has been said already. What we have to do is to think it and to say it again. The Greeks," he went on, " never bothered themselves to search for new subjects. They wrote new plays on old themes. Likewise many generations of painters found sufficient subject-matter in the Madonna and Child. I mean," he said, " to follow their example. Dr Faustus shall be for me what the Madonna and Child were to them."

We separated at the gate, after a most pleasant conversation. Herr Müller expressed a wish to see me again, and he told me that he was staying with an artist called Tishbein.

January 6.

I received this morning your letter dated December 18. I shall stay here until the Carnival, and then to Naples, where, they say, Vesuvius is in eruption. The German artist whom I met the other day turns out to be a celebrity. His real name is *Goethe*, and he is the author of *The Sorrows of Werther*, a book which you have probably not read, but of which you must certainly have heard, for it created a considerable stir about (I think) twelve years ago, and had a greater sale than any book of the kind had hitherto commanded.

HEINE IN PARIS

Fragment of an unpublished letter from Lady G—— to Lord C——

PARIS, 183—.

My dear Uncle H——,

We arrived in Paris last night. . . . (Here I omit a passage regarding the children of a family some of whom still survive.) Last night we spent a very agreeable evening at Madame Jaubert's. There were a great many people present, for we had been invited to meet the celebrated Bellini. There were many people I did not know, and many others who were introduced to me whose names did not reach me. Signor Bellini himself came early. His appearance is charming; he is just like a plump child, pink and white, amiable and good-natured, and not in the least conceited or pretentious. Soon afterwards Prince and Princess Belgiojoso arrived. This was the first time I had set eyes on the Princess. Her beauty and the grace of her person have not, indeed, been exaggerated. She resembles a classical statue, but her face has an expression which recalls later and more romantic times. Her features are regular, but there is something mysterious and rather *strange* about her face and her dark orbs. Her hair is like ebony, but her skin is very white, and she smiles with a kind of wearied look, as though she were a Chinese idol. Her hands and her hair are most beautiful, and she walks into a room as if there could not be the slightest doubt that she is the most beautiful woman there. And this is true, although perhaps she is too slender. She was elegantly dressed in violet velvet, trimmed with fur, which showed her graceful figure and disappeared in the folds of a black skirt; she wore a black lace mantilla, which she took off when she came into the room. She talks well, and her voice is musical, but, at the same time, it has a cold ring like a crystal glass being tapped. Of course one could not help seeing that she was agreeable and accomplished, but I could not restrain a wicked wish to see her dethroned from her pedestal. It is impossible to say that she gives herself airs, but at the same time there is something *irritating* about her beauty.

As soon as they arrived, Madame Jaubert took the Prince to the pianoforte and said he must sing a duet with Madame de Vergennes, and that it should be the duet out of the *Pirate*, as Bellini was there. The Prince said that he was loth to sing before the Master, but Madame Jaubert appealed to Bellini, and they both succeeded in persuading him. Madame de Vergennes herself accompanied at the pianoforte. The Prince has a real tenor voice, his *méthode* is excellent, and they sang the duet as it should be sung. Madame Jaubert said to me that if you ask musicians to a party you must let them play an active part at once in public, but if, on the other hand, you invite politicians and literary men it is best to place them in corners and let them talk.

Bellini was childish about the music: he danced with delight when they had finished, and clapped his hands and said: "Do sing it again!" Somebody suggested their singing a French song, but Bellini said: "No, no, please sing some more of my own music: I do enjoy it so much more, and you know it is much better." So they sang something from *Norma*, and after that the trio from *The Comte Ory*, in which the Prince, M. du Tillet, and a young girl took part, with Madame de Vergennes at the pianoforte.

When the trio was over, Madame Jaubert interrupted the music, although we were all anxious to hear more, I myself among others; but she took me aside and whispered to me that you must always stop music *before* people have had enough, because as soon as they have a moment too much of it they will go away with the impression that they have spent a tiresome evening. I think she was right. But there was a young man there, a M. de Musset—he writes—who was both obstinate and persistent, and never ceased for a moment asking for more. Madame Jaubert was firm and turned a deaf ear to him. The young man was introduced to me: he is good-looking and well-mannered, but sulky and overdressed. He is in love with Princess Belgiojoso, and this I suppose affected him on this occasion because she was paying but scant attention to him, and talked incessantly to Major Fraser, who was there.

Gradually the greater part of the people took their departure, and we all sat down round the table in a small room and conversed on table-turning and spirits. Then, I forget how, the conversation turned upon caricatures, and Princess Belgiojoso said, with a lovely smile, that nobody had ever been able to caricature her. Upon which M. de Musset instantly accepted the challenge and said he would make a caricature of the Princess at once. He fetched a scrap book which was in the room, and a pencil, and on a blank page drew, in four strokes, her face and figure in profile, exaggerating her thinness and making an enormous black eye. It exactly resembled her; we all craned over the table to look at it, and she took up the book and said in a tone of the utmost indifference: "Really, M. de Musset, it is unfair that you should have all the talents," and she shut the book.

Madame Jaubert took the book and put it away, and I heard her whisper to M. de Musset: "You have burnt your boats." He turned round and looked at the Princess and his eyes filled with tears, and at that moment I felt that I could have gladly chastised her.

After that we proceeded to supper. Almost all had departed; those who remained were Prince and Princess Belgiojoso, M. de Musset, Major Fraser, Mlle. de Rutières, a lovely Créole, the Comte d'Alton-Shée, Bellini, and Herr Heine, the German writer. I sat between him and Prince Belgiojoso. M. de Musset was on Madame Jaubert's left, Bellini and the Princess were sitting opposite us.

Herr Heine, like most Germans, is a trifle tiring and long-winded; of course he is cultivated and accomplished, and they say he has written most interesting books, but I cannot read a word of German. He talks French well, but he is heavy and continues a subject long after one has sufficiently discussed it. This is so different from the French, who skate over every topic so lightly and never dwell too long on any subject, and understand what you want to say before you have half said it. All the same, you see at once that he is an interesting man, and every now and then he says something truly remarkable. He wears big spectacles, and his hair, which is very fair, is cut straight and is rather long and bunches over his low collar. He astonished everybody at supper by saying that the perpetual praise of Goethe and Byron tired him.

"I cannot understand you Parisians," he said, "when you talk about poetry. You go out of the way to search out and idolize all sorts of foreign poets when you have got a real native poet who is worth all these foreigners put together." Somebody said "Victor Hugo." "Nothing of the sort," he answered, "Victor Hugo is like a wheel which turns round and round in space without any intellectual cog-wheel. It is all words, words, words. But he has no thought and no real feeling. He is screaming at the top of his voice about nothing."

"Then who is our great poet?" asked Madame Jaubert.

"Why, M. de Musset, of course," said Herr Heine.

We all laughed, and Madame Jaubert said it was a very pretty compliment. M. de Musset himself appreciated the joke quite as much as we did. But they say he really does write very well, rather in the same manner as Lord Francis Egerton.

M. de Musset remained sulky throughout supper. Once or twice he spoke across the table to Princess Belgiojoso, and she answered him as if she were an empty portfolio from which her real self was absent. We talked about music; Herr Heine said we were all barbarians as far as music was concerned; that it was true the Italians had a notion of what tune meant, but that the French, and especially the Parisians, did not know the difference between music and pastry. Somebody asked him how he could say such things after what we had heard that evening, and appealed to Bellini as to whether his music had ever been better interpreted.

"Ah, Bellini is a genius," said Herr Heine, and he turned to him and added: "You are a great genius, Bellini, but you will have to expiate your genius by an early death. You are condemned to die. All great geniuses die young—very young, and you will die like Raphael and Mozart."

"Don't talk like that! for Heaven's sake don't say that!" said Bellini. "Please do not speak about death. Forbid him to talk like that," he said to the Princess.

"Perhaps my fears are groundless," Herr Heine said to the Princess. "Perhaps Bellini is not a genius after all. Besides which I have never heard a note of his music. I purposely came in this evening after it was all over. Is he a genius, Princess? What do you think?" Then he addressed himself again to Bellini: "Let us hope, my dear friend, that the world has made a mistake about you, and that you are not a genius after all. It is a bad thing to be. It is the gift of the wicked fairy. The good fairies have given you every other gift, the face of a cherub, the simplicity of a child, and the digestion of an ostrich. Let us hope the bad fairy did not come in and spoil it all by giving you genius."

Bellini laughed, but I suspect he did not appreciate the pleasantry.

Princess Belgiojoso said that Herr Heine had no right to talk like that, for he was a poet himself.

"A poet, yes," he answered, "but not a genius. That is quite a different thing. I have never been accused of that, not even in my own country."

"But no man is a prophet in his own country," said Madame Jaubert.

"I am neither a prophet in my own country nor in any one else's," said Herr Heine. "My countrymen think I am frivolous, and the French think I am German and heavy. When I am with people like you they think I am an old professor, and when I am with professors they consider I am a frivolous *mondain.* When I am with Conservatives I am reckoned a Revolutionary, and by Revolutionaries I am considered a Reactionary. And when I am among the geniuses," he said, bowing with an ironical smile towards Bellini, "I become a pedant, a philosopher, and an ignoramus, almost as bad as M. Cousin."

"I wondered," said Madame Jaubert, "whether we should get through the evening without an allusion to M. Cousin."

"When I die," said Herr Heine, "I should like a stool to be placed on either side of my tomb, with an inscription: 'Here lies a man who fell from Heaven between two stools.'"

"Geniuses," said M. de Musset. . . .

(The end of the letter is missing.)

P.S.—Bellini died suddenly to-day, so Herr Heine's prophecy came true.

SMITH MAJOR

Letter from a Private Schoolboy to a Public Schoolboy

ST. JAMES, *March* 4, 1885.

Dear Chinee,

Thanks awfully for your letter. Eton must be jolly. I am glad I'm coming next term instead of at Micalmass. I shall be glad to leave this beastly hole. Wilson ma. has got a scholarship at Westminster and we were going to have a whole holiday extra only now its stopped worse luck! Yesterday the Head went to London and Mac sent a message to the First Div. to say we wernt to dig in Wilderness while the Head was away. Middleton brought the message and Wilson ma. told him to go and ask Mac if the message was genuine. Middleton thought he was ragging but he said: "You must take my message you Second Division squit if you don't I'll smack your head." So Middleton did. Mac was in an awful wax and sent for Wilson and asked him what he meant by it. Wilson said it was a joke—he never thought Middleton would take the message.

When the Head came back we were all sent for after tea and there was a pi-jaw. Wilson had his First Div. privileges taken away for the rest of the term, and the Holiday was stopped.

The other day Mason missed three Guatemalar green parrots from his stamp collexion which he had swoped with Jackson for a toad. It was a beastly swindel because the toad was blind. Jackson who is always sucking up to Colly sneeked about the stamps and Mac said he knew it was someone in his Div. who had bagged the stamps and if the chap didn't own up he'd give the whole Div. an electric shock with his beastly battery.

Nobody owned up and the whole Second Div. had to join hands and they said Mac gave them the biggest shock theyd ever had. They didnt carc but when it was over Middleton took the battery and threw it at Mac's head. We all thought hed be expelled but Mac didn't even sneek to the Head which was jolly decent of him. Mac can be awfully decent sometimes. After this Butler began to blub and then he said he had bagged the stamps but he meant to give them back. Mac told Butler he would find himself in Queer Street. We all knew what that meant and didnt we just tell him! Nothing happened till Monday morning--then at reeding over the Head gave the Second Div. a jaw. He said they were mutinus and as bad as feenians—a feenian is a man who eats mustard with mutton—and that Butler was a thief and a traitor worse than Gladstone. Butler's pater is a liberal and some of the chaps say he's a pal of Gladstone's and you can just think how the Head gave it him. Butler was swished. Simpson ma. and Pearse held him down and he squeeled like anything. The Head gave him fifteen from the shoulder which Gordon says is against the law. The Head had a glass of shery before the swishing.

Last week there was elexions going on. The Head got a notice from the Reding Club asking him to vote for the Lib. Wasnt he waxy! He read us out the letter at tea and jawed about the Church and State and said he would send back the letter with some coppers in it so that they would have to pay 8*d*. He said a radical was worse than a feenian. We were taken to the elexion and we all wore blue ribbons in our buttonholes. The Libs werent allowed to go. There are only seven but I believe Rowley's pater is a lib. although he swears he isnt.

Next week we are going to have athletic sports. I think I shall win the hurdel race and the high. Campbell's sister's name is Ann. Mason saw it at the end of a letter. Now we all call him Mary Ann. He's awfully sick about it.

There's a new chap called Gunter—a little beast. He's the cheekiest squit I've ever seen. Colly reported him for stealing sugar from the pantry and he was warned that if he did anything again he would be turned out of the choir and swiped although it was his first term. He *has* got cheek! He called Alston who is now top of the First Div. and captain of the Eleven, Piggy. Alston smacked his head. Fancy a Fourth Div. squit calling Alston piggy! Only the Head dares do that. He's awfully dirty too and never washes. Colly nabbed him smacking Melton mi. with a slipper and he was reported again so he was swished. The Head said it was the first time a new chap had ever been swished and afterwards he kicked the Head's straw hat through the Hall. We don't know yet what will happen but we think he'll be expeled.

I got into a row with Mac last week. While we were having tea he passed up that Bell and me were to stop talking. It never got to us and Mac sent for me afterwards and said he knew what I was up to and I'd better look out or I'd find myself in Queer Street and he stopped me talking for a week.

The Head's reading us out an awfully good Book called "Tresure Island" and he's just finished a better one called "The Last Abot of Glasconbury." In the First Div. we do have to swot but in the First Set with Colly for maths and French we don't do a stroke of work. You should hear Lambert the frenchy cheek him. He goes up to him and asks him whether one ought to pronounce *yeux* youks or yeks and Colly doesn't dare pronounce it and says he ought to know. Then Lambert says "I've forgotten Sir I really don't know how to."

Yesterday in school we lit some patent pills which you burn and a snake comes out. Colly who is awfully blind asked what I was doing. I just had time to put it in my desk and said I had dropped my pen. Only one bung and he believed it! On Valentine's Day we sent Colly some sweets with biter alows inside them the stuff Mac puts on Watson's fingers when he bites his nails and he eat them.

Last week the Choir expedition came off. They went to Reding to see the biskits made and then to Bath. If I was staying on next term I should be in the Eleven and get my flanels.

I forgot to tell you another awful row there's been. Hetherington who is a new chap sits next to Ferguson at dinner. Ferguson always bags his sausage at breakfast on Sundays. The other day the Matron found a letter in Ferguson's drawer written by Hetherington to Ferguson saying, "Deai Mister Ferguson. May I please have my sausage next Sunday. I'm so hungry." Ferguson was swished but he didn't care a rap. The Head said he's callus. I had an awfully good catty. I shot Hichens mi. in the back of his head by mistake and it bled awfully. I thought I was in for it but the Head only bagged my catty for the rest of the term. We sent for a lot of snakes and green lizzards from Covent Garden and most of us bought some. I bought a Salamander but it died. Up to the Head one can't keep a toad in one's desk as we used to when we were in Colly's div. We still have Hashed Cat and Dead Fly pudding on Thursdays and nobody eats it and Mac still asks us why we arnt hungry. But I'm in training now for the sports and don't eat pudding at all. None of us do.

Please write and tell me about the sort of things a chap ought to know before going to Eton.

Yours ever, P. Smith.

I'm Smith ma. now because my minor's here. He isnt bad.

FROM SATURDAY TO MONDAY

Letter from a Frenchwoman to an English Friend in Italy

HOTEL RITZ, LONDON, *Monday, June* 1909.

My very dear Mary,

Here is the second tome of my first impressions of your country and your compatriots, which I promised to share with you. After the town the country! After one day of the London season, the English country life, the home, the Sunday at home! I have spent what you call a Saturday week-end, or a Sunday over. I will relate you all my adventures, and tell you in all frankness the good and the bad.

The sister of our dear Jackie invited me for the Saturday week-end to her beautiful *château*. By misfortune our dear Jackie was prevented from coming himself. He was kept all Sunday at the Foreign Office to help to copy out telegrams! Is it not ignoble to spoil his holiday like that? Jackie, who has so little holiday, and who works so hard in Paris! His sister—perhaps you know her—is Lady Arlington, the wife of Sir Arlington. Their *château* is in Surrey. I had never been presented to her, but she wrote me most amiably and proposed three trains I might take. I chose the first, which arrived at half-past four, and found an auto at the station. After five minutes we arrived at the *château*, which is fine, but rather heavy:

style, Louis XIV, outside. In the interior, a mixture —Queen Elizabeth, Vandyke, Maple, Modern style, Morris. *Je n'aime pas les mélanges.* But the English comfort always seduces me. The chintzes, the flowers, the nicknacks, the thousand little nothings! Oh, it is charming! When I arrived I was shown into a large hall, all panelled (the panelling repainted) with some fine pictures (some Vandykes and a Sir Joshua) and some horrors. And a picture of Lady Arlington by a modern French painter; a nightmare like a coloured photograph! There was a large tea table and a buffet all prepared, but neither the master nor the mistress of the house there to receive me. In the corner of the room a pale young man was sitting reading a book. He got up when I entered and looked embarrassed and said nothing. I did not know whether it was Sir Arlington or not. Then he said: "It has stopped raining; I think I will go out." And he abandoned me to my fate!

I waited five minutes, ten minutes, one quarter of an hour; then Lady Arlington entered. She is not like Jackie at all, but a blonde, very tall, handsome, and striking. She was dressed simply (for games) in white serge, and I was embarrassed, because they had told me the English were all that is most elegant for Saturday week-ends, and I was very dressed, with a big hat, with a lace veil, and . . . (a page of technical details omitted). Lady Arlington was most amiable, and did not seem at all embarrassed at not having been there to receive me. She gave me tea.

Presently other guests entered; they had all been at Ascot Races—some of them had come by train, others coming in their autos from neighbouring *châteaux*. They were all simply dressed, the men in *tennis*. I felt red with shame to be the only one dressed. Lady Arlington did not present one single person to me. Two pretty young women arrived (one a real Sir Joshua and the other a Greuze), and an older lady—very handsome—who began to talk *politique*. Also a great many men, most of them bald although young; they all sat down and we drank tea. Then the master of the house arrived, a tall man with a beard, *très, très bien*, like a Vandyke. He seemed timid. Lady Arlington said to him: "You know, Madame," and then stopped, as though she had forgotten my name.

We of course talked of dear Jackie at once, but when I said it was a shame to disturb his holiday, Lady Arlington said, "Oh yes," as though she did not understand. Then a man who had not been presented to me began to talk to me. He is no longer in his first youth, but very beautiful and gentle like a seigneur in a Pinturicchio, and we discussed Sargent's pictures and art in general. I found him very well-informed, intelligent, and even erudite; he has written a book about *Villon*. Then more people arrived: an old man with a beard, who my "Italian nobleman" whispered to me was Wreathall, the celebrated novelist. He is, between us, a *raseur*, and told stories enough to make one sleep about ghosts in a kitchen. There also arrived two American ladies, one a real American, full of life; the other just like an Englishwomen, and, to speak the truth, one would not have known she was American except by her clothes; she was dressed well, just like a Frenchwoman.

Then came some sportsmen, some clubmen, and a little man with a *pince-nez*. They all talked together about their friends, calling everybody by their little names; for example, Janie, and Letty, and Tommy, and Bobbie, so all that was Greek to me. Soon everybody disappeared into the garden by twos, and I was left alone with Lady Arlington and my "Italian nobleman!" The pale young man who was there when I arrived gave a glance into the hall and went out again. Lady Arlington told me he was a celebrated M.P., and very remarkable. I continued to discuss art and history, in which he was so strong, with my "Italian nobleman," until at last Lady Arlington said she was sure I would like rest, and she conducted me to my bedroom, a ravishing room furnished with all the English comfort, looking over the superb garden with its admirable lawns.

I was glad to go to my room, so as to have plenty of time to make my toilet, because they had told me the English are so exact. I disembarrass myself of my things and put on a dressing-gown. I lie down, and presently I hear cries from the garden; I look out of the window and I see in the distance they are playing at croquet with great gaiety. I am almost tempted to go downstairs once more, but as I am already undressed I have not the energy; so I remain in my room and read a book, and at half-past seven my maid comes, so that I was ready almost before half-past eight, the dinner hour. When the dinner gong rang, and I left my room to descend, some of the men were only just coming in from the garden. I was the first downstairs.

There was no one in the salon except the little man with the *pince-nez*. He said nothing at all at first but after five minutes he said he was glad it had stopped raining, and after that not a word. We did not sit down at table until nine. Sir Arlington gave me the arm, and on the other side was an oldish distinguished man with well cut features *très bien*, with good manners, but so devoted to his neighbouress that he paid no attention to me. She was a beauty, but dressed, it is inconceivable! *Fagotée, ma chère!* If you could have seen it! It was to cry about! Her dress was made in Paris too, but all put on anyhow.

Sir Arlington is a delicious gentleman, but *distrait;* he cares only for birds and animals, and often undertakes long expeditions for sport in Africa. I asked him who all the people were, and imagine, he had no idea who was the small man with the *pince-nez,* or several of the others. He said: "Those are my wife's literary friends; they are very nice, but too clever for me." He is modest, like all the Englishmen. Lady Arlington has, it appears, the mania for *hommes de lettres* as well as for music, gardening, and a thousand other things, although, between us, she is *une sotte—bête comme une oie et poseuse!* and always making exaggerated exclamations, such as How thrilling! How darling! and always in ecstasy about nothing. I talked with Sir Arlington nearly all dinner, as my other neighbour was so occupied. There was no general conversation, and we were twenty-two at table.

After dinner, according to the British custom, the ladies went into the drawing-room; they broke up into groups, the young women sat on a sofa and two or three others—the Americans also—grouped themselves round them. The others talked *tête-à-tête.* Lady Arlington sat beside me, with another lady who seemed to be very pleased that I was French, and just as we had begun to talk Lady Arlington left us and joined the group by the sofa. The lady who remained with me talked of nothing but Paris and French things, and what a salad! Cafés chantants, Réjane, Debussy, Fursy and Maeterlinck, and all *à côté!* The men stayed very late, but came out at last, and then Lady Arlington arranged the Bridge. There were four tables; everybody played except the M.P., who sat down and began reading a book; the novelist, who went to bed; the little man with the *pince-nez*, who I discovered was a celebrated painter; my "Italian nobleman," and the political lady. She took the M.P. away from his book, and settled herself down in a corner with him for the rest of the evening.

Lady Arlington took my "Italian nobleman" apart and said something to him in a whisper, and I heard him answer: "I have been talking to her the whole afternoon." Then she went up to the painter and said something to him, and he came and sat down beside me. We talked French literature and theatres; he is intelligent, but twenty years in behind about everything French, and though I was told he was an *homme d'esprit*, I could not understand his allusions nor his pleasantries.

The Bridge went on late; it was already half-past twelve when we went to bed. Lady Arlington asked me if I would have breakfast in my room, but I, who wanted to see a real English breakfast, decided to descend. I was resolved to make no mistake about my clothes, so I came down the next morning at ten in a dress I had got for the *Mont Dore*, a simple jacket and a short skirt. Imagine my astonishment! Everybody was dressed in muslins, as elegant as possible, *grandes toilettes*. Lady Arlington was dressed in white and silver and green and gold, half *décolletée*, with a huge green hat. I am not wicked, you know, but she looked like a great white parrot with her blonde coiffure ! It is only English complexions which can support such toilettes in the morning.

After breakfast Lady Arlington and the M.P. went to the church; she said that afterwards she would show me her "Friendship's Garden," which I suppose is a garden reserved for her intimate friends. The guests went into the garden and sat under the trees in small groups; nearly every one had a book, and I found that wherever I went I made a desert, a *vide*, and everybody said they must go and write letters. After a time I went indoors, also to write letters, and in every drawing room I found a *tête-à-tête !* I waited for Lady Arlington, but Sir Arlington found me and asked me to take a walk, and he took me to see his stables and the park, which is a dream. I asked about the garden, but he said that was his wife's, and that he did not occupy himself with it; but he showed me all that was practical and interesting. It was admirable. I came in all out of breath before the lunch, and had just time to go upstairs and change my dress.

This time I thought I would be right, and I put on my most elegant Worth dress. But no ! I come downstairs, I find everybody sitting at the lunch, and they have once more changed into short skirts and flannels. It was despairing ! There was only one empty place left, between the painter and the M.P. I talked French *politique* with him; he was amiable, but I could not see what they find remarkable in him.

After lunch the tennis; it was not very hot, and Lady Arlington and some of the other guests went out, and one of the young women (she who was so pretty) quarrelled with one of the other women, and although everybody tried to calm her, she would not listen and went into the house, crying, my dear, crying hot tears, and there she remained for the rest of the afternoon! I did not know what the drama was about. Then everybody disappeared; the "Italian nobleman" (always so well meaning and so modest) proposed to me to look on at the tennis. We sat down on chairs with the painter and the novelist until tea was brought.

At tea another man arrived from London, a lord, I forget his name, middle-aged and very gay; he at once got himself presented to me; we played a new game called croquet-golf until dinner. The others did not seem to appreciate him so much, perhaps he shocked the English reserve; he is full of *en-train* and the English humour. At dinner Sir Arlington again gave me the arm. After dinner everybody played Bridge once more, but I had the joy to find my friend the new arrival, who talked to me the whole evening and regaled me with his drollery, and made a thousand farces, causing me to die of laughing, simply (imagine how!) by drawing pigs with his eyes shut!

This morning I returned to London, on which I will write you further impressions soon. I adore England, the men are so well informed and full of humour, the women are beautiful, but why do not they learn to put on clothes, and why are they so dressed and yet so untidy? Oh how different you are from us!

Your friend, JEANNE.

A RUSSIAN SAILOR

Letter from a Russian Sailor to his Brother

COWES, *July* 23 (*August* 6), 1909.
(St. Trafim's Day.)

My dear brother Ivan,

I am alive and well, and I hope you are alive and well, and that all the family are thriving, and I beg you to greet my father, my stepmother, my brother Andrew, my sister, little Peter, and all my near ones from me. Please also greet Dimitri Ivanovitch and Paul Borisovitch and Anna Nikolaevna. We arrived yesterday in this country. It belongs to the English, who possess so many countries. Their great Queen is no longer alive, but there is now a King in her place who is a blood relation of our Emperor.

We were sent on shore yesterday to buy provisions. Everything is very cheap, except *vodka,* which costs three roubles a small bottle. But the English drink a *vodka* of their own which is also very dear, and they drink a kind of beer which we do not care for much. The houses are all built of brick and warmed with coal. Even the working men live in stone houses and heat them with coal. There is no wood anywhere. The houses and the streets are kept clean, and the people, even the gentry, obey the police, and are humble when they are given orders. The English are Christians, and like white men in all respects.

They are not heathens. Most of them are rich, and they have many lacqueys who obey their masters like dumb slaves, and dare not look them in the face when they speak to them.

The English food is nasty, and there is little to eat, although all eat meat every day, except the very poor, who seldom receive alms from the passers-by. There are here many beggars in the streets, but nobody gives them food or money. We gave a cripple a quarter of a rouble and he was surprised.

There are many luxurious ships in the harbour all painted white and pretty to look at. At night they are lit up by electricity. The English Fleet is here, too, and it is very big, and the ships are fine, and we were heavy-hearted when we looked at it and thought of our brave sailors who had been obliged to fight like lions for their dear country. But there is no help for it, and if Providence wills we shall one day have another fleet bigger than the first. The tide is strong here, and dangerous for us who do not know where the rocks are, and when we ask nobody can explain, for the English do not speak Russian at all. I only know three things in English: *Plentywhisky*, which means *vodka*; *fiveoclock*, which means *shabash* (all over); and *alright*, which means "I thank you."

The English sailors are like ours, but they have little to eat or drink. The laws are strict here, and if a man who has taken drink walks about in the streets he is put in prison. If that happened in Russia we should mutiny. Moreover, it is forbidden to smoke almost everywhere. This is strange, as the English smoke a great deal; but they are an obedient people, and clean. They respect their laws.

On shore it is gay. There are many clowns and acrobats dancing and singing, just as though it were a fair. But the English do not know how to sing, and they do not dance at all, Although there is much merrymaking I have not seen one drunken man, so much afraid are they of being put in prison.

The English have a Duma, but an Englishman who speaks Russian told us that it was just like ours, and that they did nothing there but talk. He also told us that the English women had mutinied because so many of them had been put in prison for beating the police, and that they were being starved in the prisons until they should submit. This seems to us cruel, but the English are often not kind to women and animals, and they say the women interfere in what is not their business, just as they do at home.

The English have no army, only mercenaries who are paid money. Some of them are niggers. I asked the man who talked Russian why it was that if men were paid so much to be soldiers every one was not a soldier. He said that soldiers were sent away to foreign climates, and that men did not respect soldiers in England. It is also like that in China. The sailors are much respected and much loved, and they are all Englishmen, and white men, and not mercenaries. They are merry people, too.

The English naval officers are clean shaven, which makes them look very funny, but they are good officers and know their business. The police are dressed in long great-coats and carry no weapons, because the English people are docile and submissive; and they have few hooligans here, although they say that in London there are many hooligans, but these are hanged.

Yesterday we went to Portsmouth, a town, for we

could not buy what we wanted in this place, which is only a village, although all the houses are built of stone. Portsmouth is a beautiful town, with many shops, palaces, theatres, and churches, and full of beautiful women who are all married to sailors. It is the custom of the place to obey the sailors in everything, and not to rob them. The English sailors are rich, much richer than some of our generals. They spend their money generously and treat everybody. They would be robbed in Russia, but here everybody lives in terror of the police, and I am told that if a poor man is arrested there is no chance of his not being condemned to prison. They are strict, so they say, in their prisons, and the unfortunates are not allowed even to speak to each other or to smoke. Fancy this happening in Russia! If they are very bad they are sent to America! But this only happens to the very bad criminals.

The English are polite to strangers, but uncivil among themselves. They never greet each other, and even the naval officers never shake hands with each other. When I first heard this I did not believe it, as I thought only Turks behaved like that, but it is true, and they do not seem to mind. The gentry live quite apart from the common people, but the common people do not mind, and, indeed, they laugh at them openly, and call them, as I was told, fools to their faces, and abuse them and their mothers openly and without fear of any unpleasantness. All this is because they obey and respect the law, and it's very well, but we could not live in a country like this, because it would sadden us.

Everything is in order here except the railways. There the disorder is terrible. You buy no ticket for your seat, and you cannot register your luggage. But the guards are strict and never let even a poor man travel without a ticket! That would be a bad business for you, Ivan, who never take a ticket. They tell me it is impossible to make any arrangement with the railway guards because the Government is powerful and they are afraid of being put in prison.

I only travelled a short distance, but it was difficult to get a seat in the train. And if I had had any luggage it would certainly have been stolen, as they will not allow you to take much luggage in the carriage with you. The trains are bad. Their first class is more uncomfortable than our third class, because there is no room to lie down. You can get tea everywhere; but the English do not know how to make tea. It is thick and black and bitter, like soup which has been kept too long. They do not know how to make bread, and there is no black bread. Their white bread is made of starch and is not fit to eat. But since every one eats meat this does not matter.

I cannot write any more. I am glad to have travelled in foreign countries, and this is a clean country and the people are friendly and all right; but I shall be glad to get back to my native land, for which my heart is weary, and to a place where a man can do as he pleases. We always heard much of English freedom, but a man in prison in our country is freer than a man at large here. I send you a dozen postcards which are very beautiful. They did not cost much money.

Please greet my father, my stepmother, my brother, my sister, little Peter, and all who are near to me, as well as Dimitri Ivanovitch and Paul Borisovitch. Please heaven, I shall return home soon. To-day the

English King and those who are near to him will pay a visit to his Majesty the Emperor (God bless him !) and his near ones, and they will drink tea together. To-night we shall feast, and drink to their health, and if heaven pleases I shall have drink taken. Heaven bless you and all. I am, my dear brother Ivan, your affectionate brother,

BASIL.

LOST DIARIES

o*

TO

E. M.

I

FROM THE DIARY OF SMITH MINOR

St. James's School,
September, 1884.

Sunday.—Yesterday afternoon was a half-holiday we were playing prisoners base except four boys who were gardening with Mrs. Wickham. Peel hit Bell by mistake with all his force with the pic-axe on Bell's wrist.

Sunday.—Last night their was a total eclipse of the moon. We all stayed up to see it, it looked very funny. There was a shadow right over the moon. We began football yesterday. At tea the Head asked if any one had eaten chesnuts in the garden. Simes major said yes at once. Then the Head said he was sure others had too. Then Wilson stood up and after a time 7 chaps stood up. Then the Head said it would be the worse for those who didn't stand up as he knew who the culprets were. I hadn't eaten any but Anderson had given me a piece off his knife so I stood up two. The Head said we should all have two hours extra work. He was very waxy he said we were unreliabel.

Sunday.—Yesterday we were all photografed. Simes laughed and was sent to bed for misbehavier. Pork's people came down yesterday. We call Pork Hogg because he's dirty. He showed them over the school, and turned on the electrik light. The Head was looking through the curtain in the library and saw this. When his people went away Hogg was sent for and he is to be swished tomorrow. We told him he would get it hot and he blubbed.

Sunday.—We went for the choir expedition last Thursday. It was *great fun.* We went to London by the 8.35 train. We missed the train ! ! So we went by the 8.53. We got to London at 10.15. We then went to the mint we first saw the silver melted and made into thick tablets, then we saw it rolled out into thin bits then cut stamped and weighed then we had a very good luncheon and went to the Tower. We first saw the Bloody Tower were the little Princes were murdered then we saw the jewels the warder said the Queen's crown was worth over £1,000,000 then we saw the armory and the torture's, then we went to Madame Tussaus it is quite a large building now with a large stairkes then we had tea and went home.

Sunday.—I said to Anderson that we might start an aquarium but he said Ferguson had one last term and that it would be copying, he said he hates copying. So we'll have a menagery instead with lizards.

Sunday.—The lizard is very well indeed and has eat a lot of worms. White cheeked Jones ma and Mac said they must fight it out in the play-room in the hour. They fought with gloves. White gave him a bloody nose. We had a very good game of football yesterday. Williams and Pierce which left last term came from Eton to play. Pierce changed in my room. He says you don't say squit at Eton and you say Metutors not My tutors. The fireworks are in a week.

Saturday.—There was no work this morning as it was " All Saints day." There was a football matsh against another scool—Reynolds'. We won by three goals and three tries.

There was an awful row on Wednesday. Anderson cut off a piece of his hair. Mac nabbed it, and he said he hadn't as he was afraid of the consequenses. Then a search was made and they fond a piece of hair in his drawer. Mac told him he would find himself in Queer Street and Colly said when he was writing home on Sunday that he had better add that he was a liar. Nothing hapened till Monday and Anderson thought it was forgoten but at reading over when the 3nd Div came up the Head said: "Anderson I am astounded at you; you are a shufler and worse." He lost 50 marks and was swished. He would get 20 the head said if he did it again and he would be turned out of the choir.

Sunday.—When Colly was out of the room in Set 3 this morning Mason said he wouldn't sneak about me talking if I didn't sneak about him so I talked. When Colly came back Mason sneaked, Please sir will you ask Smith not to talk. I had to stand on the stool of penitence. We are going to put Mason in Coventry because he always sneaks just after he has sworn he won't. Last night we all had to play our pieces in the Drawing Room. I played a duet with Wilson mi. Astley played best. When everybody had played their pieces we had ginger beer and biscuits and went to bed. Fish played worst (on the violin).

Sunday.—We had fireworks on the 5th romman candles rockets crackers squibs and a set piece with God Save the Queen on it. They came from Broks who makes the fireworks at the Crystal palace we burnt a man in effigee a man with collars and an axe. The Head said he wouldn't say who it was meant to be but that all true Englishmen who were not traiters could guess. Rowley said it was meant to be Mister Gladstone but he only said this to get a rise out of Pork whose paters a liberal. It was reelly Guy Fawks then Pork said Anderson's father was a liberal too and Anderson hit him in the eye. The Head hates liberals.

There was another row this week. Christy said something to Broadwood at breakfast that the poridge was mighty good. That was copying Anderson who learnt it from his mater who is a Yankee. Mac asked him what he'd said. He said he'd said the porridge was good. Mac asked Is that all you've said. Christy got very red and looked as if he was going to blub and said that was all. Very well said Mac Come afterwards. Mac reported him for telling bungs. He wasn't swished as its his first term: but Mac told him he was making himself very unpopular.

On Tuesday Fatty the butler came into the 3rd Div scoolroom with a message. Some one said in a wisper Hullo Fatty. Mac nabbed it and said who said that nobody answered then Mac said he knew it was Middleton mi as he had recognised his voice Middleton swore he hadn't said a word but he was reported and swished he still swears he didn't say Fatty and I believe it was Pork. The other day at French Campbell went up to Colly and asked him what was wrong with les tables it had a pencil cross on it. Colly said that when he'd corrected it there was no S there. Campbell swore their was. Colly held the paper to the window and said he saw the ink of the S was fresh, then Christy began to blub and said he had done it and Colly said it was a forjerry and wrote forjer in white chalk on his back and said he would tell the chaps in the first Div but he didn't report him to the Head which was awfully decent of him becaus Christy is a new chap.

Sunday.—Trials are nearly over. We had Latin G and Greek G paper yesterday (set by the Head). There are only two more papers geography and Latin verse. The Consert is on Saturday. Pork's sister is called Jane ! ! Campbell saw it on the seel of a letter he got. His people were coming for the Consert but he's written to tell them not to as we told him the Head thought liberals worse than thieves.

II

FROM THE DIARY OF ISEULT OF BRITTANY

May 1.—Mamma sent me up a message early this morning to say that I was to put on my best white gown with my coral necklace, as guests were expected. She didn't say who. Nurse was in a fuss and pulled my hair when she did it, and made my face very sore by scrubbing it with pumice-stone. I can't think why, as there was no hurry. I came down punctually at noon. Mamma and papa were sitting in the hall, waiting. Fresh rushes were strewn on the floor. I was told to get out my harp, and to sit with my back to the light. I hadn't practised for weeks, and I can only play one song properly, " The Mallard," a Cornish song. When I told mamma that was the only song I knew, she said I was on no account to mention it, if I was asked to play ; but I was only to play *Breton* songs. I said I didn't know any. She said that didn't matter ; but that I could sing anything I knew and call it a Breton song. I said nothing, but I thought, and I still think, this was dishonest. Besides the only songs that I know are quite new. The stable people whistle them, and they come from Rome.

We waited a long time. Papa and mamma were both very fidgety and mamma kept on pulling me about, and telling me that my hair was badly done and that she could see daylight between the pleats of my frock. I nearly cried and papa said : " Leave the dear child alone; she's very good." After we'd been waiting about twenty minutes, the trumpets sounded and Morgan, the seneschal, walked in very slowly, and announced: "Sir Tristram of Lyoness."

Rather an oldish man walked in, with a reddish beard, and many wrinkles. One of his front teeth was broken and the other was black. He was dressed in a coat of mail which was too tight for him. He had nice eyes and seemed rather embarrassed. Mamma and papa made a great fuss about him and brought me forward and said: "This is our daughter Iseult," and mamma whispered to me: "Show your hands." I didn't want to do this, as nurse had scrubbed them so hard that they were red.

Sir Tristram bowed deeply, and seemed more and more embarrassed. After a long pause he said: "It's a very fine day, isn't it?"

Before I had time to answer, mamma broke in by saying: "Iseult has been up since six with the falconers." This wasn't true and I was surprised that mamma should be so forgetful. I hadn't been out with the hawkers for weeks.

Then dinner was served. It lasted for hours I thought, and the conversation flagged terribly. Kurvenal, Sir Tristram's Squire, had *twice* of everything and drank much more cider than was good for him. After dinner, mamma told me to fetch my harp and to sing a Breton song. I was just going to say I didn't know one, when she frowned at me so severely that I didn't dare. So I sang the Provençal orchard song about waking up too early that Kerodac the groom taught me. Sir Tristram said: "Charming, charming, that's German, isn't it; how well taught she is. I do like good singing." Then he yawned, although he tried not to, and papa said he was sure Sir Tristram was tired, and that he would take him to see the stables. Sir Tristram then became quite lively and said he would be delighted.

When they'd gone, mamma scolded me, and said that I had behaved like a ninny and that she didn't know what our guests would think of me. It seemed to me we only had one guest; but I didn't say so. Then she told me to go and rest so as to be ready for dinner.

I forgot to say that just as Sir Tristram was going out of the room he said to papa: "Your daughter's name is—er?" and papa said, "Yes, Iseult, after her aunt." And Sir Tristram said: "Oh! what a pretty name!"

May 6.—They've been here a week now and I haven't seen much of them; because Sir Tristram has been riding with papa nearly all day, and every day. But every day after dinner mamma makes me sing the Provençal song, and every time I sing it, Sir Tristram says: "Charming, charming, that's German, isn't it?" although I've already told him twice now that it isn't. I like Sir Tristram, only he's very silent, and after dinner he becomes sleepy directly, just like papa.

May 7.—I've had a most exciting day. Papa and mamma sent for me and when I came into the room they were both very solemn and said they had something particular to say to me. Then mamma cried and papa tried to soothe her and said: "It's all right, it's all right," and then he blurted out that I was to Marry Sir Tristram next Wednesday. I cried, and papa cried, and mamma cried, and then they said I was a lucky girl, and mamma said that I must see about my clothes at once.

May 8.—Nurse is in a fearful temper. She says we shall never be ready by Wednesday and that it's more than flesh and blood can stand to worrit folks like this. But mamma is in the best of tempers. Sir Tristram has gone away—to stay with some friends—he is coming back on Tuesday night. My wedding gown is to be made of silver with daisies worked on it. The weavers are working day and night, *but most of the stuff is old.* It belonged to mamma. I do think they might have given me a new gown. Blanche had a new one when she was married.

May 12.—The wedding went off very well. I had four maidens and four pages. After Mass, we had a long feast. Papa made a speech and broke down, and Tristram made a speech and got into a muddle about my name, and everybody was silent. Then he said I had beautiful hands and everybody cheered. After supper we were looking out on the sea, and just as Tristram was becoming talkative I noticed that he wore another ring besides his wedding ring, a green one, made of jasper. I said, "What a pretty ring! Who gave it you?" He said, "Oh, a friend," and changed the subject. Then he said he was very tired and went away.

May 13.—It's the 13th and that's an unlucky number. Nurse said that no child of hers should marry in May, so I suppose that's what brought it about. In any case Tristram, who has been very gloomy ever since he's been here, has got to go and fight in a tournament. He says he won't be away long and that there's no danger; not any more than crossing the sea in an open boat, which I *do* think *is* dangerous. He starts to-morrow at dawn.

May 14.—Nothing particular.

May 15.—No news.

May 16.—Kurvenal arrived this evening. He says that Tristram was slightly wounded; but would be all right in a day or two. I am very anxious.

May 17.—Tristram was brought back on a litter in the middle of the night. He has been wounded in the arm. The doctors here say he was bandaged wrong by the local doctor. They say he is suffering from slight local pain. Kurvenal says the horrid henchman hit his arm as hard as he could with a broad sword. Papa and mamma arrive to-morrow with the doctor. Tristram insists on sleeping out of doors on the beach. The doctor says this is a patient's whim and must be humoured. I'm sure it's bad for him, as the nights are very cold.

July 1.—I've been too busy to write my diary for weeks. Tristram is still just the same The doctors say there is no fear of immediate change.

August 10.—Mamma says the Queen of Cornwall (whose name is Iseult the same as mine) is coming for a few days, with her husband and some friends. I do think it's very inconsiderate, considering how full the house is already; and what with Tristram being so ill—and insisting on sleeping on the beach—it makes it very difficult for every one.

September 1.—Papa went out to shoot birds with his new cross-bow; but he came back in a bad temper as he'd only shot one, and a hen. Tristram is no better. He keeps on talking about a ship with a black sail.

September 19.—To-day I was on the beach with Tristram and he asked me if I saw a ship. I said I did. He asked me if the sail was black, and as the doctor had told me to humour him, I said it was. Upon which he got much worse, and I had to call the doctors. They said he was suffering from hypertrophy of the sensory nerves.

September 20.—Tristram unconscious. The Queen of Cornwall just arrived. Too busy to write.

III

FROM THE DIARY OF KING COPHETUA

Cophetua Castle, May 3.—We had to be married in May, after all. It was a choice between that and being married on a Friday, and Jane would not hear of that, so I gave in. Poor dear Mamma relented at the end and came to the wedding. On the whole she behaved with great restraint. She could not help saying just a word about rash promises. Jane looked exceedingly beautiful. I felt very proud of her. I regret nothing. We start for Italy to-morrow. We are to visit Milan, Florence and Rome. Jane is looking forward to the change.

Dijon, May 6.—We decided to break the journey here: but we shall probably start again to-morrow, as Jane is extremely dissatisfied with the Inn, the *Lion d'Or*. I, of course, chose the best. But she says she found a spider in her bedroom; she complained that the silver plates on which dinner was served were not properly cleaned; that the veal was tough, and that we had been given *Graves* under the guise of *Barsac*. All these things seem to me exceedingly trivial; but Jane is particular. In a way it is a good thing, but considering her early upbringing and her former circumstances, I confess I am astonished.

Lyons, May 12.—I shall be glad when we get to Italy. Jane becomes more and more fastidious about Inns. She walked out of four running, here. I was imprudent enough to say that Mamma had a vassal who was a distant connection of the Sieur Jehan de Blois and Jane insisted on my paying him a visit and asking him to lodge us, telling him who we are, as we are travelling incognito as the Baron and Baroness of Wessex. This put me in a very awkward position, as I don't know him. I did it, however, and Jane came with me. I have seldom felt so awkward, but really he could not have made things easier. He was tact itself, and while respecting our incognito, he treated us with the utmost consideration. He was most kind. Jane made me a little uncomfortable by praising a fine crystal goblet encrusted with emeralds. Sieur Jehan was of course obliged to offer it her, and, to my vexation, she accepted it.

Avignon, May 20.—Jane finds our incognito more and more irksome. I was looking forward to a real quiet holiday, where we could get away from all fuss and worry, and all the impediments of rank and riches. I wanted to pretend we were poor for a while. To send on the litters with the oxen, the horses, and the baggage, and to ride on mules—as soon as we had reached the South—but Jane would not hear of this. She said she had had enough of poverty without playing at it now. This is of course quite true, but I wish she wouldn't say such things before people. It makes one so uncomfortable. Here she has insisted on our staying with the Pope, which may put me in a very awkward position with regard to several of our allies in Italy. He has been, however, most gracious. Jane is very impulsive at times. She insisted on our making an expedition to the Bridge here, by moonlight, and dancing on it. She kicked off her shoes and danced barefooted; I asked her not to do this, whereupon she said: "If the courtiers hadn't praised my ankles you would never have married me and what's the use of having pretty ankles, if nobody can see them!" I shall be glad when we get to Italy. I am determined to preserve a strict incognito, once we are across the frontier.

Turin, June 10.—It has poured with rain every day since we crossed the frontier, and Jane won't believe that it is ever fine in Italy. It is very cold for the time of year, and the people here say that there has not been such a summer for thirty years. Every time I mention the blue sky of Italy Jane loses her temper. She spends all her time at the goldsmiths' shops and at the weavers'—I am afraid she is extravagant: and her taste in dress is not quite as restrained as I could wish. Of course it doesn't matter here, but at home it would shock people. For instance, last night she came down to supper dressed as a Turkish Sultana in pink trousers and a scimitar, and without even a veil over her face. When I remonstrated she said men did not understand these things.

Milan, June 15.—It is still raining. Jane refused to look at the Cathedral and spends her whole time at the merchants' booths as usual. To-day I broached the incognito question. I suggested our walking on foot, or perhaps riding on mules, to Florence. Jane, to my great surprise, said she would be delighted to do this, and asked when we were to start. I said we had better start the day after to-morrow. I am greatly relieved. She is really very sensible, if a little impulsive at times; but considering her early life, it might be much worse. I have much to be thankful for. She is greatly admired, only I wish she would not wear such bright colours.

Florence, June 20.—It has been a great disappointment. Just as we were making preparations to start entirely incognito—Jane had even begged that we should walk on foot the whole way and take no clothes with us—a messenger arrived from the Florentine Embassy here, saying that the Duke of Florence had heard of our intended visit and had put a cavalcade of six carriages, fifty mules, seven litters, and a hundred men-at-arms at our disposal. How he could have heard of our intention I don't know! Jane was bitterly disappointed. She cried, and said she had been looking forward to this walking tour more than to anything else. But I managed to soothe her, and she eventually consented to accept the escort of the Duke. It would have been impossible to refuse. As it was, we were very comfortable. We stopped at Bologna on the way, and Jane insisted on going to the market and buying a sausage. She tried to make me taste it, but I cannot endure the taste of garlic.

At Florence we were magnificently received, and taken at once to the Palace—where the rooms are very spacious. Jane complains of the draughts and the cold. It is still pouring with rain. There is a very fine collection of Greek statues to be seen here, but Jane takes no interest in these things. The first thing she did was to go to the New bridge, which is lined with goldsmiths' shops on both sides and to spend a great deal of money on perfectly useless trinkets. She says she must have some things to bring back to my sisters. This was thoughtful of her. The Duke is going to give a great banquet in our honour on Tuesday next.

June 23.—The feast is to-night. The gardens have been hung with lanterns; a banquet has been prepared on a gigantic scale. Five hundred guests have been bidden. Jane was greatly looking forward to it and lo and behold! by the most evil mischance a terrible vexation has befallen us. A courier arrived this morning, bearing letters for me, and among them was one announcing the death of the Duke of Burgundy, who is my uncle by marriage. I told Jane that of course we could not possibly be present at the banquet. Jane said that I knew best, but that the Duke would be mortally offended by our absence, since he had arranged the banquet entirely for us and spent a sum of 10,000 ducats on it. It would be, she pointed out—and I am obliged to admit she is right—most impolitic to annoy the Duke. After an hour's reflection I hit on what seemed to me an excellent solution—that we should be present, but dressed in mourning. Jane said this was impossible as she had no black clothes. Then she suggested that I should keep back the news until to-morrow, and if the news were received in other quarters, deny its authenticity, and say we had a later bulletin. This on the whole seemed to be the wisest course. As the etiquette here is very strict and the Dowager Duchess is most particular, I pray that Jane may be careful and guarded in her expressions.

June 25.—My poor dear mother was right after all. I should have listened, and now it is too late. The dinner went off very well. We sat at a small table on a raised dais. Jane sat between the Duke and the Prime Minister and opposite the Dowager Duchess. There was no one at the table, except myself, under sixty years of age, and only the greatest magnates were present. Jane was silent and demure and becomingly dressed. I congratulated myself on everything. After the banquet came the dance, and Jane took part with exquisite grace in the saraband : she observed all the rules of etiquette. The Dowager Duchess seemed charmed with her. Then later came supper, which was served in a tent, and which was perhaps more solemn than everything. When the time came to lead Jane to supper she was nowhere to be found. Outside in the garden the minor nobles were dancing in masks, and some mimes were singing. We waited, and then a message came that the Queen had had a touch of ague and had retired. The supper went off gloomily. At the close an enormous pie was brought in, the sight of which caused a ripple of well-bred applause. "Viva Il Re Cophetua" was written on it in letters of pink sugar. It was truly a triumph of culinary art. The mime announced that the moment had come for it to be cut, and as the Grand Duke rose to do this the thin crust burst of itself, and out stepped Jane, with no garments beside her glorious dark hair! She tripped on to the table, and then with a peal of laughter leapt from it and ran into the garden, since when she has not been heard of! My anguish and shame are too great for words. But the Duke and the Dowager have been most sympathetic.

June 26.—Jane has fled, and my jewels as well as hers are missing.

It is suspected that the attaché at the Florentine Embassy at Milan is at the bottom of the conspiracy, for Jane herself had a good heart.

IV

FROM THE DIARY OF FROISSART, WAR CORRESPONDENT

Parys, The Feast of the Epiphanie.—The astrologers say there will be plentyfull trouble in Normandy, in the spring.

June 10.—To dyner with the Cardinall of Piergourt to meet the gentyll King of Behayne and the Lorde Charles, his son. The Cardinall sayd neither the Kynge of Englande nor the Frenche Kynge desire warre, but the honour of them and of their people saved, they wolde gladly fall to any reasonable way. But the King of Behayne shook his heade and sayd: "I am feare I am a pesymyste," which is Almayne for a man who beholds the future with no gladde chere.

June 20.—The great merchaunt of Araby, Montefior, says there will be no warre. He has received worde from the cytie of London, and his friends, great merchaunts all, and notably, Salmone and Glukstyn, sayd likewise that there will be no warre.

June 30.—The currours have brought worde home, the Kynge of Englande was on the see with a great army, and is now a lande in Normandy. Have received faire offers for chronycles of the warre from London, Parys, and Rome; they offer three thousand crounes monthly, payeing curtesly for all my expenses. Have sayd I will gladly fall to their wish.

July 1.—Trussed bagge and baggage in great hast and departed towarde Normandy, the seat of warre.

July 2.—Ryde but small journeys, and do purpose, being no great horseman, every time I have to ryde a horse, to add three crounes to the expenses which my patrons curtesly pay.

Take lodgynges every day bytwene noone and thre of the clocke. Finde the contrey frutefull and reasonably suffycent of wyne.

July 3, *Cane.*—A great and ryche town with many burgesses, crafty men. They solde wyne so deare that there were no byers save myself who bought suffycent and added to the lyste which my patrons curtesly pay.

July 4, *Amyense.*—Left Cane and the englysshmen have taken the toune and clene robbed it. Right pensyve as to putting my lyfe in adventure.

Sir Godmar de Fay is to kepe note of the chronyclers and he has ordayned them to bring him their chronycles. He has curtesly made these rules for the chronyclers. Chronyclers may only chronycle the truth. Chronyclers may not chronycle the names of places, bridges, rivers, castels where batayles happen—nor the names of any lordes, knyghtes, marshals, erles, or others who take part in the batayle: nor the names of any weapons or artillery used, nor the names or numbers of any prisoners taken in batayle.

Thanks to Sir Godmar de Fay the chronycler's task has been made lyghter.

July 6, *Calys.*—The chronyclers have been ordayned by Sir Godmar de Fay to go to Calys. There are nine chronyclers. One is an Alleymayne, who is learned in the art of warre, one is a Genowayes, and one an Englysshman, the rest are Frenche. The cytie of Calys is full of drapery and other merchauntdyse, noble ladyes and damosels. The chronyclers have good wyl to stay in the cytie.

July 7.—Sir Godmar de Fay has ordayned all the chronyclers to leave the cytie of Calys and to ride to a lytell town called Nully, where there are no merchauntdyse, and no damosels, nor suffycent of wyne. The chronyclers are not so merrie as in the cytie of Calys.

July 9.—Played chesse with the Genowayse and was checkmate with a bishop.

August 6.—The chronyclers are all pensyve. They are lodged in the feldes. There has fallen a great rayne that pours downe on our tents. There is no wyne nor pasties, nor suffycent of flesshe, no bookes for to rede, nor any company.

Last nyghte I wrote a ballade on Warre, which ends, "But Johnnie Froissart wisheth he were dead." It is too indiscrete to publysh. I wysh I were at Calys. I wysh I were at Parys. I wysh I were anywhere but at Nully.

August 23.—At the Kynge's commandment the chronyclers are to go to the fronte.

August 25, *Friday*.—The Kynge of Englande and the French Kynge have ordayned all the business of a batayle. I shall watch it and chronycle it from a hill, which shall not be too farre away to see and not too neare to adventure my lyfe.

August 26.—I rode to a windmill but mistooke the way, as a great rayne fell, then the eyre waxed clere and I saw a great many Englyssh erls and Frenche knyghtes, riding in contrarie directions, in hast. Then many Genowayse went by, and the Englysshmen began to shote feersly with their crossbowes and their arowes fell so hotly that I rode to a lytell hut, and finding shelter there I wayted till the snowe of arowes should have passed. Then I clymbed to the top of the hill but I could see lytell but dyverse men riding here and there. When I went out again, aboute evensong, I could see no one aboute, dyverse knyghtes and squyers rode by looking for their maisters, and then it was sayd the Kynge had fought a batayle, and had rode to the castell of Broye, and thence to Amyense.

August 30.—The chronyclers have been ordayned to go to Calys, whereat they are well pleased save for a feare of a siege. The chronyclers have writ the chronycle of the Day of Saturday, August 26. It was a great batayle, ryght cruell, and it is named the batayle of Cressey.

Some of the chronyclers say the Englysshmen discomfyted the French; others that the King discomfyted the Englysshe; but the Englysshmen repute themselves to have the victorie; but all this shall be told in my chronycle, which I shall write when I am once more in the fayre cytie of Parys. It was a great batayle and the Frenche and the Englysshe Lordes are both well pleased at the feats of arms, and the Frenche Kynge, though the day was not as he wolde have had it, has wonne hygh renowne and is ryght pleased—likewise the Englysshe Kynge, and his son; but both Kynges have ordayned the chronyclers to make no boast of their good adventure.

August 30.—The Kynge of Englande has layd siege to Calys and has sayd he will take the towne by famysshing. When worde of this was brought to the chronyclers they were displeased. It is well that I have hyd in a safe place some wyne and other thynges necessarie.

Later.—All thynges to eat are solde at a great pryce. A mouse costs a croune.

August 31.—All the poore and mean people were constrained by the capture of Calys to yssue out of the town, men, women, and children, and to pass through the Englysshe host, and with them the poore chronyclers. And the Kynge of Englande gave them and the chronyclers mete and drinke to dyner, and every person ii d. sterlying in alms.

And the chronyclers have added to the lyst of their costs which their patrons curtesly pay: To loss of honour at receiving alms from an Englysshe Kynge, a thousand crounes.

V

FROM THE DIARY OF GEORGE WASHINGTON

WRITTEN WHEN A SCHOOLBOY

Bridges Creek, 1744, *September* 20.—My mother has at last consented to let me go to school. I had repeatedly made it quite plain to her that the private tuition hitherto accorded to me was inadequate; that I would be in danger of being outstripped in the race owing to insufficient groundwork. My mother, although very shrewd in some matters, was curiously obstinate on this point. She positively declined to let me attend the day-school, saying that she thought I knew quite enough for a boy of my age, and that it would be time enough for me to go to school when I was older. I quoted to her Tacitus' powerful phrase about the insidious danger of indolence; how there is a charm in indolence—but let me taste the full pleasure of transcribing the noble original: "Subit quippe etiam ipsius inertiæ dulcedo: et invisa primo desidia postremo amatur"; but she only said that she did not understand Latin. This was scarcely an argument, as I translated it for her.

I cannot help thinking that there was sometimes an element of pose in Tacitus' much-vaunted terseness.

September 29.—I went to school for the first time to-day. I confess I was disappointed. We are reading, in the Fourth Division, in which I was placed at my mother's express request, Eutropius and Ovid; both very insipid writers. The boys are lamentably backward and show a deplorable lack of interest in the classics. The French master has an accent that leaves much to be desired, and he seems rather shaky about his past participles. However, all these things are but trifles. What I really resent is the gross injustice which seems to be the leading principle at this school—if school it can be called.

For instance, when the master asks a question, those boys who know the answer are told to hold up their hands. During the history lesson Henry VIII was mentioned in connection with the religious quarrels of the sixteenth century, a question which, I confess, can have but small interest for any educated person at the present day. The master asked what British poet had written a play on the subject of Henry VIII. I, of course, held up my hand, and so did a boy called Jonas Pike. I was told to answer first, and I said that the play was in the main by Fletcher, with possible later interpolations. The usher, it is scarcely credible, said, "Go to the bottom of the form," and when Jonas Pike was asked he replied, "Shakespeare," and was told to go up one. This was, I consider, a monstrous piece of injustice.

During one of the intervals, which are only too frequent, between the lessons, the boys play a foolish game called "It," in which even those who have no aptitude and still less inclination for this tedious form of horse-play, are compelled to take part. The game consists in one boy being named "it" (though why the neuter is used in this case instead of the obviously necessary masculine it is hard to see). He has to endeavour to touch one of the other boys, who in their turn do their best to evade him by running, and should he succeed in touching one of them, the boy who is touched becomes " it " *ipso facto.* It is all very tedious and silly. I was touched almost immediately, and when I said that I would willingly transfer the privilege of being touched to one of the other boys who were obviously eager to obtain it, one of the bigger boys (again Jonas Pike) gave me a sharp kick on the shin. I confess I was ruffled. I was perhaps to blame in what followed. I am, perhaps, inclined to forget at times that Providence has made me physically strong. I retaliated with more insistence than I intended, and in the undignified scuffle which ensued Jonas Pike twisted his ankle. He had to be supported home. When questioned as to the cause of the accident I regret to say he told a deliberate falsehood. He said he had slipped on the ladder in the gymnasium. I felt it my duty to inform the head-master of the indirect and unwilling part I had played in the matter.

The head master, who is positively unable to perceive the importance of plain-speaking, said, " I suppose you mean you did it." I answered, " No, sir ; I was the resisting but not the passive agent in an unwarrantable assault." The result was I was told to stay in during the afternoon and copy out the First Eclogue of Virgil. It is characteristic of the head master to choose a feeble Eclogue of Virgil instead of one of the admirable Georgics. Jonas Pike is to be flogged, as soon as his foot is well, for his untruthfulness.

This, my first experience of school life, is not very hopeful.

October 10.—The routine of the life here seems to me more and more meaningless. The work is to me child's play ; and indeed chiefly consists in checking the inaccuracies of the ushers. They show no gratitude to me—indeed, sometimes the reverse of gratitude.

One day, in the English class, one of the ushers grossly misquoted Pope. He said, " A little knowledge is a dangerous thing." I held up my hand and asked if the line was not rather " A little learning is a dangerous thing," adding that Pope would scarcely have thought a little *knowledge* to be dangerous, since all *knowledge* is valuable. The usher tried to evade the point by a joke, which betrayed gross theological ignorance. He said : " All Popes are not infallible."

One of the boys brought into school a foolish toy—a gutta-percha snake that contracts under pressure and expands when released, with a whistling screech.

Jonas Pike, who is the most ignorant as well as the most ill-mannered of all the boys, suggested that the snake should be put into the French master's locker, in which he keeps the exercises for the week. The key of the locker is left in charge of the top boy of the class, who, I say it in all modesty, is myself. Presently another boy, Hudson by name, asked me for the key. I gave it to him, and he handed it to Pike, who inserted the snake in the locker. When the French master opened the locker the snake flew in his face. He asked me if I had had any hand in the matter. I answered that I had not touched the snake. He asked me if I had opened the locker ; I, of course, said " No." Questioned further as to how the snake could have got there, I admitted having lent the key to Hudson, ignorant of any ulterior purpose. In spite of this I was obliged, in company with Pike and Hudson, to copy out some entirely old-fashioned and meaningless exercises in syntax.

October 13.—A pretty little episode happened at home

to-day. The gardener's boy asked me if he might try his new axe on the old cherry-tree, which I have often vainly urged mother to cut down. I said, "By all means." It appears that he misunderstood me and cut down the tree. My mother was about to send him away, but I went straight to her and said I would take the entire responsibility for the loss of the tree on myself, as I had always openly advocated its removal and that the gardener's boy was well aware of my views on the subject. My mother was so much touched at my straightforwardness that she gave me some candy, a refreshment to which I am still partial. Would that the ushers at school could share her fine discrimination, her sound judgment, and her appreciation of character.

VI

FROM THE DIARY OF MARCUS AURELIUS

Rome. The Ides of March.—It is curious that Julius Cæsar should have considered this date to be unlucky! It was on that—for him auspicious—date that he was for ever prevented from committing the egregious folly of accepting the crown of Rome. A *king* of Rome is an unthinkable thing! An emperor of the Roman Empire is, of course, a very different matter.

April 1.—Faustina, in accordance with some ridiculous tradition, committed a grossly undignified act. She came into my study, the third hour—my busiest time, and asked me to lend her the memoirs of Remus in the Wolf's Lair. I spent a fruitless half-hour in search of the book. It then occurred to me that the whole matter was a jest—in the very worst taste, since both my secretaries were present—and I regret to say they smiled.

April 6.—Went to the games, in company with Faustina and Commodus. Commodus, as usual, too exuberant in the manner of his applause. I am all in favour of his applauding. The games are not what they used to be. The modern lions consume the Christians without the slightest discrimination. All this modern hurry and hustle is very distressing.

April 10.—Stayed at Tivoli with V. . . . and A. . . . from Saturday to Monday. Even in a country house a day may be well spent. Much interesting talk on the

Fiscal question. V. . . . deprecates Tariff Reform in all its shapes. A. . . . while remaining, as he ever was, a staunch Free Trader, considers that in some cases—and given certain conditions—retaliation is admissible—possibly in the matter of the fringes of litters and the axles of chariot-wheels—objects which exclusively concern the very rich.

April 20.—An exhilarating day. Walked to the Tiber and back. Read the preface of the new Persian grammar. Faustina interrupted me three times over purely trivial matters of domestic detail.

April 20.—Commodus is impossible. He grows more and more extravagant every day. He persists in spending his pocket money in buying absurd pets—and the gods know that Faustina has enough pets in the house already. But I am thankful to say I have drawn the line at badgers. I put my foot down. I was dignified, but firm. I endure Faustina's peacocks, because I think it is good for my better nature. Besides which they are ornamental and—if properly dressed—not unpleasant to the palate, but badgers——!

April 20.—A painful episode occurred. When I returned from my morning stroll I was aware that an altercation was taking place in the atrium. I entered and found myself face to face with two Persian merchants—of the lowest type—who were exhibiting to Faustina several ropes of pearls. Faustina, of course had had no hand in the matter. The merchants had forced themselves on her presence on some ridiculous pretext. Faustina, in spite of her faults, values jewels at their true price. She has a soul above such things. She abhors trinkets. She sees their futility.

April 23.—Re-read the Iliad. Find it too long. The character of Helen shows defective psychology.

Homer did not understand women.

April 27.—Games again. Very tame. Lions lethargic as usual. How dissatisfied Nero would have been! Nero, although a bad poet, was an excellent organiser. He understood the *psychology of the crowd.* He was essentially an altruist. Faustina insisted on making a foolish bet. Women's bets are the last word of silliness. They bet because the name of a gladiator reminds them of a pet dog, or for some such reason. They have no inkling of logic: no power of deduction. I found no difficulty in anticipating the victories of the successful candidates, but I refrained from making a wager.

May 1.—Absurd processions in the streets. Faustina painted her face black and walked round the garden in a movable bower of greenery. I could see no kind of point or sense in the episode. Under cross-examination, she confessed that the idea had been suggested to her by her nurse. All this is very trying. It sets Commodus the worst possible example. But I suppose I must endure this. The ways of Fate are inscrutable, and after all, things might have been worse. Faustina might have been a loose woman! A profligate!

May 6.—Read out the first canto of my epic on the origins of species to Faustina and Commodus. Commodus, I regret to say, yawned and finally dozed. Faustina enjoyed it immensely. She said she always thought that I was a real poet, and that now she *knew it.* She says she thinks it is far better than Homer or Virgil; that there is so much more in it. Faustina is a very good judge of literature. There is no one whose opinion on matters of art and literature I value more. For instance she thinks Sappho's lyrics are not only trivial, but coarse. She also thinks

Æschylus much over-rated, which, of course, he is. How far we have got beyond all that! Some day I mean to write a play on the subject of love. It has never yet been properly treated—on the stage. Sophocles and Seneca knew nothing of women; and Euripides' women are far too complicated.

May 12.—Meditated on religion, but was again interrupted by Faustina just as I was making a really illuminating note on the subject of Isis. Much distressed by modern free thought. Commodus pays much too much attention to the minor goddesses, but this, at his age, is excusable. He is, thank goodness, entirely untainted by the detestable Jewish or so-called "Christian" superstition, which I fear is spreading.

May 13.—V. . . . and A. . . . dined. Also a Greek philosopher whose name escapes me. The Greek was most indiscreet. He discussed the Christian question before everybody. He must have been aware by my expression that the topic is one which I consider unfit for public discussion. He not only discussed, but he actually defended this hysterical, obstinate, unpatriotic, and fundamentally criminal sect. I do not, of course, entirely credit the stories current with regard to their orgies and their human sacrifices. The evidence is not—so far—sufficiently sound; but, whatever their practices and their rites may be, the Christians are a pernicious and dangerous sect. They will prove, unless they are extirpated, the ruin of the Empire. They have no notion of civic duty; no reverence, no respect for custom or tradition. They are unfilial, and they are the enemies of the human race. They are a cancer in the State. Faustina agrees with me, I am glad to say.

May 14.—Commodus is suspected of having made

friends with a Christian slave. The rumour is no doubt a calumny. I cannot bring myself to believe that a son of mine, with the education which he has enjoyed, and the example which has ever been before his eyes, of his father's unswerving and unremitting devotion to duty and the State, can have degraded himself by dabbling in this degrading and wicked superstition. Nevertheless it is as well to be on the safe side, and, after prolonged reflection, I have decided to make a great sacrifice. I am going to allow him to take part professionally in the games: under another name of course. I think it may distract him. The games are a Roman institution. They are the expression of the Empire. They breathe the spirit of Romulus, of Brutus, of Regulus, of Fabius Cunctator, of Cincinnatus, of the Gracchi. Faustina said only yesterday that she felt she was the mother of at least one Gracchus! That was well said. I was much touched.

May 20.—Commodus has appeared with great success, but the Lions still show apathy.

VII

FROM THE DIARY OF MRS. JAMES LEE'S HUSBAND

October 1.—At last the heat wave is over. It's the first day we have been able to breathe for months.

Just as I was coming back from my morning walk, Hilda leant out of the window, and suggested I could climb up into her room like Romeo. I said I preferred the door. Hilda shut the window with a bang and was cross all through luncheon.

"Rissoles again," I said to Hilda, "you know I hate hashed meat." She said: "I know I can't give you the food you get at the Grand Hotel." That's because I went to Deauville last week.

October 5.—We lit a fire for the first time last night. Hilda said she felt cold. I thought it was rather stuffy. She said: "Do light the fire," and went out of the room. I lit it, and it smoked. This chimney always does smoke at first. When she came back she said: "What have you done?" I said: "I've lit the fire; you asked me to." She said: "But not all that wood at once, and you ought to have pushed the wood back." For the rest of the evening she complained of the heat and the smoke, although we had the window open in the dining-room and the smoke had all disappeared after a few moments.

October 7.—It's very windy. Went for a walk on the cliffs. Back through the fields. Saw a rabbit and a magpie. Wish I had had a gun.

I said to Hilda that the sea was striped to leeward like a snake, and olive-coloured, but on the weather side it was spotted with wind. Hilda said: "You are very observant about the weather." This was a hit at me and the fire. Little things rankle in her mind.

Afterwards she was sorry she had said this and she said: "What fun we shall have here in winter." I don't think it's a winter place myself, but I want to stay here till I've finished my poem. I'm getting on with it.

October 8.—I read out to Hilda a lyric I had just finished. It's to come in the Second Canto when Lancelot says good-bye to Princess Asra. The situation is roughly that the Princess bullies him and he gets sick of it and goes—and then, of course, she's sorry, when it's too late. He sings the song as he's going. She overhears it. I was rather pleased with it. Hilda said: "Oh! of course I know I worry you with my attentions." What this had got to do with the poem I can't think. It was all because last night, when I was working, Hilda came into my room and said: "Are you warm enough?" and I said "Yes," rather absent-mindedly, as I was in the middle of my work. Ten minutes later she looked in again and asked me if I wanted some beer, and I said "No," without looking up. Then very soon afterwards she came in a third time, and asked me if I was sure I wasn't cold, and whether I wouldn't have the fire lit. Rather snappishly—because it is a bore to be interrupted just when one's on the verge of getting an idea fixed—I said "No."

I'm afraid this hurt her feelings.

October 9.—Since Hilda has given up her sketching she has nothing to do. I was very busy this afternoon finishing my weekly article in time for the post. She rushed into the room and said didn't I think a butterfly settling on a rock was the ultimate symbol of love and the mind of man ? I said I thought she was very probably right. Heavens knows what she meant. Women's minds move by jerks, one never knows what they'll say next. They're so irrelevant.

October 10.—It's blowing a gale. Stuck in the poem. Hilda says it's cynical. I don't know what she means. She says she didn't know I was so bitter. I said: "It's only a kind of fairy tale." She said: "Yes; but that makes it worse." "But it's only an ordinary love story," I said. She said: "Of course I know nothing can go on being the same. It can no doubt be better, but not the same as it was before." "But Princess Asra is only an incident in my poem," I said. Hilda said nothing, but after a time she asked me whether I thought that was the meaning of the moan of the wind. I have no idea what she meant by "that." She is very cryptic sometimes.

October 11.—Lovely day. The sun came out and I suggested that I should take a holiday, and that we should go and have a picnic on the rocks. I was afraid Hilda might have something against the plan—one never knows. But she didn't. On the contrary she seemed delighted. She made a hamper and I carried it down to the rocks. We caught shrimps and threw stones into the sea just like children. I think Hilda enjoyed herself. On the way home, I asked her why she didn't go on with her drawing. I really think it's a great pity she has given it up. She has real talent. She said: "I will if you wish it." I said: "Of course I don't want you to do it, if you don't like; but I do think it's a pity to waste such a very real talent." She said: "I quite understand," and sighed. I wonder what she was thinking of. Hilda is absurdly modest. She draws extremely well, especially figures.

October 12.—Hilda has begun drawing again. I am delighted. She began copying the cast of a hand; but I suggested to her that it would be far more interesting for her to draw a real hand from nature. So she got a little girl from the village to sit for her. I am delighted. It gives her an occupation, and I really am very busy just now. After all, we came here so as not to be disturbed—to be away from people and interruptions; and I find that in the last two months I have got through less work than I did in London in June. I must make up for lost time. I can't get on with the poem. I think I shall leave it for a time. I should immensely like Hilda's opinion on what ought to happen next. She can be of the greatest help and use when she chooses. Unfortunately she has taken one of those unreasonable and entirely unaccountable dislikes to this poem, and no argument is of the slightest use. It's no good even mentioning it. I shall leave it for a time and go on with my other work. It is most unfortunate that Hilda should look upon it in this light, especially as she doesn't even know what the subject is; but she has taken an episode—in fact, one little song—as symbolic of the whole. But then logic never was Hilda's strong point.

October 13.—Hilda is getting on very well with the hand. She seems to enjoy it, which is the great thing.

October 24.—Have been too busy all these last days thinking, even to write my diary. Believe I have at last really got an idea for the poem. Shall begin to-morrow. Have not dared mention it to Hilda. Fortunately she is still utterly absorbed in her drawing.

October 27.—Great disappointment. Last night Hilda said it was no good concealing things any longer, and that one must look facts in the face. I had no idea what she meant. Then she said she had noticed for some time past how bored I was here, and how I was longing to get rid of her. Nothing I could say would persuade her of the contrary. I tried to explain that I had been searching for a new idea and that this had no doubt made me appear more absent-minded than usual. She said: "I am not going to worry you any longer. I am going to set you free." And to my intense surprise she announced that she had booked a berth on the steamer for the day after to-morrow. I knew that argument wouldn't be of any use, so I gave in at once. It is most disappointing just as I had got an idea I wanted to consult her about.

October 29.—On board the steamer *Queen Marguerite.* Saw Hilda off. She insisted on going and refused to argue. Deeply regret she is leaving. Hilda is the only woman I ever met who remains tidy even on a steamer. The sea-air suits her. It has done her a world of good, and it's a great pity she is leaving so soon—she says it's for good; but that, of course, is ridiculous.

VIII

FROM THE DIARY OF SHERLOCK HOLMES

Baker Street, January 1.—Starting a diary in order to jot down a few useful incidents which will be of no use to Watson. Watson very often fails to see that an unsuccessful case is more interesting from a professional point of view than a successful case. He means well.

January 6.—Watson has gone to Brighton for a few days, for change of air. This morning quite an interesting little incident happened which I note as a useful example of how sometimes people who have no powers of deduction nevertheless stumble on the truth for the wrong reason. (This never happens to Watson, *fortunately*.) Lestrade called from Scotland Yard with reference to the theft of a diamond and ruby ring from Lady Dorothy Smith's wedding presents. The facts of the case were briefly these: On Thursday evening such of the presents as were jewels had been brought down from Lady Dorothy's bedroom to the drawing-room to be shown to an admiring group of friends. The ring was amongst them. After they had been shown, the jewels were taken upstairs once more and locked in the safe. The next morning the ring was missing. Lestrade, after investigating the matter, came to the conclusion that the ring had not been stolen, but had either been dropped in the drawing-room, or replaced in one of the other cases; but since he had searched the room and the remaining cases, his theory so far received no support. I accompanied him to Eaton Square to the residence of Lady Middlesex, Lady Dorothy's mother.

While we were engaged in searching the drawing-room, Lestrade uttered a cry of triumph and produced the ring from the lining of the armchair. I told him he might enjoy the triumph, but that the matter was not quite so simple as he seemed to think. A glance at the ring had shown me not only that the stones were false, but that the false ring had been made in a hurry. To deduce the name of its maker was of course child's play. Lestrade or any pupil of Scotland Yard would have taken for granted it was the same jeweller who had made the real ring. I asked for the bridegroom's present, and in a short time I was interviewing the jeweller who had provided it. As I thought, he had made a ring, with imitation stones (made of the dust of real stones), a week ago, for a young lady. She had given no name and had fetched and paid for it herself. I deduced the obvious fact that Lady Dorothy had lost the real ring, her uncle's gift, and, not daring to say so, had had an imitation ring made. I returned to the house, where I found Lestrade, who had called to make arrangements for watching the presents during their exhibition.

I asked for Lady Dorothy, who at once said to me:

"The ring was found yesterday by Mr. Lestrade."

"I know," I answered, "but which ring?"

She could not repress a slight twitch of the eyelids as she said: "There was only one ring."

I told her of my discovery and of my investigations.

"This is a very odd coincidence, Mr. Holmes," she said. "Some one else must have ordered an imitation. But you shall examine my ring for yourself." Whereupon she fetched the ring, and I saw it was no imitation. She had of course in the meantime found the real ring.

But to my intense annoyance she took it to Lestrade and said to him :

"Isn't this the ring you found yesterday, Mr. Lestrade ?"

Lestrade examined it and said, "Of course it is absolutely identical in every respect."

"And do you think it is an imitation ?" asked this most provoking young lady.

"Certainly not," said Lestrade, and turning to me he added : "Ah ! Holmes, that is where theory leads one. At the Yard we go in for facts."

I could say nothing ; but as I said good-bye to Lady Dorothy, I congratulated her on having found the real ring. The incident, although it proved the correctness of my reasoning, was vexing as it gave that ignorant blunderer an opportunity of crowing over me.

January 10.—A man called just as Watson and I were having breakfast. He didn't give his name. He asked me if I knew who he was. I said, "Beyond seeing that you are unmarried, that you have travelled up this morning from Sussex, that you have served in the French Army, that you write for reviews, and are especially interested in the battles of the Middle Ages, that you give lectures, that you are a Roman Catholic, and that you have once been to Japan, I don't know who you are."

The man replied that he *was* unmarried, but that he lived in Manchester, that he had never been to Sussex or Japan, that he had never written a line in his life, that he had never served in any army save the English Territorial force, that so far from being a Roman Catholic he was a Freemason, and that he was by trade an electrical engineer—I suspected him of lying ; and I asked him why his boots were covered with the clayey and chalk mixture peculiar to Horsham ; why his boots were French Army service boots, elastic-sided, and bought probably at Valmy ; why the second half of a return ticket from Southwater was emerging from his ticket-pocket ; why he wore the medal of St. Anthony on his watch-chain ; why he smoked Caporal cigarettes; why the proofs of an article on the Battle of Eylau were protruding from his breast-pocket, together with a copy of the *Tablet* ; why he carried in his hand a parcel which, owing to the untidy way in which it had been made (an untidiness which, in harmony with the rest of his clothes, showed that he could not be married) revealed the fact that it contained photographic magic lantern slides ; and why he was tattooed on the left wrist with a Japanese fish.

" The reason I have come to consult you will explain some of these things," he answered.

" I was staying last night at the Windsor Hotel, and this morning when I woke up I found an entirely different set of clothes from my own. I called the waiter and pointed this out, but neither the waiter nor any of the other servants, after making full enquiries, were able to account for the change. None of the other occupants of the hotel had complained of anything being wrong with their own clothes.

" Two gentlemen had gone out early from the hotel at 7.30. One of them had left for good, the other was expected to return.

" All the belongings I am wearing, including this parcel, which contains slides, belong to someone else.

" My own things contained nothing valuable, and consisted of clothes and boots very similar to these ;

my coat was also stuffed with papers. As to the tattoo, it was done at a Turkish bath by a shampooer, who learnt the trick in the Navy."

The case did not present any features of the slightest interest. I merely advised the man to return to the hotel and await the real owner of the clothes, who was evidently the man who had gone out at 7.30.

This is a case of my reasoning being, with one partial exception, perfectly correct. Everything I had deduced would no doubt have fitted the real owner of the clothes.

Watson asked rather irrelevantly why I had not noticed that the clothes were not the man's own clothes. A stupid question, as the clothes were reach-me-downs which fitted him as well as such clothes ever do fit, and he was probably of the same build as their rightful owner.

January 12.—Found a carbuncle of unusual size in the plum-pudding. Suspected the makings of an interesting case. But luckily, before I had stated any hypothesis to Watson—who was greatly excited—Mrs. Turner came in and noticed it and said her naughty nephew Bill had been at his tricks again, and that the red stone had come from a Christmas tree. Of course, I had not examined the stone with my lens.

IX

FROM THE DIARY OF THE EMPEROR TITUS

Titus reginam Berenicem . . . cui etiam nuptias pollicitus ferebatur . . . statim ab urbe demisit invitus invitam.—SUETONIUS.

Rome, Monday.—The eruption at Vesuvius does not after all appear to have been greatly exaggerated, as I at first had thought on receiving Pliny's graphic letter. One never can quite trust literary men when facts are in question. It is clear that I missed a very fine and interesting spectacle. In fact I have lost a day. Good phrase, that. Must try and bring it in some time or other.

Tuesday.—I fear there is no doubt of Berenice's growing unpopularity. It is tiresome, as I was hoping that the marriage might take place soon—quietly. She insists on wearing a diadem—which is unnecessary; and her earrings—made of emeralds and gold cupids—are too large. She asked me, to-day, if I didn't think she resembled the Rose of Sharon. I said I supposed she meant the rose of Paestum. She said, "Ah! You've never read the Song of Songs." I said I had read all Sappho. She said, "It's not by Sappho, it's by Solomon." I had no idea King Solomon wrote.

Wednesday.—Berenice has asked some of her relations to stay with her. They arrived this morning. Her mother, her sister, her younger brother, and her cousin. They are very conversational. They chatter together like parrots or cockatoos. They are also insatiably inquisitive. Talked finance with Paulinus. He says that the Treasury is practically empty. Nobody in the palace appears to have any ready money. When the usual crowd of beggars came to the palace this evening for their daily allowance I had to send them away. It was the first time, Paulinus remarked, that I had let a day go by without making a gift. " Yes," I answered, " I have lost a day." The phrase, I am glad to say, was heard by everybody. I afterwards borrowed a little money from Berenice's brother, who made no difficulties. He is a nice, generous lad, if a little talkative, but then we all of us have our faults. Berenice's mother loses no opportunity of asking when the wedding day is to be. Most awkward. I temporised.

Thursday.—Berenice's relations have spread the news in the Court, by telling it to one of the matrons in strict confidence, that I am about to marry Berenice almost immediately. This is most unfortunate. The news has created a sensation, and they all say that such a match would be more than unpopular amongst the people. Berenice has not mentioned it herself. Lost heavily at dice yesterday. Accepted the offer of Berenice's brother to lend me a lump sum, instead of constantly borrowing small coins. I have no doubt that is the wiser course.

Thursday, a week later.—The strain on my purse is terrible. Had, of course, to subscribe largely to the Pompeii and Herculaneum fund, also to the pestilence relief, also to the Flavian Amphitheatre fund. Borrowed another lump sum from Berenice's brother. He is certainly very good-natured. Berenice's mother again referred to the marriage question. I said this was an unlucky month for marriages. " Not if you are born in

December," she answered. Unfortunately I was born in December.

Friday.—Do not know where to turn for money. Do not always want to be borrowing from Berenice's brother. Somehow or other it makes them all so familiar. Given the circumstances, and the extreme unpopularity of their presence here, it is awkward. Besides, it is a shame to trade on the good-nature of a youth. Have sold all the decorations of the Imperial residence and devoted a portion of the proceeds to the Relief Fund. Some one spread the rumour among the dear people that I had devoted the whole of the money to the Relief Fund. I cannot think how these rumours get about.

Saturday, a week later.—This has been a most expensive fortnight. Have had to do a lot of entertaining, and I regret to say I have been once more obliged to borrow a lump sum from Berenice's brother. How I shall ever be able to pay him back the gods alone know! Had the news of my marriage unofficially announced, followed immediately by a semi-official and ambiguous denial, made to see what effect the news would have among the public. Paulinus says the impression produced was deplorable. The Romans cannot, he says, forget that Berenice is a queen. Of course they can't, if she will wear a crown. People say, he says, that even Nero and Caligula avoided offending public opinion on this point. They refer also to Julius Cæsar's action on the Lupercal. There is no doubt that such a course will ensure me a lasting unpopularity. But what is to be done? Berenice's relations talk of the marriage as a matter of course. I have practically promised marriage. Berenice herself says nothing, but her silence is eloquent. Her brother becomes more and more familiar, and presses me to accept further loans. I do my best to refuse, and I have made a vow that the lump sum which he lent me to-day shall be positively the last one.

Monday.—Paulinus tells me that the Senate have decided to present me with a monster petition against my marriage. Since it is obviously impossible—owing to the strong feeling raised and the present excited state of popular opinion—I have resolved to anticipate events, and I have given leave to Paulinus to contradict *officially* the rumours of my impending marriage. He is to add (unofficially) that Berenice is shortly leaving Rome for change of air; and that she will probably spend the summer months in her charming villa on the Dead Sea. In the meantime I have got to break the news to Berenice before to-morrow morning. Antiochus, the king of Commagene, arrived here this morning. More expense!

Monday night, later.—The crisis is partially over. It has been extremely painful. Berenice at first was incredulous. Then she was upset, and left me, threatening to kill herself. I sent Paulinus to try and calm her. She then said she would leave Rome without setting eyes on me again, and state her reasons in an open letter which she would issue for private circulation only. This, of course, would have been most undesirable. Her mother and sister backed her up. and threw up at me the example of Antony, taunting me with cowardice, of being afraid of the Senate, and of outraging the dignity of a family, royal in rank, and of immemorial lineage. (Berenice is directly descended from King Solomon on her mother's side.) Finally, Berenice's brother came to me and said that as he would shortly be leaving Rome he would be obliged if I could pay him back the trifling loans he had favoured me with. He brought a list of them. He charges interest. It is a tradition, he says, in his family, to charge 90 per cent interest on *Royal* loans. He said that he was quite willing to apply to the Senate, if the reimbursement in any way incommoded me. This was a great shock to me. Immediate repayment was and is impossible. The marriage is equally impossible. I told Berenice frankly that I could not remain in Rome as Emperor and the husband of a foreign *Queen*. She said, "But why shouldn't I be Empress?" Woman-like, she missed the point. I said I was willing to follow her to her villa and renounce all claim to the Empire. Having offered her this alternative, I summoned Antiochus, who is an old friend of hers, to be the arbiter. As soon as the facts were put before him I left them and Antiochus had a lengthy interview with Berenice in private. I was convinced this was the best course. At the end of it, Berenice generously refused to accept my sacrifice, and while renouncing all idea of self-slaughter or retaliation announced her intention of leaving Rome. But those loans! and their terrible interest! that matter is still unsettled!

Tuesday.—All has been settled. Antiochus has lent me the whole sum due to Berenice's brother, and a handsome margin for my personal use. I restored the interest and capital of the loan to Berenice's brother. Said farewell to the family before the whole Court, and handed Berenice's brother a fine gold chain as a slight token of my esteem. "This," he said, "is too much." "No man," I answered, "should leave his prince's presence dissatisfied." Hereupon the whole Court murmured applause, and by a slight gesture I indicated that the audience was at an end. Berenice, alas! left Rome at noon, escorted by Antiochus, who is to spend the summer with her in Palestine. To-day I can say in all conscientiousness that I have not lost a day; but it seems to me that I have lost everything else that there is to lose in this life.

X

FROM THE DIARY OF HARRIET SHELLEY

George Street, Edinburgh, September 6, 1811.—Mr. Hogg arrived this morning. He seemed at first to be quite oblivious of the fact that he was in the city of the unfortunate Queen Mary. Bysshe and I conducted him to the palace of Holyrood immediately, where we inspected the instructive and elegant series of portraits of the Scottish kings. I was much affected by the sight of the unfortunate Queen's bedroom.

Mr. Hogg has not been well grounded in history; and he was on more than one occasion inaccurate. He had never heard of Fergus the Just. Bysshe was much moved, and enchanted by the objects of interest. He ran through the rooms at a great pace, now and then pointing back at an object of interest and exclaiming: "That is good." I regretted the absence of Eliza, but perhaps it is as well that she was not with us on this occasion. She would not have permitted me to contemplate the tragic stain of Rizzio's wound, for fear of the effect the sight might have on my nerves. Mr. Hogg was strangely insensible to the sorrowful associations of the spot.

After we had inspected the rooms and the relics, Bysshe with intent, I, with renewed awe, and Mr. Hogg with a somewhat inopportune levity, Bysshe was obliged to go home and write letters, and so I suggested that Mr. Hogg should conduct me to Arthur's Seat, in order to enjoy the sublime prospect which that eminence commands.

So sublime, so grand, so inspiring was the view that even Mr. Hogg was impressed. As for myself, words fail to express the manifold and conflicting emotions which were stirred in my breast. The weather was fine, clear and tranquil; but alas! no sooner had we started on our descent than the wind began to blow with great violence. It was of course impossible for me in such circumstances to risk the impropriety which might be occasioned, had the wind, as was only too probable, so disturbed my dress as to reveal to my companion the indelicate spectacle of my decently concealed ankles, so I seated myself on a rock resolving to wait until the violence of the wind should subside. Mr. Hogg, who laid unnecessary stress on the fact that he had not dined on either of the preceding days, and being deficient in a proper sense of delicacy and seemliness, vowed he would desert me and proceed home by himself. To my dismay he began to carry his threat into execution, and it was with the utmost difficulty that I succeeded in accomplishing the descent without affording him any unseemly exhibition.

Sunday.—The manner in which the Sabbath is observed in this city is repellent to my principles. Bysshe and Mr. Hogg have gone to the Kirk. I pleaded the wearisome performance would be certain in my case to bring on a headache and so I remained at home. They returned much exhausted by the wrestlings of an eminent divine with Satan. I am engaged in translating Madame Cottin's immortal "Claire D'Albe" into English prose. This occupies my morning. Bysshe is translating a treatise of Buffon, with which we were both of us charmed. In the evenings I read out "Telemachus."

I regret to say that Bysshe fell asleep while I was but half way through an instructive discourse of Idomeneius relating to the wise laws of Crete. Mr. Hogg is an attentive listener and it is a pleasure to read to him.

York, October 10, 1811.—Travelled by post-chaise from Darlington. Read "Anna St. Ives" by Holcroft in the chaise throughout the journey. Bysshe was restless and suggested my skipping certain portions of the narrative. I, of course, declined, knowing that it was the intention of the authoress that her work should be read without omissions. Bysshe is obliged to go to London. In the evenings I read out Dr. Robertson's historical works to Mr. Hogg. We are on the eve of a great event. My dear sister Eliza has consented to visit us and is about to arrive. What a privilege for Mr. Hogg, what a source of pleasure for Bysshe. I ardently regret that he should not be present to welcome her.

October 25.—Eliza has arrived. I am deeply touched by her kindness in coming and overcome when I think what a joyful surprise her presence will be for Bysshe, and how it will illuminate our household.

October 26.—Bysshe arrived from London. Eliza spent the day brushing her hair. In the evening I suggested reading aloud from Holcroft; but Eliza, such is her kind-heartedness, feared that it might upset my nerves. She felt certain too, that her esteemed friend, Miss Warne, whom she regards as a pattern and model in all things, would not approve of Holcroft.

October 26.—Eliza is certain that Miss Warne would find nothing to admire in York Minster. Changed our lodgings. Eliza thinks that the pure mountain air of the Lakes would be salutary to my nerves. Bysshe and Mr. Hogg miss our evening readings. I sometimes, however, continue to read to them in an undertone when Eliza is brushing her hair. But the pleasure is marred by the trepidation I am in lest I should disturb her. Eliza objects to the name Bysshe. She is certain Miss Warne could not endure such a name, so in future my husband shall be called Percy. It is certainly prettier and more romantic.

Keswick, November 16.—We have made the acquaintance of the Southeys. Mr. Southey is a great reader and devotes two hours daily to the study of the Portuguese and Spanish languages. Mrs. Southey is an adept at book-binding and binds her husband's books with elegance and neatness. Bysshe, I mean, Percy, has alas three times narrowly risked offending the poet. The first time by inadvertently taking a book down from one of his book-shelves, the second time by falling asleep when Mr. Southey after having locked him into his study was reading aloud to him his epic, "The Curse of Kehama," and the third time by sharply criticising his action in eating tea-cakes, and by subsequently devouring a whole plate of them, himself.

Bysshe, I mean Percy, has implored me to beg Mrs. Southey to instruct me in the art of making tea-cakes. I wish Eliza could begin to realise the existence of Bysshe, I mean Percy. She seems altogether unaware of his presence in the house ; but then Eliza is so much occupied in considering what will be best for me that she has no time to bestow any attention to anything else. Percy is contemplating the composition of a poem which is to be called "Queen Mab." Eliza said that Miss Warne had a horror of "Queen Mab" ; Bysshe explained to her that his poem was to be didactic and philosophical and had nothing to do with fairies. "That," said Eliza, "makes it worse." Bysshe ran out of the room with shrill exclamation of impatience. "Hush, hush!" said Eliza, "think of poor Harriet's nerves."

November 20.—Bysshe confessed to me that he could see neither beauty nor charm in Eliza. This is curious since her black hair has always been an object of universal admiration. I am afraid that Eliza does not understand him, I need hardly say what a disappointment this is to me.

Bysshe and I were thinking of writing a novel in collaboration. But Eliza said that Miss Warne considered that it was not seemly for a woman to dabble in fiction. Bysshe, I mean Percy—(In writing I find it difficult to accustom myself to the new name, but I am fortunately successful in the presence of Eliza in always saying Percy)—Percy and I are thinking of studying Hebrew. I have not yet told Eliza of this project. She is opposed to my reading Latin authors in their original tongue.

November 30.—We were walking this afternoon in the neighbourhood of the lake. Percy, Eliza and myself. Percy was talking of Plato's republic when Eliza interrupted him by recalling to his mind something which she had indeed often mentioned before, namely, Miss Warne's positive dislike of all the Greek authors and especially Plato. Scarcely had she uttered these words, when we looked round and found that Bysshe had vanished in silence like a ghost in the trees. We called and searched for him in vain.

But when we returned to the house we found him awaiting us buried in a book.

The incident greatly displeased Eliza and she insisted upon my taking to my bed as soon as we got home, although I confess I felt no suspicion of any ailment, nor would she hear of my reading either aloud or to myself. She sat by my bedside, brushing her hair. She grieved me by saying that she could not conceive what Miss Warne would think of Bysshe. I mean Percy.

XI

FROM THE "JOURNAL INTIME" OF THE EMPEROR TIBERIUS

February 1.—Disquieting news from Parthia. Artabanus is giving trouble again. Shall probably have to send an expedition. The military party in Rome say that there will probably be unrest in Thrace in the spring. I remember they said the same thing last year. Slept wretchedly last night. Claricles' medicine is worse than useless. Wrote three despatches and one private letter. Fed Hannibal, the tortoise. Went for a stroll in the afternoon. Picked the first wind-flower, and put it in water. The gardener says we shall have some rain shortly. Please the Gods this may be true, as the country needs it badly! Dined alone. Played spilikins after dinner with Fufius, but found it a strain.

February 2.—Woke at four and remained awake until seven, then went asleep again, and overslept myself. Scolded Balbus for not calling me. He said he did not dare call me more emphatically. Told him it must not occur again.

February 3.—Nothing particular.

February 4.—Letter from my mother begging me to come and see her. Says she is suffering from lung trouble. Women are so unreasonable. She must realise that it is impossible for me to get away just at present. Hannibal would not touch his lettuce to-day. This is the third day running it has happened. Claricles has given him some medicine. Strolled along to cliffs in the morning. Much vexed by a fisherman who pushed a lobster under my very nose. I have a horror of shellfish. Varus and Aufidius dined. Found their conversation a strain. So retired early. Read the Seventh Book of the "Æneid," but found it insipid. Virgil will certainly not live. He was a sycophant.

February 10.—Anniversary of poor Julia's death. Began to write short poem on the subject, but was interrupted by the arrival of the courier from Rome. Much vexed, as it altogether interrupted my train of thought and spoilt what would have been a fine elegy. News from Rome unsatisfactory. It rained in the afternoon, so I did not go out. Sorted my specimens of dried herbs, which are in a sad state of confusion. Dined alone. Dictated a despatch to Sejanus. Read some of the "Alcestis" (Euripides) before going to bed. Alcestis reminds me of Julia in many ways. She had the same fervid altruism and the same knack of saying really disagreeable things. But they both meant well. . . .

March 1.—A lovely spring day. Went for a stroll, and jotted down a few ideas for a poem on Spring. The birds were singing. Listened for some time to the babbling of the brook. Think of alluding to this in the poem. "Desilientis aquae" would make a good ending to a pentameter. Mentioned it to Fufius when I came in, casually. He said he did not think it was very original. Fufius is hyper-critical. He does not *feel* verse. Finished the memorial lines on Julia ending "Ave atque Vale." Shall not show them to Fufius. He would be certain to say something disparaging. Positively haunted by the sight of the wild tulips in the hills, fluttering in the breeze. Sights like this live in the memory. Disturbed early in the morning by a noise of hammering. It is strange that where ever I go this happens. Made inquiries, and ascertained that the stable roof is being repaired. If it is not the stable roof it is sure to be something else. Last week it was a strayed cow which woke me at five. Find it very difficult to get sleep in the early morning, whatever precautions I take. In a month's time the nightingales will begin, and then sleep will be out of the question. Thinking of writing a poem called "To Sleep."

March 10.—Claricles says I am over-worked and need a change. Have decided to go for a short walking tour, quite by myself. Thought of taking Fufius, but knowing how self-willed he is, decided not to. Packed my knapsack. Took an extra pair of sandals, a worsted scarf, an ivory comb, two gold toothpicks, and a volume of Sappho's Songs. Find this light, feminine verse suitable for outdoor life. Shall start early to-morrow. Had my hair cut. The slave was clumsy when cutting round the ears. They still smart. Find this fault to be universal among haircutters. Shall take tablets with me in order to jot down any ideas for future poems, although Claricles advises me to give up writing for two or three weeks.

March 13.—Returned earlier than I expected. Walking tour successful on the whole. Visited Sorrentum, an idyllic spot. Not sure I don't prefer it to Capreæ. It is a curious thing that man is always discontented with what he has, and hankers after what he has not got. Walked leisurely the first day, stopping every now and then for light refreshment. Found the country people very civil and anxious to please. Nobody knew who I was, and I was intensely gratified by many spontaneous and frank experiences of loyalty and devotion to the Emperor. This is refreshing in this sceptical age. It is a comfort to think that although I may not go down to posterity as a great military genius like Julius Cæsar, I shall at least leave a blameless name, as far as my domestic life is concerned, and an untarnished reputation for benevolence, kindness, and unswerving devotion to duty. Without being conceited, I think that some of my verse will live. I think I shall be among the Roman poets when I die; but this is not saying much, when one considers the absurd praise given to poetasters such as Virgil and Ponticus. Strolling along the seashore near Sorrentum a very pretty little episode occurred. A woman, one of the fishermen's wives, was sitting by her cottage door, spinning. Her child, a little girl about six years old, was playing with a doll hard by.

I said "Good day" to the fisherman's wife, and she offered me a glass of wine. I declined, as Claricles has forbidden me red wine, but I said I would gladly accept a bowl of milk. She immediately went to fetch it, and the child went with her. When they returned the child offered me the bowl, lisping in a charming manner. I drank the milk, and the mother then said to the child:

"Tell the kind gentleman whom you love best in the world."

"Papa and mamma," lisped the child.

"And after that?" asked the mother.

"After that the divine Emperor Tiberius, who is the father and the mother of us all," she said.

I gave the mother a gold piece. Fufius says it is a mistake to give money to the poor, and that it pauperises them. He says one does more harm than good by indiscriminate charity. But I think it cannot be a bad thing to follow the impulses of the heart. I should like this to be said of me: "Although he had many faults, such as discontent and want of boldness, his heart was in the right place." It is little incidents like the one I noted above which make up for the many disappointments and trials of a monarch's life. The second day of my tour was marred by a thunder-shower, but I found a thrush's nest and three eggs in it. There are few things which move me so inexpressibly as the sight of a thrush's nest with the eggs lying in it. It is curious that the nightingale's egg should be so ugly. Owing to the bad weather, and the rheumatism in my joints which it brought on, I was obliged to cut short my tour.

(*This extract probably belongs to a later period*)

June.—Asinius Gallus has again sent in a petition about the prison fare. It appears he has a conscientious objection to eating veal. The officials say they can do nothing. If they make an exception in his favour they will be obliged to do so in many less deserving cases. I confess these little things worry me. Our prison system seems to me lacking in elasticity; but it is dreadfully difficult to bring into effect any sweeping reform; because if the prison disciplinary system is modified to meet the requirements of the more cultivated prisoners, the prisons would be crowded with ruffians who would get themselves arrested on purpose. At least this is the official view, and it is shared by Sejanus, who has gone into the matter thoroughly. I confess it leaves me unconvinced. I am glad to say we are ahead of the Persians in the matter. In Persia they think nothing of shutting up a prisoner—of whatever rank—in a cell and keeping him isolated from the world sometimes for as long as three months at a time. This seems to me barbarous.

July 6.—The heat is overpowering. Agrippina threatens to come home and to bring her daughter. I wrote saying I thought it is very unwise to bring children here at this time of year, owing to the prevalence of fever. She answered that her daughter was looking forward to the sea-bathing. If they come it will mean that my summer will be ruined.

July 7.—I went to the home farm this afternoon. The farmer's wife is very ill. There is little or no hope of her recovery. Spent two hours there reading out passages of the "Odyssey." She does not understand Greek; but it seemed to soothe her. Her husband told her that he felt confident that she could not get worse after this. The faith of these simple folk is most touching. How unlike Fufius and all his friends.

August 1.—There is no news except that, as always occurs at this time of year, the Phœnix is reported to have been seen in Egypt.

August 3.—One of those distressing little incidents happened to-day which entirely spoil one's comfort and peace of mind for the moment: just like a piece of dust getting into one's eye. My old friend Lucius Anuseius came all the way from Rhodes to see me. By some mistake he was shown into the Chamber, where prisoners are examined, and before the error was rectified he was rather rudely interrogated. It turned out afterwards that Balbus mistook him for Titus Anuseius, the informer. Balbus is growing more and more stupid; he forgets everything. I ought to send him away; on the other hand, he knows my habits, and I should feel lost without him. As it is, Claricles says that Lucius is likely to feel it for several days. He is so sensitive and the slightest thing upsets his nerves. All his family are touchy, and I am afraid he will look upon the matter as a deliberate slight. If it had happened to anyone else it would not have mattered. They would have understood at once. This has quite put me out. But, as Fufius says, how little I shall think of this in a year's time.

August 7.—Lucius Anuseius left the island in a huff. It is most regrettable.

August 12.—Agrippina arrives to-morrow. There is nothing to be done. How pleasant life would be were it not for one's relations.

XII

FROM THE DIARY OF ŒDIPUS REX

Corinth. The Feast of the Minotaur.—My birthday and coming-of-age. All went off very successfully. Papa gave me a chariot and mamma a pocket toothpick, set in gold, with an Egyptian inscription on it (two flamingoes and a water-rat, which means in Egyptian " Be merry and wise"). Nausicaa, my nurse, gave me a stylus-wiper with " A Present from Corinth " beautifully worked into it in silk. Polyphemus, our faithful old messenger (who has only one eye), gave me a pair of sandal strings. Very useful, as I'm always losing mine.

In the morning, after I had received all the family congratulations and tokens, at the first meal, there was a public presentation of gifts in the palace.

The town of Corinth sent a deputation, headed by the Priest of the Temple of Castor and Pollux, which presented me, on behalf of the city, with a silver vase, symbolic of the freedom of the city, beautifully embossed, and engraved with a suitable inscription.

The priest made a long speech, and papa, who never cared for oratory, kept on muttering, " By Demeter, be brief," but the priest wasn't brief. He spoke for nearly an hour.

Then I had to respond. I said I would earnestly endeavour to follow in my father's footsteps and to deserve the good-will and esteem of my future subjects, which was being manifested in so touching and patriotic a fashion. My speech had all been written out for me beforehand by Zoroaster, my Persian tutor; but I flatter myself I added a few unexpected and telling touches.

For instance, I began by saying: "Unaccustomed as I am to speaking in public——" They cheered this to the echo.

I also managed to bring in rather an amusing anecdote about how a foreign merchant called Abraham tried to get the better of a Corinthian merchant in a bargain and how the Corinthian got the best of him by guile. This provoked loud laughter.

My peroration, ending with the words:

"What do they know of Corinth who only Corinth know?"

(a quotation from Tyrtæus) was loudly cheered. But my cousin Thersites almost spoilt the effect by adding audibly, "Quite enough."

In the afternoon there were games, and an ox was roasted whole for the όι πολλόι. Papa says, now I am of age, I must go and pay my respects to the oracle at Delphi. It is a family tradition.

Delphi.—(What is the date?)—Arrived at last after a tedious journey. The inn is very uncomfortable. This is too bad, as in the guide book (Odysseus') it is marked with a constellation of the Pleiades, which means very good. The wine tastes of tar. And the salt is a chemical compound called Σερεβος. I made a scene and asked for ordinary slaves' salt, and they hadn't got any.

Shall not stay at this inn again, and I shall warn others not to. It is called ΞΕΝΩΔΟΧΕΙΟΝ ΒΑΓΟΝΔΗ. Disappointed in the Temple (very *late* architecture) and still more in the Oracle. I suppose it thought I didn't pay enough. But because one happens to be a prince, I don't see why one should be robbed. Besides which I am travelling incognito as Kyrios Ralli. But the priests bowed, and they all called me, "your Shiningness." The Oracle was quite absurd, and evidently in a very bad temper. It said I would kill my father and marry my mother. It only shows how absurd the whole thing is. I hate superstition, and oracles ought to be stopped by law. Gypsies on the roadside are put in gaol. Why should oracles be supported by the State? I shall write to the *False Witness* about it.

In the afternoon went to the theatre. Saw the tragedy of Adam and Eve, a historical drama, translated from the Hebrew. Very long. The part of the Archangel, danced by Thepsis, was very bad, and the man who danced Eve was too old; but the snake was good. Scenery fine, especially the tree (which had real leaves).

Daulis, Tuesday.—Arrived this morning. Very disappointing; the famous Daulian nightingale is not singing this spring. Just my luck. Rather an amazing incident happened yesterday on the way. My chariot was run into by a stranger. He was on the wrong side of the road, and, of course, entirely in the wrong. Also, his charioteer was not sober. We shouted, and we gave them ample room, and time, but he ran straight into us and his chariot was upset. The owner and charioteer were both taken to the Æsculapian Home, which is under the management of the Red Serpent. The doctor said it was serious. We did all we could, but had to go on, as I was due at Daulis to-day.

Thebes, a year later.—Staying with Queen Jocasta, a charming widow. All very comfortable. Everybody is concerned about the Sphinx, who is really causing great annoyance, asking impertinent riddles, and playing dangerous practical jokes on people who can't answer. They want me to go. Very tiresome, as I never could answer a riddle ; but it's difficult to refuse.

Wednesday.—Saw the Sphinx. Guessed the riddle first shot. It asked what was that which runs on two legs, has feathers and a beak, and barks like a dog. I said " pheasant," and I added, " You put that in about the barking to make it more difficult." The Sphinx was very angry and went off in a huff, for good.

Thursday.—As a reward for getting rid of the Sphinx I am allowed to marry the Queen ; we are engaged. Everybody thinks it an excellent thing. She is a little older than I am ; but I don't think that matters.

* * * *

(*Ten years later*)

Thebes.—Rather a severe epidemic of plague. They say it is not bubonic, however. In fact, it is what they call plagueen. Still, there are a great many deaths.

Thebes, a week later.—The plague increasing. Have sent for Tiresias to find out what it comes from.

Tuesday.—Tiresias arrived. Very cross and guarded. Don't believe he knows anything about it. Doesn't want to commit himself. He loves making mysteries.

Saturday.—Insisted on Tiresias speaking out. Regret having done so now. He flew into a passion, and threatened the whole court with " exposure " and " revelations." That's the last thing we want now.

Monday.—Had it all out with Tiresias. He told the most absurd cock and bull story. Utterly preposterous but very disagreeable even to have such things hinted.

Said nothing to Jocasta, as yet. Luckily, there are no proofs. Tiresias has raked up an old shepherd, who is ready to swear I am not the son of the King of Corinth, but the son of Laius, King of Thebes, and of Jocasta (my wife !) ; and that Laius was the man I accidentally killed years ago on the road to Daulis !

Tiresias says this is the sole cause of the plague, which is getting worse. They now say it *is* Asiatic.

Thursday.—I interviewed and cross-examined the shepherd in the presence of Tiresias. There seems to be no doubt whatsoever about the facts. But I cannot see that any good can be done now, after all these years, by making a public scandal. It is, after all, a family matter. Tiresias says the plague will not stop unless the whole truth is published. Very awkward. Don't know how to break it to Jocasta.

Friday (*dictated*).—Jocasta overheard me discussing the matter with Tiresias and jumped, rashly, to conclusions. She had hysterics, and, losing all self-control, seriously injured both my eyes with a pin. I may very likely be blind for life. She was very sorry afterwards, and is now laid up. I and the children leave for Colonnus to-morrow, and it is settled that I am to abdicate in favour of Creon on the plea of ill-health and overwork. The children have been told nothing ; but Antigone, who is far too precocious, alluded to Jocasta as grandmamma. The matter will be hushed up as far as possible.

Citium Colonnus, two months later.—The air here is delicious. Must say the change is doing me good.

XIII

FROM THE DIARY OF WILLIAM THE CONQUEROR

Rouen, 1066.—Disquieting news from London. My friend, benefactor and relation, my brother Sovereign, Edward of England, has again had one of his attacks. It comes, I am sure, from not eating meat. Were anything to happen to him, I should be obliged to go over to London at once and settle as to the carrying on of the Government with Harold. Nothing could be more inconvenient at the present moment. Have the utmost confidence in Harold; but I fear the influence of the English nobility. I like the English; but they are not to be trusted in foreign politics. They are naturally perfidious, and they don't know it. They think they are more virtuous than other people; or rather that they are exempted from the faults and the vices which are common to us all. The European situation seems unsatisfactory.

Among other things Father Anselm writes that a certain party among the Englishwomen want to be admitted to the Witenagemot. The majority of the women are against it. The agitators sent a deputation to Westminster, but the King said it would not be according to the precedents to receive them. They were so annoyed at this that they made a dastardly attack on the beautiful old Druid Temple of Stonehenge, almost completely destroying it. F. Anselm says only a few blocks of stone are left, and that the place is unrecognisable.

The ringleaders were taken and claimed the ordeal by fire and the matter was referred to the Archbishop of Canterbury, who said that it was not a matter to be dealt with by ordeal. (Quite right !) He put the case into the hands of a select body of matrons, chosen from all classes. These decided that the offenders should be publicly whipped by women, and sent home. This was done, much to the satisfaction of everybody.

Rouen.—Heard Mass and went out hunting. Excellent sport. Shot a fox and six thrushes. Had thrush-pie for dinner. Find it difficult to get on horseback without aid.

Rouen.—Received a letter from the Pope. He says that should anything happen to King Edward—he is, of course, far from suggesting such a thing, but one must take everything into consideration—I must be very firm about claiming the succession. H.H. says that although, of course, it would be indelicate for him to raise the question *just now,* he knows it is the King's wish that I should succeed him. He seems to think Harold may give trouble. But Harold is bound to me by oath. Also I saved his life.

Rouen.—Took William out hunting. His red hair frightens the ducks. Have told him over and over again to get a close-fitting green cap. The boys are always quarrelling. I don't know what is to be done with them. Robert broke his new battle-axe yesterday in a fit of passion.

My only consolation is that Henry is really making some progress with his tutor. He last learnt the alphabet as far as the letter F.

Rouen.—A fisherman arrived last night from Southampton with the news that King Edward is dead. The news, he said, was confirmed by the appearance of a strange star with a tail to it in the sky. I have questioned the courier and gathered he had only got the news at second-hand. The rumour is probably baseless.

Rouen.—The regular courier did not arrive this evening. The bag was brought by an Englishman. The official bulletin states that the King is slightly indisposed owing to a feverish cold, which he caught while inspecting the newly-raised body of archers, in the New Forest. A private letter from the archbishop tells me, in strict confidence, that the King's illness is more dangerous than people think. The children again quarrelled to-day. Matilda, as usual, took Henry's part, and said I was to blame. These domestic worries are very trying at such a critical moment. As a matter of fact, Henry teases his elder brothers, and boasts to them of his superior scholarship; they retaliate, naturally enough, by cuffing the boy, who complains at once to his mother. Since Henry has mastered the rudiments of the alphabet, his conceit has been quite beyond bounds. Of course, I admit it is clever of him. He is a clever boy. There is no doubt about that, but he shouldn't take advantage of it.

Rouen.—Again the regular courier has not arrived. The bag again brought by an Englishman. According to a bulletin the King is going on well. Received a very friendly note from Harold, putting Pevensey Castle at my disposal, should I visit England in the autumn—and suggesting sport in the New Forest.

Rouen.—Messenger arrived direct from London, *via* Newhaven. He says the King died last week, and that Harold has proclaimed himself King. Matilda said this would happen from the first. I think there can be no doubt that the news is authentic. The messenger, who is an old servant of mine, is thoroughly to be trusted. He saw the King's body lying in state. This explains why the regular messengers have not arrived. Harold had them stopped at the coast. This, in itself, is an unfriendly act. Matilda says I must invade England at once. Think she is right. But wish war could be avoided. Have written to the Pope asking for his moral support. Invasion a risky thing. Discussed the matter with General Bertram, who is an excellent strategist. He says he can devise fifty ways of landing troops in England, but not one way of getting them out again. That is just it. Supposing we are cut off? The English army is said to be very good indeed.

Rouen.—Invasion of England settled. Must say have great misgivings on the subject. If we fail, the King of France is certain to attack us here. Matilda, however, won't hear of any other course being taken. Have privately sent a message to Harold proposing that we should settle the matter in a friendly fashion—I offer him nearly all Wessex, Wales and Scotland and the North—I taking the rest of the Kingdom, including London and Winchester. His situation is by no means entirely enviable. His brothers are certain to fight him in the North, and the King of Norway may also give trouble.

Rouen.—Received letter from the Pope entirely approving of invasion. Sends me back banner, blessed. Received a letter from Harold also. Very insulting. Answers vaguely and commits himself to nothing. Ignores the past. Seems to forget I saved him from shipwreck and that he solemnly swore to support my claims. Seems also to forget that I am the lawful heir to the English throne. The crowning insult is that he addressed the letter to Duke William the Bastard.

Have ordered mobilisation to take place at once. The war is popular. Matilda and I were loudly cheered when we drove through the market place this afternoon. War will be a good occupation for the boys. Robert wants to stop here as Regent. Do not think this wise.

Hastings.—Very disagreeable crossing. Took medicine recommended by Matilda (nettle leaves and milk and cinnamon), but did no good. Harold apparently defeated his brother in the North. Expect to fight to-morrow. Temper of the troops good. Terrain favourable, but cannot help feeling anxious.

London.—Everything sadly in need of thorough reorganisation. Have resolved to carry out following initial reforms at once :

1. Everybody to put out their lights by 8. Bell to ring for the purpose. The people here sit up too late, drinking. Most dangerous.

2. Enroll everybody in a book. Make it compulsory for the leeches to attend the poor, and dock serfs of a part of their wage, in order to create a fund for paying the leeches. (Think this rather neat.)

Shall tolerate no nonsense from the women. Matilda agrees that their complaints are ridiculous.

News from Normandy disquieting. Robert seems to be taking too much upon himself. Something must be done.

Going next week to New Forest to hunt. Very fine wild pony hunting there.

XIV

FROM THE DIARY OF MARY, MRS. JOHN MILTON (*née* POWELL)

Aldersgate Street, July 1, 1643.—Housekeeping not quite such fun as I thought it would be. John is very particular. He cannot eat mutton, or any kind of hashed meat. He compares the cooking here unfavourably with that of Italy. He says the boys in the school are very naughty and that, during the Latin lesson this morning, one boy, called Jones minor, put a pin on his chair, just before he sat down on it. I couldn't help laughing; and this made John cross. He is thinking of writing a poem about King Arthur (*sic*) and the burnt cakes.

July 6.—John has begun his poem. He makes it up during meals, which makes him forget to eat, and makes the meal very gloomy; he writes it down afterwards. He read me a long piece of it last night; but as it is in Latin I did not understand very much of it.

July 7.—John and I quarrelled. It was about Jones minor. John announced the news of a reported rebel success during the boys' Greek lesson, and told the boys to give three cheers for the rebel army, which, of course, they all did, as they would never dare to disobey, except one brave *hero*, I call him, called Jones minor (the son of a tinker, bless him!), who called out as loud as he could: "Long live King Charles and death to all traitors!" John told him to repeat what he had said, and he did, and John caned him. I think this was very wrong on John's part, because, of course, the rebels *are* traitors. I took the part of the boy, and this made John angry. Then I said: "Of course, if all loyalists are so wicked, why did you marry me? My father is loyal and I am heart and soul for the King and the Church." John said that women's politics didn't count; but that the young must be taught discipline; that he was tolerant of all *sincere* opinion, however much he disagreed with it; but that the boy had merely wished to be insolent, by flying in the face of public opinion and the will of the school, which was the will of the *people*, and therefore the will of God, merely to gain a cheap notoriety. I said that probably all the boys felt the same, but didn't dare say so, as they knew that he, John, was on the other side. John said there are only seven "malignants" in the school. He said the boys were very angry with Jones minor and kicked him. I said they were a set of cowards. John said did I mean he was a coward, and quoted Greek. I said I didn't understand Greek and didn't want to. "That comes from your false education," said John; "your parents deserve the severest blame." I said that if he said anything against my parents, I would leave the house, and that my father knew Latin as well as he did. John said I was exaggerating. I said that I had often heard Papa say that John's *Latin* verses were poor. John said when his epick on King Alfred and the Lady of the Lake would be published, we should see who knew how to write Latin. I said: "Who?" John said I was flighty and ignorant. I said I might be ignorant, but at least I wasn't a rebel. John said I was too young to understand these things, and that, considering my bringing up, I was right to hold the opinions I did. When I was older I would see that they were false. Then I cried.

July 6.—We made up our quarrel. John was ashamed of himself, and very dear, and said he regretted that he had used such vehement language. I forgave him at once.

July 9.—We had some friends to dinner. Before we sat down, John said: "We will not mention politicks, as we might not all agree and that would mar the harmony of the symposium." But towards the end of dinner, I drank the King's health, quite unwittingly and from force of habit, forgetting——

This made John angry and led to a discussion, some of our guests taking the King's part and others saying that he was quite wrong. The men became very excited, and a young student, called Wyatt, whom John had invited because he is very musical and cultivated, threw a glass of wine in the face of Mr. Lely, the wine-merchant, who is a violent rebel, and this broke up the party. John said that all "malignants" were the same; and that they none of them had any manners; that they were a set of roystering, nose-slitting, dissolute debauchees. When I thought of my dear father, and my dear brothers, this made me very angry; but I thought it best to say nothing at the time, as John was already annoyed and excited.

July 10.—John says he can't make up his mind whether to write his epick poem in Latin or in Hebrew. I asked him whether he couldn't write it in English. He told me not to be irrelevant. The city is very dreary. John disapproves of places of public amusement. He is at the school all day; and in the evening he is busy thinking over his poem. Being married is not such fun as I thought it would be, and John is quite different from what he was when he courted me in the country. Sometimes I don't think he notices that I am there at all. I wish I were in the country.

July 11.—John was in good temper to-day, because a scholar came here yesterday who said he wrote Italian very well. He asked me for my advice about his epick poem—which I thought was the best subject for an epick, King Arthur and the Cakes or the story of Adam and Eve. This made me feel inclined to laugh very much. Fancy writing a poem on the story of Adam and Eve! Everybody knows it! But I didn't laugh out loud, so as not to hurt his feelings, and I said "Adam and Eve," because I felt, somehow, that he wanted me to say that. He was so pleased, and said that I had an extraordinarily good judgment, when I chose. We had some cowslip wine for dinner which I brought from the country with me. John drank my health in Latin, which was a great favour, as he never says grace in Latin, because he says it's Popish.

July 14.—John is thinking of not writing an epick poem after all, at least not yet, but a history of the world instead. He says it has never been properly written yet.

July 15.—John has settled to translating the Bible into Latin verse. I am afraid I annoyed him; because when he told me this, I said I had always heard Papa say that the Bible was written in Latin. He said I oughtn't to talk about things which I didn't understand.

July 28.—I am altogether put about. There are two Irish boys in the school; one is called Kelley and comes from the North, and the other is called O'Sullivan and comes from the South. They had a quarrel about politicks and O'Sullivan called Kelley a rebel, a heretick, a traitor to his country, a renegade, a coward and a bastard; and Kelley said that O'Sullivan was an idolator and a foreigner, and ended up by saying he hoped he would go and meet the Pope.

"Do you mean to insult the Pope before me?" said O'Sullivan.

"Yes," said Kelley, "to hell with your Pope."

I could hear and see all this from my window, as the boys were talking in the yard.

Kelley then shouted, "To hell with the Pope!" as loud as he could three times, and O'Sullivan turned quite white with rage, but he only laughed and said quite slowly:

"Your father turned traitor for money, just like Judas." Then the boys flew at each other and began to fight; and at that moment John, who was thinking over his epick poem in the dining-room, rushed out and stopped them. Then he sent for both the boys and asked them what it was all about, but they both refused to say a word. Then John sent for the whole school, and said that unless some boy told him exactly what had happened, he would stop all half-holidays for a month. So Pyke, a boy who had been there, told the whole story. John caned both O'Sullivan and Kelley for using strong language.

In the evening Mr. Pye came to dinner, from Oxford. He teaches the Oxford boys physic or Greek philosophy; I forget which. But no sooner had we sat down to dinner than he began to abuse the rebels, and John, who was already cross, said that he did not suppose Mr. Pye meant to defend the King. Mr. Pye said he had always supposed that that was a duty every true-born Englishman took for granted; and John became very angry. I never heard anybody use such dreadful language. He said the King was a double-faced, lying monkey, full of Popish anticks, a wolf disguised as a jackass, a son of Belial, a double-tongued, double-faced, clay-footed, scarlet Ahithophel, and Mr. Pye was so shocked that he got up and went away. I said that people who insulted the King were rebels, however clever they might be, and that it was dreadful to use such language ; and when I thought of his beating those two little boys this morning for using not half such strong language it made me quite mad. John said that I was illogical. I said I wouldn't hear any more bad language ; and I ran upstairs and locked myself in my room.

August 1, *Oxfordshire.*—I have come home. I couldn't bear it. John was too unjust. Whenever I think of those two Irish boys and of John's language at dinner, my blood boils. Went out riding this morning with the boys. Papa says the war news is better, and that the rebels will soon be brought to heel.

XV

FROM THE DIARY OF MARK ANTONY

Alexandria (*undated*).—The reception went off very well. The Queen came to meet me by water in her State barge. She is different from what I remember her long ago, when I caught a glimpse of her in Rome. Then she was rather a colourless young girl, who had the reputation of being very well read, and rather affected. But now . . . when you look at her face and you look away, you see green from the flash, as though you had been staring at the sun. She dazzles and blinds you. I received her in the market place. Her curtsey was a miracle of grace. She was very civil and dignified. After I had received her in the market placc, I went to her palace. Such is the etiquette. I invited her to supper; but she insisted on my being her guest. I accepted. Supper in her palace. Semi-state, as the court is in mourning for Archilaus, the King of Cappadocia's eldest son, the Queen's first cousin. The ladies in waiting wore gold ornaments only. One of them, Charmian, pretty. The Queen, dropping all formality, was very lively and excellent company. The supper was good (the boars *well* roasted) and not so stiff as those kind of entertainments are as a rule.

After supper we had music and some dancing. Egyptian Bacchanals, who did a modern thing called *Ariadne in Naxos*. Very noisy and not much tune in it ; but the dancing good, although hardly up to the Scythian standard.

Mardian, who has a fine contralto voice (he has been admirably trained), sang a piece from a ballet on the siege of Troy arranged by Æschylus. Very good. I like those old-fashioned things much better. They say it's conventional and out of date ; but I don't care. The Queen told me in confidence that she quite agreed with me, but that even classical music bored her, so after we had listened to one or two odes, she asked Mardian to sing something light, some songs in dialect, which he did. Very funny, especially the one which begins :

"As I was going to Brindisi, upon a summer's day."

We made him sing that one twice. The Greeks know how to be witty without even being in the least vulgar.

Alexandria, three weeks later.—Time has passed very quickly. Everybody is being so kind, and the Queen has taken immense pains to make everything a success. Most amusing improvised banquet in fancy dress last night. The Queen disguised as a fish-wife. She made me dress up, too. I put on a Persian private soldier's uniform. After supper we went into the town, in our disguises. Nobody recognised us, and we had the greatest fun. I threw pieces of orange-peel on the pavement. It was too comic to see the old men trip up over them. Then we went into a tavern on the first floor, and ate oysters. The Queen heated some coppers at the fire, and, after putting them on a plate with a pair of pincers, threw them out of the window. It was quite extraordinarily funny to see the beggars pick them up and then drop them with a howl ! I don't think I ever laughed so much ! The Queen has a royal sense of humour. And I who thought beforehand she was a blue-stocking ! It shows how mistaken one can be.

Alexandria.—Time seems to fly. No news from Rome. Wish the Queen would not be quite so ostentatiously lavish on my account. Eight wild boars for breakfast is too much. And the other night at supper she wasted an immense pearl in drinking my health in vinegar. This kind of thing makes people talk. She is wonderfully witty. She can mimic exactly the noises of a farmyard. Nothing seems to tire her, either. She will sit up all night and be ready early the next morning to go out fishing, sailing or anything else. She must have a constitution of steel. Wonderful woman !

Alexandria, later.—News from Rome. Fulvia is dead : must go at once.

Rome, a month later.—Engaged to be married to Octavia, Cæsar's sister, a widow. Purely a political alliance. Cleopatra is sure to understand the necessity of this. It is a great comfort to think that she is reasonable and has a real grip of the political situation.

Athens, a month later.—Political situation grows more and more complicated. Octavia is very dutiful and most anxious to please. Do not think the climate here agreeable. The wind is very sharp and the nights are bitterly cold. Never did care for Athens.

Think that if I went to Egypt for a few days I could (*a*) benefit by change of air, (*b*) arrange matters with the Eastern Kings. Cæsar and Lepidus are trying to do me in the eye.

Athens, a day later.—Octavia has very kindly offered to go to Rome, so as to act as a go-between between myself and Cæsar. She says she is quite certain it is all only a misunderstanding and that she can arrange matters. Thought it best not to mention possibility of Egyptian trip, as I may not go, after all.

Alexandria.—Back here once more after all. Doctors all said change of air was essential, and that the climate of Athens was the very worst possible for me, just at this time. They said I should certainly have a nervous breakdown if I stayed on much longer. Besides which, it was absolutely necessary for me to be on the spot, to settle the Eastern Question. It is now fortunately settled. Cleopatra delighted to see me; but most reasonable. Quite understood everything. She did not say a word about Octavia. Reception in Alexandria magnificent. Ovation terrific. Shows how right I was to come back. Settled to proclaim Cleopatra Queen of Egypt, Lower Syria, Cyprus and Lydia. Everybody agrees that this is only fair.

Alexandria.—Public proclamation in the market place. Settled to keep Media, Parthia and Armenia in the family, so divided them among the children. Ceremony went off splendidly. Cleopatra appeared as the Goddess Isis. This was much appreciated, as it showed the people she really is *national.* The cheering was terrific.

Staying with us at present are the King of Libya, the King of Cappadocia, the King of Paphlagonia, the King of Thrace, the King of Arabia, the King of Pont, the King of Jewry, the King of Comagena, the King of Mede, and the King of Lycaonia. Question of precedence a little awkward. Herod, the King of Jewry, claimed precedence over all the other Kings on the grounds of antiquity and lineage. The King of Mede contested the claim, and the King of Arabia said that he was the oldest in years. There is no doubt about this, as he is 99. It was obvious the first place belonged to him.

Question very neatly settled by Cleopatra. That they should rank according to the number of years they have reigned. She said this was the immemorial Egyptian custom, established by the Pharaohs and written out very carefully on a step of the great Pyramid. Everybody satisfied. King of Arabia takes precedence, but *not* on account of his age. Herod still a little touchy, but had to give in.

Played billiards with Cleopatra. Gave her 20. Won with difficulty. Cæsar is certain to make war on us. Have written to Octavia explaining everything fully.

In Camp near Actium.—Nothing doing. One wonders whether Cæsar means to fight after all. The mosquitoes are very annoying. Impossible to get any milk.

In Camp near Actium, later.—Cleopatra has arrived. She is used to camp life and does not mind roughing it. Everybody advises me to fight on land and not by sea, but Cleopatra and myself think we ought to fight by sea. Cæsar has taken Toryne. We have sixty sail. The thing is obvious; but soldiers are always prejudiced. Enobarbus worrying me to death to fight on land.

Cleopatra won't hear of it, and I am quite certain she is right. A woman's instinct in matters of strategy and tactics is infallible; and then—what a woman!

Alexandria, later.—Very glad to be home again. Cleopatra was perfectly right to retreat. Played billiards. Gave Cleopatra 25. She beat me. She will soon be able to give me something. She is a surprising woman. Last night the Greek envoy dined. Too clever for me, but Cleopatra floored him over Anaxagoras. Wonderful woman! She sang, or rather hummed, in the evening a little Greek song, the burden of which is

'Εγὼ δὲ μόνα καθεύδω.

I cannot get the tune out of my head.

XVI

FROM THE DIARY OF IVAN THE TERRIBLE

Moscow, September 1, 1560.—I drove to the village of O——, 24 versts. On one side of the river is the village, with its church, on the other a lonely windmill. The landscape flat and brown, the nearer houses and the distant trees sharp in the clear autumn air. The windmill is maimed; it has lost one of its wings. It is like my soul. My soul is a broken windmill which is rusty, stiff, and maimed; it groans and creaks before the winds of God, but it no longer turns; and no longer, cheerfully grumbling as of yore, it performs its daily task and grinds the useful corn. The only spots of colour in the landscape were the blue cupolas of the church; a blue and red shirt hanging up to dry on an apple-tree near a wooden hut, and the kerchiefs of the women who were washing linen in the river. A soldier talked to the women, and laughed with them. I would that I could laugh like that with men and women. I I can only laugh alone and bitterly. I had never been there before. But when lazily, a cock crew, and a little boy made music on a wooden pipe, and a long cart laden with sacks creaked by, the driver walking by its side, I knew that I had seen all this before, not something like unto it, but this very thing, that same windmill, that same creaking cart, that same little boy playing that very tune on that very pipe.

It was a mournful tune, and it said to my soul,

"Why art thou so dusty and rusty, O my soul, why art thou sorrowful? Crusted with suspicion; uneasy and fearful, prompt to wrath and slow to trust, inhospitable towards hope, and a stranger to gladness?"

The world is a peep-show, and I have satisfied my expectation. I am weary of the sights of the fair, and the mirth of the crowd to me is meaningless. The bells, and the tambourines, and the toy trumpets, the grating of the strings, and the banging of the drum jar upon me. Like a child, who has spent a whole day in frolic and whose little strength is utterly exhausted, I desire to go home and to rest.

Rest, where is there any rest for thee, Ivan, Ivan the Restless? Everywhere have I sought for peace and found it nowhere, save in a cell, and on my knees, before the Image.

September 10.—Why was I born to be a King?

Why was I cast, a frail and fearful infant, to that herd of ravenous wolves, those riotous nobles, that band of greedy, brutal, and ruthless villains who bled my beloved country and tore my inheritance into shreds? I think I know why I was sent thither. Out of the weakness came forth strength; a little boy was sent forth to slay the giant. I was sent to deliver the Russian people, to break the necks of the nobles, and to cast the tyrants from their stronghold. I was sent to take the part of the people, and they will never forget this or me; in years to come, ages after I am dead, mothers will sing their children to sleep with songs about the great Tsar of Moscow, Ivan the well-beloved, Ivan the people's friend, Ivan the father of the fatherless, the brother of the needy, the deliverer of the oppressed.

But the proud and the mighty, the rich and the

wicked, shall hate me and vilify me, and blacken my name. I know you, ye vipers, and all your ways. I would that not one of you could escape me ; but, like the hydra, you have a hundred heads, that grow again as fast as they are cut off. When I am gone, O vile and poisonous nobility, you will raise your insolent head once more, and trample again upon my beloved people.

Would that I could utterly uproot you from the holy soil of Russia, and cast you to perish like weeds into a bottomless pit.

October 1.—I dreamed last night a fearful dream. I dreamed that I had done an abominable thing, and that I bore stains on my hands that the snows of the mountains and the waves of the sea could not wash out. I dreamed that all mankind shunned me, and that I wandered alone across the great plain till I came to the end of the world and the gates of Heaven. I knocked at the gates, but they were shut ; and round me there was a multitude, and there arose from it a sound of angry voices, crying, " He has slain our fathers, and our brothers, and our mothers, by him our houses were burnt and our homes were laid waste, let him not enter " ; and I knocked at the gate, and then there came a man with a mark on his brow, and he said, " This man has killed his son, let him not in." And I knew that man was Cain. And the howling of the voices grew louder, and the cries of hate surging round me deafened me. I knocked, and prayed, and cried, and wept, but the gate remained shut. And all at once I was left alone in the great plain deserted even by my enemies, and I shivered in the darkness and in the silence. Then, along the road, came a pilgrim, a poor man, begging for alms, and when he saw me, he knelt before me, and I said, " Wherefore dost thou kneel to me, who am deserted by God and man?" And he answered, "Is not sorrow a holy thing? Thou art the most sorrowful man in the whole world, for thou hast killed what was dearer to thee than life, and bitter is thy sorrow, and heavy is thy punishment." And the pilgrim kissed my hand, and the hot tears that he shed fell upon it.

And at that moment, far away I heard a noise as of gates turning on a great hinge, and I knew that the doors of Heaven were open.

Then I awoke, and I crept up the stairway to my little son's bedroom. He lay sleeping peacefully. And I knelt down and thanked Heaven that the dream was but a dream; but when the sun rose in the morning, like a wave from out of infinity, apprehension rolled to my soul and settled on it. I am afraid, and I know not of what I am afraid.

February 13, 1570.—Thanks to God Novgorod is no more. I have utterly destroyed its city and its people for its contumacy. So fare all the enemies of Russia and of Moscow.

XVII

FROM THE PRIVATE LOG OF CHRISTOPHER COLUMBUS

On Board the *Santa Maria*.

August 3, 1492, *Friday*.—At five in the morning made the signal to weigh: but in less than half an hour the wind shifting to the southward and blowing fresh, I furled the topsails. The wind came in the afternoon to S. by W.; we weighed, but did not get far, the flood tide making against us.

August 4.—Little wind, or calm, all day. Send-off very fine; but now that we have started wonder whether I have been wise after all. Wonder whether we shall reach Western India and China.

August 5.—Took the meridian observation at mid-day; wind northerly with a great swell. Ship's company in good spirits: but the doctor says we have started on a wild goose chase.

August 8.—Stood close in with the land. At noon the latitude by observation was 28 degrees 18 minutes. Stood in to a small bay to the southward of Teneriffe. Anchored with the stream anchor, and sent the boat for water. Went ashore with the astronomer and instruments. All the liberty men came on board the worse for liquor, which is, on the whole, fortunate, as we shall have no trouble in getting them to continue the voyage.

August 9.—Several of the men confined with colds,

and complain of pains in their bones. But from the careful attendance given them, doses of "Skulker's Mixture" being administered by the doctor all round, few continued in the sick list. The air very warm.

September 9.—Thick fog. At five the officer informed me that we were near an iceberg. I ordered the ship to be kept N. by W. and hauled farther in. At noon I steered north, seeing nothing of the ice; soon after I was told that they saw the ice: I went upon deck and perceived something white upon the bow, and heard a noise like the booming of surf. I hauled down the studding sails and hailed the *Niña* and the *Pinta*: I desired that they would keep close to us, the fog being so thick, and have everybody up ready to follow our motions instantaneously, determining to stand under such sail as should enable us to keep the ships under command, and not risk parting company. Soon afterwards, we saw something on the bow, which from the appearance we took to be islands, and thought we had not stood far enough out. The ship's company raised a cheer. I hauled up immediately to the N.N.W., and was soon undeceived, finding it to be a moderate-sized sea serpent, which we could not clear upon that tack; we tacked immediately, but the wind and sea both setting directly upon it, we neared it very fast, and were within a little more than a cable's length of the animal whilst in stays.

The doctor, who has always scoffed at the idea of the sea serpent, which, he said, was a travellers' tale (adding, sarcastically, and, I think, very inconsiderately, "like the western passage to China"), was silent all the evening.

Prefer this to his irritating reiteration of that silly Andalusian song:

> And if we ever get back to Spain
> We will never, never, never go to sea again.

which he is so fond of indulging in. Sea serpent of the ordinary kind, with a white ring round its neck and a tufted crest. Not so large as the Icelandic specimens. Expect to reach China in ten days' time, should the weather be favourable. Officers and ship's company in decidedly less good spirits since the foggy weather began. Sea serpent incident also caused a good deal of disappointment, the men being convinced we had reached the coast of China, although I had repeatedly explained that we could not possibly make that land for some time yet.

September 10.—Lost the *Niña* and the *Pinta* twice in the night from the very thick fog. The situation of the men from the very fatiguing work made most minute precautions necessary. Double allowance of Manzanilla served round to-day.

September 11.—No land in sight. Calm all day, with a great swell from the S.W., and the weather remarkably mild. Confess am disappointed; wonder whether there is such a country as China after all. Confess I have no satisfactory evidence for thinking so. But am concealing my anxiety, of course, from the officers and the doctor, who grow more and more sarcastic every day. He said at dinner yesterday that we might come home by the Nile, as we should certainly encounter its source in China. Want of taste. It is only too plain that both officers and ship's company are growing sceptical as to the practical results of our voyage. Wish the King and Queen of Spain had been a little less sanguine. We shall indeed look very foolish if we come back having accomplished nothing.

September 12.—Ship's company distressingly sulky. If matters continue like this it will end in a mutiny. Have been obliged to fake the observations, measuring the ship's way so that the ship's company should remain in ignorance of the distances traversed, and think that they are much less than they are in reality.

This faking has been an easy task, since the log, being only a mean taken every hour and consequently liable to error from the variations in the force of the wind during the intervals, from which an arbitrary correction is made by the officer of the watch ; as this allowance must from its nature be inaccurate, it is very easy to make it more inaccurate still, now, that is to say, that I have squared Roderigo.

September 13.—Have made a startling and disagreeable discovery. There is something wrong or odd about the compass. The axis of the needle no longer coincides with the geographical meridian it occupies—but makes an angle. This matter must be investigated.

September 17.—The ship's company discovered at dawn to-day the vagaries of the compass. Situation alarming. They at once said we must go home. Doctor and surgeon both say that they are not surprised. Roderigo has constructed an instrument, hanging by a universal joint on a triangular stand, adjusted so as to hang in a plane perpendicular to the horizon, by means of a plumb line, which is suspended on a pin above a divided circle. The length of the magnetic needle is 12 inches, and its axis is made of gold and copper.

Roderigo says he can now observe the variation. Most ingenious (if true).

September 18.—Everybody expects to see land to-day. Why, I can't think. Sailors sometimes have strange superstitions.

September 25.—We are now 475 leagues from the Canaries. No sign of land. I am quite convinced personally that there is no chance of our ever reaching land this voyage. I knew from the first the affair was hopeless. Feel certain we cannot be near China or India. Unfortunately, my conviction, which I have never expressed, is shared by the ship's company, who showed signs of positive mutiny to-day. Calmed them as best I could with soothing words and old sherry. Steered S. to W.

September 26.—Steered W. No sign of anything. Wish we had never left Spain. The Alguazil disgracefully drunk again last night, and rude in his cups. Doctor sarcastic. Surgeon sea-sick. Ship's company mutinous. Have a bad headache. Never did like the sea. It never agreed with my liver.

October 7.—I ordered the allowance of liquor to be altered, serving the ship's company one-fourth of their allowance in Manzanilla and the other three-fourths in brandy. One half of this allowance was served before dinner, and the other half in the evening. Result satisfactory.

Altered course W. to S.W.

October 10.—Mutiny. Ship's company refuse to go on. Insist on returning to Spain. If I refuse they threaten to kill me ; but I fear they will kill me if I consent. Otherwise the matter would be simple. Have asked for three days respite. Roderigo saw a piece of driftwood and a small bird called a red-poll. Thinks we are not far from land. Too good to be true.

October 11.—Saw a light on starboard bow, but am not quite certain that it wasn't a star.

October 12.—Roderigo saw the land at two in the

morning. The King promised a reward of 10,000 Maravedises to whoever saw land first. Clearly this reward is mine, as the light I saw on Thursday night was not a star. Explained this to Roderigo, who lost his temper, and said that if he didn't get the reward he would turn Mahommedan. The land is, of course, the coast of China. I always said it was somewhere about here.

Stood in to make the land. Anchored with the best bower in eleven fathoms, soft clay. Hoisted Spanish flag; took possession of the country, which seems to be India, and not China, after all. Call it West India or Hispaniola. Natives talk in a drawling sing-song, chew tobacco and gum, and drink Manzanilla and Vermouth mixed, icing the drink. This is a very gratifying mixture. It is called a *Cola de gallo*. They have a round game of cards with counters, called chips, in which you pretend to hold better cards than you do hold in reality. Played and lost. Natives very sharp.

XVIII

FROM THE DIARY OF THE MAN IN THE IRON MASK

Pignerol, August 21, 1669.—Have at last, I think, attained my heart's desire. Arrived last night under the pseudonym of *Eustache Danger*. Found everything fairly satisfactory. That is to say, the King's promises to me with regard to the absolute solitude I crave have been carried out as far as was possible in the time. The prison is not finished, and this accounts for a fact which annoyed me not a little on my arrival. I found that the walls of my room were not of the thickness promised, so that, should any one be lodged next door to me, which Heaven forfend! he might have the bad taste to try and communicate with me by knocking on the wall. I wear a black velvet mask and the King solemnly promised me that if any officer were to dare to ask me who I was he would be instantly dismissed.

August 22, 1669.—So far so good. Saint Mars, the Governor of the Prison, is certainly doing his best. But last night, when he brought me my dinner, he forgot himself and said, "Bon Soir, Monsieur." If he does this again he will have to be removed. I did not come here to be bothered with conversation.

August 25.—I am enjoying myself immensely. The relief of waking up in the morning and of gradually becoming conscious that it will not be necessary—

(*a*) To dress in Court clothes.

(*b*) To go out hunting.

(*c*) To attend the King's *lever*, or still worse, his *coucher*.

(*d*) To play cards and lose.

(*e*) To listen to a play performed in a private house.

(*f*) To laugh at Madame ——'s chaff.

(*g*) To make love to J——.

(*h*) To pretend to enjoy the beauties of nature.

(*i*) To hear and give opinions on Molière.

(*j*) To sit through the long, long dinner.

(*k*) To talk philosophy with Mademoiselle.

(*l*) To find fault with my servant for giving me the wrong stockings.

(*m*) To wait for hours in the crown of the *Œil-de-Bœuf*.

(*n*) To be taken to the window by the English Ambassador and asked if I think the Spaniards really mean business.

(*o*) To talk internal politics with Louvois.

(*p*) To listen to Le Nôtre's account of Lord Carlisle's new garden.

(*q*) To listen to Bossuet's sermon on Sunday.

(*r*) Not to annoy the Duchesse de La Vallière.

(*s*) To have to look as if I thought the King an amusing conversationalist.

(*t*) To say that a *Bal Masqué* is great fun.

(*u*) To go to the opera at the back of a box.

(*v*) To pretend I like Dutch pictures.

(*w*) To dance all night in a room like a monkey cage.

(*x*) To read the Gazette.

(*y*) To be civil to the German Ambassadress.

(*z*) To change my clothes three times a day.

That is my alphabet of negation. It is incomplete.

Yet to write it and read it over and over again fills me with ecstasy.

March, 1670.—A most annoying incident happened to-day. The upper tower, at the western angle of the Castle, is occupied by Fouquet and Lauzun. The King promised me solemnly that neither of them should be allowed to hold any communication with me. To-day one of Fouquet's servants entered my room and spoke to me, asking me whether I had anything of importance to communicate. I told him very sharply to go to the devil. If this happens again I shall ask to be removed to a quieter prison.

It is extraordinary that even in a place like this one cannot be free from the importunity and the impertinence of human curiosity.

April 3, 1670.—As the days go on, I enjoy myself more and more. A cargo of books arrived yesterday from Paris, sent by the King, but Saint Mars had the good sense not to bring them to me. He merely notified the fact on a slip of paper, which he left on my plate. I scribbled a note to the effect that he could throw them to the bottom of the sea, or read them himself, or give them to Fouquet's servant. Books indeed ! It is no longer, thank God, necessary for me to read books, or to have an opinion on them !

November 1, 1671.—Lauzun has been sent here. The prison is getting far too crowded. It will soon be as bad as Versailles.

November 10.—Lauzun is being very tiresome. He taps on my ceiling. I wrote a short note to Saint Mars that if this annoyance continued I should be constrained to leave his prison.

March 3, 1680.—The situation was intolerable. Lauzun and Fouquet found some means of communication and they carried on interminable conversations. What they can have to talk about passes my understanding. I bore it patiently for some days. At last I complained to Saint Mars in writing, he took some steps and it appears that Fouquet has had an attack of apoplexy and died. I cannot endure the neighbourhood of Lauzun, and I have written to the King saying that unless I am transferred to a quieter dungeon I shall leave the prison.

April 8, 1680.—Matters have been arranged satisfactorily, and I have been moved into the lower chamber of the *Tour d'en bas*. But the whole fortress is far too crowded. There are at least five prisoners in it. Also I found a tame mouse here, left I suppose by a former occupant. Had the nuisance removed at once. It is delicious to be safely in prison just now that the spring is beginning and to think that I shall not have to spend chilly evenings in wet gardens and to speak foolishly of the damp April weather.

January, 1681.—Caused much annoyance by a tiresome Italian fellow prisoner called Mattioli, who, feigning either madness or illness, or both, caused a commotion in the prison, necessitating the arrival of doctors and priests. Kept awake by noise of bolts being drawn, and the opening and shutting of doors. Wrote to the King complaining of this which is a direct infringement of his promise. Asked to be moved to a quieter spot.

September 2, 1681.—Moved to the Fortress of Exiles. Prison said to be empty. Hope this will prove true.

October 10, 1681.—Saint Mars very nearly spoke to me to-day. He was evidently bursting with something he longed to communicate. However, I made such a gesture, that I think he felt the frown through my velvet mask and withdrew.

January 5, 1687.—After months, and indeed years of peace, perfect peace, with loved ones far away, I have again been subjected to intolerable annoyance. Fouquet's valet fell ill, and *Saint Mars informed me of the fact.* I wrote to the King at once saying that either Saint Mars or I must go.

April 30, 1687.—King has granted my request. Arrived at Sainte Marguerite in a chair with wheels covered with wax-cloth. I think I shall be quieter here. I have been promised that no other prisoner shall be lodged here at all, but the promises of Kings are as iridescent and as brittle as Venetian glass.

January, 1690.—Alas! Alas! for the vanity of human wishes. Here I was perfectly contented, and, as I thought, quiet at last. Day followed day of perfect enjoyment, unmarred by conversation, undisturbed by study, unvexed by the elements, when the peace of my solitude is rudely shattered by the arrival of two Protestant ministers. It is true I am never to see them, but the mere fact of knowing that there are two Protestant ministers in the same building is enough to poison life!

June 1, 1698.—More Protestant ministers have arrived, worse than the last. They sing hymns. I have written to the King asking him to transfer me to the Bastille at once. I always said that the Bastille was the only tolerable dwelling-place in France.

September 13, 1698.—Arrived at the Bastille this afternoon. Lodged on the third floor of the *Bertandière* tower—the *thickest* tower. Really quiet.

September 19.—A man hammered over my head

at four o'clock this morning. It is intolerable. Shall I ever find a place where I can sleep from 4 to 8 a.m. without being disturbed ? As it is, I might just as well be living in a fashionable inn.

XIX

FROM THE DIARY OF AN ENGLISH GOVERNESS RESIDING IN PARIS DURING THE FRENCH REVOLUTION

Paris, October 7, 1789.—I arrived this afternoon after a rapid and satisfactory journey. To my amazement found that neither the Count nor the Countess were here to receive me. The Hotel was deserted save for the presence of an old servant, and his wife, who appears to be the cook of the household, and to combine with this office the duties of hall porter. As I have no command over even the elementary rudiments of the French language, and as the French never trouble to learn any language but their own, communication is a sorely difficult task and results in perpetual misunderstanding. Nevertheless, I succeeded in apprehending from the voluble expostulations and the superfluous gesticulation of the old servant, whose name appears to be Pierre, but whom I have decided to call Peter, that the family had left Paris. That they had departed but recently and in haste, my senses were able to inform me. All over the house were traces of disorder. Some but half-packed boxes had been left behind ; cupboards were open, clothes were strewn on the floor, and everywhere traces of precipitate packing and sudden departure were manifest. I made as if I would depart also, but Peter made it plain by signs that I was expected to remain, and indeed he conducted me to my room, which is airy and commodious enough, and where, after partaking of a light supper, insufficient and badly cooked as all French meals, and accompanied by the sour " wine " of the country, I fell into a comfortable slumber.

October 10, 1789.—I have now been here three days, and as yet I have received neither message, nor token, nor sign from the departed family, nor can I ascertain from Peter or his wife, the obtuse menials who are the sole occupants of this in some respects elegant mansion, whither they have gone: whether they are loitering in their country seat, or whether they have started on a longer peregrination. Paris is very full. The streets are ill-kept and ill-lit, a strange contrast to the blaze (at night) and tidiness (by day) of the London streets. It is a dingy city, and I think it must certainly be insanitary. The French understand no word of English, and if indeed one ventures to address them, all they reply is: " Rosbeef, plom pudding," a form of address which they consider facetious. The house is spacious enough, although inconveniently distant from the centre of the city, but it has the advantage of an extensive garden surrounded by high walls. As for myself, I am well cared for by Peter and his wife. She talks at me with great volubility, but I cannot understand a word of what she says. French is an unmusical language, very sharp and nasal, but not ill-suited to a backward people.

July 14, 1790.—Went for a long walk in the city. The streets quiet and deserted. Peter and his wife went out for the day. She is very handy with her needle. I find altogether that the French are quite amenable to reason, if well treated. Of course, one cannot expect them to work like English people, but they are willing and do their best. It is unfortunate they do not speak English. Received last quarter's salary through the usual channel. No further views.

March 4, 1792.—Went out in the evening with Peter and his wife. They took me to the Opera House, having apparently received tickets from a friend connected with theatrical affairs. *Castor and Pollux* was the name of the opera. The scenery was gorgeous, and the ballets very skilfully performed. The opera was given in French, so that I could not follow the words. Weather grey and dark. The Boulevards as usual ill-lit; but crowded with people coming from the coffee-houses, the theatres and the out-of-door dining houses—all singing at the top of their voices. Returned home between nine and ten.

March 6, 1792.—Again to the Opera House to hear the *Alcestis* of Gluck, and to see the celebrated Vestris dance in a ballet called *Psyche*. Scenery as usual gorgeous, singing nasal and most unpleasing.

August 13, 1792.—Nothing worth recording. Spend most of the days in the garden. Weather hot. French people vulgar and loud in their holiday-making, partial also to fireworks, explosives, firing of guns, etc. I now make a point of staying at home on Feast days and holidays, of which there are far too many.

Sunday, September 2, 1792.—Read the morning service in the garden. Sultry.

January 21, 1793.—Shops shut this morning, although it is Monday. No salary received for the last two quarters.

November 10, 1793.—Sunday. Started out to walk along the river in spite of the damp weather. Streets very muddy. A great crowd of people near the Cathedral. Caught in the crowd and obliged to follow with the stream. Borne by the force of the crowd right into the church. Deeply shocked and disgusted at the display of Romish superstition. A live woman resembling a play actress throned near the altar, representing no doubt the Virgin Mary. Most reprehensible. Was obliged to assist at the mummery until the crowd departed. Think I have taken cold.

November 11, 1793.—Have indeed taken cold in consequence of yesterday's outing. Remained indoors all day. Peter and his wife most obliging. They made me some hot negus flavoured with black currant, not unpalatable.

November 12, 1793.—Cold worse. Suffering from ague in the bones as well. Shall not get up to-morrow. Peter's wife spent much time in talking and screaming at me. Gathered from her rapid and unintelligible jargon that she wished me to see a doctor. Shook my head vehemently. Shall certainly not put myself in the hands of a French doctor. One never knows what foreigners may prescribe.

January 1, 1794.—Came downstairs for the first time since I have been laid up. Made many good resolutions for the New Year. Among others to keep my journal more diligently.

May 30, 1794.—Walked in the garden for the first time since my relapse. Peter's wife has nursed me with much care and tenderness. Still very weak.

July 30, 1794.—First walk in the city since my long illness. Feel really better. Bought a lace kerchief.

October 1, 1794.—The family, that is to say, the Countess and her two daughters, arrived unexpectedly in the night. Countess simple and kindly, can scarcely speak any English. Begin lessons to-morrow.

October 2, 1794.—The eldest girl Amelia, aged seven,

speaks English but has been shamefully ill-taught during her stay in England (for it appears the family have been in England !). She is sadly backward in spelling : but she has a fair accent and is evidently an intelligent child. Unfortunately, she has picked up many unseemly expressions. The Countess suggested my learning French, but I respectfully declined. Reading Pope's *Essay on Man* in the evenings. It is improving as well as elegant.

XX

FROM THE DIARY OF HAMLET, PRINCE OF DENMARK, DURING HIS STAY AT ENGLAND, WHITHER HE WAS SENT TO STUDY AT THE UNIVERSITY AT OXFORD, UNDER THE SPECIAL CARE OF POLONIUS

Balliol College, Monday.—Read aloud my Essay on Equality to the Master. It began: "Treat all men as your equals, especially the rich." The Master commented on this sentence. He said, "Very ribald, Prince Hamlet, very ribald."

In training for the annual fencing match between the Universities of Oxford and Cambridge. Doing my utmost to reduce my flesh which is far too solid.

Tuesday.—Went to Abingdon for the day. When I came back I found that havoc had been made of my rooms: both the virginals broken to pieces—all the furniture destroyed, and all my pictures including a signed portrait of Ophelia.

Have my suspicions as to who has done this. Shall first make certain and then retaliate terribly. In the meantime it will be politic to conceal my annoyance.

Friday.—Dined last night with a society of Undergraduates who meet together in a Barn to discuss Falconry and French verse. Rhenish wine served in great quantities. Feigned drunkenness in order to discover who was guilty of taking liberties with my furniture. As I suspected, Rosencrantz and Guildenstern were the culprits. They as good as admitted it in their cups.

Intend to be revenged some day, and that royally.

Saturday.—When we returned home from the barn last night, it was of course necessary for me to keep up the false semblance of intoxication with which I had started the evening.

This I did by improvising and singing quaint rhymeless couplets as we strutted across the Quadrangle of the College. It so chanced that we encountered the Dean, who addressed me. I answered, keeping up the part: "Buzz. Buzz."

Monday.—A College meeting was held this morning and I was summoned to appear on the charges:—

(*a*) Of having been intoxicated.

(*b*) Of having insulted the Dean.

(*c*) Of having persuaded and finally compelled the younger members of the College to drink more than was good for them.

To which I replied (*a*) that seeing that I was in strict training it was obvious that the charge of intoxication was unfounded; (*b*) that so far from insulting the Dean I had addressed him in Danish, and that familiar as I knew him to be with all the languages of Europe and especially the Scandinavian tongues, he had probably not realized to the full the exact shade of deference, respect, and awe which the expression I used implied; (*c*) that as far as the charge of corrupting the young was concerned, I was not ashamed to stand in the same dock with Socrates, and I would cheerfully if the College authorities and my Royal parents thought fit, share the doom of my august master. Finally I reminded the noble and learned assembly that were I to be expelled, even temporarily, from the College I should be unable (*a*) to represent the *Alma Mater* with the rapier against the University of Cambridge, who had a powerful champion of the noble art in Laertes, a fellow-countryman of mine ; and (*b*) I should not be able to row in the College boat. I concluded by saying that certain as I was that my royal parents would endorse any decision which should be arrived at by the Master and his Colleagues, I was convinced that were I to be sent down from the College, my royal father, in order that my studies might not be interrupted, would immediately send me to Cambridge.

The net result of all this is that I am admonished.

Later in the Day I received a note from the Dean asking me to dine with him next Thursday.

Sunday.—Breakfasted with the Master to meet the Poet Laureate, the Archbishop of York, the Lord Chancellor, the French ambassador, and Quattrovalli, a celebrated Italian juggler. The poet laureate read out an Ode he had just composed on the King's sixth marriage. Very poor.

Monday.—Took part in the debate held by the College Debating Society. The subject being whether Homer's Epics were written by Homer or by a Committee of Athenian Dons.

Took what seemed to the audience a paradoxical view that they were written by Homer.

Tuesday.—Gave a small dinner party in my rooms. Horatio and a few others. Again compelled to feign intoxication, so as not to mar the harmony of the evening. Burnt a small organ, and rather a complicated printing press, belonging to a German undergraduate named Faustus, in the Quadrangle.

Wednesday.—The master commenting on last night's bonfire said he thought it was not humorous, and fined us heavily. Have as yet found no opportunity of revenging myself on Rosencrantz and Guildenstern.

Thursday.—Coached by Polonius for two hours in Scottish history. Very tedious. In the afternoon went on the river in my boat the *Ophelia*. Faustus has been sent down for trying to raise the Devil in the precincts of the College. It appears this is strictly against the rules. His excuse was that he had always understood that the College authorities disbelieved in a personal devil. To which the Dean replied: "We are all bound to believe in the Devil in a *spiritual* sense, Mr. Faustus." And Faustus imprudently asked in what other sense you could believe in him.

Friday.—Must really settle this business of Rosencrantz and Guildenstern soon. It is beginning to prey upon my mind. They are quite insufferable. Have lost one stone since the term began, which is satisfactory. Fencing match is to take place next week, here.

Saturday.—The man who has the rooms opposite mine is a Spaniard. A nobleman very cultivated and amiable. His name is Quixote. Consulted him last night as to what to do about Rosencrantz and Guildenstern. Quixote said it was entirely a point of honour. That if I were certain they were guilty, and certain likewise that they had purposely insulted me, I should challenge them each, separately, to personal combat, with sword and rapier. I pointed out, however, that whereas I was a champion swordsman, and indeed had been chosen to represent the University, they had no skill at all. Moreover, I considered that to challenge them to fight would be doing them too much honour. Quixote said I must indubitably take action of some kind, or else I would incur the suspicion of cowardice.

At that moment—we were talking by the open casement—I saw in the darkness, walking stealthily along the wall a man whom I took to be Guildenstern. Seizing a bottle of white wine from Xeres with which Quixote had entertained me, I flung it out of the window on to the head of the skulker, but alas ! it was not Guildenstern but the Dean himself !

Monday.—Again appeared before a College meeting. Accused of having wantonly wounded, and almost murdered the Dean. Protested my innocence in vain. It was further suggested I was intoxicated. Lost my temper, which was a mistake, and called the Dean a villain, losing control over my epithets.

Sent down for the rest of the term. Polonius is very angry. He has written to my father suggesting that I should not go back to Oxford, nor seek to enter Cambridge either, but go to Wittenberg instead. Owing to my abrupt departure the fencing match with Laertes will not come off. No matter, a day will come, when maybe I shall be revenged on Rosencrantz and Guildenstern. We go to London to-day.